Bullying, Victimization, and Peer Harassment
A Handbook of Prevention and Intervention

D1003630

HAWORTH School Psychology
Charles A. Maher
Editor

Bullying, Victimization, and Peer Harassment: A Handbook of Prevention and Intervention edited by Joseph E. Zins, Maurice J. Elias, and Charles A. Maher

Books of Related Interest

Bullying, Peer Harassment, and Victimization in the Schools: The Next Generation of Prevention edited by Maurice J. Elias and Joseph E. Zins

Multicultural Issues in School Psychology edited by Bonnie K. Nastasi

School Sport Psychology: Perspectives, Programs, and Procedures edited by Charles A. Maher

Bullying, Victimization, and Peer Harassment
A Handbook of Prevention and Intervention

Joseph E. Zins, PhD
Maurice J. Elias, PhD
Charles A. Maher, PsyD
Editors

The Haworth Press
New York • London • Oxford

KH

For more information on this book or to order, visit
http://www.haworthpress.com/store/product.asp?sku=5808

or call 1-800-HAWORTH (800-429-6784) in the United States and Canada
or (607) 722-5857 outside the United States and Canada

or contact orders@HaworthPress.com

The Haworth Press, Inc. 10 Alice Street, Binghamton, NY 13904-1580.

PUBLISHER'S NOTE
The development, preparation, and publication of this work has been undertaken with great care. However, the Publisher, employees, editors, and agents of The Haworth Press are not responsible for any errors contained herein or for consequences that may ensue from use of materials or information contained in this work. The Haworth Press is committed to the dissemination of ideas and information according to the highest standards of intellectual freedom and the free exchange of ideas. Statements made and opinions expressed in this publication do not necessarily reflect the views of the Publisher, Directors, management, or staff of The Haworth Press, Inc., or an endorsement by them.

This book contains articles previously published in the *Journal of Applied School Psychology, 19*(2) (2003) published by The Haworth Press, Inc.

Cover design by Lora Wiggins.

Library of Congress Cataloging-in-Publication Data

Bullying, victimization, and peer harassment : a handbook of prevention and intervention / Joseph E. Zins, Maurice J. Elias, Charles A. Maher, editors.
    p. cm.
    Includes bibliographical references and index.
    ISBN-13: 978-0-7890-2218-9 (case : alk. paper)
    ISBN-10: 0-7890-2218-4 (case : alk. paper)
    ISBN-13: 978-0-7890-2219-6 (soft : alk. paper)
    ISBN-10: 0-7890-2219-2 (soft : alk. paper)
    1. School violence—Prevention. 2. Bullying in schools—Prevention. I. Zins, Joseph E. II. Elias, Maurice J. III. Maher, Charles A., 1944-

LB3013.3.B83 2007
371.7'82—dc22

    2006022962

1/3/08

CONTENTS

SECTION II: EMPIRICAL RESEARCH AND OTHER IMPORTANT EVIDENCE

SECTION III: EMPIRICALLY VALIDATED AND PROMISING PREVENTIVE AND SUPPORTIVE INTERVENTIONS

SECTION IV: GUIDELINES FOR PRACTICE: PROFESSIONAL ISSUES AND LEGAL CONSIDERATIONS

ABOUT THE EDITORS

Joseph E. Zins, PhD, was a psychologist and professor in the College of Education, Criminal Justice, and Human Services at the University of Cincinnati. He was recognized nationally and internationally as an expert on social and emotional learning, prevention, individual and organizational consultation, and psychological service delivery systems. He has over 150 publications, and included among his twelve books are *Building Academic Success on Social and Emotional Learning; Bullying, Peer Harassment, and Victimization in the Schools* (Haworth); *Promoting Social and Emotional Learning,* and *Helping Students Succeed in the Regular Classroom.* Dr. Zins passed away in 2006.

Maurice J. Elias, PhD, is Professor in the Department of Psychology at Rutgers University and directs the Rutgers Social-Emotional Learning Lab. He is Vice Chair of the Leadership Team of the Collaborative for Academic, Social, and Emotional Learning and Senior Advisor for Research, Policy, and Practice to the New Jersey Center for Character Education. He served as a member of the expert panel that advised the development of the NASP/CECP Early Warning Signs, Timely Response book on violence prevention and subsequent materials, and he is the author of numerous books and articles on prevention. His books include *Emotionally Intelligent Parenting: How to Raise a Self-Disciplined, Responsible, and Socially Skilled Child,* and *Raising Emotionally Intelligent Teenagers: Guiding the Way for Compassionate, Committed, Courageous Adults.*

Charles A. Maher, PsyD, is a Professor of Psychology, Graduate School of Applied and Professional Psychology, Director of the Sport Psychology Concentration, and also a Contributing Faculty of the Center of Alcohol Studies at Rutgers University. For thirty years, he has worked with children, adolescents, youths, and adults with emotional and behavioral disorders. He has helped school districts and related education agencies in the United States and elsewhere with the design, implementation, and evaluation of programs, services, and systems for children and youth who are impatient, impulse-disordered, physically violent, and dangerous to the safety and health of others. In addition, he has consulted with adult and juvenile correctional facilities on prevention and maintenance of psychological problems of inmates including hostage negotiation. He is a licensed psychologist, fellow and diplomate of various societies and boards, author of books and articles, and Editor of the *Journal of Applied School Psychology.*

CONTRIBUTORS

Jennifer Angelucci, The Children's Hospital of Philadelphia and The University of Pennsylvania School of Medicine.

Moira Atria, Division of Educational Psychology and Evaluation, Department of Psychology, University of Vienna.

Amy Bellmore, University of California-Los Angeles.

Noel A. Card, St. John's University.

LeeAnn Cardaciotto, The Children's Hospital of Philadelphia and The University of Pennsylvania School of Medicine.

Paulette Tam Cary, University of Nebraska-Lincoln.

Antonius H. N. Cillessen, University of Connecticut.

Jennifer Connolly, York University.

Kim Coyle, Rock Solid Foundation, Victoria, BC.

Wendy M. Craig, Queen's University.

Melissa E. DeRosier, 3-C Institute for Social Development and University of North Carolina at Chapel Hill.

Dorothy L. Espelage, University of Illinois at Urbana-Champaign.

Karla Fischer, University of Illinois at Urbana-Champaign.

Harry S. Freeman, Division of Counseling and Psychology in Education University of South Dakota.

Suzanne Goldbaum, Queen's University.

Amy B. Goldstein, The Children's Hospital of Philadelphia and The University of Pennsylvania School of Medicine.

Sandra Graham, University of California-Los Angeles.

Bullying, Victimization, and Peer Harassment
© 2007 by The Haworth Press, Inc. All rights reserved.
doi:10.1300/5808_b

Michael B. Grossman, The Children's Hospital of Philadelphia and The University of Pennsylvania School of Medicine.

Denise L. Haynie, National Institute of Child Health and Human Development.

Ernest V. E. Hodges, St. John's University.

Wendy Hoglund, Department of Psychology, University of Victoria.

Melissa K. Holt, Family Research Laboratory, University of New Hampshire.

Shelley Hymel, University of British Columbia.

Jenny Isaacs, St. John's University.

Jaana Juvonen, University of California-Los Angeles.

Howard M. Knoff, Director, State Improvement Grant/Project ACHIEVE, Arkansas Department of Education, Little Rock, Arkansas.

Bonnie Leadbeater, Department of Psychology, University of Victoria.

Stephen S. Leff, The Children's Hospital of Philadelphia and The University of Pennsylvania School of Medicine.

Patricia McDougal, University of Saskatchewan.

Linda M. Raffaele Mendez, University of South Florida.

Grace A. Mims, Division of Counseling and Psychology in Education University of South Dakota.

Richard J. Morris, University of Arizona Department of Special Education, Rehabilitation, and School Psychology College of Education.

Tonja R. Nansel, National Institute of Child Health and Human Development.

Maury Nation, Vanderbilt University.

Brooke Paskewich, The Children's Hospital of Philadelphia and The University of Pennsylvania School of Medicine.

Jennifer J. Paul, University of Connecticut.

Debra Pepler, York University.

Stephanie Rahill, Fairfax County (Virginia) Public Schools.

Philip C. Rodkin, University of Illinois at Urbana-Champaign.

Lee Rothman, Prince Georges County (Maryland) Public Schools.

Bruce G. Simons-Morton, National Institute of Child Health and Human Development.

Christiane Spiel, Division of Educational Psychology and Evaluation, Department of Psychology, University of Vienna, Austria.

Dagmar Strohmeier, University of Vienna, Austria.

Árni Víkingur Sveinsson, University of Arizona Department of Special Education, Rehabilitation, and School Psychology College of Education.

Susan M. Swearer, University of Nebraska-Lincoln.

Hedwig Teglasi, University of Maryland Fr.

Tracy Vaillancourt, McMaster University.

Tom Woods, Rock Solid Foundation, Victoria, BC.

Ellie L. Young, Brigham Young University.

Acknowledgments

Both ME and CM acknowledge our utmost respect for Dr. Joe Zins, who passed away suddenly on March 1, 2006, prior to completing the final stages of work on this book. Joe was the driving force behind this book. Without Joe's typical enthusiasm, effort, ease, good humor, and attention to technical and procedural detail, this work would not have come to fruition. Joe was a scholar, researcher, practitioner, and friend to both of us. We feel privileged to have been part of this work and his life. We miss him profoundly.

Completion of this book also was made possible by the generous and dedicated effort of each of the contributors, and we are grateful for their patience and collaborative spirit. It was a pleasure working with each of these talented researchers and leaders, and we learned immensely from them. As part of an earlier version of these acknowledgments, JEZ expressed his "love and thanks to my wonderful partner, Charlene R. Ponti, PhD, and our fantastic children, Lauren, Michael, and Ryan. They are valued far more than words can express." MJE wishes to thank his wife, Ellen, daughters, Sara Elizabeth and Samara Alexandra, and parents, Agnes and Sol, for their continuing inspiration and unwavering support. Finally, CM acknowledges the co-editors of this book, Maurice Elias and Joseph Zins, for their dedication and contributions to the social and emotional learning of children, adolescents, and adults, and for being there, as colleagues.

Bullying, Victimization, and Peer Harassment
© 2007 by The Haworth Press, Inc. All rights reserved.
doi:10.1300/5808_c

SECTION I:
THEORY AND CONCEPTUAL ISSUES

Chapter 1

Prevention and Intervention in Peer Harassment, Victimization, and Bullying: Theory, Research, and Practice

Joseph E. Zins
Maurice J. Elias
Charles A. Maher

Emerging research into areas of peer harassment, bullying, and other forms of student intimidation and threat in schools yields remarkable and deeply disturbing convergences. The chapters in this book represent the latest stages of a wave of groundbreaking work in theory, research, and practice that will influence the direction of both researchers and practitioners for at least the next decade. From our perspective as psychologists involved in school, clinical, and community psychology fields, the focus of this book is long overdue.

A PERVASIVE AND SERIOUS ISSUE FOR SCHOOL MENTAL HEALTH AND ACADEMIC ACHIEVEMENT

Despite some inconsistencies in how bullying and harassment are defined (see Chapter 2 by Sveinsson and Morris), these clearly are pervasive problems in schools, worldwide. Swearer and Cary (Chapter 5), Nansel, Haynie, and Simons-Morton (Chapter 4) and Holt and Espelage (Chapter 6)

This chapter was adapted from "Bullying, Other Forms of Peer Harassment, and Victimization in the Schools: Issues for School Psychology Research and Practice" by Maurice J. Elias and Joseph E. Zins, *Journal of Applied School Psychology*, 2003, *19*(2), pp. 1-6.

found that 70 percent of the student body is affected, and surprisingly large numbers of children are subjected to sexual harassment (see Chapter 17 by Young and Raffaele Mendez). As several of the chapters indicate, bullying traditionally has been and continues to be overlooked, ignored, or viewed as a "normal" developmental behavior. Statements such as, "Boys will be boys," "She shouldn't dress like that if she doesn't want the attention," and "She shouldn't just listen to that stuff, she should give it right back, and more," were and are made openly by supervising adults. Victims frequently are blamed, almost as if they were the perpetrators. "What's wrong with you that you'd just let him get under your skin?" However, we now know that even actions as common as teasing, "dissing," and shunning can have significant effects on perpetrators and victims, and can result in missed school, poor grades, depression, low self-esteem, aggression, and suicide. Further, as Freeman and Mimms point out (see Chapter 10), relational aggression and intimidation are witnessed by a majority of students, suggesting that their impact may reach far beyond the at-risk groups typically targeted by prevention programs. And finally, as reported by Holt and Espelage in Chapter 6, students who experience multiple forms of victimization are impacted especially strongly.

RESEARCH FINDINGS

The research presented in this book significantly contributes to the literature. It includes descriptions of relevant theory, concepts, and empirical findings necessary to promote an understanding of the most salient aspects of the problem, as well as to draw related implications for intervention. A majority of the text reviews a wide range of innovative, evidence-based practices. These interventions range from a focus on individuals and peers to broad, systems-level change within schools, related educational settings and communities that target both victims and perpetrators. Included in the forthcoming chapters are suggestions regarding the need to make changes in the culture and climate of our schools, using an expanded, ecological, and developmental perspective so that these organizations are safe, caring, supportive places of academic, social, and emotional learning. A number of the studies address middle school issues and involve multiethnic populations, including those from Canada and Europe, as well as within the United States. The research supporting interventions for victims is particularly notable because, as Nation notes in Chapter 14, many programs and other interventions that are in place have not been evaluated. In addition, other chapters clearly integrate peer sexual harassment and dating-related aggression into discussions that previously have been predominantly oriented to traditional views of bullying and peer intimidation, and accordingly serve to expand our knowledge of the issues. The various chapters also identify important directions for future research and practice, and legal and ethical practice guidelines. They also cross socioeconomic lines and take a longitudinal perspective. The strategies described demonstrate the development of key social and emotional learning (SEL) skills related to success in school and life (e.g., Elias et al., 1997; Greenberg et al., 2003; Zins, Weissberg, Wang, & Walberg, 2004). For instance, building social awareness and relationship skills can help develop positive peer relationships, and being able to resist inappropriate peer pressure can help deal with bystander motivational issues. And, we know that other SEL outcomes such as having high-quality friendships and fewer aggressive behaviors may serve as protective factors from bullying.

Developmental studies are especially important because they begin to allow some inferences about directionality of effects. A persistent question, for example, is the extent to which preexisting psychological difficulties lead to victimization, which in turn leads to poor school outcomes, versus victimization leading to psychological destabilization, which then results in deteriorating academic functioning. Data in Chapter 3 by Paul and Cillessen, as well in Chapter 9 by Goldbaum et al. and Chapter 4 by Nansel, Haynie, and Simons-Morton suggest that the latter is a more prevalent model than the former. That is, victimization, as well as being a bully-victim, seems highly deleterious to children. Indeed, those who cease being victimized have outcomes more similar to those who were never victims than to those who remain in that status. Future research needs to understand much more about the conditions under which victim status is changed.

DIRECTIONS FOR RESEARCH AND PRACTICE

Among the important directions for research and practice that this book suggests are the following:

- Better agreement about defining bullying is needed to facilitate comparisons across studies, cultures, and countries.
- We must continue to take a more differentiated and developmental perspective on bullies, victims, and bully-victims. The continuity of bullying and victimization over time and across different school settings, as well as changes in status on the part of a given student, are salient factors in understanding risk.

- More psychometrically sound measures and consistency in use of similar instruments across studies will lead to better understanding as noted by Sveinsson and Morris in Chapter 2.
- Victims are truly victimized by what happens to them. Their outcomes are worse than those of the bullies. Furthermore, there is no doubt that some bullies, perhaps as many as half, enjoy positive status, not only from peers but from teachers. Those victims who then become bullies (while and while not also remaining victims) are a group at the early stages of being understood by researchers; their situation may well be the most problematic of all the subgroups, although some data suggest that continued victimization produces the worst outcomes.
- Methodologically, it is important to recognize that different data sources may yield different conclusions about who is perpetrating and receiving harassment. Teachers, other students, and the self-report of the child reflect distinctive perspectives that may or may not converge, for reasons that Graham, Bellmore, and Juvonen (Chapter 8), and Sveinsson and Morris (Chapter 2) explore in detail.
- Research must continue to examine differential effects as a function of gender, ethnic and cultural group, socioeconomic status (SES), and type of school. Information about the latter is relatively lacking in the research base thus far, other than confirming the prevalence of significant peer harassment across a wide range of school contexts. Findings by Strohmeier and Spiel (Chapter 7), Atria and Spiel (Chapter 11), Leff et al. (Chapter 12), and Graham, Bellmore, and Juvonen indicate that subgroups can be selected out for greater victimization, or at least a lower degree of social integration.

The focus of efforts to decrease bullying and harassment must move beyond individuals and specific programs to include systemic change that includes the culture and climate of the school. The overreliance on the use of negative consequences and social control techniques found in many schools and homes should be replaced with development of SEL skills, school-home-community partnerships, and development of safe and caring environments with a sense of belonging and community, backed by relevant policies and system support.

LORD OF THE FLIES *REVISITED IN OUR SCHOOLS?*

Disquieting, however, is what the data suggest about life in schools. It would appear as if there is a culture (indeed, it is too prevalent to call a sub-culture but might even approach a "norm") of intimidation in schools that does not emerge in discussions of school reform and school change, and also does not surface as a primary organizational concern of school psychologists and other school support personnel. The accumulated research, in this book and elsewhere, suggests a very serious and pressing need to examine peer culture in schools and the roles of adults in inadvertently and often unknowingly creating and enabling its negative elements.

Consider this quote: "Girls who physically fight back may not only be punished by the boys who attack them, but unfairly and unevenly by school authorities. The narratives of girls who are harassed and who respond actively to that harassment are filled with stories of unjust punishment" (see Chapter 16 by Rodkin and Fischer). This report represents a highly complex situation, since other data suggest that those who fight back are headed for especially poor outcomes, and many bullies are seen as popular and admirable by both peers and teachers. Also think about Swearer and Cary's data on where most bullying takes place: classrooms, hallways, after school, gym, and recess. In four of these five contexts, adults should be providing supervision and de facto protection.

Is this *The Lord of the Flies* revisited? In the absence of adult structure, are children creating a society based on social power? Is the prevalence of bullying and harassment a sign of how many students feel disconnected from the subculture of academic, athletic, and artistic performance successes in schools and the star culture that fuels each? Debates about school safety and legislative and programmatic antibullying interventions would do well to be informed by the findings of the research presented in this book. This research speaks to the role of adults in schools, the interpersonal structure of school safety, and the pervasive and harmful nature of the trends observed. All this has happened on the watch of school psychologists; so what shall the response be? In Chapter 21 Knoff notes that focusing on individuals and programs rather than the culture and climate of schools is the road too often traveled. Perhaps a warning from Seymour Sarason in *The Culture of the Schools and the Problem of Change* (1982) is in order: Only by taking an expanded, ecological, and developmental perspective is the field likely to make major and lasting contributions to research and practice around how our schools can become more caring, supportive, safe, and effective places of academic, social, and emotional learning.

BRIEF OVERVIEW

This handbook presents a thorough overview of theory, research, and practice related to prevention and intervention in peer harassment, victimization, and bullying in schools and related settings. It includes original chapters plus all of the articles in a thematic issue of the *Journal of Applied School Psychology* (Elias & Zins, 2003). The contents reflect an in-depth, state-of-the-art, and insightful examination of important aspects of peer harassment, victimization, and bullying not found elsewhere. The goal of the handbook is to provide valuable information about theory, empirical research, practice guidelines, and suggestions for preparing schools for programmatic initiatives in the content domains covered by the various chapters. The contents reflect a concise but thorough and up-to-date examination of key aspects of the overall topic. We hope you will find the contents to be as informative and useful.

REFERENCES

Elias, M. J., & Zins, J. E. (Eds.) (2003). *Bullying, peer harassment, and victimization in the schools: The next generation of prevention.* New York: Haworth.

Elias, M. J., Zins, J. E., Weissberg, R. P., Frey, K. S., Greenberg, M. T., Haynes, N. M., et al. (1997). *Promoting social and emotional learning: Guidelines for educators.* Alexandria, VA: Association for Supervision and Curriculum Development.

Greenberg, M. T., Weissberg, R. P., O'Brien, M. U., Zins, J. E., Fredericks, L., Resnik, H., & Elias, M. J. (2003). Enhancing school-based prevention and youth development through coordinated social and emotional learning. *American Psychologist, 58,* 466-474.

Sarason, S. B. (1982). *The culture of the schools and the problem of change* (2nd ed.). Boston: Allyn & Bacon.

Zins, J. E., Weissberg, R. P., Wang, M. C., & Walberg, H. J. (Eds.) (2004). *Building academic success on social and emotional learning: What does the research say?* New York: Teachers College Press.

Chapter 2

Conceptual and Methodological Issues in Assessment and Intervention with School Bullies

Árni Víkingur Sveinsson
Richard J. Morris

Interest in the study of "bullying" has increased tremendously over the past twenty years. The original research was conducted in Sweden where Olweus (1978) initiated a series of longitudinal studies of twelve- to four-teen-year-old boys in Swedish schools. The research generated interest in other Scandinavian countries, and when a series of childhood suicides in the early 1980s in Norway were linked to bullying experiences, the Norwegian government asked Olweus to conduct a nationwide study on bullying in Norwegian schools (Olweus, 1991). These early studies, as well as a European conference on bullying in Stavanger, Norway in 1987 (Smith & Brain, 2000), stimulated further discussion and research in other countries in the late 1980s and early 1990s, including the United Kingdom (e.g., Boulton & Underwood, 1992; Whitney & Smith, 1993), Australia (e.g., Rigby & Slee, 1991), Canada (e.g., Pepler, Craig, Ziegler, & Charach, 1994), Italy (e.g., Genta, Menesini, Costabile, & Smith, 1996), Ireland (e.g., O'Moore, Kirkham, & Smith, 1997), and the United States (e.g., Hoover, Oliver, & Hazler, 1992). It has only been relatively recently, however, that interest in bullying has become more prevalent in the United States, with

Preparation of this chapter was supported, in part, by the David and Minnie Meyerson Foundation's "Project on Research, Advocacy, and Policy Studies on Disability" at the University of Arizona.

the majority of research studies being published since 1998. This area of study has also been highlighted recently in publications of the American Psychological Association (e.g., Crawford, 2002) and the National Association of School Psychologists (e.g., Furlong, Morrison, & Greif, 2003; Lieberman, 2001), and was a topic area addressed during the November 2002 "The Future of School Psychology" online conference (Crockett, 2003).

Emerging international research has documented bullying to be a substantial problem within different school systems and seemingly independent of country or culture. Prevalences, however, have varied considerably between different countries, with rates of bullying (i.e., being victimized by bullies) ranging from 8 percent in Norway (Olweus, 1993) to 77-78 percent in the United States (Crockett, 2003; Hoover et al., 1992). Although cultural and linguistic differences may explain some of the wide range in prevalence percentages, considerable variation has also been reported within the same countries. For example, recent research within the United States by Nansel et al. (2001) found a prevalence value of 16.9 percent for bullying—a value appreciably smaller than the 77-78 percent values reported by Crockett (2003) and Hoover et al. (1992). Similar variability has also been reported in studies in the United Kingdom, where prevalence values range from 12.2 percent (Smith & Shu, 2000) to almost 50 percent (Wolke, Woods, Bloomfield, & Karstadt, 2000). Differences in the age range of the samples may account for some of this variability, where younger children tend to report higher rates of being victimized than do older children (e.g., Nansel et al., 2001; Olweus, 1993; Whitney & Smith, 1993). The main source of variability, however, appears to be differences in the assessment methods used and the conceptualizations of bullying. For example, the research studies reporting the higher prevalence data in the United States and United Kingdom employed different assessment instruments than those reporting lower values. Furthermore, conceptualizations of bullying varied substantially between these studies, where Wolke et al. (2000) and Hoover et al. (1992) used a much broader definition of bullying. Such variation in definitions between research studies is not uncommon, as there appears to be no one agreed-upon standard definition of bullying in the bullying literature (see, e.g., Arora, 1996; Ross, 2003).

In this chapter we discuss the conceptual and methodological issues associated with assessment and intervention research on bullying. Specifically, we address the definitional issues in regard to bullying and discuss some of the methodological and conceptual issues associated with the assessment methods currently used as well as the intervention procedures being practiced.

DEFINITIONAL ISSUES

While there has been considerable variation in how different research studies and other publications have defined bullying, there appears to be some consensus regarding the fundamental understanding of bullying (e.g., Greene, 2000; Olweus, 1999b; Salmivalli, Lagerspetz, Björkqvist, Österman, & Kaukiainen, 1996; Smith & Brain, 2000). For example, most writers agree that bullying is *intentional* and *unprovoked* aggression that involves *disparity of power* between the victim and his or her perpetrator(s). In this regard, Olweus (1999b) defines bullying as a repeated exposure to negative acts by one or more students, consisting of intentional aggression repeated over time (as opposed to one incident) and within a context of a disproportionate power relationship. Ross (2003) provides a variation of the same theme, but questions the element of repetition, maintaining that a child's perception of being bullied should be considered, regardless of whether the incident occurred once or several times. Similarly, Arora (1996) maintains that the long-term effects on the victim rather than the component of repetition is a more essential feature of bullying, because a victim is likely to experience emotional trauma as a result of even one such incident. Besag (1989), on the other hand, includes elements of repetition and power dominance similar to those in Olweus's definition, but also adds a component of highly competitive yet socially acceptable behavior. Crick and Dodge (1999), however, have proposed a more restrictive definition. They view bullying as "a type of proactive aggression in which aggressive acts are employed to achieve interpersonal dominance over another" (p. 129).

A number of writers have also proposed a distinction between "direct" and "indirect" forms of bullying (e.g., Olweus, 1999b; Salmivalli et al., 1996; Wolke et al., 2000). Direct bullying refers to face-to-face physical or verbal confrontations, while indirect bullying is usually described as less visible harm-doing, such as spreading rumors and social exclusion. In practice, however, this distinction does not appear to be applied when bullying is assessed in school settings. For example, the operational definition of bullying used in the Olweus Bully/Victim Questionnaire (Olweus, 1999a) includes acts of verbal and physical aggression ranging from hitting to teasing, but does not appear to include behavioral referents associated with "indirect bullying." Similarly, Bosworth, Espelage, and Simon (1999) include both "physical" and "psychological" harm in their definition, but do not differentiate between these forms of bullying in their operationalization of the construct in which behavioral referents include acts ranging from physical aggression to making fun of others. Thus, the distinction between direct and indirect forms of bullying does not appear to be intended to differentiate between the two types of bullying, but rather to justify the inclusion of less overt forms of aggression. This tendency to expand bullying beyond direct behavioral acts may be an attempt on the part of some writers to capture the full range of harmful behaviors that some children direct toward their peers. For example, Besag (1989) argues against more rigid definitions, stating that "some of the most traumatic and terrifying instances of bullying have been seemingly innocuous acts, such as giving the victim 'the wink' or 'the look'" (p. 4). The use of such inclusive definitions of bullying, however, may be counterproductive. For example, Espelage, Bosworth, and Simon (2000) report that only 19.5 percent of the middle school students in their study indicated that they had not bullied their peers in the last thirty days. In other words, approximately 80 percent of the sample engaged in bullying behaviors as defined by the study, including such behaviors as, "I called other students names"; "I teased students"; and "I said things about students to make other students laugh" (p. 328). Prevalence rates indicating that about 80 percent of a student population engages in bullying appear to suggest that having such an inclusive operationalization of bullying may result in the failure to discriminate bullying from more "normative peer conflicts."

Other nonbullying research that has focused on peer aggression and victimization (e.g., Crick & Bigbee, 1998; Crick & Grotpeter, 1996; Grotpeter & Crick, 1996) has employed a clearer distinction between overt aggression and the more indirect or relational forms of aggressive behaviors. Specifically, "overt aggression" in this literature is construed as a set of behaviors that is intended to harm others through physical hurt or a threat thereof (i.e., shoving and/or threatening to beat up a peer), while "relational aggression" is viewed as involving behaviors that intentionally harm another through manipulations of peer relationships (i.e., maliciously spreading lies or rumors; social exclusion). This latter categorization of forms of peer aggression has received empirical support, and the concepts of direct and indirect types of aggression have been shown to be highly related to gender. For example, Crick and Bigbee (1998) reported significantly higher rates of overt aggression for boys than girls, while the reverse was true for relational aggression.

Consistent with the findings of Crick and Bigbee (1998), bullying research reports much higher rates of overt aggression for boys (e.g., Boulton & Underwood, 1992; Genta et al., 1996; Olweus, 1993; O'Moore et al., 1997; Pelegrini, Bartini, & Brooks, 1999; Whitney & Smith, 1993). Based on these gender differences in the literature, as well as research distinguishing between direct and indirect forms of aggression, it would seem that research on bullying would benefit from a more specific and restricted definition. That is, definitions of bullying may not need to include behaviors that are better described by other terms, such as "peer rejection," "ostracism," and "relational aggression."

A more restricted definition of bullying would also assist in the comparability of research across cultures, since the term is shaped by English colloquialism, and an exact meaning is generally not found in the lexicon of other languages. For example, in France, school bullying is referred to as "faits de violence" (i.e., acts of violence), and includes all forms of violence in the schools, as well as disruptive behaviors that interfere with school activities (Fabre-Cornali, Emin, & Pain, 1999). This conceptualization also appears to hold for Poland (Janowski, 1999) where direct translation of bullying is somewhat difficult. Similarly, in Spain, Ortega and Mora-Merchan (1999) reported problems with defining the term within their cultural environment. In this regard, Smith, Cowie, Óafsson, and Liefooghe (2002), after studying the comparability in bullying terminology across fourteen countries and thirteen languages, suggested that prevalence of bullying in some countries (e.g., Italy) may be inflated because of the use of more inclusive "translations." In order to make comparisons across cultures more meaningful, it appears that future research would benefit from an increased specificity in the definition and operationalization of bullying.

ASSESSMENT ISSUES

Bullying research has used various methods of assessment to gather information regarding prevalence rates, attitudes, and sociometric status of those involved (i.e., popularity of perpetrators and victims), as well as information on a range of other psychosocial issues. These assessment methods have included structured interviews (Wolke et al., 2000), direct observations (Craig & Pepler, 1997), teacher's ratings (Olweus, 1978), peer nominations (Salmivalli et al., 1996), and self-reports (Nansel et al., 2001; Olweus, 1993; Pelegrini et al., 1999; Whitney & Smith, 1993).

The vast majority of the bullying research, however, has used self-reports to establish prevalence data and to explore other demographics related to bullying. The most commonly used self-report has been a translated and/or adapted version of the Olweus Bully/Victim Questionnaire (e.g., Genta et al., 1996; O'Moore et al., 1997; Whitney & Smith, 1993). This questionnaire provides a definition of bullying through brief examples of various forms of verbal and physical aggression in the context of disproportionate power relationships, where participants are asked various questions regarding frequency and circumstances of such bullying incidents. Greene (2000) maintains that this method of assessment relies on participants' retention of the definition presented at the outset of administration of the instrument, but this underlying assumption may not be valid. Respondents, for example, might revert to their own personal definition as they complete the questionnaire and provide answers reflecting behavioral referents different from those explained in the research definition. There is some evidence for this assertion, where Smith et al. (2002) found that when younger children (i.e., eight-year-olds) were asked to discriminate between different forms of aggression (e.g., bullying versus physical aggression) in various "cartoon scenarios," they primarily contrasted aggressive and nonaggressive behaviors but generally did not differentiate between the different terms (e.g., bullying, social exclusion, verbal aggression) presented to them.

In terms of the psychometric properties associated with the Olweus Bully/Victim Questionnaire, only a few published studies address the reliability and validity of this assessment instrument within or across various countries. For example, Olweus (1991) indicates that in his early Swedish studies, "self report items on being bullied or bullying or attacking others respectively correlated in the range .40-.60 (unpublished) with reliable peer ratings on related dimensions" (p. 432). Olweus (1991) also reported that in his postintervention assessment in Norway (1991) he had each participant estimate the number of students in his or her class who were involved in bullying. Class means were then correlated with the results from the Bully/Victim Questionnaire resulting in correlations of .61 (victimization) and .58 (bullying). Little additional psychometric data were published by Olweus and his colleagues until 2003 when Solberg and Olweus (2003) reported correlations for prevalence estimation between specific item clusters at .79 for being bullied and .77 for bullying other students. Specifically, these item clusters consisted of the two key items generally used from the Olweus Bully/Victim Questionnaire to establish prevalence (i.e., Have you been bullied/bullied other students?) on the one hand, and seven items about the various forms of victimization/bullying (e.g., being bullied verbally, being excluded from a group) on the other. Solberg and Olweus (2003) argue against using composite scale scores for prevalence estimation, and specifically state "a single variable/item with quite specific response alternatives is the 'method of choice' for prevalence estimation," explaining that composite scores from a scale or index are "typically somewhat more abstract and general than an estimate derived from a single variable" (p. 242). They interpret their findings to show clear discriminant value for the two key variables, and conclude that these variables show "functionality" in terms of construct validity and psychometric properties for estimating prevalence of bullying and victimization.

Although Solberg and Olweus (2003) interpret their recent findings as showing adequate construct validity for prevalence estimation of bullying and victimization in Norwegian schools, available information on the psychometric properties on the Olweus Bully/Victim Questionnaire remains limited to the Norwegian version of this assessment instrument. For example, studies that have translated and/or modified the Olweus Bully/Victim Questionnaire tend not to report reliability or validity data for the modified versions of the questionnaire (see, e.g., Borg, 1999; Genta et al., 1996; Olafsen & Viemerö, 2000).

In summary, although the majority of the available data on bullying are based on self-report data using primarily the Olweus Bully/Victim Questionnaire, it appears that the psychometric properties associated with this instrument have not been examined in detail by independent researchers within or across various countries. This apparent lack of established and readily available information on the psychometric properties of instruments like the Olweus Bully/Victim Questionnaire limits the utility and resultant decision making associated with this assessment instrument. It is, therefore, critical that future research place greater importance on establishing reliability and validity information on those instruments used to assess bullying behaviors, and make sure that these assessment tools are standardized within the particular countries and school environments in which they are used.

INTERVENTION ISSUES

A number of intervention programs are available for bullying, but relatively few have been empirically validated. One of the first programs to be evaluated was a "whole school policy approach" developed in Norway by Olweus in the early 1980s in connection with a nationwide campaign against bullying (Olweus, 1993). The program was based on "a limited set of key principles" (Olweus, 1993, p. 115), which centered on creating a school environment characterized by positive adult interest, warmth, and involvement, while setting firm limits regarding unacceptable student behavior enforced by adult supervision and nonphysical punishments. The core components at the school level included questionnaire surveys, school conference days, and better supervision during recess. The class level involved class rules against bullying and class meetings, and the core components at the individual level were "serious talks with bullies and victims" and "serious talks with parents of involved students" (Olweus, 1993, p. 127). The nationwide implementation of the intervention generally relied on existing resources at the school level (i.e., teachers and other school personnel), emphasizing the role of nonmental health professionals in the whole school policy approach to bullying.

The effectiveness of Olweus's intervention program has been documented in the literature (e.g., Olweus, 1991, 1992, 1993, 1994a, 1999a), where its success has prompted other schools (e.g., Björkqvist & Österman, 1999; Pepler et al., 1994) to implement similar procedures to curb bullying. In Olweus's study, approximately 2,500 students in Grades 4 through 7 in one Norwegian city (Bergen) were administered the Olweus Bully/Victim Questionnaire at three intervals over a two-year period. A "time-lagged contrasts between age equivalent groups" was used where only one grade/age cohort was assessed on all three occasions (Olweus, 1991). The results, presented in summarized formats in various publications (e.g., Olweus, 1991, 1992, 1993, 1994b, 1996, 1997, 1999a, 2003; Olweus & Alsaker, 1991) reported marked reductions of up to 50 percent in the frequency of bullying problems in most comparisons. However, the data and relevant analyses upon which these comparisons are based do not appear to be readily available in an English language research publication by Olweus.

The Toronto Board of Education piloted Olweus's program in four elementary schools with minor adaptations (Pepler et al., 1994). The Olweus Bully/Victim Questionnaire was administered to all enrolled students at pretest ($n = 1052$) and after eighteen months of intervention ($n = 1041$). Comparisons across measurements indicated a slight increase in the number of children reporting at least two incidents of victimization by bullies during the current school term, while there was a significant reduction (5 percent) in the number of children reporting victimization within the last five days. Contrary to the expected decrease, significantly more children also reported bullying others after eighteen months of intervention (Pepler et al., 1994). These results are in contrast to the reported success of this intervention in Bergen, Norway (e.g., Olweus, 1991).

In a review of the Norwegian Nationwide Campaign, Roland (2000) cites another evaluation study in Rogaland County, Norway, following three years of a nationwide plan to implement Olweus's program. In contrast to Olweus's results in Bergen, Norway (Olweus, 1991), Roland reports that the results of the Rogaland County study showed a slight increase in the rates of bullying. Roland indicates, however, that the two different findings may be explained in terms of implementation support, where schools in Bergen received support and direct feedback from the research team, while schools in Rogaland County received the typical national campaign procedure, consisting of a package of antibullying materials and program description.

Stevens, De Bourdeaudhuij, and Van Oost (2000) also designed a treatment outcome study in Flemish schools to evaluate the effectiveness of the Olweus's intervention program in comparison to a control condition. They also addressed Roland's concerns in regard to the availability of professional support. The study included two treatment conditions, one with extensive support from the research team, while the other condition did not receive support beyond the intervention materials. Eighteen schools were selected from a pool of fifty schools willing to participate in the study, and randomly assigned to experimental and control conditions. Measures were taken at baseline, after five months of intervention, and at a one-year follow-up. The results revealed significant differences between both treatment conditions and the control condition for students' self-reports of bullying in primary schools, while this effect was not significant at the secondary level. The significant treatment effect, however, may be somewhat misleading, since mean scores in both treatment conditions remained constant or decreased only slightly over time, while mean scores in the control groups-increased. Contrast analyses of reported victimization showed only a significant main effect for time in primary schools, where a small decrease was noted across all conditions.

In their review of the effectiveness of school-based interventions, Smith and Ananiadou (2003) cite two German publications (Hanewinkel & Knaack, 1997; Hanewinkel & Eichler, 1999), which evaluated antibullying programs in Germany that closely followed the blueprint of Olweus's intervention program. According to Smith and Ananiadou's review, pre- and posttest measures were obtained from thirty-seven schools using a German version of the Olweus Bully/Victim Questionnaire, where reductions in victimization averaged 2 percent for being bullied "now and then or more frequently" for students up to Grade 10; however, bullying increased in Grades 11 and 12.

Although one might conclude that the relative effectiveness of Olweus's intervention program has not been substantiated, more recent literature by Olweus (2003) reports the successful use of his program. Specifically, Olweus (2003) indicates that two additional replication studies in Norway (1997-1998; 1999-2000) demonstrate "clear improvements with regard to bully/victim problems" (p. 15). The first study (conducted in 1997-1998) involved thirty Norwegian schools where Olweus's program was implemented with a sample of 3,200 students, and showed reductions of 21 to 38 percent in regard to bully/victim problems. The second study (conducted in 1999-2000) reported an even better outcome with a sample of 2,300 students in ten schools, resulting in ". . . an average reduction by around 40 percent with regard to 'being bullied' and by about 50 percent for 'bullying other students'" (Olweus, 2003, p. 16).

Another whole school policy approach has also been developed and empirically evaluated in England (Smith, 1997). Designed by Sheffield University with support from the English Department of Education, the Sheffield Anti-Bullying Project provided guidelines for participating schools to develop a framework of whole school policy against bullying, within which "optional interventions" could be implemented. These were categorized into curriculum-based strategies, direct intervention for bullying situations, and playground interventions (Whitney, Rivers, Smith, & Sharp, 1994). The curriculum-based strategies included a video film about bullying for classroom discussion, drama techniques with support from a theater company, children's literature specific to bullying, and student group problem solving. Direct interventions involved assertiveness training for victims, work with bullies in line with the "Method of Shared Concern" derived from Pikas (1989), school tribunals where students were elected to sit with staff on a "court" on bullying, and peer counseling where students provided a listening service to their victimized peers. The third category, playground interventions, involved training lunchtime supervisors in recognizing and dealing with bullying, and improving the playground environment (Smith, 1997; Whitney et al., 1994).

Twenty-three schools participated in the project, and received professional support for development and implementation of the bullying interventions. Each school, however, made individual choices regarding which components of the optional interventions were implemented at its site (Whitney et al., 1994). Hence, although all schools adopted a similar "whole school policy" approach to bullying, there were differences between schools regarding which particular aspects of the treatment program would comprise their particular intervention.

An English version of the Olweus Bully/Victim Questionnaire was administered to the students enrolled in the participating primary and secondary schools several months prior to the intervention, and again two years later, at which time some schools had made good progress on policy development with about a year of implementation, while others had not achieved the program implementation stage. Consequently, the results varied considerably across schools, where twelve of the sixteen primary schools showed significant reduction in bullying rates, or an average reduction of 17 percent in the number of students reporting victimization, and an average reduction of 14 percent in the reported frequency of bullying. The effects for secondary schools, however, were substantially smaller, or typically around 5 percent (Smith, 1997).

Since these schools varied in their selection of particular aspects of the intervention package, and implementation varied across schools at the time of postintervention assessment, it is difficult to pinpoint which particular factors contributed to the positive outcome results. Whitney et al. (1994) point out, however, that based on significant correlations between input measures (i.e., effort by school) and students' ratings of perceived change (i.e., improvements in regard to bullying), schools in which intervention efforts were higher appeared to achieve more reductions in bullying. It should also be noted that the significant correlations that were found were not maintained with regard to student ratings of actual victimizations. In explaining this finding, Whitney et al. indicate that the lack of significant correlations in this area may be a result of heightened student awareness about bullying in those schools that expended higher effort, and, therefore, led a greater number of students to "recognize that they were experiencing some form of bullying which they might previously have discounted" (p. 54). In summary, these authors maintain that the overall results indicate considerable evidence for the efficacy of policy development and antibullying work. With schools being able to choose which programmatic components they want to include in their respective intervention plan, the question that arises is what aspects of the "whole school policy" approach are both necessary and sufficient for reducing bullying and victimization.

A number of "whole school policy" interventions have also been evaluated in Italy. For example, Gini (2004) reports a general decrease in bullying and victimization following these interventions; however, similar to the Sheffield project, the success and the components of these interventions varied between schools. Other intervention approaches for reducing school bullying have also been emerging from different countries over the past several years. These include "The Common Concern Method" in Sweden (Pikas, 1989), "The No-Blame Approach" in the United Kingdom (Young, 1998), and "The Bully Free Classroom" (Beane, 1999) and "Bully Proofing Your School" (Garrity, Jens, Porter, Sager, & Short-Camilli, 2000) in the United States, to name a few. However, empirical studies based on these respective approaches have generally not been published in the current research literature.

Although one could argue that whole school policy approaches appear to show some potential for curbing bullying and victimization problems in the school environment, the level of reported success appears to vary considerably. One of the reasons for this variation, as stated earlier, may be the lack of clear detail in both design and implementation of a whole school policy approach and related lack of standardization of interventions within evaluation studies. These factors have important implications for both internal validity and external validity, as well as replicability of research findings. Further specification is needed regarding the different components of the "whole school policy" approach, how school personnel are trained to implement such interventions, which materials are disseminated throughout schools, how the various components are integrated, and what controls are in place to maintain treatment fidelity and integrity.

CONCLUSIONS AND FUTURE DIRECTIONS FOR RESEARCH

Although there has been a tremendous increase in research and related scholarship on bullying in recent years, a number of areas need further study. First, while there is some agreement in regard to what constitutes "bullying," definitions are rather broad and tend to include a wide range of aggressive behaviors. As a result, behavioral referents may vary considerably from one study to another, resulting in potentially inaccurate comparisons across research studies. In order to address this concern, research on bullying needs to adopt a clearer and more specific definition of bullying. For example, current definitions of bullying include behavioral referents that describe both direct and indirect forms of aggression. Since research has shown that these two forms of aggression are highly related to gender and, therefore, are carried out differently by males versus females (e.g., Crick and Bigbee, 1988; Crick & Grotpeter, 1996; Grotpeter & Crick, 1996), we recommend that future research make a clearer distinction between direct and indirect forms of bullying with denotative operations associated with each.

A second area of concern in bullying research is related to the lack of attention to psychometric qualities in assessment. For example, the vast majority of the available data on bullying are based on the Olweus Bully/ Victim Questionnaire, for which there appear to be few published studies on reliability and validity within or across countries. Without such basic psychometric information, the validity of various research findings using this instrument within particular countries may be in question. Future assessment research in this area should be directed at establishing psychometrically sound assessment instruments where a clear distinction is made between direct and indirect forms of bullying behaviors. In addition, by relying only on victim and bully self-report data, bullying researchers may not always receive the most accurate information (e.g., Gottheil & Dubow, 2001; Perry, Kusel, & Perry, 1988). Information from other sources, such as peers and teachers, is likely to both improve accuracy of assessment and provide useful information for cross-validation studies.

Only a few different intervention programs for reducing bullying behaviors have been empirically assessed. Additional controlled comparison outcome research is needed in this area, using multiple outcome measures and including follow-up assessment periods. Although the "whole school policy" approach appears to be promising as an intervention procedure, further specification is needed in order to better evaluate this method and to maximize the replicability of the research findings, as well as to make cross-cultural comparisons easier. While it is widely understood that research within school contexts usually imposes some methodological constraints such as lack of control (see, e.g., Christenson, Carlson, & Valdez, 2002), this should not limit the consistency under which an intervention is implemented between one school and another. Hence, "whole school policy" approaches can and should provide more specific implementation guidelines, such as a teacher training manual and specification of the method for training key school personnel. In this regard Olweus (2003) has described a rigorous training method for key personnel for his program in Norway, and an unpublished "teacher handbook" is now available directly from Olweus. It is unclear, however, how this method should be adapted for schools in different cultures and for schools that may not have the same teacher-student ratio or the same classroom teaching philosophy as Norwegian schools.

Intervention studies would also benefit from added clarity in focus, such as whether or how an intervention addresses the different forms of bullying (i.e., direct and indirect) inherent in current definitions. In addition to making a distinction between direct and indirect forms of bullying, future research should consider separating out "reactive aggression" children from "proactive aggression" children (Dodge, 1991) to determine whether certain interventions are more effective for one group of bullies versus another group. Research on social information-processing has identified differences in processing patterns for the aforementioned two types of aggression (e.g., Dodge & Coie, 1987; Dodge & Crick, 1990), where proactive-aggressive children have been shown to evaluate verbally and physically aggressive behavior in significantly more positive ways than those children who were not proactive-aggressive, while reactive-aggressive children have exhibited a higher frequency of hostile attributions to ambiguous provocation than their nonaggressive counterparts (Crick & Dodge, 1996). Since bullying is a form of proactive aggression, it may be important for future intervention research to address the associated information-processing bias (i.e., expectation of positive outcomes and sense of efficacy regarding aggressive acts) with emphasis on changing the reinforcement contingencies in the bully's environment. This approach is consistent with the prescriptive- oriented research in the child psychotherapy literature (see, e.g., Morris & Kratochwill, 1998).

Bullying research is a relatively young field of study where great progress has been made in recent years. As a result, there is now an increased awareness of the negative effect bullying has on children's psychosocial adjustment, as well as recognition on the part of school authorities that there is a need for interventions (e.g., Nansel et al., 2001; Smith & Shu, 2000). In light of the increase in the research on bullying over the past several years, as well as the current emphasis on evidence-based interventions in the schools (e.g., Gutkin, 2002), we fully expect continuing progress in the areas of assessment research and comparison outcome intervention research.

REFERENCES

Arora, C. M. J. (1996). Defining bullying: Towards a clearer general understanding and more effective intervention strategies. *School Psychology International, 17,* 317-329.

Beane, A. L. (1999). *The bully free classroom: Over 100 tips and strategies for teachers K-8.* Minneapolis, MN: Free Spirit Publishing, Inc.

Besag, V. E. (1989). *Bullies and victims in schools: A guide to understanding and management.* Philadelphia: Open University Press.

Björkqvist, K., & Österman, K. (1999). Finland. In P. K. Smith, Y. Morita, J. Junger-Tas, D. Olweus, R. Catalano, & P. Slee (Eds.), *The nature of school bullying: A cross-national perspective* (pp. 56-67). New York: Routledge.

Borg, M. G. (1999). The extent and nature of bullying among primary and secondary schoolchildren. *Educational Research, 41,* 137-153.

Bosworth, K., Espelage, D. L., & Simon, T. R. (1999). Factors associated with bullying behavior in middle school students. *Journal of Early Adolescence, 19,* 341-362.

Boulton, M. J., & Underwood, K. (1992). Bully/victim problems among middle school children. *British Journal of Educational Psychology, 62,* 73-87.

Christenson, S. L., Carlson, C., & Valdez, C. R. (2002). Evidence based interventions in school psychology: Opportunities, challenges, and cautions. *School Psychology Quarterly, 17,* 466-474.

Craig, W. M., & Pepler, D. J. (1997). Observations of bullying and victimization on the school yard. *Canadian Journal of School Psychology, 2,* 41-60.

Crawford, N. (2002, October). New ways to stop bullying. *Monitor on Psychology, 33,* 64-66.

Crick, N. R., & Bigbee, M. A. (1998). Relational and overt forms of peer victimization: A multiinformant approach. *Journal of Consulting and Clinical Psychology, 66,* 337-347.

Crick, N. R., & Dodge, K. A. (1996). Social information-processing mechanisms in reactive and proactive aggression. *Child Development, 67,* 993-1002.

Crick, N. R., & Dodge, K. A. (1999). "Superiority" is in the eye of the beholder: A comment on Sutton, Smith, and Swettenham. *Social Development, 8,* 128-131.

Crick, N. R., & Grotpeter, J. K. (1996). Children's treatment by peers: Victims of relational and overt aggression. *Development and Psychopathology, 8,* 367-380.

Crockett, D. (2003, February). Critical issues children face in the 2000's. *Communiqué, 31.*

Dodge, K. A. (1991). The structure and function of reactive and proactive aggression. In D. J. Pepler, & K. H. Rubin (Eds.), *The development and treatment of childhood aggression* (pp. 201-218). Hillsdale, NJ: Lawrence.

Dodge, K. A., & Coie, J. D. (1987). Social-information-processing factors in reactive and proactive aggression in children's peer groups. *Journal of Personality and Social Psychology, 53,* 1146-1158.

Dodge, K. A., & Crick, N. R. (1990). Social information-processing bases of aggressive behavior in children. *Personality and Social Psychology Bulletin, 16,* 8-22.

Espelage, D. L., Bosworth, K., & Simon, T. R. (2000). Examining the social context of bullying behaviors in early adolescence. *Journal of Counseling & Development, 78,* 326-333.

Fabre-Cornali, D., Emin, J. C., & Pain, J. (1999). France. In P. K. Smith, Y. Morita, J. Junger-Tas, D. Olweus, R. Catalano, & P. Slee (Eds.), *The nature of school bullying: A cross-national perspective* (pp. 128-139). New York: Routledge.

Furlong, M. J., Morrison, G. M., & Greif, J. L. (2003). Reaching an American consensus: Reactions to the special issue on school bullying. *School Psychology Review, 32,* 456-471.

Garrity, C., Jens, K., Porter, W., Sager, N., & Short-Camilli, C. (2000). *Bully proofing your school: A comprehensive approach for elementary schools* (2nd ed.). Longmont, CO: Sopris West.

Genta, M. L., Menesini, E., Fonzi, A., Costabile, A., & Smith, P. K. (1996). Bullies and victims in schools in central and southern Italy. *European Journal of Psychology of Education, 11,* 97-110.

Gini, G. (2004). Bullying in Italian schools: An overview of intervention programmes. *School Psychology International, 25,* 106-116.

Greene, M. B. (2000). Bullying and harassment in schools. In R. S. Moser, & C. E. Frantz (Eds.), *Shocking violence: Youth perpetrators and victims—A multidisciplinary perspective* (pp. 72-101). Springfield, IL: Charles C. Thomas Publisher, Ltd.

Grotpeter, J. K., & Crick, N. R. (1996). Relational aggression, overt aggression, and friendship. *Child Development, 67,* 2328-2338.

Gottheil, N. F., & Dubow, E. F. (2001). The interrelationships of behavioral indices of bully and victim behavior. In R. A. Geffner, M. Loring, & C. Young (Eds.), *Bullying behavior: Current issues, research, and interventions* (pp. 75-93). New York: The Haworth Press, Inc.

Gutkin, T. B. (Ed.). (2002). Evidence-based interventions in school psychology: The state of the art and future directions [Special issue]. *School Psychology Quarterly, 17*(4).

Hoover, J. H., Oliver, R., & Hazler, R. J. (1992). Bullying: Perceptions of adolescent victims in the Midwestern USA. *School Psychology International, 13*, 5-16.

Janowski, A. (1999). Poland. In P. K. Smith, Y. Morita, J. Junger-Tas, D. Olweus, R. Catalano, & P. Slee (Eds.), *The nature of school bullying: A cross-national perspective* (pp. 264-275). New York: Routledge.

Juvonen, J., Nishina, S., & Graham, S. (2000). Peer harassment, psychological adjustment, and school functioning in early adolescence. *Journal of Educational Psychology, 92*, 349-359.

Lieberman, R. (2001). Bullying: A slow fuse to childhood rage. *Communiqué, 29*.

Morris, R. J., & Kratochwill, T. R. (Eds.). (1998). *The practice of child therapy* (3rd ed). Boston: Allyn & Bacon.

Nansel, T. R., Overpeck, M., Pilla, R. S., Ruan, W. J., Simons-Morton, B.,. & Scheidt, P. (2001). Bullying behaviors among US youth: Prevalence and association with psychosocial adjustment. *JAMA: Journal of the American Medical Association, 285*, 2094-2100.

Olafsen, R. N., & Viemerö, V. (2000). Bully/victim problems and coping with stress in school among 10- to 12-year-old pupils in Åland, Finland. *Aggressive Behavior, 26*, 57-65.

Olweus, D. (1978). *Aggression in the schools: Bullies and whipping boys.* Washington DC: Hemisphere Publishing Corporation.

Olweus, D. (1991). Bully/victim problems among school children: Basic facts and effects of a school based intervention program. In D. J. Pepler, & K. H. Rubin (Eds.), *The development and treatment of childhood aggression* (pp. 411-448). Hillsdale, NJ: Lawrence Erlbaum Associates, Publishers.

Olweus, D. (1992). Bullying among school children: Intervention and Prevention. In R. D. Peters, R. J. McMahon, & V. L. Quinsey, (Eds.), *Aggression and violence throughout the lifespan* (pp. 100-125). Newburry Park, CA: Sage.

Olweus, D. (1993). *Bullying at school: What we know and what we can do.* Oxford, UK: Blackwell Publishers.

Olweus, D. (1994a). Annotation: Bullying at school: Basic facts and effects of a school based intervention program. *Journal of Child Psychology and Psychiatry, 35*, 1171-1190.

Olweus, D. (1994b). Bullying at school: Long-term outcomes for the victims and an effective school-based intervention program. In L. R. Huesmann (Ed.), *Aggressive behavior: Current perspectives* (pp. 97-130). New York: Plenum Press.

Olweus, D. (1996). Bully/victim problems at school: Facts and effective intervention. *Journal of Emotional and Behavioral Problems, 5*, 15-22.

Olweus, D. (1997). Tackling peer victimization with a school-based intervention program. In D. P. Fry, & K. Björkqvist (Eds.), *Cultural variation in conflict resolution: Alternatives to violence* (pp. 251-231). Mahwah, NJ: Lawrence Elrbaum Associates, Inc.

Olweus, D. (1999a). Norway. In P. K. Smith, Y. Morita, J. Junger-Tas, D. Olweus, R. Catalano, & P. Slee (Eds.), *The nature of school bullying: A cross-national perspective* (pp. 28-48). New York: Routledge.

Olweus, D. (1999b). Sweden. In P. K. Smith, Y. Morita, J. Junger-Tas, D. Olweus, R. Catalano, & P. Slee (Eds.), *The nature of school bullying: A cross-national perspective* (pp. 7-27). New York: Routledge.

Olweus, D. (2003). A profile of bullying at school. *Educational Leadership, 60,* 12-17.

Olweus, D., & Alsaker, F. D. (1991). Assessing change in a cohort longitudinal study with hierarchical data. In D. Magnusson, L. R. Bergman, G. Rudinger, & B. Törestad (Eds.), *Problems and methods in longitudinal research: Stability and change* (pp. 107-132). New York: Cambridge University Press.

O'Moore, A. M., Kirkham, C., & Smith, M. (1997). Bullying behavior in Irish schools: A nationwide study. *The Irish Journal of Psychology, 18,* 141-169.

Ortega, R., & Mora-Merchan, J. A. (1999). Spain. In P. K. Smith, Y. Morita, J. Junger-Tas, D. Olweus, R. Catalano, & P. Slee (Eds.), *The nature of school bullying: A cross-national perspective* (pp. 157-173). New York: Routledge.

Pellegrini, A. D., Bartini, M., & Brooks, F. (1999). School bullies, victims, and aggressive victims: Factors relating to group affiliation and victimization in early adolescence. *Journal of Educational Psychology, 91,* 216-224.

Pepler, D. J., Craig, W. M., Ziegler, S., & Charach, A. (1994). An evaluation of an anti-bullying intervention in Toronto schools. *Canadian Journal of Community Mental Health, 13,* 95-110.

Perry, D. G., Kusel, S. J., & Perry, L. C. (1988). Victims of peer aggression. *Developmental Psychology, 24,* 807-814.

Pikas, A. (1989). A pure concept of Mobbing gives the best results for treatment. *School Psychology International, 10,* 95-104.

Rigby, K., & Slee, P. T. (1991). Bullying among Australian school children: Reported behavior and attitudes toward victims. *The Journal of Social Psychology, 131,* 615-627.

Roland, E. (2000). Bullying in school: Three national innovations in Norwegian schools in 15 years. *Aggressive Behavior, 26,* 135-143.

Ross, D. M. (2003). *Childhood bullying, teasing, and violence: What school personnel, other professionals, and parents can do* (2nd ed.). Alexandria, VA: American Counseling Association.

Salmivalli, C., Lagerspetz, K., Björkqvist, K., Österman, K., & Kaukiainen, A. (1996). Bullying as a group process: Participant roles and their relations to social status within the group. *Aggressive Behavior, 22,* 1-15.

Smith, P. K. (1997). Bullying in schools: The UK experience and the Sheffield anti-bullying project. *The Irish Journal of Psychology, 18,* 191-201.

Smith, P. K., & Ananiadou, K. (2003). The nature of school bullying and the effectiveness of school-based interventions. *Journal of Applied Psychoanalytic Studies, 2,* 189-209.

Smith, P. K., & Brain, P. (2000). Bullying in schools: Lessons from two decades of research. *Aggressive Behavior, 26,* 1-9.

Smith, P. K., Cowie, H., Ólafsson, R. F., & Liefooghe, A. P. D. (2002). Definitions of bullying: A comparison of terms used, and age and gender differences, in a fourteen-country international comparison. *Child Development, 73,* 1119-1133.

Smith, P. K., & Shu, S. (2000). What good schools can do about bullying: Findings from a survey in English schools after a decade of research and action. *Childhood, 7,* 193-212.

Solberg, M. E., & Olweus, D. (2003). Prevalence estimation of school bullying with the Olweus bully/victim questionnaire. *Aggressive Behavior, 29,* 239-268.

Stevens, V., De Bourdeaudhuij, I., & Van Oost, P. (2000). Bullying in Flemish schools: An evaluation of anti-bullying intervention in primary and secondary schools. *British Journal of Educational Psychology, 70,* 195-210.

Whitney, I., & Smith, P. K. (1993). A survey of the nature and extent of bullying in junior/middle and secondary schools. *Educational Research, 35,* 3-25.

Whitney, I., Rivers, I., Smith, P. K., & Sharp, S. (1994). The Sheffield project: Methodology and findings. In P. K. Smith, & S. Sharp (Eds.), *School bullying: Insights and perspectives* (pp. 20-56). New York: Routledge.

Wolke, D., Woods, S., Bloomfield, L., & Karstadt, L. (2000). The association between direct and relational bullying and behavior problems among primary school children. *Journal of Child Psychology & Psychiatry & Allied Disciplines, 41,* 989-1002.

Young, S. (1998). The support group approach to bullying in schools. *Educational Psychology in Practice, 14,* 32-39.

SECTION II:
EMPIRICAL RESEARCH
AND OTHER IMPORTANT EVIDENCE

Chapter 3

Dynamics of Peer Victimization in Early Adolescence: Results from a Four-Year Longitudinal Study

Jennifer J. Paul
Antonius H. N. Cillessen

Early adolescence is a crucial period of development due to the many biological, cognitive, and social changes that occur during this time. Peer relationships and interactions during the middle school years greatly influence differentiation and individuation of self-concepts. It is during early adolescence that an extremely fragile sense of self begins to unfold. Adolescents in this stage of development are able to recognize contradictions in their self-concepts and in how they conceptualize others, but they are not yet able to explain or reconcile these contradictions (Harter, 1998). Experiences during this time of social development will shape eventual identity formation in later adolescence and early adulthood.

Considering the impact of peer relations on normative social development during early adolescence, it follows that studying peer harassment or victimization that occurs during this time is critical. Peer relations researchers have considered various forms of peer harassment, including being a victim of physical, direct verbal, and indirect verbal aggression (Underwood, Galen,

This chapter was adapted from "Dynamics of Peer Victimization in Early Adolescence: Results from a Four-Year Longitudinal Study" by Jennifer J. Paul and Antonius H. N. Cillessen, *Journal of Applied School Psychology, 19*(2), pp. 25-43.

& Paquette, 2001). Although researchers in this area of study have often explored victimization in elementary school samples (e.g., Crick & Bigbee, 1998; Hodges, Boivin, Vitaro, & Bukowski, 1999; Kochenderfer-Ladd & Wardrop, 2001), less is known about this phenomenon in adolescence. One reason for this is that victimization is often assessed using peer nominations, and sociometric methods had not been used very often in early adolescent groups until recently. It is, however, crucial to explore victimization further in the early adolescent years because the experience of victimization may be especially detrimental at this time of identity formation and development of peer interactions and relationships.

STABILITY OF VICTIMIZATION

The stability of physically aggressive behavior is a well-documented finding (Coie & Dodge, 1998). Individual differences in aggression are stable over time and consistent across changes in peer group composition. Less is known, however, about the stability of being the target of peer aggression or victimization. Understanding the stability of victimization is crucial because victimization is a serious problem for students who are frequently its targets.

Most research on the stability of victimization has focused on frequency rather than chronicity (Boulton & Smith, 1994; Boulton & Underwood, 1992). Kochenderfer-Ladd and Wardrop (2001) examined physical, verbal, indirect verbal, and general victimization, and suggested that chronic victimization is not as common as might be expected based on frequency studies. This finding may be due in part to their focus on children in early elementary school only. Victimization may become more stable over the course of development and especially in early adolescence (Hodges & Perry, 1999). The stability of victimization needs to be considered not only across time, but also across contexts, keeping in mind potential changes in peer group composition. In this respect, the change from elementary to middle school, especially when it results in a new peer group, is an important developmental transition. If victimization is highly stable across time and contexts, it is critical to intervene at the earliest sign of victimization rather than believing that victimization is an experience that will pass.

Correlates and Consequences of Victimization

Research has shown that the experience of victimization is tied to emotional distress such as loneliness, anxiety, and depression (see, for a review, Kochenderfer-Ladd & Ladd, 2001) and to maladjustment as reflected in poor school achievement, self-confidence, self-esteem, and prosocial skills (Kochenderfer & Ladd, 1996; Perry, Perry, & Kennedy, 1992). These correlates of victimization have been explored in not only North American children, but also children in other cultures. For children between nine and twelve years old in Greece (Andreou, 2001), in China (Schwartz, Chang, & Farver, 2001), and Turkish children living in The Netherlands (Verkuyten & Thijs, 2001), the experience of victimization has been found to be negatively correlated with self-worth and academic functioning, and positively correlated with behavior problems. Researchers in England (Mynard, Joseph, & Alexander, 2000) and South Australia (Rigby, 2000) studied twelve-to sixteen-year-old adolescents and found victimization to be correlated with increased psychological distress (e.g., anxiety, depression) and diminished self-worth. Since many of the present studies of the concurrent correlates of victimization rely solely on self-report, however, researchers must continue to explore these by building upon the few studies that have used a multi-informant approach (e.g., Boivin, Hymel, & Hodges, 2001; Schwartz et al., 2001).

While it is clear that social maladjustment occurs concurrently with the experience of victimization, a number of studies have suggested that many of the concurrent correlates of victimization are also short-term consequences of victimization. For example, Hodges et al. (1999) found that victimized children without a mutual best friend experience both internalizing and externalizing problems one year later. In addition, increased truancy and a decline in academic performance in the spring of one academic year have been identified as short-term consequences of being victimized the previous fall (Kochenderfer & Ladd, 1996).

Furthermore, the experience of victimization at the hands of peers predicts retaliatory violence by the victims, who may imitate the aggression to which they have been chronically subjected. Various studies have demonstrated an association between victimization and aggression; between 5 and 10 percent of children who are the victims of peer aggression are themselves aggressive toward others (Olweus, 1978; Pellegrini, Bartini, & Brooks, 1999; Perry et al., 1992; Schwartz, Dodge, Pettit, & Bates, 1997). These children often become involved in emotionally charged conflicts that they tend to mismanage (Perry et al., 1992). Reports in the media of teenagers who have been involved in school shootings have suggested that these students often had a history of peer victimization before they became violent themselves. Isaacs, Card, and Hodges (2000) shed further light on this anecdotal information by showing that early adolescent boys (girls report never carrying weapons) who score high on both victimization and aggression are the most likely to carry weapons to middle school. Thus, victimization may play an important role in the occurrence of violence in school.

Predictors of Victimization

In addition to examining the concurrent behavioral and sociocognitive correlates and short-term consequences, the predictors of victimization are equally important. Elementary school students have been the focus of most of the current studies on the predictors of victimization. These studies have suggested that low self-perceived social competence, poor peer relations, internalizing and externalizing problems, and physical weakness may be predictors of elementary school victimization (see, for a review, Perry, Hodges, & Egan, 2001).

Hodges and Perry (1999) conducted one of the few studies that included older children when they examined the antecedents of victimization in third through seventh graders across a one-year interval. They found that internalizing problems, physical weakness, and peer rejection each contributed to later victimization. However, relatively little is known about the antecedents of victimization over longer intervals and into adolescence. This information is important from an early intervention perspective. Knowledge of the early predictors helps school administrators to identify students who are most likely to become victims later and to plan interventions accordingly. Intervention should address not only victimization in a proactive manner, but bullying as well. Teaching and encouraging children to embrace and value diversity, acquire team-building skills, and develop effective anger management and conflict resolution strategies at an early age are key in this effort.

Current Study

Given these considerations, the goal of the current study was to contribute to what is known about the role of victimization in adolescent development, and identify potential points of prevention and intervention by examining in detail the correlates, outcomes, and predictors of victimization in early adolescence. General victimization, including physical, direct verbal, and indirect verbal forms, was examined. The specific research predictions were as follows: (1) victimization is expected to be stable across four consecutive school years (Grades 4-7), including the transition from elementary to middle school; (2) victimization is expected to be related to concurrent measures of social and academic functioning at school in early adolescence (Grade 6); (3) victimization is expected to be negatively related to short-term adjustment outcomes in early adolescence (Grade 7); (4) both internalizing withdrawal behaviors and externalizing disruptive behaviors in elementary school (Grades 4-5) are expected to be predictors of early adolescent victimization, while self-efficacy and positive peer relationships are expected to protect against later victimization; and (5) previous research has indicated that the dynamics of peer victimization may differ for boys and girls, but the reported differences are highly variable from study to study, making it difficult to hypothesize specific differences. Therefore, the examination of gender differences within the dynamics of peer victimization is treated as exploratory.

METHOD

Participants and Design

Data collection took place in the spring of four consecutive school years as students from one cohort were followed longitudinally from Grade 4 to Grade 7. In each year, all students were invited to participate in the study. The participation rate was 95 percent or higher in each year, resulting in sample sizes of 658, 638, 600, and 600, for Grades 4-7, respectively. In Grades 4 and 5, participants were enrolled in twenty-eight classrooms of ten elementary schools. In Grades 6 and 7, they converged into two middle schools. No formal bullying interventions were taking place at any of these schools at the time of the study. About 50 percent of the students in each year were girls. The ethnic composition of the sample at the beginning of the study (Grade 4) was 77 percent white, 14 percent black, 8 percent Latino, and 1 percent of other origin. The data collection in each year included a peer sociometric measure as well as self- and teacher-report measures; these are discussed later.

Peer Sociometric Measures

Victimization was assessed in each year using unlimited peer nominations with grade as the reference group, allowing same-sex and other-sex choices. Confidentiality was discussed preceding the peer nominations. Students were instructed to work by themselves and respect each other's privacy, and researchers monitored the data collection to ensure that students complied with these guidelines. Information about individual students was not accessible to teachers or school administrators.

In each grade, a general victimization question was used ("Name the people in your grade who get picked on and teased by other kids"). In Grades 6 and 7, two additional questions were used, one for physical victimization ("Name the people who get hit, pushed, or kicked by others") and one for relational victimization ("Name the people who have lies, rumors, or mean things said about them"). In each year, nominations received were counted and standardized within school by computing z-scores. This method is consistent with the usual procedures for processing peer nomination data (cf. Cillessen & Bellmore, 1999). In Grades 4 and 5, each student's victimization score was the standardized number of general victimization nominations received. In Grades 6 and 7, the standard scores for the three victimization items were highly correlated (all $rs > .75$). Therefore, they were averaged to one victimization composite score in each year. In order to identify victimization status in Grade 6, students with a z-score larger than 1 for general, physical, or relational victimization were identified as victims ($n = 68$; 46 boys, 22 girls). The remaining sixth graders ($n = 531$; 260 boys, 271 girls) formed the nonvictimized comparison group.

Teacher Ratings

As part of the larger study, teachers rated students on a variety of constructs each year. Teachers completed the teacher report forms while students completed the peer nomination and self-report forms. Of interest for the present study were teacher ratings of disruptive conduct, school competence, and peer sociability. Items for each construct were selected from existing instruments that were age-appropriate for each grade and, therefore, varied somewhat from year to year. To place all resulting scores on a comparable metric scale, scores were standardized to z-scores in each year.

In Grades 4 and 5, three items were available for each construct from the teacher form of the Child Rating Scale (T-CRS; Hightower, Work, Cowen, Lotyczewski, Spinell, Guare, & Rohrbeck, 1986), except that one item was available for peer sociability in Grade 4. All items were rated on a 9-point scale to indicate how much they described a student (1 = not at all, 9 = very much). Internal consistencies (Cronbach's α) were .83 and .88 (disruptive conduct) and .88 and .92 (school competence) in Grades 4 and 5, respectively, and .94 for sociability (Grade 5).

In Grades 6 and 7, six items were available to measure disruptive conduct from the teacher form of the Child Behavior Checklist (CBCL; Achenbach, 1991a). Four items from the Multidimensional Self-concept Scale (MSCS; Bracken, 1992) were available to measure school competence and peer sociability. All items were rated on a 7-point scale indicating how much they were true for each student (1 = not at all, 7 = very much). Internal consistencies (Cronbach's α) were .90 and .91 (disruptive conduct), .88 and .87 (school competence), and .92 and .91 (peer sociability) in Grades 6 and 7, respectively.

Self-Report Measures

Students rated themselves in each year on six constructs within the larger longitudinal study that were of interest for the purpose of the present study: internalizing problems (loneliness or depression), disruptive conduct, anxiety/withdrawal, peer sociability, social self-efficacy, and academic self-efficacy. In addition, because self- and other-awareness become important in adolescence, meta-perceptions of victimization, cooperation, aggression, and withdrawal were also assessed in middle school. Items for each construct were selected from existing instruments that were age-appropriate for each age group and, therefore, varied somewhat from year to year. To correct for variation in the metrics of ratings between years, scale scores in each year were standardized to z-scores. The measures selected for the present study are described next.

Internalizing Problems

In Grades 4 and 5, loneliness was assessed with the 24-item Loneliness and Social Dissatisfaction Inventory (Asher & Wheeler, 1985) (α = .88 and .91 in Grades 4 and 5, respectively). In Grade 6, depression was assessed with the 26-item Child Depression Inventory (CDI; Kovacs, 1992; α = .77). In Grade 7, depression was assessed with the 12-item Beck Depression Inventory (BDI; Beck, Steer, & Garbin, 1988; α = .85).

Behavior Ratings

In Grades 4 and 5, participants rated their disruptive conduct, anxiety/withdrawal, and peer sociability with six items (Grade 4) or four items (Grade 5) per construct selected from the child form of the Child Rating Scale (CRS; Hightower, Cowen, Spinell, Lotyczewski, Guare, Rohrbeck, & Brown, 1987). Items were rated on a 5-point scale indicating how well they described the student (1 = not at all true, 5 = always true). Internal consistencies were .84 and .79 (disruptive conduct), .81 and .67 (anxious-withdrawn), and .82 and .81 (peer sociability) in Grades 4 and 5, respectively.

In Grades 6 and 7, participants rated their disruptive conduct on 12 items selected from the child form of the CBCL (Achenbach, 1991b). Twelve items derived from the MSCS (Bracken, 1992) were available for school competence and peer sociability. All items were rated on a 7-point scale indicating how much they were true for a student (1 = not at all, 7 = always). Internal consistencies were .83 and .86 (disruptive conduct), .87 and .91 (anxious-withdrawn), and .66 and .84 (peer sociability) in Grades 6 and 7, respectively.

Self-Efficacy

Social and academic self-efficacy were measured in Grades 5, 6, and 7 with items from the Student Self-concept Scale (SSCS; Gresham, Elliot, & Evans-Fernandez, 1993). These constructs were not assessed in Grade 4. Twenty items measuring social self-efficacy were available in Grades 5 and 7 (α = .89 and .93), and 11 items in Grade 6 (α = .89). Academic self-efficacy was measured with 18 items in Grades 5 and 7 (α = .89 and .92) and with 9 items in Grade 6 (α = .91). Students rated all items on a 5-point scale (Grade 5) or 7-point scale (Grades 6 and 7), indicating how confident they were in their ability to engage in the behavior described by each item (1 = not at all confident, 5 or 7 = very confident). Scale scores were averaged across items and standardized to z-scores to make them comparable between measures and years.

Meta-Perceptions

Adolescents' beliefs about how others saw them were assessed in Grades 6 and 7 for victimization ("How many people in your grade think that you get picked on and teased by other kids?"), prosocial behavior ("How many people in your grade think that you cooperate, share, or help others?"), aggression ("How many people in your grade think that you start fights, say mean things, or tease others?"), and social withdrawal ("How many people in your grade think that you are hard to get to know because you stay by yourself a lot?"). Students rated each item on a 7-point scale (1 = almost no one, 7 = almost everyone).

RESULTS

Stability of Victimization

First, correlations were computed between the continuous peer-nomination-based victimization scores for Grades 4 through 7. All correlations were significant ($p < .05$). The one-year stability of victimization was about equally high in elementary school (.70) and in middle school (.68). Despite the change in social context and peer group, the one-year stability of victimization across the transition from elementary to middle school was high as well (.62). The two-year stabilities that included the school transition were almost as high (.60 and .58). The stability of victimization from Grades 4 to 7 was lower (.44), but still substantial.

Second, stability of victimization was examined categorically. Consistent with previous approaches, students with a victimization z-score larger than $+1$ in each year were classified as victims. Of the students who were victims in Grade 4, 65 percent were also victims in Grade 5, 49 percent in Grade 6, and 34 percent in Grade 7. Of the Grade 5 victims, 42 percent and 43 percent were also victims in Grades 6 and 7, respectively. Finally, 48 percent of the victims in Grade 6 were also victims in Grade 7. Both the continuous and categorical approaches indicated significant stability of victimization across the four years of the study. The continuous and categorical stabilities for boys and girls separately were identical to each other and to the results for the total sample.

Concurrent Correlates of Adolescent Victimization

A 2 (Grade 6 Victimization Status; Victim versus Nonvictim) $\times$ 2 (Gender) ANOVA was conducted on the Grade 6 teacher- and self-report measures. Multiple ANOVAs were run following the statistical argumentation of Huberty and Morris (1989). A significant effect of victimization was found for teacher ratings of disruptive behavior, $F(1, 446) = 13.49$, school competence, $F(1, 445) = 15.27$, and peer sociability, $F(1, 446) = 9.14$, and for self-ratings of disruptive behavior, $F(1, 464) = 15.00$, withdrawal, $F(1, 464) = 5.48$, peer sociability, $F(1, 464) = 9.39$, perceived aggression, $F(1, 456) = 18.20$, perceived victimization, $F(1, 450) = 16.55$, all $ps < .003$, and academic self-efficacy, $F(1, 431) = 4.01$, $p = .046$. As can be seen in Table 3.1, victims scored higher than nonvictims on disruptive behavior (teacher and self), withdrawal, and perceived aggression and victimization. Victims scored lower than nonvictims on school competence, peer sociability (teacher and self), and academic self-efficacy.

Several significant effects of gender were found. Teachers rated girls ($M = .19$, $SD = .97$) higher than boys ($M = -.18$, $SD = .99$) on peer sociability, $F(1, 446) = 7.04$, $p = .008$. They also rated girls ($M = .16$, $SD = .91$) higher than boys ($M = -.16$, $SD = 1.06$) on school competence, $F(1, 445) = 5.39$, $p = .021$. On self-reports of disruptive behavior, boys ($M = .15$, $SD = 1.06$) scored higher than girls ($M = -.16$, $SD = .90$), $F(1, 464) = 4.19$,

TABLE 3.1. Means and standard deviations in Grade 6 and adjusted means and standard errors in Grade 7 for students who were victims and nonvictims in Grade 6.

| | Grade 6 | | | | Grade 7 | | | |
| | M | | SD | | M | | SE | |
	V	NV	V	NV	V	NV	V	NV
Disruptive (T)	.54	−.06	1.17	.96	−.04	−.04	.15	.05
School competence (T)	−.62	.07	1.10	.96	−.04	.06	.17	.05
Peer sociability (T)	−.50	.06	1.00	.98	−.57	.10	.16	.05
Disruptive (S)	.57	−.07	1.08	.97	.28	−.02	.12	.04
Anxious-withdrawn (S)	.27	−.03	.99	.10	−.27	−.04	.13	.04
Peer sociability (S)	−.45	.05	1.15	.97	−.34	.08	.14	.05
Depression (S)	.19	−.02	.93	1.01	.19	−.06	.14	.05
Social self-efficacy (S)	−.05	.011	.10	.99	−.16	.14	.14	.05
Academic self-efficacy (S)	−.25	.03	1.21	.97	.03	.07	.14	.04
Perceived prosocial (S)	−.12	.01	.98	1.00	−.38	.06	.15	.05
Perceived aggression (S)	.60	−.07	1.30	.93	.21	−.08	.15	.05
Perceived withdrawal (S)	.05	−.01	1.00	1.00	.20	−.06	.15	.05
Perceived victimization (S)	.63	−.07	1.34	.93	.21	.02	.17	.06

Note. V = victim; NV = nonvictim; T = teacher-report; S = self-report. Means (Grade 6) and adjusted means (Grade 7) that are underlined are significantly different between victims and nonvictims.

$p = .041$. On self-reports of anxiety-withdrawal, girls ($M = .13$, $SD = .98$) scored higher than boys ($M = −.13$, $SD = 1.00$), $F(1, 464) = 4.82$, $p = .029$. On perceived prosocial behavior, girls ($M = .22$, $SD = .91$) also scored higher than boys ($M = −.21$, $SD = 1.04$) did, $F(1, 457) = 4.42$, $p = .036$.

The effect of victimization on academic self-efficacy was qualified by an interaction with gender, $F(1, 431) = 5.97$, $p = .015$. Victimization influenced academic self-efficacy for girls only, $F(1, 217) = 11.01$, $p < .001$. Victimized girls ($M = −.52$, $SD = 1.35$) had lower academic self-efficacy expectations than nonvictimized girls ($M = .20$, $SD = .80$) did. Victimized boys ($M = −.08$, $SD = 1.09$) did not differ from other boys ($M = −.15$, $SD = 1.10$).

To further examine the concurrent associations of victimization, a stepwise regression analysis was conducted in which the continuous victimization score in Grade 6 was regressed on the concurrent teacher- and self-report measures. The final model included six predictors explaining 22 percent of the variance in victimization, $F(6, 316) = 15.06$, $p < .001$. Not surprisingly, self-reported disruptive conduct ($\beta = .22$) and perceived victimization ($\beta = .19$) positively predicted victimization, whereas teacher-reported school competence ($\beta = -.30$) and self-reported peer sociability ($\beta = -.14$) negatively predicted victimization.

Interestingly, social self-efficacy was also a positive predictor ($\beta = .21$), and social isolation a negative predictor of victimization ($\beta = -.12$). These effects seem counterintuitive at first, as self-efficacy is typically associated with positive outcome and social isolation with negative outcome. In the context of victimization, however, they make sense when considering that both are related to the frequency with which students expose themselves to peer interaction. Socially self-efficacious students engage themselves frequently in interactions with peers, thereby also increasing the risk that some of these interactions may be met with rebuff. Isolated students limit their interactions, and thereby decrease the risk that some interactions turn out negative. Thus, we predict that these effects are mediated by frequency of interaction, and will disappear when it is controlled for, a hypothesis to be tested in further research.

Short-Term Consequences of Adolescent Victimization

A 2 (Grade 6 Victimization Status) $\times$ 2 (Gender) ANCOVA was conducted on each Grade 7 teacher- and self-report measure, using the equivalent Grade 6 measure as a covariate. Thus, we tested whether Grade 6 victims and nonvictims were significantly different from one another one year later in Grade 7, after controlling for their initial differences in Grade 6. Multiple ANCOVAs were run, following the arguments of Huberty and Morris (1989). A significant effect of Grade 6 victimization was found on Grade 7 teacher-rated peer sociability, $F(1, 363) = 16.72, p < .001$, and self-rated disruptive behavior, $F(1, 362) = 5.21, p = .023$, anxiety-withdrawal, $F(1, 363) = 5.24, p = .023$, peer sociability, $F(1, 362) = 7.45, p = .007$, social self-efficacy, $F(1, 324) = 4.00, p = .046$, and perceived prosocial behavior, $F(1, 358) = 7.98, p = .005$, controlling for these variables in Grade 6. The interpretation of these effects is aided by the adjusted means in Table 3.1, indicating which group scored higher and which group scored lower compared to one another. Compared to nonvictims, being a victim in Grade 6 was associated with decreased sociability and social self-efficacy in Grade 7, increased disruptive and anxious-withdrawn behavior, and enhanced beliefs of being viewed negatively by peers (as anxious-withdrawn and not prosocial).

A significant effect of gender was found for self-ratings of depression, $F(1, 357) = 13.67$, anxiety-withdrawal, $F(1, 363) = 15.62$, and perceived prosocial behavior, $F(1, 358) = 6.86, ps < .009$. Girls had higher scores than boys for depression (M_{adj} = .34 versus −.21, SE = .11 versus .10) and anxiety-withdrawal (M_{adj} = .38 versus −.15, SE = .10 versus .09). Boys were less likely to think that peers saw them as prosocial (M_{adj} = −.36 versus .05, SE = .10 versus .12). A significant victim by gender interaction was found for depression, $F(1, 357) = 10.79$, $p = .001$, anxiety-withdrawal, $F(1, 363) = 9.13$, $p = .003$, self-rated disruptive behavior, $F(1, 362) = 11.19$, $p < .001$, peer sociability, $F(1, 362) = 4.67$, $p = .031$, and perceived anxiety-withdrawal, $F(1, 354) = 6.26$, $p = .013$. These interactions reflected that victimized girls stood out from the other groups. As seen in Table 3.2, victimized girls were more depressed and withdrawn than all other groups, who did not differ from each other. Victimized girls believed that peers saw them as more anxious-withdrawn than did nonvictimized girls, whereas victimized and nonvictimized boys did not differ. Victimized girls rated themselves as more disruptive and less sociable with peers than did nonvictimized girls and boys. Among nonvictims, boys were more disruptive than girls; among victims, girls were more disruptive than boys.

To further examine the effect of victimization on later adjustment, a series of hierarchical regressions was run in which each Grade 7 measure was predicted from its equivalent Grade 6 measure in Step 1, after which the incremental effect of Grade 6 victimization (continuous score) was tested in Step 2. Being victimized in Grade 6 significantly and incrementally predicted lower teacher ratings of peer sociability ($\beta = -.21$), and self-ratings reflecting more disruptive conduct ($\beta = .11$), less social self-efficacy ($\beta = -.11$), and beliefs of being seen more negatively by peers as less prosocial ($\beta = -.17$), more aggressive ($\beta = .14$), and more socially isolated ($\beta = .14$).

TABLE 3.2. Adjusted means and standard errors for self-ratings in Grade 7 for victimized and nonvictimized girls and boys.

| | M_{adj} | | | | SE | | | |
| | Girls | | Boys | | Girls | | Boys | |
	V	NV	V	NV	V	NV	V	NV
Depression	.70a	−.03b	−.32b	−.09b	.21	.07	.18	.07
Anxious-withdrawn	.74a	.03b	−.20b	−.10b	.20	.06	.17	.06
Perceived withdrawal	.51a	−.14b	−.12b	.01b	.23	.07	.19	.07
Peer sociability	−.61a	.13b	−.07ab	.02b	.22	.07	.19	.07
Disruptive	.58a	−.15b	−.03bc	.11c	.19	.06	.16	.06

Note. V = victim; NV = nonvictim. Means in the same row that do not share subscripts differ at $p < .05$ in a post hoc comparison test.

Risk and Protective Factors of Adolescent Victimization

To examine the effects of potential risk and protective factors on adolescent victimization, composite scores were computed for nine measures assessed in elementary school by averaging them across the Grade 4 and 5 assessments (except for efficacy measures, which were only assessed in Grade 5). Loneliness, anxiety, and disruptive behavior (teachers and self) were considered risk factors of adolescent victimization. School competence, social and academic self-efficacy, and peer sociability (teachers and self) were considered protective factors. All nine factors were entered into a discriminant analysis to examine their ability to determine victim status in Grade 6, following the transition to middle school. The discriminant analysis was run twice, once for boys and once for girls.

A significant linear discriminant function was found for girls, $F(9, 229) = 2.11$, $p = .029$, correctly classifying 68 percent of Grade 6 victims, and 72 percent of nonvictims. Consistent with the expectations, function coefficients for the classification of victim status were positive for the risk factors loneliness (.19, ns.), anxiety-withdrawal (.40, $p = .071$), disruptive behavior-self (.54, $p = .014$), and disruptive behavior-teacher (.41, $p = .060$), and negative for the protective factors social self-efficacy ($-.16$, ns.), academic self-efficacy ($-.55$, $p = .013$), peer sociability-self ($-.52$, $p = .017$), peer sociability-teacher ($-.42$, $p = .056$), and school competence ($-.43$, $p = .052$). Thus, disruptive behavior in elementary school was the strongest risk factor for later victimization for girls, followed by anxious-withdrawn behavior. Academic self-efficacy, school competence, and peer sociability were the strongest protective factors against victimization for girls. A significant linear discriminant function was also found for boys, $F(9, 243) = 2.08$, $p = .032$, correctly classifying 60 percent of Grade 6 victims, and 70 percent of nonvictims. Again, consistent with the expectations, function coefficients for the classification of victim status were positive for the risk factors loneliness (.30, $p = .049$), anxiety-withdrawal (.11, ns.), disruptive behavior-self (.34, $p = .027$), and disruptive behavior-teacher (.42, $p = .006$), and negative for the protective factors social self-efficacy ($-.19$, ns.), academic self-efficacy ($-.26$, $p = .091$), peer sociability-self ($-.37$, $p = .015$), peer sociability-teacher ($-.57$, $p = .001$), and school competence ($-.48$, $p = .001$). Thus, disruptive behavior in elementary school was the strongest risk factor for later victimization for boys, followed by loneliness. School competence and peer sociability were the strongest protective factors for boys.

DISCUSSION

The goal of this study was to examine the dynamics of peer victimization in a large sample of students as they were followed from elementary school across the transition to middle school. The stability, concurrent correlates, short-term consequences, and predictors of victimization in early adolescence were examined.

The stability of victimization was high across all years of the study. The stability of aggression is often reported to be in the .50-.60 range (see Coie & Dodge, 1998). Remarkably, the stability of victimization in the current study exceeded these estimates. Thus, peer victimization is a highly stable phenomenon across the middle childhood and early adolescent years. We found correlations exceeding .70 across consecutive years, even when this included an important change in social context (and corresponding composition of the peer group). A correlation of .70 translates into a proportion of shared variance of about 50 percent between consecutive measurement points, indicating that change also occurred in the midst of stability. On the other hand, the .70 stability coefficients are among the highest found for any construct in the social development literature (stabilities of aggression and social preference average around .60), and thus should be taken very seriously. The proportion of stable victims ranged from about two-thirds across the shortest interval (one year) to one-third across the longest interval (four years).

The concurrent correlates of victimization in our current sample corroborate and extend what has been found in previous research. As before, victimized adolescents are characterized by a number of psychosocial adjustment problems that include high levels of internalizing and externalizing behaviors, and low academic expectations (about themselves) and competencies (as reported by their teachers). It should be noted that low academic self-efficacy expectations were particularly characteristic of victimized girls, much more so than of boys and nonvictimized girls. This may be related to some of the other unique characteristics of girls who are victims of peer aggression that are detailed later.

Beyond the concurrent correlates of victimization, a question of great importance is that of causality. Does victimization by peers lead to the maladjustment problems described, or do underlying maladjustment problems predispose a child or adolescent to become an easy target for others? Disentangling causality is complex given the quasi-experimental nature of the majority of research in this field, yet is becoming increasingly possible with advanced statistical methods. The current study made a contribution to this issue by examining whether victimization is associated with later behavior problems when controlling for earlier levels of the outcome variables. In this respect, our study demonstrated a number of important findings strongly suggestive of an effect of victimization on negative outcomes.

The negative short-term consequences of victimization in early adolescence were found for girls, but not for boys. Victimized girls had higher levels of depression, anxiety, negative social self-perceptions, as well as self-reported disruptive behavior after one year than any other group. The question of importance is why this finding is so pronounced for early adolescent girls. Several explanations are possible. One is that girls are generally more accurate social perceivers and more sensitive to rejection than are boys (see, e.g., Cillessen & Bellmore, 1999). In addition, the forms of victimization among adolescent girls are more likely to be socially rather than physically aggressive in nature (Galen & Underwood, 1999). Combining their heightened awareness of social processes with the relational nature of the aggression may explain why victimization is associated with such negative outcomes for girls, particularly in the internalizing domain.

Our results also shed light on the elementary school variables that can be considered risk and protective factors of victimization in adolescence. For both girls and boys, the protective factors had a social and an academic component. For both genders, peer sociability was a protective factor against adolescent victimization. This effect may be direct or indirect. Directly, being more socially skilled enables adolescents to deal more effectively with the social pressures of the peer system. Indirectly, more sociable students are more likely to have friends or belong to social groups that may serve as a buffer against victimization. Teacher ratings of school competence and academic self-efficacy were associated with reduced risk of victimization for both genders. Academic achievement and confidence may be related to a more general sense of self-confidence in the school environment that may make students less vulnerable to peer harassment.

Early risk factors were also quite similar for girls and boys, and included both an externalizing and an internalizing component. For both genders, disruptive behavior in elementary school was associated with victim status in middle school. Disruptive behavior may be a risk factor because it is associated with poor behavioral and emotional regulation, making children easy to antagonize. Also, the disregulated reactions of these children are reinforcing for peers who victimize them. It is also possible that students may turn to disruptive behavior as a reaction to being victimized. Thus, disruptive behavior may become both a cause and consequence within the dynamics of victimization. The same may hold true for the internalizing risk factors; specifically, anxious-withdrawn behavior for girls and loneliness for boys. Being anxious or withdrawn and lacking a peer support network make a child defenseless, vulnerable, and an easy target for bullying. Again, these internalizing behaviors may be not only risk factors for future victimization, but also a result of previous victimization, thus placing the child in a vicious cycle of victimization experiences from which it is difficult to escape.

Strengths and Limitations

A number of strengths and limitations of the current study warrant mention. Strengths of the current study are the large sample size and the ability to make gender comparisons. Also, the longitudinal nature of the research design, spanning an extended period of time, enabled us to examine predictors as well as consequences in the context of a single study. Finally, by using peer nominations, self-report measures, and teacher reports, the current study followed a multi-informant approach that is important for work in this area. Limitations of the current study need to be examined as well. One limitation is that, although often developmentally appropriate, the change in number of items used to measure certain constructs over the course of the study may hinder some comparisons. Also, because the study was limited to one cohort, it cannot speak to potential differences across cohorts. Finally, there is a limitation in the causal interpretation of the data due to potential mediating and moderating factors (e.g., family influences) that are unknown. Further examination of mediating and moderating factors is an important direction for future research.

Implications for Research and Intervention

From a prevention standpoint, our data demonstrated that there are a number of behaviors of children in elementary school that function as risk and protective factors of later victimization. Risk factors included both internalizing and externalizing behaviors. Elementary school children who experience problems in these domains would be selected for intervention efforts aimed at alleviating these problems. The fact that these behaviors are also related to later victimization makes early intervention even more important. On the positive side, protective factors for victimization included school competence and peer sociability. Again, while the strengthening of academic and social skills are obviously of primary importance in and of themselves, the fact that these skills are also protective factors for later victimization contributes further to the importance of their pursuit. Unfortunately, high levels of risk factors tend to co-occur with low levels of protective factors. Children with externalizing or internalizing problems tend also to score low on peer sociability and academic achievement. Thus, children who demonstrate a profile of negative scores across all four of these domains should be considered as particularly at risk for later problems in relationships with peers.

From an intervention perspective, our data clearly indicate and confirm the negative social ramifications of victimization. Interventionists will need to take into consideration and target the internalizing problems of victimized adolescents. Efforts at reducing these problems will be ineffective if the processes of bullying in the peer group are allowed to continue and are not addressed directly as well. Furthermore, it seems likely that labeling the victim as a "problem student" or "someone who needs help" will not contribute to eliminating the targeting of this person by peers in her or his daily life in school. Thus, intervention needs to be systemic, focusing on the peer system as a whole, rather than only examining the individual. It may be possible to address bullying and victimization directly through student initiatives and peer-run groups or clubs (see Peterson & Rigby, 1999). Incorporating team-building and conflict-management skill development into these groups or clubs may serve to improve social skills and, in turn, impede the cycle of bullying and victimization.

REFERENCES

Achenbach, T. M. (1991a). *Manual for the Teacher's Report Form and 1991 Profile.* Burlington, VT: University of Vermont Department of Psychiatry.

Achenbach, T. M. (1991b). *Manual for the Youth Self-Report and 1991 Profile.* Burlington, VT: University of Vermont Department of Psychiatry.

Andreou, E. (2001). Bully/victim problems and their association with coping behaviour in conflictual peer interactions among school-age children. *Educational Psychology, 21,* 59-66.

Asher, S. R., & Wheeler, V. A. (1985). Children's loneliness: A comparison of rejected and neglected peer status. *Journal of Consulting and Clinical Psychology, 53,* 500-505.

Beck, A. T., Steer, R. A., & Garbin, M. (1988). Psychometric properties of the Beck Depression Inventory: Twenty-five years of evaluation. *Clinical Psychology Review, 8,* 77-100.

Boivin, M., Hymel, S., & Hodges, E. V. E. (2001). Toward a process view of peer rejection and harassment. In J. Juvonen & S. Graham (Eds.), *Peer harassment in school: The plight of the vulnerable and victimized* (pp. 265-289). New York: Guilford Press.

Boulton, M. J., & Smith, P. K. (1994). Bully/victim problems in middle-school children: Stability, self-perceived competence, peer perceptions, and peer acceptance. *British Journal of Developmental Psychology, 12,* 315-329.

Boulton, M. J., & Underwood, K. (1992). Bully/victim problems among middle school children. *British Journal of Educational Psychology, 62,* 73-87.

Bracken, B. A. (1992). *The multidimensional self-concept scale.* Austin, TX: PRO-ED.

Cillessen, A. H. N., & Bellmore, A. D. (1999). Accuracy of social self-perceptions and peer competence in middle childhood. *Merrill-Palmer Quarterly, 45,* 650-676.

Coie, J. D., & Dodge, K. A. (1998). Aggression and antisocial behavior. In W. Damon (Series Ed.), & N. Eisenberg (Vol. Ed.), *Handbook of child psychology: Vol. 3. Social, emotional, and personality development* (5th ed., pp. 779-862). New York: Wiley.

Crick, N. R., & Bigbee, M. A. (1998). Relational and overt forms of peer victimization: A multi-informant approach. *Journal of Consulting and Clinical Psychology, 66,* 237-347.

Galen, B. R., & Underwood, M. K. (1997). A developmental investigation of social aggression among children. *Developmental Psychology, 33,* 589-600.

Gresham, S. M., Elliot, S. N., & Evans-Fernandez, S. E. (1993). *Student self-concept scale.* Circle Pines, MN: American Guidance Service, Inc.

Harter, S. (1998). The development of self-representations. In W. Damon (Series Ed.), & N. Eisenberg (Vol. Ed.), *Handbook of child psychology: Vol. 3. Social, emotional, and personality development* (5th ed., pp. 553-617). New York: Wiley.

Hightower, A. D., Cowen, E. L., Spinell, A. P., Lotyczewski, B. S., Guare, J. C., Rohrbeck, C. A., et al. (1987). The Child Rating Scale: Development of a self-rating scale for elementary school children. *School Psychology Review, 16,* 239-255.

Hightower, A. D., Work, W. C., Cowen, E. L., Lotyczewski, B. S., Spinell, A. P., Guare, J. C., et al. (1986). The Teacher-Child Rating Scale: A brief objective measure of elementary school children's problem behaviors and competencies. *School Psychology Review, 15,* 393-409.

Hodges, E. V. E., Boivin, M., Vitaro, F., & Bukowski, W. M. (1999). The power of friendship: Protection against an escalating cycle of peer victimization. *Developmental Psychology, 35,* 94-101.

Hodges, E. V. E., & Perry, D. G. (1999). Personal and interpersonal antecedents and consequences of victimization by peers. *Journal of Personality and Social Psychology, 7,* 677-685.

Huberty, C. J., & Morris, J. D. (1989). Multivariate analysis versus multiple univariate analyses. *Psychological Bulletin, 105,* 302-308.

Isaacs, J., Card, N. A., & Hodges, E. V. E. (2000, June). *Aggression, peer victimization, social cognitions, and weapon carrying in schools.* Paper presented at the annual meeting of the American Psychological Society, Miami Beach, FL.

Kochenderfer, B. J., & Ladd, G. W. (1996). Peer victimization: Cause or consequence of school maladjustment? *Child Development, 67,* 1305-1317.

Kochenderfer-Ladd, B., & Ladd, G. W. (2001). Variations in peer victimization: Relations to children's maladjustment. In J. Juvonen & S. Graham (Eds.), *Peer harassment in school: The plight of the vulnerable and victimized* (pp. 25-48). New York: Guilford Press.

Kochenderfer-Ladd, B., & Wardrop, J. L. (2001). Chronicity and instability of children's peer victimization experiences as predictors of loneliness and social satisfaction trajectories. *Child Development, 72,* 134-151.

Kovacs, M. (1992). *Children's Depression Inventory (CDI) Manual.* New York: Multi-Health Systems, Inc.

Mynard, H., Joseph, S., & Alexander, J. (2000). Peer victimization and posttraumatic stress in adolescents. *Personality and Individual Differences, 29,* 815-821.

Olweus, D. (1978). *Aggression in the Schools: Bullies and Whipping Boys.* Washington, DC: Hemisphere Press.

Pellegrini, A. D., Bartini, M., & Brooks, F. (1999). School bullies, victims, and aggressive victims: Factors relating to group affiliation and victimization in early adolescence. *Journal of Educational Psychology, 91,* 216-224.

Perry, D. G., Hodges, E. V. E., & Egan, S. K. (2001). Determinants of chronic victimization by peers: A review and a new model of family influence. In J. Juvonen & S. Graham (Eds.), *Peer harassment in school: The plight of the vulnerable and victimized* (pp. 73-104). New York: Guilford Press.

Perry, D. G., Perry, L. C., & Kennedy, E. (1992). Conflict and the development of antisocial behavior. In C. U. Shantz & W. W. Hartup (Eds.), *Conflict in child and adolescent development* (pp. 301-329). New York: Cambridge University Press.

Peterson, L., & Rigby, K. (1999). Countering bullying at an Australian secondary school with students as helpers. *Journal of Adolescence, 22,* 481-492.

Rigby, K. (2000). Effects of peer victimization in schools and perceived social support on adolescent well-being. *Journal of Adolescence, 23,* 57-68.

Schwartz, D., Chang, L., & Farver, J. M. (2001). Correlates of victimization in Chinese children's peer groups. *Developmental Psychology, 37,* 520-532.

Schwartz, D., Dodge, K. A., Pettit, G. S., & Bates, J. E. (1997). The early socialization of aggressive victims of bullying. *Child Development, 68,* 665-675.

Underwood, M. K., Galen B. R., & Paquette, J. A. (2001). Top ten challenges for understanding gender and aggression in children: Why can't we all just get along? *Social Development, 10,* 248-266.

Verkuyten, M., & Thijs, J. (2001). Peer victimization and self-esteem of ethnic minority group children. *Journal of Community and Applied Social Psychology, 11,* 227-234.

Chapter 4

The Association
of Bullying and Victimization
with Middle School Adjustment

Tonja R. Nansel
Denise L. Haynie
Bruce G. Simons-Morton

INTRODUCTION

The transition from elementary to middle school is an important developmental task for early adolescents. It is a time typically characterized by increased academic demand, decreased personal attention in school, increased social stressors, and a shift from adult-focused to peer-focused relationships (Eccles, 1999; Elias, Gara, & Ubriaco, 1985; Lynch & Cicchetti, 1997). An important component of adaptation to middle school is the youth's development of healthy social relationships with peers. Peer relationships may influence school adjustment through both affective and social processes. Youths' peer relationships at school function as either supports or stressors in their adjustment to the demands of a new school environment (Birch & Ladd, 1996; Ladd & Price, 1987; Ladd, Kochenderfer, & Coleman, 1997). Difficulties in peer relationships are associated with negative changes in self-concept and feelings of self-worth (Fenzel, 2000; Haynes, 1990; Wenz-Gross, Siperstein, Untch, & Widaman, 1997), which may impair subsequent

This chapter was adapted from "The Association of Bullying and Victimization with Middle School Adjustment" by Tonja R. Nansel, Denise L. Haynie, and Bruce G. Simons-Morton, *Journal of Applied School Psychology, 19*(2), pp. 45-61.

Bullying, Victimization, and Peer Harassment
doi:10.1300/5808_04

school adjustment. Conversely, healthy peer relationships may promote positive school adjustment by creating a sense of relatedness that serves a motivational function for youth in school (Connell &Wellborn, 1991; Anderman & Anderman, 1999; Ryan & Powelson, 1991).

A common maladaptive type of peer interaction among middle school youth is that of bullying. Bullying is typically defined as aggressive peer-to-peer behavior in which (1) there is an intention to harm or disturb the victim; (2) the aggression occurs repeatedly over time; and (3) there is an imbalance of power, with a more powerful person or group attacking a less powerful one (Olweus, 1993). The aggressive behavior may be verbal (e.g., name-calling, threats), physical (e.g., hitting), or psychological (e.g., rumors, shunning/exclusion). Bullying is a relatively common phenomenon among early adolescents. In a nationally representative study of U.S. youth in Grades 6-10, 29.9 percent reported involvement in moderate or frequent bullying, with 13.0 percent bullying others, 10.6 percent being bullied, and 6.3 percent reporting both bullying others and being bullied. Bullying occurred more frequently among sixth to eighth grade youth than among those in Grades 9 and 10 (Nansel, Overpeck, Pilla, Ruan, & Simons-Morton, 2001).

Involvement in bullying during the transition to middle school may represent an important risk factor for subsequent school adjustment. Both bullying others and being victimized represent maladaptive peer relationships, which could predispose the youth involved to increased difficulty during the middle school transition. However, the relationship between bullying/victimization and school adjustment has not been adequately addressed in previous research. The purpose of this study was to determine the relationship of bullying and being victimized during the first year of middle school with school adjustment and perceived school climate at the end of the first and second years of middle school. We examined the continuity of bullying behaviors over time, and investigated the extent to which bullies, victims, and bully-victims differed from noninvolved youth in their adjustment to middle school.

REVIEW OF RELEVANT LITERATURE

The developmental challenges associated with the transition to middle school may result in personal and academic difficulties for youth. Overall, students typically experience an increase in psychological distress and a decrease in academic motivation and achievement during the transition to middle school (Blyth, Simmons, & Carlton-Ford, 1983; Crockett, Peterson,

Graber, Schulenberg, & Ebata, 1989; Guttman & Midgley, 2000; Hirsch & Rapkin, 1987; Simmons & Blyth, 1987; Wigfield, Eccles, Maclver, Reuman, & Midgley, 1991). While these findings occur across racial and socioeconomic status groups, individual students vary in the extent to which they experience such transition difficulties (Chung, Elias, & Schneider, 1998; Crockett et al., 1989; Fenzel & Blyth, 1986; Hirsch & Rapkin, 1987; Simmons & Blyth, 1987). Thus, it is likely that various risk and protective factors may influence the degree of difficulty experienced.

Previous research indicates that one important factor influencing middle school adjustment may be that of the youth's peer relationships. In a predominantly middle-class sample of Canadian youth, McDougall and Hymel (1998) found that transition differences between youth were predicted by both social adjustment and school attitudes/behaviors, with social adjustment playing a potentially critical role. In a study of low-income black children, adjustment during the first year of middle school was predicted by both aggression and peer rejection (Coie, Lochman, Terry, & Hyman, 1992). Support for various mechanisms linking peer relationships to academic adjustment has been found. One study conducted with youth in a working-class, ethnically diverse Midwestern community, found support for the mediating role of prosocial behavior (Wentzel & Caldwell, 1997). Another conducted with a sample of ethnically diverse urban middle-school youth supported an explanatory model in which peer harassment negatively influences psychological adjustment, which subsequently affects school adjustment (Juvonen, Nishina, & Graham, 2000).

There is much support for the assertion that peer harassment has a negative effect on psychological adjustment. Research conducted across countries and with diverse samples has consistently found that both bullies and victims of bullying demonstrate poorer psychosocial functioning than their noninvolved peers. Youth who bully others tend to demonstrate higher levels of conduct problems and externalizing behaviors, whereas youth who are bullied generally show higher levels of internalizing behaviors, including anxiety, depression, loneliness, unhappiness, and low self-esteem, as well as increased physical symptoms (Austin & Joseph, 1996; Boulton & Underwood, 1992; Forero, McLellan, Rissel, & Bauman, 1999; Hawker & Boulton, 2000; Haynie et al., 2001; Hodges & Perry, 1999; Kaltiala-Heino, Rimpela, Rantanen, & Rimpela, 2000; Kumpulainen, Rasanen, & Henttonen, 1999; Nansel et al., 2001; Olweus, 1978, 1993; Rigby, 1999; Salmon, James, & Smith, 1998; Williams, Chambers, Logan, & Robinson, 1996). Moreover, youth who both bully others and are victims of bullying demonstrate even poorer psychosocial functioning than youth who only bully or are only victimized (Andreuo, 2000; Austin & Joseph, 1996; Forero et al., 1999;

Kaltiala-Heino et al., 2000; Kumpulainen et al., 1998; Haynie et al., 2001; Nansel et al., 2001). Studies conducted to date, then, suggest that peer relationships influence psychological adjustment, and subsequently, psychological adjustment affects school adjustment. This relationship may be especially acute during the middle school years, when youth are shifting emphasis from adult-focused to peer-focused relationships. If maladaptive peer relationships do in fact have a negative impact on school adjustment due to their detrimental effect on psychosocial functioning, youth who bully others and youth who are bullied would be at risk for school adjustment problems. This study focuses on bullying that occurs during the sixth grade year—when students are in the middle school transition period.

METHODS

Participants

Self-report survey data were obtained from two cohorts of students in four middle schools (grades 6-8) in one suburban Maryland school district. The county in which this school district resides is somewhat racially diverse, with 69 percent of residents white, 26 percent African American, 2 percent Hispanic, and 2 percent Asian (U.S. Census Bureau, 1990). The 1997 model-based estimates for the percent of people of all ages in poverty in the county is 7 percent, and median income is $54,110, according to the U.S. Census Bureau. Students starting sixth grade in the fall of 1996 and the fall of 1997 were recruited to participate in the study. Special education students with reading disabilities ($n = 119$) were considered ineligible. Data were obtained in the fall of sixth grade, the spring of sixth grade, and the spring of seventh grade. The four schools had been randomly assigned a nonintervention status as part of a district-wide study evaluating the effects of a school-based program targeting multiple problem behaviors. The school district had no other special interventions occurring in the middle schools at the time of the study, as part of their agreement to be the site for the research. From a total of 1,490 eligible sixth grade students, 1,267 (85 percent) completed the baseline survey. Nonparticipants included 118 parent refusals, 47 nonreturned consent forms, 55 absences on both assessment dates, and 3 incomplete/unusable surveys. Of the 1,267 baseline participants, 939 (74 percent) were also assessed at the following two time points. Lost to follow-up were 116 students who moved out of the county, 42 parent refusals, 60 nonreturned consent forms, 43 absences, 33 who moved to a treatment condition school, 27 who were later classified as special education students, and 7 who failed sixth grade. The final sample comprised 47.1 percent boys and 52.9 percent girls. The ethnic composition of the sample was 73.7 percent white students, 16.7 percent black students, and 9.6 percent students of other racial/ethnic backgrounds.

Procedures

Parents and students were informed that the survey was the measurement component of the intervention evaluation study. Written consent was obtained from all parents of the participating students. Students' assent was also obtained. Students completed questionnaires during their homeroom classroom, with makeup assessments scheduled the following week for students who were absent on the day of assessment. The survey was administered in each classroom by two trained proctors. Study investigators and project staff served as trainers and team leaders, each supervising several pairs of proctors. Teachers remained in the classroom to supervise student discipline but were otherwise uninvolved in the survey procedures. To ensure confidentiality, students first completed and turned in a cover page that included their name, survey identification number, birth date, and homebase classroom teacher's name. Students' names were not on the questionnaires. The study was reviewed by the National Institute of Child Health and Human Development Institutional Review Board and authorized by representatives of the school district.

Measures

The questionnaire was designed to assess behaviors and attitudes targeted by the intervention program. Measures were either selected or created based on extensive review of the relevant published literature. Prior to implementation in this study, a pilot study ($n = 130$ sixth-grade students) was conducted to ascertain the readability of items and internal consistency of scales. The survey used in the current study consisted of 116 items assessing student background, psychosocial, school, and parent variables, as well as involvement in problem behaviors, a subset of which included questions about bullying and victimization. For the measures of school adjustment and climate, if a student completed at least of the items comprising a scale, the value for any missing items was imputed based on the item mean for students of the same grade and gender. Scale scores were then computed (Kessler, Little, & Groves, 1995). A summary of each measure follows.

Bullying

Bullying was assessed by asking "How many times in the last year have you bullied or picked on someone younger, smaller, or weaker (not including your brothers and sisters")? Response categories were 0 = zero, 1 = 1 or 2 times, 2 = 3 to 5 times, and 3 = 6 or more times.

Victimization

Victimization during the last year was assessed by asking how many times the respondent had (1) something taken from them by force or threats, (2) been made to do something they did not want to do, (3) been threatened to be physically hurt, and (4) been actually physically hurt. Response categories were 0 = zero, 1 = 1 or 2 times, 2 = 3 to 5 times, and 3 = 6 or more times.

School Adjustment

This eleven-item scale measured the student's adjustment in the activities of school, such as doing well on schoolwork, getting along with classmates, following rules, doing homework, etc. Students rate how well the item describes them on a 4-point scale: really true, sort of true, sort of false, or really false.

School Climate

This seventeen-item scale, adapted from Pyper and colleagues (1987), includes items measuring perceived teacher support, rule clarity and enforcement, and student respect for one another. Items are rated from strongly agree to strongly disagree on a 4-point scale.

Analysis

As the focus of this study is on bullying/victimization that occurs during the first year of middle school, students were classified as victims, bullies, bully-victims, or comparisons, based on their reports in the spring of sixth grade regarding bullying and victimization during the previous year (i.e., during sixth grade). Victims reported having been victimized three or more times in the past year and having never or rarely (two or fewer times) bullied. Bullies reported bullying others three or more times in the past year and never or rarely having been victimized. Bully-victims reported both having bullied and having been victimized three or more times in the past year. Comparison youth were those who reported no bullying or victimization. Students who reported rarely bullying and/or being victimized were not classified in any of the four groups, as the focus of this study is on repeated bullying and victimization during the first year of middle school. Students missing data on either bullying or victimization measures ($n = 9$; 0.01 percent) were excluded from the analysis.

Because bullying behaviors may persist over time (Kumpulainen et al., 1999), students who bullied or were victimized during the first year of middle school may have differed from noninvolved youth at baseline (fall of sixth grade). Therefore, potential baseline group differences were assessed by analyses of variance (ANOVA) conducted on baseline measures of bullying, victimization, school adjustment, and school climate using the four-group classification. To control for these baseline differences, analysis of covariance (ANCOVA) was selected as the analytic technique for subsequent analyses. Analysis of covariance adjusts the means on each dependent variable (school adjustment or climate) to their expected levels if all subjects had scored equally on the covariates (baseline bullying, victimization, and the corresponding school measure) (Tabachnick & Fidel, 1996). A series of ANCOVAs were conducted on spring sixth and seventh grade measures of school adjustment and school climate with baseline bullying, victimization, and the corresponding school measure as covariates.

RESULTS

Variable means, standard deviations, range of responses, coefficient alphas, and correlations are presented in Table 4.1. As anticipated, school adjustment and perceived school climate showed a mean decrease from fall to spring of sixth grade. In addition, perceived school climate declined further by spring of seventh grade. School adjustment and perceived school climate were positively associated with each other, and negatively associated with bullying and victimization. A total of 199 students (21.4 percent) reported being victimized repeatedly (three or more times) during their first year of middle school, 25 (2.7 percent) reported repeatedly bullying others, and 23 (2.5 percent) reported both repeatedly bullying others and repeatedly being victimized (Table 4.2). Almost half of the students ($n = 419$, 45.1 percent) reported no bullying or victimization. In addition, 264 (28.4 percent) reported bullying and/or being victimized once or twice.

TABLE 4.1. Ranges, means, standard deviations, and correlations among variables.

Variable†	Range	Alpha	Mean	SD	1	2	3	4	5	6	7	8	9	10	11
1. F6 Victimization	0-18	.82	1.27	2.43											
2. S6 Victimization	0-24	.84	1.82	3.16	.37										
3. S7 Victimization	0-24	.84	1.79	3.25	.30	.48									
4. F6 Bullying	0-3	-	.21	.57	.30	.20	.10								
5. S6 Bullying	0-3	-	.28	.64	.15	.16	.18	.21							
6. S7 Bullying	0-3	-	.39	.75	.15	.16	.28	.28	.42						
7. F6 School adjustment	15-44	.85	35.91	5.81	-.22	-.17	-.17	-.24	-.15	-.10					
8. S6 School adjustment	11-44	.85	33.68	6.26	-.21	-.29	-.20	-.26	-.22	-.18	.49				
9. S7 School adjustment	14-44	.78	33.21	5.94	-.19	-.28	-.25	-.28	-.19	-.31	.38	.62			
10. F6 School climate	23-68	.91	59.50	7.38	-.18	-.12	-.13	-.23	-.14	-.09	.41	.34	.26		
11. S6 School climate	17-68	.92	54.90	9.22	-.14	-.24	-.19	-.20	-.18	-.16	.29	.52	.38	.49	
12. S7 School climate	17-68	.92	52.18	9.06	-.13	-.20	-.21	-.17	-.13	-.20	.21	.35	.49	.40	.57

†Note. F6 = fall of sixth grade; S6 = spring of sixth grade; S7 = spring of seventh grade.

TABLE 4.2. Sixth grade bully and victim groups' reports of bullying and victimization during seventh grade.

	Sixth grade group		Seventh grade group		
	None	Minimal†	Victim	Bully	Bully-Victim
Nonbully/nonvictim (n = 419)‡	62.5% (260)	25.3% (105)	9.4% (39)	1.9% (8)	1.0% (4)
Victim (n = 199)‡	23.2% (46)	24.2% (48)	46.0% (91)	2.5% (5)	4.0% (8)
Bully (n = 25)	32.0% (8)	8.0% (2)	8.0% (2)	32.0% (8)	20.0% (5)
Bully/Victim (n = 23)	0.0% (0)	17.4% (4)	47.8% (11)	8.7% (2)	26.1% (6)

Note. † Those who bullied and/or were victimized only "once or twice."
‡ Four participants were missing data on bullying/victimization at the spring seventh grade assessment. As such, table percentages are calculated based on an *n* of 416 on the nonbully/nonvictim group and 198 in the victim group.

Analysis of the four groups who reported bullying and victimization during seventh grade showed considerable continuity from spring of sixth to spring of seventh grade. (The sixth Grade measures were done seven months apart; thus, continuity from fall to spring of sixth grade was not assessed due to overlap in the twelve-month time frame of these two measures.) As seen in Table 4.2, most students who reported no bullying or victimization during sixth grade also reported two or fewer such incidents during seventh grade. About half of the sixth grade victims reported seventh grade victimization and half of the sixth grade bullies reported seventh grade bullying. Among the sixth grade bully-victims, almost all were bullies, victims, or both in seventh grade.

A series of ANOVAs for bullying, victimization, school adjustment, and school climate at the fall of sixth grade showed significant baseline differences between the four groups ($F = 40.34$ for victimization, 18.35 for bullying, 12.38 for school adjustment, and 4.19 for school climate; $p < .01$ for all variables). That is, students who bullied others and/or were victimized during their first year of middle school were significantly different on these measures when they entered middle school. Therefore, adjusting for baseline scores on these measures is warranted.

The results of the ANCOVAs demonstrated poorer adjustment to middle school at both spring of sixth grade and spring of seventh grade among victims, bullies, and bully-victims after controlling for baseline scores on these measures (Table 4.3). Bully and victim group status demonstrated a significant effect on school adjustment and climate at spring of sixth and seventh grades above that explained by baseline scores. Bullies, victims, and bully-

TABLE 4.3. Adjusted and unadjusted means for bully and victim groups on school measures at spring of sixth and seventh grade.

Sixth-grade bully and victim group	Spring of sixth grade				Spring of seventh grade			
	School adjustment $F = 16.63$**		School climate $F = 8.69$**		School adjustment $F = 15.29$**		School climate $F = 5.48$**	
	Unadjusted mean	Adjusted mean[†]	Unadjusted mean[‡]	Adjusted mean	Unadjusted mean	Adjusted mean[†]	Unadjusted mean	Adjusted mean[‡]
Nonbully/Nonvictims	35.57	34.97[a]	56.96	56.37[a]	35.11	34.65[a]	53.74	53.31[a]
Victims	30.70	31.65[b]	51.80	52.70[b]	30.86	31.56[b]	49.73	50.41[b]
Bullies	30.42	30.91[b]	52.30	53.74[ab]	31.00	31.46[b]	50.83	51.85[ab]
Bully/Victims	30.32	32.31[b]	50.00	51.35[b]	29.64	31.21[b]	48.00	48.78[b]

Note. ** $p < .01$.
[†] Adjusted for baseline values on victimization, bullying, and school adjustment. Adjusted means reflect the value that would be expected if all subjects had the same scores at baseline.
[‡] Adjusted for baseline values on victimization, bully, and school climate. Adjusted means reflect the value that would be expected if subjects had the same scores at baseline.
[a,b] Means with different superscripts are significantly different from each other.

victims all demonstrated poorer school adjustment than their noninvolved peers even after controlling for their poorer baseline scores on these measures. These differences were present at spring of sixth grade and persisted through spring of seventh grade. Victims and bully-victims also reported a more negative perceived school climate at spring of both sixth and seventh grades than noninvolved students.

DISCUSSION

Overview of Findings

Findings from this study indicate that bullying and victimization are common problems among youth. More than one-half of sixth grade youth reported some level of bullying, victimization, or both, and over one-fourth reported repeated bullying and/or victimization. Both bullying and victimization demonstrated continuity over time, with over half of students who were involved in repeated bullying and/or victimization in sixth grade reporting repeated involvement in seventh grade as well. In contrast, among youth not involved in bullying or victimization during sixth grade, almost 12 percent reported repeated bullying and/or victimization during seventh grade. This suggests that bullying and/or victimization is a continuing problem for youth who are involved in these behaviors during their first year of middle school.

Results of this study suggest that involvement in bullying others or being a victim of bullying may be a risk factor for poorer adjustment to middle school. Youth who were classified as bullies, victims, or bully-victims during sixth grade all reported poorer school adjustment at both spring of sixth grade and spring of seventh grade than their noninvolved peers, even after adjusting for their baseline scores on bullying, victimization, and school adjustment. Similarly, those who were victims or bully-victims during sixth grade reported a more negative perceived school climate at spring of both sixth and seventh grade than bullies or comparison youth. These youth were less adapted to middle school upon entry, but showed even poorer later school adjustment than would be expected from their initial scores. This suggests that the failure to develop positive peer relationships may be an issue not only of social and emotional development, but also may hinder adaptation to the middle school environment as well. This effect may be mediated by poorer psychosocial adjustment for both bullies and victims. In addition, for bullies, it may reflect difficulties with the social constraints and limits placed by the school environment. In previous studies, bullies have been found to like school less (Rigby & Slee, 1991) and to be less popular with teachers (Slee & Rigby, 1993) than other youth. For victims, the lack of safety in the school environment may also contribute to poorer adjustment to school.

In the past, bullying has often been viewed as a minor problem among youth–as a negative but normative and unavoidable aspect of peer interaction (Arora & Thompson, 1987; Hoover & Oliver, 1996). Findings from the current study add to the body of research indicating that bullying is associated with detrimental outcomes for both bullies and victims. As such, it should be treated as a significant issue for youth, especially during the middle school transition years, warranting efforts to promote youth and adult norms intolerant of bullying.

Strengths and Limitations

This study is one of the few to address the relationship between bullying and school adjustment over time. The longitudinal nature of the data provides several strengths. Continuity of bullying/victimization over time was assessed. Baseline differences on the variables of interest were controlled for in the analysis, and outcomes were measured during spring of both the first and second years of middle school. Nevertheless, the study's limitations must be recognized as well. Variables associated with bullying and victimization were assessed through self-report, and measures used were brief, as bullying was not the main focus of the survey. Further, the measure of bullying in this study might have tapped primarily direct, aggressive, bullying, and not other behaviors, such as teasing or exclusion, which are not as commonly associated with the word "bully." As such, the number of youth in the bully and bully-victim groups were small, limiting the power of the study. The youth in this study, while ethnically diverse, were from a primarily suburban area of an eastern city, and may differ from youth in rural or urban areas and those from other parts of the country. Finally, this study did not investigate causes of bullying or potential variables that might account for both bullying/victimization and school adjustment problems (e.g., family socialization, individual character, etc.), nor did it test the potential pathway of the effect of peer harassment on school adjustment through psychological adjustment.

Implications for Research and Practice

While much research has been conducted on aggressive behavior among U.S. youth, little attention has been paid specifically to bullying. However, a large body of international research provides a foundation for future study and intervention in this area (Smith & Brain, 2000). Research conducted in Norway and England has demonstrated that the incidence of bullying in schools can, in fact, be reduced substantially through school-based interventions that create changes within the school and classroom environment (Olweus, 1993, 1994; Sharp & Smith, 1991; Smith, 1997). Findings from these studies demonstrate the importance of creating a school environment (1) characterized by warmth, positive interest, and involvement from adults— where students feel they are cared about and expected to do well; and (2) where there are clear, firm limits to peer harassment and bullying that areconsistently enforced. Important components of these bullying prevention programs include clear and explicit expectations regarding the treatment of others, the use of classroom meetings addressing peer relationships, the incorporation of activities promoting respect for others into day-to-day curriculum, adequate supervision of youth, adult intervention in bullying situations, individual intervention with bullies and victims as needed, ongoing staff training/development, and the facilitation of parental involvement.

Findings from this study support the need for these types of programs in the United States and highlight the importance of early prevention, before these behavior patterns become entrenched, and concomitant adjustment problems occur. Bullying prevention information and materials for educators are becoming increasingly available and may provide a useful start for the promotion of school-based bullying prevention efforts (e.g., Committee for Children, 2001; Froschl, Sprung, & Mullin-Rindler, 1998; Garrity, Jens, Porter, Sager, & Short-Camilli, 2001; Hoover & Oliver, 1996; Olweus, Limber, & Mihalic, 1999). However, as little research has been done on the effectiveness of bullying prevention programs in the United States, these efforts should include efficacy and effectiveness trials to determine effective and feasible models for U.S. schools. Adaptations of programs based on school size, grade levels served, geographic location, and culture also need to be addressed. In addition, the hypothesized model linking peer relationships to school adjustment through psychological adjustment needs to be more fully tested in future studies. Adjustment to school represents an important task of youth, one that may parallel later adaptation to the work world and other adult responsibilities. Promoting positive peer relationships and preventing abuse and harassment among youth may be an essential element of healthy youth development.

REFERENCES

Anderman, L. H., & Anderman, E. M. (1999). Social predictors of changes in students' achievement goal orientations. *Contemporary Educational Psychology, 24*(1), 21-37.

Andreuo, E. (2000). Bully/victim problems and their association with psychological constructs in 8- to 12-year-old Greek schoolchildren. *Aggressive Behavior, 26*(1), 49-56.

Arora, C. M., & Thompson, D. A. (1987). Defining bullying for a secondary school. *Educational and Child Psychology, 4*(3-4), 110-120.

Austin, S., & Joseph, S. (1996). Assessment of bully/victim problems in 8- to 11-year-olds. *British Journal of Educational Psychology, 66*, 447-456.

Birch, S. H., & Ladd, G. W. (1996). Interpersonal relationships in the school environment and children's early school adjustment: The role of teachers and peers. In J. Juvonen & K. R. Wentzel (Eds.), *Social Motivation: Understanding Children's School Adjustment* (pp. 199-225). Cambridge: Cambridge University Press.

Blyth, D. A., Simmons, R. G., & Carlton-Ford, S. (1983). The adjustments of early adolescents to school transitions. *Journal of Early Adolescence, 3*(1-2), 105-120.

Boulton, M. J., & Underwood, K. (1992). Bully/victim problems among middle school children. *British Journal of Educational Psychology, 62*, 73-87.

Chung, H., Elias, M., & Schneider, K. (1998). Patterns of individual adjustment changes during middle school transition. *Journal of School Psychology, 36*(1), 83-101.

Coie, J. D., Lochman, J. E., Tery, R., & Hyman, C. (1992). Predicting early adolescent disorder from childhood aggression and peer rejection. *Journal of Consulting and Clinical Psychology, 60*(5), 783-792.

Committee for Children (2001). Steps to Respect: A bullying prevention program. Seattle, Washington: Committee for Children. Available at http://www.cfchildren.org/str.html.

Connell, J. P., & Wellborn, J. G. (1991). Competence, autonomy, and relatedness: A motivational analysis of self-system processes. In M. R. Gunnar & L.A. Sroufe (Eds.), *Self processes in development: Minnesota symposium on child psychology* (Vol. 23, pp. 43-77). Hillsdale, NJ: Erlbaum.

Crockett, L. J., Peterson, A. C., Graber, J. A., Schulenberg, J., & Ebata, A. (1989). School transitions and adjustment during early adolescence. *Journal of Early Adolescence, 9*(3), 181-210.

Eccles, J. S. (1999). The Development of Children Ages 6 to 14. *The Future of Children, 9*(2), 30-44.

Elias, M. J., Gara, M., & Ubriaco, M. (1985). Sources of stress and support in children's transition to middle school: An empirical analysis. *Journal of Clinical Child Psychology, 14*(2), 112-118.

Fenzel, L. M. (2000). Prospective study of changes in global self-worth and strain during the transition to middle school. *Journal of Early Adolescence, 20*(1), 93-116.

Fenzel, L. M., & Blyth, D. A. (1986). Individual adjustment to school transitions: An exploration of the role of supportive peer relations. *Journal of Early Adolescence, 6*(4), 315-329.

Forero, R., McLellan, L., Rissel, C., & Bauman, A. (1999). Bullying behaviour and psychosocial health among school students in New South Wales, Australia: Cross-sectional survey. *British Medical Journal, 319,* 344-348.

Froschl, M., Sprung, B., & Mullin-Rindler, N. (1998). *Quit it: A teacher's guide on teasing and bullying for use with students in grades K-3.* New York: Educational Equity Concepts.

Garrity, C., Jens, K., Porter, W., Sager, N., & Short-Camilli, C. (2001). *Bully proofing your school: A comprehensive approach for elementary schools.* Longmont, Colorado: Sopris West.

Guttman, L. M., & Midgley, C. (2000). The role of protective factors in supporting the academic achievement of poor African American students during the middle school transition. *Journal of Youth and Adolescence, 29*(2), 223-248.

Hawker, D. S. J., & Boulton, M. J. (2000). Twenty years' research on peer victimization and psychosocial maladjustment: A meta-analytic review of cross-sectional studies. *Journal of Child Psychology and Psychiatry, 41,* 441-455.

Haynes, N. M. (1990). Influence of self-concept on school adjustment among middle- school students. *Journal of Social Psychology, 13*(2), 199-207.

Haynie, D. L., Nansel, T. R., Eitel, P., Crump, A. D., Saylor, K. E., Yu, K., et al. (2001). Bullies, victims, and bully/victims: Distinct groups of youth at risk. *Journal of Early Adolescence, 21*(1), 29-50.

Hirsch, B. J., & Rapkin, B. D. (1987). The transition to junior high school: A longitudinal study of self-esteem, psychological symptomatology, school life and social support. *Child Development, 58*(5), 1235-1243.

Hodges, E. V. E., & Perry, D. B. (1999). Personal and interpersonal antecedents and consequences of victimization by peers. *Journal of Personality and Social Psychology, 76*(4), 677-685.

Hoover, J. H., & Oliver, R. L. (1996). *The bullying prevention handbook: A guide for principals, teachers, and counselors.* Bloomington, Indiana: National Educational Services.

Juvonen, J., Nishina, A., & Graham, S. (2000). Peer harassment, psychological adjustment, and school functioning in early adolescence. *Journal of Educational Psychology, 92*(2), 349-359.

Kaltiala-Heino, R., Rimpela, M., Rantanen, P., & Rimpela, A. (2000). Bullying at school: An indicator of adolescents at risk for mental disorders. *Journal of Adolescence, 23*(6), 661-674.

Kessler, R. C., Little, R. J. A., & Groves, R. M. (1995). Advances in strategies for minimizing and adjusting for survey nonresponse. *Epidemiologic Reviews, 17*(1), 192-204.

Kumpulainen, K., Rasanen, E., & Henttonen, I. (1999). Children involved in bully-ing: Psychological disturbance and the persistence of the involvement. *Child Abuse and Neglect, 23*(12), 1253-1262.

Kumpulainen, K., Rasanen, E., Henttonen, I., Almqvist, F., Kresanov, K., Linna, S. L., et al. (1998). Bullying and psychiatric symptoms among elementary school-age children. *Child Abuse and Neglect, 22*(7), 705-717.

Ladd, G. W., Kochenderfer, B. J., & Coleman, C. C. (1997). Classroom peer accep-tance, friendship, and victimization: Distinct relational systems that contribute uniquely to a children's school adjustment? *Child Development, 68*(6), 1181-1197.

Ladd, G. W., & Price, J. M. (1987). Predicting children's social and school adjust-ment following the transition from preschool to kindergarten. *Child Develop-ment, 58*(5), 1168-1189.

Lynch, M., & Cicchetti, D. (1997). Children's relationships with adults and peers: An examination of elementary and junior high school students. *Journal of School Psychology, 35*(1), 81-99.

McDougall, P., & Hymel, S. (1998). Moving into middle school: Individual differ-ences in the transition experience. *Canadian Journal of Behavioural Science, 30*(2), 108-120.

Nansel, T. R., Overpeck, M., Pilla, R. S., Ruan, W. J., & Simons-Morton, B. G. (2001). Bullying behaviors among US youth: Prevalence and association with psychosocial adjustment. *Journal of the American Medical Association, 285* (16), 2094-2100.

Olweus, D. (1978). *Aggression in the schools, bullies and whipping boys.* Washing-ton, DC: Hemisphere Publishing Corporation.

Olweus, D. (1993). *Bullying at school: What we know and what we can do.* Oxford: Blackwell.

Olweus, D. (1994). Bullying at school: Long-term outcomes for the victims and an effective school-based intervention program. In L. R. Huesmann (Ed.), *Aggres-sive behavior: Current perspectives* (pp. 97-130). New York: Plenum Press.

Olweus, D., Limber, S., & Mihalic, S. F. (1999). *Blueprints for violence prevention, book nine: Bullying prevention program.* Boulder, CO: Center for the Study and Prevention of Violence.

Pyper, J. R., Freiberg, H. J., Ginsburg, M., & Spuck, D. W. (1987). *Instruments to measure teacher, parent, and student perceptions of school climate.* Bloom-ington, ID: Phi Delta Kappa.

Rigby, K. (1999). Peer victimisation at school and the health of secondary school students. *British Journal of Educational Psychology, 69,* 95-104.

Rigby, K., & Slee, P. T. (1991). Dimensions of interpersonal relations among Aus-tralian children and implications for psychological well-being. *The Journal of Social Psychology, 133*(1), 33-42.

Ryan, R. M., & Powelson, C. L. (1991). Autonomy and relatedness as fundamental to motivation and education. *Journal of Experimental Education, 60*(1), 49-66.

Salmon, G., James, A., & Smith, D. M. (1998). Bullying in schools: Self-reported anxiety, depression, and self-esteem in secondary school children. *British Medical Journal, 317,* 924-925.

Sharp, S., & Smith, P. K. (1991). Bullying in UK schools: The DES Sheffield Bullying Project. *Early Child Development & Care, 77,* 47-55.

Simmons, R. G., & Blyth, D. A. (1987). *Moving into adolescence: The impact of pubertal change and school context.* New York: Aldine.

Slee, P. T. & Rigby, K. (1993). Australian school children's self-appraisal of interpersonal relations: The bullying experience. *Child Psychiatry and Human Development, 23*(4), 273-282.

Smith, P. K. (1997). Bullying in schools: The UK experience and the Sheffield Anti-Bullying Project. *The Irish Journal of Psychology, 18,* 191-201.

Smith, P. K., & Brain, P. (2000). Bullying in schools: Lessons from two decades of research. *Aggressive Behavior, 26*(1), 1-9.

Tabachnick, B. G., & Fidel, L. S. (1996). *Using multivariate statistics.* New York: Harper Collins.

U.S. Census Bureau (1990). Charles County, Maryland: 1990 Census population, demographic, and housing information. Retrieved August 8, 2002, from http:// quickfacts.census.gov/ cgi-bin/cnty_QuickLinks?24017.

Wentzel, K. R., & Caldwell, K. (1997). Friendships, peer acceptance, and group membership: Relations to academic achievement in middle school. *Child Development, 68*(6), 1198-1209.

Wenz-Gross, M., Siperstein, G. N., Untch, A. S., & Widaman, K. F. (1997). Stress, social support, and adjustment of adolescents in middle school. *Journal of Early Adolescence, 17*(2), 129-151.

Wigfield, A., Eccles, J. S.,Maclver, D., Reuman, D., & Midgley, C. (1991). Transitions during early adolescence: Changes in children's domain specific self-perceptions and general self-esteem across the transition to junior high school. *Developmental Psychology, 27,* 552-565.

Williams, K., Chambers, M., Logan, S., & Robinson, D. (1996). Association of common health symptoms with bullying in primary school children. *British Medical Journal, 313,* 17-19.

Chapter 5

Perceptions and Attitudes Toward Bullying in Middle School Youth: A Developmental Examination Across the Bully/Victim Continuum

Susan M. Swearer
Paulette Tam Cary

Bullying, including both verbal and physical behaviors, may be the most prevalent type of school violence (Batsche, 1997). Reported incidence rates, with populations from the United States, range from a conservative 10 percent for "extreme victims" of bullying (Perry, Kusel, & Perry, 1988) to a high of 75 percent of school-aged children who reported being bullied at least one time during their school years (Hoover, Oliver, & Hazler, 1992). More recent studies within the United States have found 8.4 percent (Nansel, Overpeck, Pilla, Ruan, Simons-Morton, & Scheidt, 2001) to 20 percent (Limber & Small, 2000) of children reporting being victimized several times per week while 24.2 percent (Nansel et al., 2001) to 44.6 percent (Haynie et al., 2001) report being bullied at least once during the past year. Recent rates of bullying other students are less variable; approximately 9 percent (Nansel et al.) to 13 percent (Limber & Small) of students report bullying other students several times per week while 24 percent (Nansel et al.) to 25 percent (Haynie et al.) report bullying other students at least once in the past year.

This chapter was adapted from "Perceptions and Attitudes Toward Bullying in Middle School Youth: A Developmental Examination Across the Bully/Victim Continuum" by Susan M. Swearer, and Paulette Tam Cary, *Journal of Applied School Psychology,* *19*(2), pp. 63-79.

Bullying, Victimization, and Peer Harassment
Published by The Haworth Press, Inc., 2007. All rights reserved.
doi:10.1300/5808_05

Within the past decade, the phenomenon of bullying has been recognized as a serious problem for the quality of school life among children (Berthold & Hoover, 2000). Data from the Centers for Disease Control and Prevention Youth Risk Behavior Surveillance survey indicated that 7.4 percent of American youth reported having been threatened or injured with a weapon on school grounds one or more times within the past year (Kann et al., 1998). In addition, 4 percent reported missing school within the last thirty days because they feared being intimidated or bullied. Hoover et al. (1992) found that a significant number of victims reported experiencing social and academic trauma resulting from bullying. Batsche and Knoff (1994) reported that victims commonly respond to bullying through escape/avoidance behaviors, such as not going to school, refusing to go to certain places, running away from home, and in some extreme cases, attempting suicide.

Studies have documented that children involved in the bully/victim continuum experience impaired psychosocial functioning (Bosworth, Espelage, & Simon, 1999; Juvonen, Nishina, & Graham, 2000). Research has found that victims experience impaired physical and mental health (Rigby, 1999), internalizing problems (Swearer, Song, Cary, Eagle, & Mickelson, 2001), and psychosomatic symptoms (Kumpulainen et al., 1998). On the other end of the continuum, bullies report feelings of depression (Kaltiala-Heino, Rimpela, Marttunen, Rimpela, & Rantanen, 1999; Swearer et al., 2001), and suicidal ideation and behavior (Bailey, 1994; Kaltiala-Heino et al., 1999). Students who both bully others and are bullied (bully-victims) experience psychological distress (Duncan, 1999); anxiety (Craig, 1998); loneliness (Forero, McLellan, Rissel, & Bauman, 1999); and depression (Craig; Kaltiala- Heino et al., 1999; Swearer et al., 2001). In fact, these youth may be the most impaired subgroup along the bully/victim continuum (Swearer et al., 2001).

Bullying and victimization appear to pose negative consequences not only at the time they occur within a youth's life, but also, potentially, for their future. Potential long-term negative effects for bullies include an increased risk for becoming involved in delinquent and criminal activity (Loeber & Dishion, 1983; Olweus, 1993). Victims of bullying are more at risk for symptoms of depression and low self-esteem as young adults than compared to their nonvictimized peers (Olweus, 1993).

Researchers have suggested that bullying behavior tends to peak in middle school and generally decreases with age (Hoover et al., 1992; Pellegrini & Bartini, 2000). Pellegrini and Bartini note that the increase in bullying behavior occurs when students make the transition into middle school. Thus, bullying behaviors appear to reflect the needs of students to establish social status as they transition into a new peer group. In addition to transitioning into new peer groups, early adolescence is also a time when cross-gender contacts and interactions become an important goal. Breaking the well-established norms of same-sex interactions from early childhood can prove risky; therefore, young adolescents may try to minimize the risks by using playful and/or ambiguous overtures, such as pushing, poking, and teasing, which can be interpreted as bullying (Pellegrini, 2001). In addition, this study found that sexual harassment in seventh grade was predicted by bullying in sixth grade.

With the plethora of potential negative consequences resulting from bullying and victimization (e.g., internalizing psychopathology, delinquent pathways, sexual harassment), examining the cognitions and attitudes of students toward bullying may assist researchers and educators in the effort toward developing effective prevention and intervention programs that reduce bullying behaviors. This information may help illustrate the reasons why some students bully and why others do not, as well as identify any beliefs that may contribute to or perpetuate the bullying phenomenon among school-aged youth.

One of the first studies exploring students' perceptions toward bullying was conducted by Olweus (1978). Olweus found that rather than being bullied due to prototypical "nerd" or social-outcast characteristics (e.g., wore glasses, different clothing, spoke differently, overweight, etc.), students were bullied because they appeared physically and/or emotionally weak. Rigby and Slee (1991) found that the majority of Australian children were opposed to bullying and tended to support the victims; however, the children's attitudes toward victims became less supportive as they became older. Specifically, they tended to dislike victims of bullying and admire the bullies. More recently, Rigby (1997) found that as Australian students matured, up to the age of sixteen, their attitudes became more supportive of bullying, and they reported more participation in bullying. Additionally, males tended to possess more pro-bullying attitudes than females. Similarly, a large-scale survey study from Italy and England found that in both countries the majority of children were opposed to bullying and supportive toward victims with females tending to be more distressed by bullying than males (Menesini et al., 1996). Bullies were found to be more inclined to understand other bullies, feel less sympathetic toward victims' suffering, less likely to intervene when witnessing a bullying episode, and more likely to join in bullying other children they did not like.

Within the United States, Oliver, Hoover, and Hazler (1994) surveyed middle and high school students in Midwestern schools. They found that 64 percent of students tended to agree that victims brought teasing on themselves, 51 percent of students felt that teasing was done in fun, and 39 percent of students felt that bullying "helped" the victim by making him or her tougher. In addition, when compared to males, 34 percent of females believed that bullies had higher social status than victims (compared to 24 percent of males). In an earlier study examining victim characteristics, physical weakness was significantly more likely to motivate bullying if the victim was male while the victims' peer group was more likely to motivate bullying if the victim was female (Hazler, Hoover, & Oliver, 1991). Males have been found to engage in bullying behavior more frequently than girls, while girls have been found to hold more negative attitudes toward bullying than boys (Hazler et al., 1991; Pellegrini & Bartini, 2000).

Pellegrini, Bartini, and Brooks (1999) found that bullies possessed more positive attitudes toward bullying than other groups (i.e., victims and controls). More recently, Pellegrini and Bartini (2000) found that cognitions about bullying did not predict bullying status; therefore, these researchers suggested that positive attitudes toward bullying, especially among bullies, may serve as a strategy to reduce the cognitive dissonance associated with feelings that are inconsistent with the dominant peer and/or cultural norms. However, while this study examined attitudes toward bullying among bullies, victims, and aggressive victims, students who did not experience bullying were not included.

Previous research has documented some patterns of beliefs and attitudes about bullying that students may hold. However, research examining the attitudes and perceptions toward bullying along the bully/victim continuum including not only bullies and victims, but also bully-victims and students not involved in bullying, has not been conducted. The purpose of this study was to examine the attitudes and perceptions of middle school students about bullying and to examine attitudes toward bullying across bullies, victims, bully-victims, and students who are neither bullies nor victims (i.e., no status). This study investigated the attitudes and perceptions of students toward bullying throughout their middle school years, the time in which bullying behavior has been found to peak.

Data were collected over the first three years of a five-year longitudinal study examining ecological factors in bullying in middle school youth. Ecological factors examined in the larger study include internal psychological factors (depression, anxiety, hopelessness, aggression, locus of control), school climate, teacher and peer nominations of bullies and victims, and prosocial behaviors. Data are presented on the attitudes toward the value of bullying, perceptions of bullying behaviors, and the reasons youth cite for their bullying behaviors across the bully-victim continuum. It was predicted that attitudes supportive of bullying would be associated with external attributions for bullying and that these attitudes would differ across the bully/victim continuum. In addition, it was predicted that attitudes toward bullying would become more positive as students progressed through middle school.

METHOD

All students at a Midwestern middle school (Grades 6 through 8) were eligible to participate in a longitudinal study of bullying and victimization. A letter describing the study, which was signed by the principal investigator and the principal of the school, was sent to all parents of sixth-grade students along with the parental consent form. Active parental consent and youth assent were obtained for each participant in the study. Students in cohort 1, with parental consent to participate in the study, were administered a series of instruments during April 1999 (sixth grade), April 2000 (seventh grade), and April 2001 (eighth grade). Students in cohort 2, with parental consent to participate in the study, were administered a series of instruments during April 2000 (sixth grade) and April 2001 (seventh grade). The Bully Survey was administered in the spring of every year so that participants had time to get to know their classmates. Results from responses on a survey of bullying and victimization were examined to elucidate changes in perceptions and attitudes toward bullying that students reported throughout middle school.

Participants

Data are presented from sixth-, seventh-, and eighth-grade students in one middle school. In April 1999, eighty-three sixth-grade students (thirty-six male and forty-seven female) participated in the study. This reflects a 41 percent participation rate. Out of the original eighty-three participants, sixty-six seventh-grade students (thirty-three male and thirty-three female) continued in the study. In eighth grade, fifty-seven students (twenty-eight male and twenty-nine female) continued in the study. In all cases, when students did not continue in the study, it was due to moving to another school. In April 2000, fifty sixth-grade students (twenty-nine male and twenty-one female) participated in the study. This reflects a 29 percent participation rate. One hypothesis for this lower participation rate is that the increased media attention to school violence and bullying that occurred after the school shooting in Colorado made parents wary of participating in research on bullying. In fact, several parents expressed concern over allowing their child to participate in a study on bullying. Of these fifty participants, forty seventh-grade students (twenty-one male and nineteen female) continued in the study. Again, the students who did not continue in the study moved to other schools. All participants were assigned a code number to maintain confidentiality, and these code numbers were used to track the data across the three points in time. Thus, 133 sixth-grade, 106 seventh-grade, and 57 eighth-grade students participated in this study.

Demographic characteristics for the participants across grades included ages ranging from eleven to thirteen years old ($M = 11.67$; $SD = .55$; $n = 133$) for the sixth graders; twelve to fourteen years old ($M = 12.60$; $SD = .58$; $n = 106$) for the seventh graders; and thirteen to fifteen years old ($M = 13.54$; $SD = .54$; $n = 57$) for the eighth-grade students.

The racial distribution across cohorts was as follows: 64 percent Caucasian, 14 percent African American, 9 percent Asian/Asian American, 6 percent Latino(a), 5 percent Biracial, 1 percent Eastern European, and 1 percent Middle Eastern. These demographic characteristics are consistent with the overall school population.

Participants were grouped according to status (i.e., bully, bully-victim, victim, or no status) based on ratings from their responses on the Bully Survey (see Table 5.1). In sixth grade the bully/victim distribution was 5 percent bullies ($n = 7$); 39 percent victims ($n = 52$); 30 percent bully-victims ($n = 40$); and 26 percent no status (i.e., does not experience victimization and/or bullying others) ($n = 34$). In seventh grade the bully/victim distribution was 6 percent bullies ($n = 6$); 43 percent victims ($n = 46$); 20 percent bully-victims ($n = 21$); and 31 percent no status ($n = 33$). In eighth grade the bully/victim distribution was 7 percent bullies ($n = 4$); 40 percent victims ($n = 23$); 21 percent bully-victims ($n = 12$); and 32 percent no status ($n = 18$).

Instrumentation

The Bully Survey (Swearer, 2001).[1]

The Bully Survey is a three-part, thirty-one-question survey that queries students regarding their experiences with bullying, perceptions of bullying,

TABLE 5.1. Bully/victim status across year.

Status	Time 1 (Sixth)		Time 2 (Seventh)		Time 3 (Eighth)	
	%	*n*	%	*n*	%	*n*
Bully	5	7	6	6	7	4
Victim	39	52	43	46	40	23
Bully-victim	30	40	20	21	21	12
No status	26	34	31	33	32	18
Total		133		106		57

and attitudes toward bullying during the school year in which the survey is administered. The Bully Survey was developed and pilot tested in 1998 with a sixth grade cohort ($n = 169$), including both regular and special education students. The survey was based on other well-known surveys of bullying; however, items were also included that were of interest to the local school district. Since 1998, the Bully Survey has been used in three middle schools in the Midwest and in a school district in Virginia. It has also been used internationally in Germany, Guatemala, and Peru. Bullying is defined in each section of the survey as follows:

> Bullying is anything from teasing, saying mean things, or leaving someone out of a group, to physical attacks (hitting, pushing, kicking) where one person or a group of people picks on another person over a long time. Bullying refers to things that happen in school, on the school grounds, or going to and from school.

In Part A of the survey, students answered questions about when they were victims of bullying during the past year. Additionally, there are two questions in Part A that ask students whether they have experienced bullying at home. If the participants reported they had not been victims of bullying, they were instructed to skip Part A and begin Part B. Part B of the survey addressed questions about the participants' observations of bullying behavior among their peers during the past year. If they reported that they had not observed bullying behavior, the participants were instructed to skip Part B. Part C of the survey requested information from the participants about when they bullied other students. If the participants indicated that they had not bullied other students within the last year, they skipped Part C and completed the final section of the survey. The final section of the survey contained a scale that measures attitudes toward bullying. In the present study, the internal consistency reliability using coefficient alpha was .69 for the total attitude score for Time 1, .55 for Time 2, and .74 for Time 3.

RESULTS

Results will be described in terms of examining perceptions and attitudes toward bullying among bullies, victims, bully-victims, and no-status students across their middle school years. SPSS version 10.1 was used to analyze the data.

Given that previous research has found differences between males and females regarding bullying behaviors, analyses were run to determine whether gender differences existed across status groups. Interestingly, there were no differences across status with respect to gender in sixth grade ($\chi^2 = 4.46$, $p = .21$), seventh grade ($\chi^2 = 1.33$, $p = .72$), and eighth grade ($\chi^2 = 1.33$, $p = .85$). This suggests that within this sample, there were no differences between boys and girls across status groups (bullies, victims, bully-victim, and no-status participants) during middle school.

An integrity check of the status groups was conducted in order to validate participants' status as reported on the Bully Survey. We examined office referral data across the four status groups across their middle school years (see Table 5.2). Students in this school receive office referrals for insubordination, violation of school rules, physical aggression, and verbal aggression. As expected, on average across the middle school years, bullies had the highest number of office referrals, followed by bully-victims, no-status students, and victims. These data also serve as an indicator of the validity of the Bully Survey, reflecting the fact that students who bully others are more likely to be sent to the office as a disciplinary measure.

Students' experiences with bullying and victimization across their middle school years were examined. Specifically, perceptions regarding the top locations where bullying was reported, who was involved in the bullying, if students were bullied at home, how students felt the school responded to the bullying, and participants' attitudes toward bullying are presented.

Main Locations Where Bullying Occurred

The top three locations across status groups where students felt that bullying occurred are reported (see Table 5.3). The majority of students across the status groups reported that bullying occurred most frequently in classrooms, hallways, after school, and gym or recess. Across all three years, bully-victims endorsed more locations than the other groups.

TABLE 5.2. Office referrals across status and year.

Status	Time 1 (sixth)		Time 2 (seventh)		Time 3 (eighth)	
	M	*SD*	*M*	*SD*	*M*	*SD*
Bully	1.43	2.15	4.83	4.50	7.75	4.57
Victim	.69	1.45	3.15	5.89	2.87	4.35
Bully-victim	2.67	5.27	4.50	7.16	6.17	7.77
No status	3.00	5.77	3.37	8.78	1.24	1.64

TABLE 5.3. Main locations participants reported bullying to occur.

Location	Time 1 (sixth)				Time 2 (seventh)				Time 3 (eighth)			
	Bully	Victim	Bully-victim*	No status	Bully	Victim	Bully-victim*	No status	Bully	Victim	Bully-victim*	No status
Classroom	43% (#1)	15% (#3)	28% (#1) / 15% (#2)	32% (#1)	17% (#2)	11%	35% (#1) / 10% (#3)	0%	25% (#3)	39% (#2)	25% / 17%	42% (#2)
Hallway	29% (#2)	19% (#1)	20% (#2) / 15% (#2)	16% (#2)	0%	41% (#1)	20% (#2) / 14% (#2)	29% (#1)	50% (#2)	61% (#1)	67% (#1) / 42% (#1)	58% (#1)
After school	14% (#3)	17% (#2)	8% / 18% (#1)	11%	0%	15% (#2)	10% / 5%	18% (#2)	75% (#1)	30%	42% (#2) / 25%	33% (#3)
Gym	14% (#3)	10%	3% / 15% (#2)	11%	33% (#1)	15% (#2)	15% (#3) / 4% (#2)	6%	50% (#2)	35% (#3)	33% (#3) / 33% (#2)	25%
Recess	0%	14%	13% (#3) / 5%	16% (#3)	17% (#2)	15% (#2)	20% (#2) / 24% (#1)	12% (#3)	25% (#3)	26%	33% (#3) / 33% (#2)	25%
Cafeteria	0%	12%	8% / 8% (#3)	5%	0%	13% (#3)	20% (#2) / 4% (#2)	12% (#3)	50% (#2)	30%	17% / 8%	58% (#1)

* Note. Locations where bully-victims reported bullying others are listed first, followed by where bully-victims reported being victimized.

Who Was Involved in Bullying Incidents?

Tables 5.4 and 5.5 summarize who students report are involved in bullying. It appears that bullying includes a power differential (older students bullying younger students) and that bullying occurs equally among males and females. Bullying is a ubiquitous phenomenon occurring across grade, gender, status, and year.

Perceptions of Bullying

Students' perceptions of why they were bullied or why they bullied others were examined across sixth, seventh, and eighth grades. Interestingly, there was some consistency across status groups concerning students' per-

TABLE 5.4. Victims as reported by bullies and bully-victims.

	Time 1 (sixth)		Time 2 (seventh)		Time 3 (eighth)	
Victims	Bullies (%)	Bully-victims (%)	Bullies (%)	Bully-victims (%)	Bullies (%)	Bully-victims (%)
Younger boys	71	45	67	43	0	33
Younger girls	71	43	67	38	0	33
Same grade boys	57	63	83	62	50	75
Same grade girls	57	55	33	38	50	58
Older boys	43	45	67	38	25	17
Older girls	57	40	33	33	0	8

TABLE 5.5. Bullies as reported by victims, bully-victims, and no-status students.

	Time 1 (sixth)			Time 2 (seventh)			Time 3 (eighth)		
Bullies	Victims	Bully-victims	No status	Victims	Bully-victims	No status	Victims	Bully-victims	No status
Younger boys	19	35	42	24	29	47	0	8	17
Younger girls	28	30	42	20	14	35	0	17	17
Same-grade boys	48	50	74	59	62	71	67	33	92
Same-grade girls	52	43	58	37	29	59	30	42	42
Older boys	60	60	53	48	62	71	22	8	25
Older girls	44	33	47	30	33	47	9	0	17

ceptions of why the bullying behaviors occurred. External attributes such as being different, being weak, and wearing certain clothes were cited across all four status groups as reasons for bullying. Bullies endorsed perceived physical attributes such as the way someone talks, the clothes they wear, or being weak as reasons for bullying. Victims endorsed getting good grades, being weak, overweight, different, and wearing certain clothes as reasons for being bullied. Bully-victims endorsed the same reasons as victims for being bullied and the same reasons for being bullied as a rationale to bully others. No-status students endorsed being weak, overweight, different, and wearing certain clothes as reasons for students being bullied.

Congruence Between Bullying at School and Being Bullied at Home

We were also interested in knowing whether or not students who experienced bullying at school were also bullied at home. Approximately 70 percent of the victims across all three points in time reported that they were not bullied at home, while bully-victims reported being bullied at home by their siblings (53 percent; sixth grade), (28 percent; seventh grade), and (50 percent; eighth grade).

Perceptions of the Schools' Responses to Bullying

Across all three points in time, bullies, victims, and no-status students felt that when school staff knew the bullying occurred, they responded in a satisfactory fashion. However, bully-victims felt that the school did not address bullying issues well (when they were either victims or bullies). The majority of the sample across their middle school years felt that schools should worry about bullying (80 percent). However, 80 percent of the sample reported that the school staff did not know that the bullying occurred.

Attitudes Toward Bullying Across Middle School

Over time, the participants' attitudes toward bullying were fairly consistent with a trend toward having more favorable attitudes toward bullying by the eighth grade. There were significant differences between groups on attitudes toward bullying in seventh and eighth grades. In seventh grade, victims had less favorable attitudes toward bullying than the bullies or the no-status students ($F = 3.35$; $p = .02$). In eighth grade, victims had less favorable attitudes toward bullying than the bully-victims ($F = 2.65$; $p = .05$).

DISCUSSION

Several interesting patterns emerged from the current study. Specifically, there were no differences in terms of gender across bullies, victims, bully-victims, and no-status groups. When one considers our use of the definition of bullying that includes both verbal and physical behaviors, this finding is consistent with previous research that has found that girls and boys are equally involved in bullying when bullying includes both overt and covert behaviors (Ahmad & Smith, 1994; Boulton & Smith, 1994; Hoover et al., 1992) and that students include both verbal and physical aggression in their definition of bullying (Espelage & Asidao, 2001).

When asked about the location of bullying incidents, most participants reported that they were bullied in more than one location in and around the school building. Bullying was reported to occur most frequently in hallways, academic classrooms, gym and/or recess, and after school. This is consistent with previous research that has found that bullying occurs in those same locations (Limber & Small, 2000). This finding has implications for program development, as schools can implement interventions such as increasing the number of hall monitors, monitoring the school grounds, and adopting teacher training programs that help teachers identify bullying behaviors.

In examining the participants' reports of who is involved in bullying incidents, it appears that both boys and girls are equally involved in bullying incidents over the three years. Previous research suggests that the relationship between predictor variables such as school and family functioning are similar for boys and girls (Haynie et al., 2001). Thus, while the forms of bullying may look different in boys and girls, the phenomenon of bullying may occur consistently across gender and grade.

Open-ended responses on the bully survey were examined to add a descriptive element to the perceptions and attitudes that the participants reported. Several of the bullies commented that they bullied other students in response to internal feelings they were experiencing (e.g., "bullying releases my stress" and "when I have a bad day I feel like I need to pick on someone"). Bullies also acknowledged that bullying "proves I'm stronger" and they bully to "fit in." Bullies also stated that they bully others "because they hate me" and "they were making fun of me and talking behind my back." Internal factors have been hypothesized to be related to erroneous attributional style in youth who are aggressive toward others (Dodge & Frame, 1982). In situations where the social interaction is actually neutral, aggressive youth have been found to interpret those interactions as hostile (Dodge, 1993). Some of these comments underscore the research that has examined reasons behind bullying and aggressive behavior in youth and suggest that interventions that target cognitive distortions may be best directed toward bullies and bully-victims.

Victims' open-ended comments support research findings that have concluded that victims are persecuted for external attributions (Bernstein & Watson, 1997; Hazler et al., 1991; Ma, 2001). Victims stated that they are bullied because "I am fat," "I'm smarter than a lot of people," "how I dress," "how I look," and "because of my teeth." As expected, in this study, victims and no-status students held the least favorable attitudes toward bullying. Thus, interventions that include social perspective-taking and that include both victims and bystanders may be important prevention and intervention components.

Bully-victims in this study report that they are also bullied at home and that their siblings are the primary perpetrators of the bullying. Previous research has found that youth with more siblings are more likely to bully others in the school setting (Eslea & Smith, 2000; Ma, 2001). While we did not examine family constellation, it would be interesting to determine whether bully-victims come from larger families. The bully-victims' open-ended responses were associated with feelings of getting even. For example, "They bullied me, so I bullied them." Given the connection to being bullied at home for bully-victims, this could be associated with sibling relationships where issues of fairness may be prevalent.

Participants in this study began middle school in the sixth grade. According to Pellegrini and Bartini (2000), bullying may serve a function of establishing dominance and may assist students in the transition to middle school. Because the grade in which students transition to middle school differs across school districts, school administrators and staff may wish to focus on intervention efforts for students in their first year of middle school. This may be the most difficult year in terms of bullying for middle school youth.

This study represents part of a larger longitudinal study examining bullying and victimization in middle school youth and is not without limitations. First, we examined self-report data for attitudes and perceptions of bullying for which we do not have external data to validate the participants' responses. For example, we validated status by examining office referral data from school records; however, we could not validate attitudes toward bullying by using another source of data. Second, the cell sizes in this data set continue to be small, which precludes submitting these data to more rigorous statistical analyses. Another problem related to cell size is the inability to examine differences across status by gender. When these analyses were conducted, the cell sizes were too small to make meaningful conclusions. Finally, these data were collected from one Midwestern middle school and thus cannot be generalized to other populations.

Implications for Practice and Policy

Results suggest that an important element of bullying prevention and intervention programs should include components that address perceptions and attitudes toward bullying. Additionally, teacher and staff training programs should include training on the complexity behind bullying behaviors. The participants in this study stated that school staff typically did not know that the bullying had occurred. This is consistent with research that has found that students do not feel the school staff is interested in reducing bullying (Harris, Petrie, & Willoughby, 2002). If students feel that the school staff does not care about bullying or that the staff is unaware that bullying occurs, then they may not feel hopeful that these behaviors can change.

Many state legislatures are mandating that schools adopt antibullying policies. While policies are helpful to standardize procedures for responding to problems, schools must be given the tools and the financial support to implement these policies. Schools must also be partners with researchers to conduct research on bullying in their unique school ecology. Each school ecology is unique, and effective research that can be translated into effective practice should guide the development and implementation of prevention and intervention programs.

Bullying should be viewed as an interaction between the individual and his or her peers, school, family, culture, and community (Swearer & Doll, 2001). This definition of bullying presumes an ecological understanding of the phenomenon. Thus, bullying is not simply a behavior, and the titles of "bully" "victim," and "bully-victim" do not represent an innate characteristic of a person. Results from this study reinforce this framework by examining bullying behaviors by utilizing a comprehensive assessment of perceptions and attitudes toward bullying. As researchers, educators, and youth begin to understand the complexities behind bullying, inclusion of ecological contexts will help guide effective intervention and prevention programs.

NOTE

1. The Bully Survey (Swearer, 2001) can be obtained from the first author.

REFERENCES

Ahmad, Y., & Smith, P. K. (1994). Bullying in schools and the issue of sex differences. In J. Archer (Ed.), *Male violence* (pp. 70-83). London: Routledge.

Bailey, S. (1994). Health in young persons' establishments: Treating the damaged and preventing harm. *Criminal Behavior and Mental Health, 3,* 349-367.

Batsche, G. M. (1997). Bullying. In G. G. Bear, K. M. Minke, & A. Thomas (Eds.), *Children's Needs II: Development, Problems, and Alternatives* (pp. 171-179). Bethesda, MD: National Association of School Psychologists.

Batsche, G. M., & Knoff, H. M. (1994). Bullies and their victims: Understanding a pervasive problem in the schools. *School Psychology Review, 23,* 165-174.

Bernstein, J. Y., & Watson, M. W. (1997). Children who are targets of bullying: A victim pattern. *Journal of Interpersonal Violence, 12,* 483-498.

Berthold, K. A., & Hoover, J. H. (2000). Correlates of bullying and victimization among intermediate students in the Midwestern USA. *School Psychology International, 21,* 65-78.

Bosworth, K., Espelage, D. L., & Simon, T. R. (1999). Factors associated with bullying behavior in middle school students. *Journal of Early Adolescence, 19,* 341-362.

Boulton, M. J., & Smith, P. K. (1994). Bully-victim problems in middle-school children: Stability, self-perceived competence, peer perceptions, and peer acceptance. *British Journal of Developmental Psychology, 12,* 315-329.

Craig, W. M. (1998). The relationship among bullying, victimization, depression, anxiety, and aggression in elementary school children. *Personality and Individual Differences, 24,* 123-130.

Dodge, K. A. (1993). Social-cognitive mechanisms in the development of conduct disorder and depression. *Annual Reviews of Psychology, 44,* 559-584.

Dodge, K., & Frame, C. L. (1982). Social cognitive biases and deficits in aggressive boys. *Child Development, 53,* 467-489.

Duncan, R. D. (1999). Maltreatment by parents and peers: The relationship between child abuse, bully victimization, and psychological distress. *Child Maltreatment, 4,* 45-55.

Eslea, M., & Smith, P. (2000). Pupil and parent attitudes towards bullying in primary schools. *European Journal of Psychology of Education, 15,* 207-219.

Espelage, D. L., & Asidao, C. S. (2001). Conversations with middle school students about bullying and victimization: Should we be concerned? *Journal of Emotional Abuse, 2,* 49-62.

Forero, R., McLellan, L., Rissel, C., & Bauman, A. (1999). Bullying behaviour and psychological health among school students in New South Wales, Australia: Cross sectional survey. *British Medical Journal, 319,* 344-348.

Harris, S., Petrie, G., & Willoughby, W. (2002). Bullying among 9th graders: An exploratory study. *NASSP Bulletin, 86,* 3-14.

Haynie, D. L., Nansel, T., Eitel, P., Crump, A. D., Saylor, K., Yu, K., et al. (2001). Bullies, victims, and bully/victims: Distinct groups of at-risk youth. *Journal of Early Adolescence, 21,* 29-49.

Hazler, R. J., Hoover, J. H., & Oliver, R. (1991). Student perceptions of victimization by bullies in school. *Journal of Humanistic Education and Development, 29,* 143-150.

Hoover, J. H., Oliver, R., & Hazler, R. J. (1992). Bullying: Perceptions of adolescent victims in the Midwestern U.S.A. *School Psychology International, 13,* 5-16.

Juvonen, J., Nishina, A., & Graham, S. (2000). Peer harassment, psychological adjustment, and school functioning in early adolescence. *Journal of Educational Psychology, 92,* 349-359.

Kaltiala-Heino, R., Rimpela, M., Marttunen, M., Rimpela, A., & Rantanen, P. (1999). Bullying, depression, and suicidal ideation in Finnish adolescents: School survey. *British Medical Journal, 319,* 348-351.

Kann, L., Kinchen, S. A., Williams B. I., Ross, J. G., Lowry, R., Hill, C. V., et al. (1998). *Youth Risk Behavior Surveillance, 1997.* Atlanta, GA: Centers for Disease Control and Prevention. CDC Surveillance Summaries, August 14, 1998. MMWR; 47 (No. SS-3).

Kumpulainen, K., Rasanen, E., Henttonen, I., Almqvist, F., Kresanov, K., Linna, S., et al. (1998). Bullying and psychiatric symptoms among elementary school-age children. *Child Abuse & Neglect, 22,* 705-717.

Limber, S. P., & Small, M. A. (2000, August). *Self-reports of bully-victimization among primary school students.* Paper presented at the annual meeting of the American Psychological Association, Washington, D.C.

Loeber, R., & Dishion, T. J. (1983). Early predictors of male delinquency: A review. *Psychological Bulletin, 94,* 68-99.

Ma, X. (2001). Bullying and being bullied: To what extent are bullies also victims? *American Educational Research Journal, 38,* 351-370.

Menesini, E., Eslea, M., Smith, P. K., Genta, M. L., Giannetti, E., Fonzi, A., et al. (1996). Cross-national comparison of children's attitudes towards bully/victim problems in school. *Aggressive Behavior, 23,* 245-257.

Nansel, T. R., Overpeck, M., Pilla, R. S., Ruan, W. J., Simons-Morton, B., & Scheidt, P. (2001). Bullying behaviors among U.S. youth: Prevalence and association with psychosocial adjustment. *Journal of the American Medical Association, 285,* 2094-2100.

Oliver, R., Hoover, J. H., & Hazler, R. J. (1994). The perceived roles of bullying in small-town Midwestern schools. *Journal of Counseling and Development, 72,* 416-420.

Olweus, D. (1978). *Aggression in the schools: Bullies and whipping boys.* New York: Wiley.

Olweus, D. (1993). *Bullying at school: What we know and what we can do.* Oxford, UK: Basil Blackwell.

Pellegrini, A. D. (2001). A longitudinal study of heterosexual relationships, aggression, and sexual harassment during the transition from primary school through middle school. *Applied Developmental Psychology, 22,* 119-133.

Pellegrini, A. D., & Bartini, M. (2000). A longitudinal study of bullying, victimization, and peer affiliation during the transition from primary school to middle school. *American Educational Research Journal, 37,* 699-725.

Pellegrini, A. D., Bartini, M., & Brooks, F. (1999). School bullies, victims, and aggressive victims: Factors relating to group affiliation and victimization in early adolescence. *Journal of Educational Psychology, 91,* 216-224.

Perry, D. G., Kusel, S. J., & Perry, L. C. (1988). Victims of peer aggression. *Developmental Psychology, 24,* 807-814.

Rigby, K. (1997). Attitudes and beliefs about bullying among Australian school children. *Irish Journal of Psychology, 18,* 202-220.

Rigby, K. (1999). Peer victimization at school and the health of secondary school students. *British Journal of Educational Psychology, 69,* 95-104.

Rigby, K., & Slee, P. T. (1991). Bullying among Australian school children: Reported behavior and attitudes toward victims. *Journal of Social Psychology, 131,* 615-627.

Swearer, S. M. (2001). *The Bully Survey.* Unpublished manuscript, University of Nebraska-Lincoln.

Swearer, S. M. & Doll, B. (2001). Bullying in schools: An ecological framework. *Journal of Emotional Abuse, 2,* 7-23.

Swearer, S. M., Song, S. Y., Cary, P. T., Eagle, J. W., & Mickelson, W. T. (2001). Psychosocial correlates in bullying and victimization: The relationship between depression, anxiety, and bully/victim status. *Journal of Emotional Abuse, 2,* 95-121.

Chapter 6

A Cluster Analytic Investigation of Victimization Among High School Students: Are Profiles Differentially Associated with Psychological Symptoms and School Belonging?

Melissa K. Holt
Dorothy L. Espelage

INTRODUCTION

Sexual harassment and dating violence are pervasive forms of victimization within our society. Initial efforts aimed at better understanding these phenomena focused on college students and adults. Results derived from such studies showed that upward of 50 percent of women have experienced sexual harassment in their working lives (Fitzgerald & Ormerod, 1993) and as many as 50 percent have been physically abused by a dating partner (Neufeld, McNamara, & Ertl, 1999). More recently, research endeavors have examined the prevalence of sexual harassment and dating violence among adolescents, although the literature base for this population is less

This chapter was adapted from "A Cluster Analytic Investigation of Victimization Among High School Students: Are Profiles Differentially Associated with Psychological Symptoms and School Belonging?" by Melissa K. Holt and Dorothy L. Espelage, *Journal of Applied School Psychology, 19*(2), pp. 81-98.

Bullying, Victimization, and Peer Harassment
Published by The Haworth Press, Inc., 2007. All rights reserved.
doi:10.1300/5808_06

extensive. Extant literature suggests that it is during adolescence when sexual harassment and dating violence begin to emerge (e.g., American Association of University Women [AAUW], 1993; Burcky, Reuterman, & Kopsky, 1988). Moreover, studies have documented that 80 percent of high school students have experienced sexual harassment in the form of unwelcome sexual behaviors of a physical and verbal nature (AAUW, 2001). Furthermore, between 10 percent (Roscoe & Callahan, 1985) and 55 percent have incurred physical or emotional abuse from a dating partner (O'Keefe, 1998).

The need to understand the dynamics of sexual harassment and dating violence is pressing given the psychological, educational, and career-related outcomes many targets face. For example, individuals who have been sexually harassed often suffer from depression, posttraumatic stress, decreased interest in school- and work-related activities, and self-doubt (AAUW, 1993; Dansky & Kilpatrick, 1997; Schneider, Swan, & Fitzgerald, 1997). Similarly, experiencing dating violence can produce outcomes such as feelings of anger and sadness (Carlson, 1987), posttraumatic stress, and anxiety (Harned, 2001). Although some existing research explores sexual harassment and dating violence among adolescents, a comprehensive analysis of how such victimization is linked to psychological functioning is lacking. Furthermore, additional information is needed regarding the effects of experiencing sexual harassment and dating violence in conjunction with other forms of victimization. Understanding multiple types of victimization affecting an individual is particularly important for two reasons. First, studies have demonstrated that when individuals are victimized once, they are at increased risk for future victimization (e.g., Harned, 2000). For example, students who reported experiencing sexual harassment were more likely to report dating violence victimization than those students who had not experienced sexual harassment (Connolly, McMaster, Craig, & Pepler, 1997). Second, victims of multiple types of violence are at greater risk for negative outcomes (e.g., Follette, Polusny, Bechtel, & Naugle, 1996). For instance, college females who had experienced sexual harassment, sexual abuse/assault, and physical abuse reported significantly more posttraumatic stress, anxiety, and disordered eating symptoms than women who had experienced only one type of victimization (Harned, 2000). Given that studies of repeated victimization have focused primarily on college-aged and adult populations, however, we know little about the effects of multiple victimization among adolescents. In the case of middle and high school students, a comprehensive model of victimization would be strengthened through the inclusion of peer victimization and childhood sexual abuse in addition to sexual harassment and dating violence.

Peer Victimization

Peer victimization in the form of bullying is a particularly salient factor to consider due to the frequency with which it occurs (Espelage, Bosworth, & Simon, 2000; Hoover, Oliver, & Hazler, 1992). For example, 88 percent of junior high and high school students reported having observed bullying and 77 percent reported being a victim of bullying during their school years (Hoover et al., 1992). Although there is substantial variation in how students respond to victimization from their peers (Kochenderfer-Ladd & Ladd, 2001), at least 14 percent of the Hoover et al. sample reported significant distress as a result of the harassment. Additional research has been directed at understanding why some students experience adverse outcomes to victimization and others do not (Kochenderfer-Ladd & Ladd). Specifically, these authors postulate that students who lack adaptive coping resources to draw from when they are harassed might experience negative outcomes.

Childhood Sexual Abuse

Childhood sexual abuse is another important form of victimization to evaluate among adolescents for a number of reasons. First, since approximately 20 percent of females and between 5 and 10 percent of males experience sexual abuse in childhood or adolescence (Finkelhor, 1994), it is probable that some participants in this investigation have been sexually abused. Second, a childhood sexual abuse history might heighten an individual's likelihood of experiencing subsequent victimization. For example, one study documented that women who had been sexually abused as children were more likely to experience sexual victimization and sexual harassment as adults than women without histories of childhood sexual abuse (Frazier & Cohen, 1992). A similar pattern might exist for adolescents. Third, childhood sexual abuse has been linked to comparable psychological outcomes as those associated with sexual harassment and dating violence, including depression, decreased involvement in school, anxiety, and substance abuse (e.g., Garnefski & Arends, 1998; Luster & Small, 1997; Trickett & McBride-Chang, 1995).

Hypotheses

The high rates of sexual harassment and dating violence among high school students necessitate that further research is conducted within this population to delineate more clearly the dynamics associated with these types of victimization. Moreover, it is essential to consider multiple forms of victimization simultaneously so as to better understand the influence of repeated victimization on psychological and educational functioning. As such, the current investigation evaluated the effects of sexual harassment, dating violence, peer victimization, and childhood sexual abuse on adolescents.

We hypothesized that groups of students would emerge with similar victimization patterns (e.g., no victimization, victimization in multiple realms), and that these groups would differ with respect to psychological functioning and sense of school belonging. Specifically, we predicted that, on average, students in groups characterized by greater victimization would report more symptoms of psychological distress and a lower sense of school belonging than students in groups characterized by less victimization.

The current investigation adds to existing literature by providing a unique perspective on victimization among adolescents. Findings are essential for school employees and clinicians who work with adolescents. Results provide school personnel with a framework for understanding that the victimization experiences of students are heterogeneous and as such victimization might differentially affect students.

METHOD

Participants

Participants were 504 students (grades 9 through 12) from the sole high school in a Midwestern town nearby a large university community. Total enrollment at this school was 1,555. Students enrolled in physical education classes were targeted; given enrollment characteristics of these classes each grade was not proportionally represented, although on other demographic characteristics participants were representative of the school population. One hundred eighty-eight participants were Freshmen (37 percent), 35 were Sophomores (7 percent), 158 were Juniors (31 percent), 119 were Seniors (24 percent), and 4 did not report their grades (<1 percent). The mean age for the sample was 16 ($SD = 1.3$). There were 228 (45 percent) males, 273 (54 percent) females, and 3 (<1 percent) students who did not report their gender. With respect to race there were 131 African American (26 percent), 313 Caucasian (62 percent), 29 Hispanic (6 percent), 6 Asian American (1 percent), 5 Native American (1 percent), 18 "Other" (4 percent), and two students (<1 percent) who did not report their race.

Procedure

Parental Consent

Passive parental consent was used in this investigation to maximize participation. Parents of all students enrolled in physical education classes were sent letters informing them about the purpose of the study. Furthermore, parents were asked to sign the form and return it only if they were unwilling to have their child participate in the investigation; no forms were returned. In addition to passive parental consent, students were asked to consent to participate in the study through an informed consent form included in the questionnaire packet.

Survey Administration

Six trained research assistants, the primary researcher, and a faculty member collected data. At least two of these individuals administered surveys to each physical education class, which ranged in size from twenty-five to fifty. Students were first informed about the general nature of the investigation. Next, researchers made certain that students were sitting far enough from one another to ensure confidentiality. Students were then given survey packets and asked to answer all questions honestly, and were told that no identifying information would be associated with their responses. Researchers were available to answer questions that emerged once students began responding to survey items. When students had completed the surveys, they were given the opportunity to have their data removed from analyses if they had not carefully considered each question. Each participant was also provided with a list of phone numbers to call (e.g., community counseling agencies) should they experience an emotional reaction to the questionnaires. Last, a raffle was held in each group in which one student won a $10 gift certificate to a local mall. On average it took students approximately forty-five minutes to complete the survey.

Measures

Each participant first completed a demographic questionnaire that included questions about his/her gender, age, grade, and race. For race, participants were given six options: African American (not Hispanic), Asian American, white (not Hispanic), Hispanic, Native American, and Other (with a space to write in the most appropriate racial descriptor).

Peer Sexual Harassment

The AAUW Sexual Harassment Survey (AAUW, 1993) is a 14-item inventory designed to measure the frequency with which students are victimized by sexually harassing behaviors. Participants are asked to indicate how often other students engaged in particular behaviors aimed at the participants (e.g., made sexual comments, jokes, gestures, or looks) within the previous year. Items reflect verbal and physical harassment. Response options are as follows: Not sure, Never, Rarely, Occasionally, and Often. Coefficient alpha for this sample was .90 for peers.

Physical Victimization in Dating Relationships

The Victimization in Dating Relationships scale (Foshee, Linder, Bauman, & Langwick, 1996) is an eighteen-item inventory designed to measure physically violent victimization within dating relationships. Participants are asked to indicate how often individuals they went on dates with engaged in particular behaviors (e.g., scratched me, kicked me) and are instructed to count only behaviors that their partners inflicted on them first. Violence inflicted due to self-defense, therefore, is not measured by the Victimization in Dating Relationships scale. There are four response options: Never, one to three times, four to nine times, and ten or more times. For the current sample the coefficient alpha was .95.

Psychological Abuse in Dating Relationships

The Abusive Behavior Inventory (ABI; Shepard & Campbell, 1992) is a thirty-item inventory designed to measure participants' perceptions of physical and psychological abuse in dating relationships. For the purpose of this investigation, a modified version of the ABI was used. Specifically, ten items tapping psychological abuse (e.g., "How often has a dating partner called you a name and/or criticized you?") were selected on the basis of appropriateness for a high school sample. Response options offered ranged from zero (Never) to four (Often), and participants were also given the opportunity to select "Not sure" as a response. The resulting alpha coefficient for the current study was .90.

Peer Victimization

A four-item victimization scale was used to assess peer victimization (Espelage & Holt, 2001). This scale was developed through in-depth interviews with middle school students. Items derived from the interviews emerged as a distinct dimension in a factor analysis of 422 middle school students and converged with peer nomination data. Students are asked how often they have been picked on, made fun of, called names, and hit or pushed in the last thirty days. Response options are "never," "one or two times," "three or four times," "five to six times," and "seven or more times." Coefficient alpha in this sample was .85.

Childhood Sexual Abuse

The seven-item sexual abuse scale from the Childhood Trauma Questionnaire was used (CTQ; Bernstein & Fink, 1994). Items on the scale inquire specifically about sexual abuse (e.g., "Someone molested me") and ask about behaviors consistent with sexual abuse (e.g., "Someone tried to make me do sexual things or watch sexual things"). Respondents were asked to think about how often these behaviors occurred throughout their entire lives. Response options are "Never true," "Rarely true," "Sometimes true," "Often true," and "Very often true." Coefficient alpha for the sexual abuse scale was .85 in this sample.

Psychological Functioning

The anxiety/depression scale from the Youth Self-Report (YRS; Achenbach, 1991) was used to assess psychological functioning. This scale consists of sixteen self-report items and students are asked to indicate the degree to which particular statements apply to them (e.g., "I feel lonely," "I am nervous or tense"). Response options are "Not true," "Somewhat or sometimes true," and "Very true or Often true." For the current investigation coefficient alpha was .90.

Two scales from the Weinberger Adjustment Inventory's (WAI; Weinberger & Schwartz, 1990) Psychological Distress Scale were also used, self-esteem and low well-being. Response options are on a 5-point scale ranging from "Not at all true" through "Always true." For the current sample, coefficient alpha was .77.

Sense of School Belonging

Perceived belonging at school was assessed with a revised version of the Psychological Sense of School Membership scale (Goodenow, 1993). This scale was a result of a factor analysis based on 558 middle school students; for a more detailed description of the development, refer to Bosworth,

Espelage, and Simon (1999). Students are asked how much they agree with the following statements: "I feel proud of belonging to my school," "I am treated with as much respect as other students are," "The teachers here respect me," and "There is at least one teacher or other adult in this school I can talk to if I have a problem." Response options include "Strongly disagree," "Disagree," "Neither agree nor disagree," "Agree," and "Strongly agree." Coefficient alpha for the current sample was .66.

RESULTS

First, frequencies of victimization were computed. Analyses indicated that 70 percent of the adolescents surveyed had experienced peer sexual harassment at least "rarely" and 54 percent had experienced peer sexual harassment at least "occasionally" within the last year. With respect to dating violence, 66 percent of the students endorsed psychological abuse in dating relationships and 40 percent reported incurring physical violence from a dating partner. Finally, 54 percent of respondents noted that they had been bullied during the last thirty days. Frequencies by gender and grade are delineated in Table 6.1.

Second, correlations among study variables were examined. As delineated in Table 6.2, for males and females victimization variables were positively correlated with one another, with correlations ranging from low to moderate in strength. In addition, victimization was related to psychological functioning; greater victimization tended to be associated with greater psychological distress. Finally, a diminished sense of school belonging was positively correlated with victimization and psychological symptoms.

Third, we used cluster analytic techniques to identify types of victimization profiles yielded by high school students. The following scales were entered into the SYSTAT program using a k-means cluster analytic procedure: peer sexual harassment, physical dating violence, psychological abuse in dating relationships, peer victimization, and childhood sexual abuse. Sufficient scale data were available for 491 participants. Results of cluster analyses utilizing these methods suggested that a five-cluster solution was appropriate for the data (see Table 6.3).

Designated labels for each cluster were as follows: (1) "No victimization" (Cluster 1), a group characterized by scores below the mean on all victimization measures; (2) "Sexual harassment" (Cluster 2), a group characterized by scores one standard deviation above the mean on peer sexual harassment and scores within one standard deviation of the mean on all other victimization indicators; (3) "Revictimization" (Cluster 3), a group

TABLE 6.1. Victimization frequencies by grade and gender.

	Total sample		Grade 9		Grade 10		Grade 11		Grade 12	
	M (N = 228)	F (N = 273)	M (N = 83)	F (N = 105)	M (N = 22)	F (N = 13)	M (N = 70)	F (N = 87)	M (N = 52)	F (N = 66)
Peer sexual harassment										
Rarely (%)	60	75	52	71	60	85	60	75	69	79
Occasionally (%)	42	54	31	49	46	69	41	56	56	56
Physical abuse in dating relationships (%)	43	41	34	33	50	61	39	52	50	38
Emotional abuse in dating relationships (%)	59	71	46	71	64	92	59	79	77	71
Peer victimization (%)	57	52	48	50	50	62	70	52	58	56

TABLE 6.2. Correlations among study variables by gender.

	CSA	DV	PA	PSH	PV	LSE	LWB	Anx/Dep	Belong
CSA		0.40**	0.25**	0.22**	0.06	0.08	0.06	0.37**	−0.23**
DV	0.45**		0.39**	0.32**	0.14*	0.23**	0.18**	0.48**	−0.20**
PA	0.36**	0.65**		0.33**	0.07	0.19**	0.11	0.31**	−0.24**
PSH	0.51**	0.42**	0.43**		0.00	−0.03	−0.03	0.10	−0.16*
PV	0.20**	0.12*	0.27**	0.22**		0.18**	0.10	0.26**	−0.06
LSE	0.18**	0.22**	0.30**	0.17**	0.20**		0.56**	0.57**	−0.32**
LWB	0.17**	0.22**	0.28**	0.17**	0.15*	0.55**		0.49**	−0.24**
Anx/Dep	0.35**	0.34**	0.40**	0.28**	0.33**	0.61**	0.50**		−0.30**
Belong	−0.09	−0.11	−0.17**	−0.10	−0.03	−0.25**	−0.25**	−0.13*	

Note. Upper right quadrant represents males and lower left quadrant represents females. *$p < .05$. **$p < .01$. CSA = Childhood sexual abuse from Childhood Trauma Questionnaire; DV = Physical dating violence from the Victimization in Relationships Scale; PA = Psychological abuse in dating relationships from the Abusive Behavior Inventory; PSH = Peer sexual harassment from the AAUW Sexual Harassment Inventory; PV = Peer victimization from the Self-reported Victimization Scale; LSE = Low self-esteem scale from the Weinberger Adjustment Inventory; LWB = Low well-being scale from the Weinberger Adjustment Inventory; Anx/Dep = Anxiety/Depression scale from the Youth Self Report; Belong = Sense of School Belonging from Psychological Sense of School Membership Scale.

characterized by scores one standard deviation above the mean on all victimization measures *except* peer victimization; (4) "Psychological abuse in dating relationships" (Cluster 4), a group characterized by scores one standard deviation above the mean on psychological abuse in dating relationships and scores within one standard deviation of the mean on all other victimization measures; (5) "Physical dating violence and childhood sexual abuse" (Cluster 5), a group characterized by scores three standard deviations above the mean on physical dating violence, one standard deviation above the mean on childhood sexual abuse, and within one standard deviation of the mean on all other victimization measures.

Chi-square analyses revealed that these clusters did not differ by grade or race, but that they did differ by gender (c^2 (1, $N = 493$) = 12.69, $p < .01$). Specifically, a greater percentage of females were in the "Psychological abuse in dating relationships" cluster than males, and a greater percentage of males were in the "Physical dating violence and childhood sexual abuse" cluster than females.

Next, we evaluated the extent to which the cluster groups differed on psychological symptoms, including sense of school belonging, depression/anxiety scores from the Youth Self-Report (Achenbach, 1991) and psychological low well-being and self-esteem scores from the Weinberger Adjust-

TABLE 6.3. Means and standard deviations for each victimization scale across clusters.

Scale	Total Sample[a]		"No victimization" (Cluster 1)[b]		"Peer sexual harassment" (Cluster 2)[c]		"Revictimization" (Cluster 3)[d]		"Psychological abuse in dating relationships" (Cluster 4)[e]		"Physical dating and childhood sexual abuse" (Cluster 5)[f]	
	M	SD	M	SD	M	SD	M	SD	M	SD	M	SD
Childhood sexual abuse	7.59	4.28	6.36	3.13	8.94	4.23	15.58	5.10	7.68	4.10	13.06	5.24
Psychological abuse in dating relationships	5.22	6.13	1.84	2.34	5.60	4.34	17.21	7.15	13.37	4.54	8.78	6.54
Physical dating violence	3.28	7.33	0.48	1.36	2.21	2.72	19.05	10.34	4.83	5.01	27.72	11.08
Peer sexual harassment	5.78	7.53	1.82	2.24	14.68	5.37	27.68	7.61	5.29	4.10	12.94	6.76
Peer victimization	6.26	3.42	5.76	2.93	6.65	3.93	7.26	4.15	6.85	3.66	9.06	4.61

Note. [a]n = 491, [b]n = 295, [c]n = 72, [d]n = 22, [e]n = 82, [f]n = 20.

ment Inventory (Weinberger & Schwartz, 1990). Given that these variables were correlated moderately with one another, we conducted a MANOVA with cluster membership as the independent variable and school belonging, anxiety/depression, low well-being, and self-esteem as dependent variables. A significant group difference emerged from this analysis (Wilks's $l = .75$, $F = 9.16$, $p < .05$, eta-squared = .07). Follow-up univariate tests indicated that there was a significant group difference for each of the seven dependent variables ($Fs = 4.70$-31.27, $ps < .01$; see Table 6.3).

A number of key findings emerged. Not surprisingly, the "No victimization" cluster group had lower scores on psychological distress than the remaining four cluster groups. In addition, the "Revictimization" group reported a significantly lower sense of school belonging than the "Peer sexual harassment" and "Psychological abuse in dating relationships" groups and lower self-esteem than the other four groups. Moreover, members of the "Revictimization" group revealed significantly more depression and lower well-being than individuals in the "No Victimization" and "Peer sexual harassment" groups, and more anxiety/depression than individuals in all groups except for the "Physical dating violence and childhood sexual abuse" group. Finally, to determine which psychological variable was the most predictive of cluster membership, a discriminant function analysis (DFA) was calculated. Only one discriminant function was statistically significant (Wilks's $l = .75$, $c^2 = 140.42$, $p < .001$). Interpretation of the structure coefficients indicated that the Depression/Anxiety (.92) had the highest correlation with the discriminant function, followed by low self-esteem (.52), school belonging ($-.47$), and low well-being (.35). This is consistent with the effect size data presented in Table 6.4. Although the small sample sizes in the cluster groups prohibit additional analyses, these results suggest that anxiety and depression significantly differentiate several of the groups, particularly clusters 3 and 5.

DISCUSSION

The current investigation examined sexual harassment, dating violence, peer victimization, and childhood sexual abuse among racially diverse adolescents. Objectives were (1) to gain a better understanding of prevalence rates, and (2) to delineate psychological and educational effects of victimization patterns. Results indicated that adolescents from the high school surveyed incur frequent victimization across multiple realms. Within this sample, 70 percent of the participants reported that they had been sexually harassed by peers. This rate is similar to those cited in previous studies. For

TABLE 6.4. Means and standard deviations for sense of school belonging and psychological symptoms across clusters.

	Total Sample[a]		"No victimization" (Cluster 1[b])		"Peer sexual harassment" (Cluster 2[c])		"Revictimization" (Cluster 3[d])		"Psychological abuse in dating relationships" (Cluster 4[e])		"Physical dating violence and childhood sexual abuse" (Cluster 5[f])		F	Eta-Squared
	M	SD	M	SD	M	SD	M	SD	M	SD	M	SD		
School belonging	14.63	3.24	15.19	2.84	14.34	3.54	12.14	4.59	13.91	3.16	13.05	3.87	8.32*	.06
Low self-esteem	13.73	5.62	12.65	5.02	14.10	5.85	19.23	4.93	15.54	6.50	14.95	4.56	11.62*	.09
Low well-being	13.53	5.83	12.76	5.43	13.88	6.19	16.90	7.02	14.57	6.32	15.55	4.50	4.70*	.04
Anxiety/Depression	6.56	6.63	4.68	5.12	6.72	6.43	15.50	8.00	8.95	6.76	14.10	8.13	31.27*	.21

Note. [a]$n = 491$, [b]$n = 295$, [c]$n = 72$, [d]$n = 22$, [e]$n = 82$, [f]$n = 20$, *$p < .01$.

School Belonging from the Psychological Sense of School Membership Scale; Low Self-Esteem from the Weinberger Adjustment Inventory; Low Well-Being from the Weinberger Adjustment Inventory; Anxiety from the Youth Self-Report.

example, in the AAUW (1993) sample, 79 percent of the adolescents surveyed endorsed peer sexual harassment. With respect to dating violence, 40 percent of the respondents in this investigation indicated that they had been physically abused by a dating partner and 66 percent revealed that they had experienced emotional abuse from a dating partner. These rates are also consistent with existing literature (e.g., Bookwala, Frieze, Smith, & Ryan, 1992; Roscoe & Callahan, 1985). Finally, in line with past research (Nansel et al., 2001), 54 percent of the high school students in this study noted that they had been victimized by peers within the last month.

Findings also supported the hypothesis that there is heterogeneity in victimization experiences among these high school students. Five distinct groups of students with similar victimization histories were identified using cluster analysis. These groups included (1) students with minimal victimization experiences, (2) adolescents who reported only significant peer sexual harassment, (3) participants who revealed only significant psychological abuse in dating relationships, (4) respondents with significant physical dating violence and childhood sexual abuse experiences, and (5) a small number of adolescents who reported experiencing multiple forms of victimization. As such, our findings suggested that while some students are victimized in primarily one realm (e.g., they are sexually harassed), other adolescents are the targets of multiple types of victimization. This supports limited existing literature that sexual harassment and dating violence in particular are likely to co-occur (e.g., Connolly et al., 1997).

Interestingly, resulting clusters did not differ by grade or race, but did differ by gender. In support of previous literature indicating that females experience more psychological abuse in dating relationships than males (e.g., Foshee, 1996), girls in this sample were more likely than boys to be classified in the group characterized by high levels of psychological abuse in dating relationships. Surprisingly, males were somewhat more likely than females to be members of the "Physical dating violence and Childhood sexual abuse" group; this counters previous literature finding that either gender differences on physical dating violence did not exist (e.g., Malik, Sorenson, & Aneshensel, 1997) or females were more often the targets of physical dating violence than males (e.g., Roscoe & Callahan, 1985).

As expected, victimization patterns were differentially related to psychological functioning and sense of school belonging. For instance, members of the "No victimization" group were less distressed than individuals in the other four groups, suggesting that being the target of even one type of victimization produces deleterious psychological symptoms. Consistent with hypotheses, negative outcomes were heightened, however, for adolescents in the "Revictimization" group. Importantly, not only did these adolescents reveal more psychological symptoms (e.g., more depression) than individuals in some of the other groups, but they also reported feeling disconnected to the school environment. These findings support the notion advocated by Follette and colleagues (1996) that individuals who are revictimized tend to suffer more distress. Coupled together these risk factors might result in students disengaging in school activities or dropping out. As such, it is critical to identify students who might have multiple victimization experiences to provide support structures for them.

Limitations of the Study

Future studies are needed to replicate findings from the current investigation and to further our understanding of multiple victimization among adolescents. Results from the present study are limited to a suburban population and, therefore, might not be applicable to urban youth. Furthermore, a restricted range of outcomes was considered; the effects of victimization on areas such as academic performance and social functioning with peers and family are also important to evaluate. Finally, this investigation was cross-sectional in nature and, therefore, it was impossible to discern whether students with multiple victimization experiences had changes in functioning after they first were victimized or whether changes occurred as a result of cumulative effects.

Implications for Research and Practice in Applied Psychology

In sum, individuals are faced with multiple forms of victimization during their high school years, including sexual harassment, dating violence, peer victimization, and childhood sexual abuse. These experiences are not to be taken lightly; adolescents are negatively affected when they are targets of such victimization. Furthermore, although school personnel might believe that girls are victimized more frequently than males, this study documents that males are also frequently targets. In particular, it appears that males are more likely than females to report a combination of physical dating violence and childhood sexual abuse.

Findings from the current investigation also underscore the importance of understanding adolescents' overall victimization experiences rather than considering specific types in isolation from one another. Similarly, results highlight the salience of addressing a range of victimization types in educational or intervention programming. Furthermore, school psychologists should be aware that students presenting with one victimization concern might also have been victimized in additional arenas.

Given the developmental importance of adolescence it is possible that psychological distress resulting from victimization will have deleterious effects on myriad aspects of these individuals' lives as they transition into adulthood. It is, therefore, incumbent upon researchers and educators to promote awareness of these issues, and to create environments that feel safe enough for high school students to approach school staff to obtain help in curbing violent behaviors directed toward them and to seek psychological counseling if necessary.

REFERENCES

Achenbach, T. M. (1991). *Manual for the Youth Self-Report and 1991 Profile.* Burlington, VT: University of Vermont, Department of Psychiatry.

American Association of University Women Educational Foundation (1993). *Hostile hallways: The AAUW survey on sexual harassment in America's schools* (Research Report 923012). Washington, DC: Harris/Scholastic Research.

American Association of University Women Educational Foundation (2001). *Hostile hallways: Sexual harassment and bullying in schools.* Washington, DC: Harris/Scholastic Research.

Bernstein, D. P., & Fink, L. (1998). *Childhood trauma questionnaire: A retrospective self-report manual.* San Antonio: The Psychological Corporation.

Bookwala, J., Frieze, I. H., Smith, C., & Ryan, K. (1992). Predictors of dating violence: A multivariate analysis. *Violence and Victims, 7,* 297-309.

Bosworth, K., Espelage, D. L., & Simon, T. (1999). Factors associated with bullying behavior in middle school students. *Journal of Early Adolescence, 19,* 341-362.

Burcky, W., Reuterman, N., & Kopsky, S. (1988). Dating violence among high school students. *The School Counselor, 35,* 353-358.

Carlson, B. E. (1987). Dating violence: A research review and comparison with spouse abuse. *Social Casework: The Journal of Contemporary Social Work,* 16-23.

Connolly, J., McMaster, L., Craig, W., & Pepler, D. (1997). Dating, puberty, and sexualized aggression. In A. Slep (Chair), *Dating Violence: Predictors and Consequences in Normative and At-Risk Populations.* Symposium conducted at the annual meeting of the Association for the Advancement of Behavior Therapy, Miami, FL.

Dansky, B. S., & Kilpatrick, D. G. (1997). Effects of sexual harassment. In W. T. O'Donohue (Ed.), *Sexual harassment: Theory, research, and treatment* (pp. 152-174). Needham Heights, MA: Allyn & Bacon.

Espelage, D. L., Bosworth, K., & Simon, T. (2000). Examining the social environment of middle school students who bully. *Journal of Counseling and Development, 78,* 326-333.

Espelage, D. L., & Holt, M. K. (2001). Bullying and victimization during early adolescence: Peer influences and psychosocial correlates. *Journal of Emotional Abuse, 2*(3), 123-142.

Finkelhor, D. (1994) Current information on the scope and nature of child sexual abuse. *Future of Children, 4,* 31-53.

Fitzgerald, L. F., & Ormerod, A. J. (1993). Breaking the silence: The sexual harassment of women in academia and the workplace. In F. L. Denmark & M. A. Paludi (Eds.), *Psychology of women: A handbook of issues and theories* (pp. 553-581). Westport, CT: Greenwood Press/Greenwood Publishing Group, Inc.

Follette, V. M., Polusny, M. A., Bechtle, A. E., & Naugle, A. E. (1996). Cumulative trauma: The impact of child sexual abuse, adult sexual assault, and spouse abuse. *Journal of Traumatic Stress, 9,* 25-35.

Foshee, V. A. (1996). Gender differences in adolescent dating abuse prevalence, types, and injuries. *Health Education Research: Theory and Practice, 11,* 275-286.

Foshee, V. A., Linder, G. F., Bauman, C. E., & Langwick, S. A. (1996). The safe dates project: Theoretical basis, evaluation, design, and selected baseline findings. *American Journal of Preventive Medicine, 12,* 39-47.

Frazier, P. A., & Cohen, B. B. (1992). Research on the sexual victimization of women: Implications for counselor training. *The Counseling Psychologist, 20,* 141-158.

Garnefski, N., & Arends, E. (1998). Sexual abuse and adolescent maladjustment: Differences between male and female victims. *Journal of Adolescence, 21,* 99-107.

Goodenow, C. (1993). The psychological sense of school membership among adolescents: Scale development and educational correlates. *Psychology in the Schools, 30,* 79-90.

Harned, M. (2001). Abused women or abused men? An examination of the context and outcomes of dating abuse. *Violence and Victims, 16,* 269-285.

Harned, M. S. (2000, May). *The extent and impact of repeated and multiple victimization.* Paper presented at the 72nd Annual Meeting of the Midwestern Psychological Association, Chicago, IL.

Hoover, J. H., Oliver, R., & Hazler, R. J. (1992). Bullying: Perceptions of adolescent victims in the midwestern USA. *School Psychology International, 13,* 5-16.

Kochenderfer-Ladd, B., & Ladd, G. W. (2001). Variations in peer victimization: Relations to children's maladjustment. In J. Juvonen & S. Graham (Eds.), *Peer harassment in school: The plight of the vulnerable and victimized* (pp. 25-48). New York: Guilford Press.

Luster, T., & Small, S. A. (1997). Sexual abuse history and problems in adolescence: Exploring the effects of moderating variables. *Journal of Marriage and the Family, 59,* 131-142.

Malik, S., Sorenson, S. B., & Aneshensel, C. S. (1997). Community and dating violence among adolescents: Perpetration and victimization. *Journal of Adolescent Health, 21,* 291-302.

Nansel, T. R., Overpeck, M., Pilla, R. S., Ruan, W. J., Simons-Morton, B., & Scheidt, P. (2001). Bullying behaviors among US youth: Prevalence and association with psychosocial adjustment. *Journal of the American Medical Association, 285,* 2094-2132.

Neufeld, J., McNamara, J. R., & Ertl, M. (1999). Incidence and prevalence of dating partner abuse and its relation to dating practices. *Journal of Interpersonal Violence, 14,* 125-137.

O'Keefe, M. (1998). Factors mediating the link between witnessing interparental violence and dating violence. *Journal of Family Violence, 13,* 39-57.

Roscoe, B., & Callahan, J. E. (1985). Adolescents' self-report of violence in families and dating relations. *Adolescence, 20,* 1985.

Schneider, K. T., Swan, S., & Fitzgerald, L. F. (1997). Job-related psychological effects of sexual harassment in the workplace: Empirical evidence from two organizations. *Journal of Applied Psychology, 82,* 401-415.

Shepard, M. F., & Campbell, J. A. (1992). The Abusive Behavior Inventory: A measure of psychological and physical abuse. *Journal of Interpersonal Violence, 7,* 291-305.

Trickett, P. K., & McBride-Chang, C. (1995). The developmental impact of different forms of child abuse and neglect. *Developmental Review, 15,* 311-337.

Weinberger, D. A., & Schwartz, G. E. (1990). Distress and restraint as superordinate dimensions of self-reported adjustment: A typological perspective. *Journal of Personality, 58,* 381-417.

Chapter 7

Immigrant Children in Austria: Aggressive Behavior and Friendship Patterns in Multicultural School Classes

Dagmar Strohmeier
Christiane Spiel

As a consequence of worldwide waves of immigration, a growing number of immigrant children are attending public schools together with native borns in countries all over the world. This development leads to an increase of ethnically mixed school classes. There, children are challenged to learn cooperative forms of interethnic interactions by crossing cultural group boundaries.

At the moment, scientific knowledge about the quality of interethnic relationships in children is very limited, because the main focus of research lay on prejudices and interethnic attitudes. Interethnic relationships in contact situations were hardly ever studied (e.g., Vedder & O'Dowd, 1999). This study deals with this topic. To get insights into quality of relationships between immigrant and native children, positive and negative aspects of interactions in multicultural school classes were investigated. Thus, the brief

This chapter was adapted from "Immigrant Children in Austria: Aggressive Behavior and Friendship Patterns in Multicultural School Classes" by Dagmar Strohmeier and Christiane Spiel, *Journal of Applied School Psychology, 19*(2), pp. 99-116. Parts of this paper were presented at the fifth workshop on aggression in Hannover, Germany, November 2000.

Bullying, Victimization, and Peer Harassment
Published by The Haworth Press, Inc., 2007. All rights reserved.
doi:10.1300/5808_07

review of the literature incorporates two fields of research: (1) research on aggression, in particular on bullying, and (2) research on friendship, both with the focus on interethnic interactions.

PROBLEMATIC INTERETHNIC INTERACTIONS—PEER AGGRESSION

In the literature dealing with multicultural school classes, one important factor for the formation and maintenance of interactions between pupils from various cultural backgrounds was seen in the proficiency in a common language (Vedder & O'Dowd, 1999). It was argued that a lack of common language skills might hamper the contact between pupils and might be a reason for problematic interethnic relationships in children. To test this hypothesis, Vedder and O'Dowd conducted a study in ethnically mixed school classes in Sweden. Immigrant children divided into two groups depending on their proficiency in Swedish and Swedish children were compared in peer-rated aggressive-disruptive behavior, isolation/withdrawal, and sociability/leadership. No differences between the three groups were found in aggressiveness and withdrawal. However, immigrant children with weaker Swedish comprehension were found to score lower in leadership/sociability compared to their Swedish peers. The importance of good language proficiency for high social status is not limited to immigrant children. In a sociometric study, Rost and Czeschlik (1994) showed the general importance of good verbal comprehension for high social status. Even in monocultural settings, children with higher verbal ability are more accepted by their peers than others. These findings support the impact of language proficiency on peer acceptance but not on negative aspects of interethnic relationships such as aggression.

In general, scientific knowledge concerning immigrant children's involvement in peer aggression is very limited. Only a few studies provide data of prevalence rates. However, these studies never distinguished between the countries of origin of the children (they were uniformly labeled as "foreigners") and did not reveal consistent results. While Fuchs (1999) observed a higher level of aggression in immigrant children than in native-born children, some studies revealed no significant differences (Loesel, Bliesener, & Averbeck, 1999; Popp, 2000). In the study conducted by Klicpera and Gasteiger-Klicpera (1996) immigrant children were shown to be less often engaged in bullying than native borns. However, it was argued (e.g., Fuchs, 1999; Popp, 2000) that immigrant children are more likely to attend schools with generally high aggression rates and thus, comparisons of children with different nationalities without controlling for school might be biased. These inconsistencies may also trace back to conceptual differences between the studies concerning peer aggression or to the heterogeneity within the sample of "foreign" children investigated.

The literature on peer aggression shows a high variability in the conceptualization of aggression and the categorization of negative acts. In the last decade more and more empirical studies conducted in schools are based on the concept of bullying according to Olweus (1993) which describes a subcategory of aggression. In this concept a specific relationship between a victim and its perpetrator(s) is defined. The main characteristics of this harmful relationship are imbalance of power, long duration, and the bully's intention to hurt the victim. Bullying is a widespread phenomenon in schools that takes place in almost every class in school (Schuster, 1999; Strohmeier & Spiel, 2001). Bullying is also considered as a social phenomenon determined not only by characteristics of bullies and victims but also by social relationships in the group, which were studied between pupils taking different roles (e.g., Salmivalli, Lagerspetz, Bjoerqvist, & Oestermann, 1996; Sutton & Smith, 1999). Furthermore, bullying includes a variety of negative acts, which can be delivered face-to-face or by indirect means. Whereas physical or verbal insults are mostly visible and thus categorized as direct bullying, in the last decade various forms of indirect aggressive acts have gained attention (Bjoerqvist, Lagerspetz, & Kaukiainen, 1992; Lagerspetz, Bjoerqvist, & Peltonen, 1988). While Olweus (1993) defines indirect aggression as social exclusion, Lagerspetz et al. (1988) and Bjoerqvist et al,, (1992) suggest social manipulation as the main characteristic of indirect bullying. Recently, social manipulative forms of aggression were intensely investigated and found to be typical for girls (e.g., Crick & Grotpeter, 1995; Lagerspetz & Bjoerqvist, 1994; Rys & Bear, 1997). Due to the fact that both gender and race segregation is quite prevalent in children's social lives (Maccoby, 1988, 1990), social exclusion might be more typical for interethnic relationships than social manipulation. Thus, in this study, indirect aggression was defined in terms of social exclusion (Olweus, 1989, 1993).

Cooperative Forms of Interethnic Interactions—Friendships

Scientific knowledge about cooperative forms of interethnic relationships in children is also very limited. However, gender and race were found to be important dimensions along which children form peer groups and dyadic friendships (e.g., Brown, 1990; Boulton & Smith, 1996; Graham & Cohen, 1997). Brown (1995) noted that children are usually able to discriminate between in-group and out-group members at the age of three years. Here, gender appeared to be a more salient factor than race for children's friendship choices (Graham, Cohen, Zbikowski, & Secrist, 1998). The proportion of same gender and same race relationships increases with age (Graham et al., 1998; Maharaj & Connolly, 1994). That means, children exist in different subcultures that are determined by social categories, especially by gender (Maccoby, 1988, 1990). Moreover, the similarity-attraction hypothesis (Berscheid, 1985) could be confirmed for children. Children were shown to be similar to their friends with respect to demographic, behavioral, and academic attributes (e.g., Kupersmidt, DeRosier, & Patterson, 1995). Furthermore, the absence of cooperative forms of social relationships is strongly associated with the concept of indirect bullying, according to Olweus (1989, 1993).

Although the development and maintenance of social relations with members of other cultural groups is a major dimension in acculturation models (e.g., Berry, 1980; Bourhis, Moise, Perreault, & Seneca, 1997), neither interethnic friendship patterns nor peer acceptance were yet investigated in children from different countries of origin. This lack of research is hard to understand, as the formation of close interpersonal relationships is considered an important factor for the social integration of an individual into the peer group (Laireiter & Baumann, 1992).

It is the main goal of this study to overcome these deficiencies in the research on immigrant children and (1) to distinguish immigrants with respect to their countries of origin, and (2) to focus on both problematic interethnic interactions and cooperative forms of interethnic interactions. Concretely, we addressed the following questions:

- Do children of various immigrant groups (e.g., Turkish, Yugoslavian) differ from each other with respect to demographic and academic attributes (e.g., place of birth, age, last school grade in German language) that are considered to be important for social integration (similarity-attraction hypothesis)?
- Do children from various immigrant groups differ from each other and from native borns in direct and indirect forms of bullying?
- Are there differences in friendship patterns and peer acceptance between native children and immigrant children from various countries of origin?

METHOD

Procedure and Participants

Research was conducted in twenty-nine classes (sixth and seventh grades) of six general secondary schools situated in a middle-sized city in the southern part of Austria.[1] General secondary schools serve predominantly lower middle-class families, and show higher aggression levels of pupils than academic secondary schools (e.g., Gasteiger-Klicpera & Klicpera, 1997). This study included general secondary schools with a considerably high number of immigrant children.

Participation in the study was voluntary; strict confidentiality for both pupils and schools was guaranteed. After the study was accepted by the local school council, school principals provided alphabetic class rosters of participating classes. Based on these rosters, every child was assigned to a code. These rosters were projected onto the wall in the classrooms during data collection. While filling in the questionnaire, pupils were asked to use the presented codes instead of names to assure their confidentiality. Data collection was done by two trained bilingual (German and Serbian/Croatian and Turkish) research assistants during a regular lesson and lasted about two hours.

In sum, 326 native and 242 immigrant children (258 girls and 310 boys) participated in the study. According to the official statistics of the local school council, 886 pupils of general secondary schools in this district were immigrant children (Kerschbaumer, 2000). That means, 27 percent of the population of immigrant children who attended a general secondary school in this school district participated in the study. The children of the immigrant subsample spoke twenty-two different mother-tongues, which were shown to represent the population well. For theoretical and practical reasons, participants were divided into four groups: native children (57 percent), children from the former Yugoslavia (22 percent), Turkish and Kurdish children (14 percent), and a heterogeneous rest group (7 percent). Whereas children of the first three groups are considered as similar regarding their cultural backgrounds, children of the rest group are mostly the only representatives of their immigrant group in the school class and thus are considered as similar with respect to their social situation. We acknowledge that the group labels are imprecise and that there is additional heterogeneity within these categories. However, it is likely that these broad categories, rather than more narrow subgroups, are particularly salient to the peer group. Similar group distinctions were made by Hanish and Guerra (2000a, 2000b) for various ethnic groups in the United States.

INSTRUMENTS

Bully/Victim Behavior

In this study, "bullying" was defined according to Olweus (1993). Because of the fact that an exact translation of the term "bullying" into German is not possible (Spiel, 2000; Spiel & Atria, 2001; Strohmeier & Spiel, 2000) instead of an ambiguous translation the English term "bullying" was used and was explained to the pupils in a very careful and standardized way. In addition, participants were presented with the German version of the definition of "bullying" provided in the Olweus Bullying Inventory (1989).[2]

Self-Ratings

Participants were presented with four subscales of the Bully/Victim Questionnaire (BVQ; Olweus, 1989). Previous checks of psychometric properties of the German version of these subscales showed satisfying results. Reliability estimates (Cronbach's α) ranged between .61 and .85 (Robier, 1997; Singer, 1998). The subscales are as follows: (1) Victim Scale of Indirect Bullying (4 items; e.g., How much do you like recess time?), (2) Victim Scale of Direct Bullying (4 items; e.g., How often have you been bullied at school this term?), (3) Bully Scale (5 items; e.g., How often have you taken part in bullying other young people at school this term?), and (4) Attitude to Bullying Scale (3 items; e.g., What do you think about pupils who join in bullying other young people?). The response scales in this inventory are paraphrased verbally and range from 1 (low feature characteristic) to 5 (high feature characteristic). Several of the response alternatives are fairly specific, such as "about once a week," and "several times a week" and thus, more objective than alternatives like "often" and "very often."

Peer Ratings

According to the definition of "bullying" provided in the BVQ (Olweus, 1989; see earlier) participants were asked to nominate every classmate they regarded (1) as a bully and/or (2) as a victim. To control for the varying class sizes (ranged between sixteen and twenty-seven pupils) participants were classified as "victims" or "bullies," when they were nominated by more than 33 percent of their classmates. Similar cut-off points were used, for example, by Boulton and Smith (1994) and Salmivalli, Huttunen, and Lagerspetz (1997).

Friendship Patterns and Peer Acceptance

To assess children's level of peer acceptance, a sociometric nomination technique was used (Coie, Dodge, & Copotelli, 1982). Self-ratings were applied to get insights into participants' friendship patterns.

Self-Ratings

Participants were asked to write down name, country of origin, and gender of their friends (both classmates and others). They were requested to think of a person as a "friend" if they liked that person very much, felt emotionally close to that person, spent lots of their leisure time with that person, told secrets to that person, and if they thought that their lives would be very different without that person. For each child, the number of friends differentiated by her/his country of origin (Austria, former Yugoslavia, Turkey, and other countries) was calculated.

Peer Ratings

Participants were asked to nominate the three classmates they liked most (LM) and the three classmates they liked least (LL). Based on this information, these two indicators were combined to a "social preference (SP)" score (SP = LM − LL; see Peery, 1979). Social preference scores are used to index a child's actual peer acceptance (number of positive nominations minus number of negative nominations). Sociometric classifications based on social preference scores were shown to exhibit good one-year stability (Coie & Dodge, 1983). To control for the varying class sizes, the index used was z, standardized by class.

In addition, information about demographic and academic attributes considered to be important for the social integration of immigrant children was collected (Berscheid, 1985; Laireiter & Baumann, 1992). These variables are as follows: age, place of birth, midterm marks in German language, mother-tongue instruction, and duration of stay in Austria.[3]

RESULTS

In the first step, children from the three immigrant groups were compared in demographic and academic attributes. Results of analyses are shown in Table 7.1.

Univariate ANOVAS, c^2 tests, and Alpha-corrected Bonferroni post hoc tests showed that age, place of birth, midterm marks in German language, duration of stay in Austria, and the attendance of additional mother-tongue

TABLE 7.1. Description of immigrant and native children.

Groups of children	Native children		Rest group children		Turkish/Kurdish children		Children of the former Yugoslavia	
Age	M	SD	M	SD	M	SD	M	SD
	12.70	.97	12.89	1.06	13.42	.93	12.71	1.05
Place of birth	Austria	Elsewhere	Austria	Elsewhere	Austria	Elsewhere	Austria	Elsewhere
	$n = 324$	$n = 2$	$n = 6$	$n = 30$	$n = 1$	$n = 79$	$n = 16$	$n = 110$
	99.4%	.6%	16.7%	83.3%	1.2%	98.8%	12.7%	87.3%
Mid-term marks in German language	M	SD	M	SD	M	SD	M	SD
	3.12	.94	3.83	1.41	3.92	1.25	3.19	.92
Mother-tongue instruction			Yes	No	Yes	No	Yes	No
			$n = 12$	$n = 23$	$n = 41$	$n = 38$	$n = 19$	$n = 105$
			34.3%	65.7%	51.9%	48.1%	15.3%	84.7%
Duration of stay in Austria (in months)			M	SD	M	SD	M	SD
			69.67	55.45	52.29	34.07	94.11	34.63

instruction are not equal between groups (see Table 7.1). Turkish and Kurdish children were older than children of the other groups, $F(3/559) = 11.54, p < .001$. Furthermore, Turkish and Kurdish children and children of the rest group achieved lower marks in German compared to Austrians and children from the former Yugoslavia, $F(3/539) = 16.59, p < .001$. Children of the former Yugoslavia and children of the rest group were more often born in Austria than Turkish children, $c^2 (2) = 9.98, p < .01$. In addition, children of the former Yugoslavia stayed longer in Austria than Turkish children and children of the rest group, $F(2/235) = 29.49, p < .001$. In addition, groups differed with respect to additional mother-tongue instruction: 52 percent of the Turkish children, 34 percent of the rest group children, and 15 percent of the children from the former Yugoslavia attended these voluntary lessons, $c^2 (2) = 30.91, p < .001$.

PROBLEMATIC INTERETHNIC INTERACTIONS

Bully/Victim Status: Peer Ratings

In sum, 9.1 percent of the participants were classified as bullies and 6.7 percent as victims. Statistically significant differences between immigrant and native-born children were found in the distribution of both bullies,

c^2 (3) = 7.77, p = .05, and victims, c^2 (3) = 8.13, p = .04. Thus, 11.8 percent of the native Austrian, 7.2 percent of the former Yugoslavian, but only 3.8 percent of the Turkish/Kurdish and 2.8 percent of the rest group children were classified as bullies. For the victim status, a slightly different picture emerged: 9.0 percent of the native Austrian, 8.3 percent of the rest group, 5.1 percent of the Turkish/Kurdish, and only 1.6 percent of the former Yugoslavian children were identified as victims based on peer ratings.

Bully/Victim Behavior: Self-Ratings

To make reliable comparisons between the groups of children, the psychometric properties of the Bully/Victim Questionnaire (BVQ) (Olweus, 1989) in native and all groups of immigrant children were checked.

For each group, the internal consistency of the four subscales of the BVQ was examined using Cronbach's a. Analyses revealed satisfying consistency scores for all groups of children in the Victim Scale of Direct Bullying, the Bully Scale, and the Attitude to Bullying Scale (Cronbach's a ranged between .54 and .83). However, striking differences in internal consistency were found for the Victim Scale of Indirect Bullying between native children and all groups of immigrant children (see Table 7.2).

As shown in Table 7.2, item-total correlations were very low in the subsamples of immigrant children. Thus, the concept of indirect aggression, defined as (1) liking recess times; (2) feeling lonely at school; (3) being alone during recess times; and (4) being as well liked as the other students in class (Olweus, 1989) does not fit well for immigrant children.

TABLE 7.2. Olweus scale of indirect bullying—internal consistencies (a) and item reliabilities *(rit)* for groups of children.

	Groups of children			
Reliability scores	Native children	Rest group children	Turkish/ Kurdish children	Children of the former Yugoslavia
How do you like recess time?	.20	−.01	−.09	.05
Do you feel lonely at school?	.55	.25	.04	.44
How often does it happen that other students don't want to spend recess time with you and you end up being alone?	.46	.40	.15	.39
Do you feel you are less well liked than other students in your class?	.44	.16	−.01	.15
Internal consistency (Cronbach a for Scale)	.63	.36	.04	.44

When investigating differences in bully/victim behavior between immigrant and native children, results of psychometric analyses were taken into account. First, we conducted a 2×4 MANOVA with gender and group (native Austrian, former Yugoslavian, Turkish/ Kurdish, and rest group) as factors and the three internally consistent subscale scores of the BVQ (Victim Scale of Direct Bullying, Bully Scale, and Attitude to Bullying Scale) as dependent variables. Application of multivariate tests using the Pillais Criterion did not identify a main effect group or an interaction effect. However, a gender effect was observed, $F(3,539) = 3.59$, $p = .02$, $\eta^2 = .02$. Follow-up univariate tests revealed differences between boys and girls regarding the Attitude to Bullying Scale, $F(1,541) = 7.20$, $p < .01$, $\eta^2 = .01$. Boys reported more positive attitudes toward bullying ($M = 7.49$, $SD = 3.06$) than girls did ($M = 6.77$, $SD = 2.77$).

To explore differences in indirect forms of bullying, a second 2×4 MANOVA with the factors gender and group and the four single items of the Victim Scale of Indirect Bullying as dependent variables was conducted. Multivariate tests using the Pillais Criterion identified both main effects group, $F(12,1647) = 5.91$, $p < .001$, $\eta^2 = .04$, and gender, $F(4,547) = 4.59$, $p < .001$, $\eta^2 = .03$, to be significant. No significant interaction was found. Follow-up univariate tests revealed differences between immigrant groups in the items "How do you like recess times?" $F(3,550) = 3.32$, $p = .02$, $\eta^2 = .02$, and "Do you feel lonely at school?" $F(3,550) = 11.52$, $p < .001$, $\eta^2 = .06$. Alpha-corrected Bonferroni post hoc tests showed that Turkish/Kurdish children liked recess less ($M = 1.54$, $SD = 1.08$) than native children ($M = 1.23$, $SD = .69$). Furthermore, Turkish/Kurdish children ($M = 2.35$, $SD = 1.38$), and rest group children ($M = 2.17$, $SD = 1.07$) reported feeling lonely more often at school than native ($M = 1.68$, $SD = .86$) and former Yugoslavian children ($M = 1.69$, $SD = 1.02$).

COOPERATIVE FORMS
OF INTERETHNIC INTERACTIONS

Peer Acceptance

To compare the four groups (native Austrian, former Yugoslavian, Turkish/ Kurdish, and rest group) in peer acceptance, a 2×4 ANOVA was conducted with the standardized social acceptance score as dependent variable and gender and group as factors. The two main effects, gender, $F(1,554) = 4.73$, $p = .03$, $\eta^2 = .01$, and group, $F(3,554) = 5.70$, $p = .02$, $\eta^2 = .03$, were statistically significant. Alpha-corrected Bonferroni post hoc tests revealed that Turkish/Kurdish children ($M = -.46$, $SD = .96$) were less accepted by their peers than both native ($M = .06$, $SD = 1.00$) and former Yugoslavian children ($M = .14$, $SD = .84$). Furthermore, boys ($M = -.10$, $SD = 1.04$) were less accepted than girls ($M = .12$, $SD = .87$).

Friendship Patterns

On average, 68.52 percent of the friends nominated by the participants were their classmates. In this percentage no group differences were found. To compare the four groups (native Austrian, former Yugoslavian, Turkish/Kurdish, and rest group) in their nomination of classmates as friends, a 2 × 4 ANOVA was conducted with gender and group as factors and the number of classmates nominated as friends as dependent variable. The main effect group, $F(3,547) = 5.97$, $p < .001$, $\eta^2 = .03$, appeared to be statistically significant. Post hoc tests according to Bonferroni revealed that Turkish/Kurdish children nominated fewer classmates as friends ($M = 2.71$, $SD = 2.47$) than did native ($M = 4.00$, $SD = 2.87$) and former Yugoslavian children ($M = 4.50$, $SD = 3.29$).

To get insights into children's interethnic friendship patterns, the total number of Austrian, former Yugoslavian, Turkish/Kurdish, and other friends were counted for each participant. A repeated measures MANOVA with the country of origin of the friends (Austria, former Yugoslavia, Turkey, other countries) as the within-subject factor and the own-group membership (native, former Yugoslavia, Turkish/ Kurdish, and rest group) as the between-subject factor was conducted. The number of friends was used as dependent variable. Multivariate tests using the Pillais Criterion showed a significant main effect on the within-factor country of origin of friends, $F(3,562) = 84.24$, $p < .001$, $\eta^2 = .31$, and a significant interaction effect, $F(9,1692) = 56.78$, $p < .001$, $\eta^2 = .23$. The between-factor group was also statistically significant, $F(3,564) = 17.08$, $p = .01$, $\eta^2 = .02$.

As shown in Figure 7.1, children had specific friendship patterns depending on their group membership. Whereas native and Turkish/Kurdish children showed a strong preference for friends from their own group, this was not the case for children of the former Yugoslavia and of the rest group.

DISCUSSION

The focus of this study lay on the investigation of both negative and positive aspects of interethnic interactions of children from various countries of origin in ethnically mixed school classes. In particular, we compared preva-

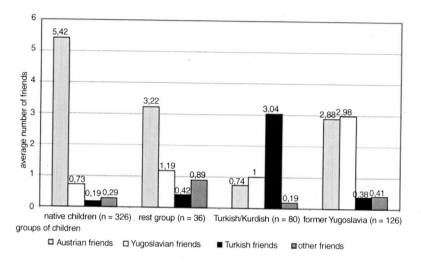

FIGURE 7.1. Interethnic friendship patterns.

lence rates of bullying (for both victims and perpetrators) in native and immigrant children, which were divided into three groups (former Yugoslavia, Turkish/Kurdish, heterogeneous rest group). We also investigated direct and indirect forms of bullying, peer acceptance, and friendship patterns in native borns and children of the three immigrant groups. Results provide support for the hypothesis that interethnic interactions of children vary systematically depending on their country of origin.

Prevalence Rates of Bullying

The design of this study differs in several aspects from previous studies on peer aggression in immigrant children (e.g., Fuchs, 1999; Klicpera & Gasteiger-Klicpera, 1996; Loesel et al., 1999; Popp, 2000). *First,* immigrant children were not uniformly labeled as one homogeneous group of "foreign children," but were distinguished into three immigrant groups. Contrary to the majority of previous studies, primary analyses were conducted to check for particularities regarding demographic and academic attributes between groups. Data suggest that children of various immigrant groups differ considerably from each other. Analyses revealed that children of the former Yugoslavia are more similar to natives than other immigrants. *Second,* bullying according to Olweus (1993) was examined not only via self-ratings but also via nomination techniques. Peer ratings are considered as reliable and valid data source and nomination techniques are frequently used (e.g., Schuster, 1999; Salmivalli et al., 1996; Perry, Kusel, & Perry, 1988). *Third,* to reliably identify victims and perpetrators of bullying and to control for varying class sizes, a rather strict criterion was used. A child was labeled as "bully" and/or "victim" if he/she was identified by more than 33 percent of his/her classmates.

In sum, 9 percent of the children were found to be bullies and 7 percent to be victims. Analyses revealed that native children were more often nominated as victims (9 percent) and perpetrators (12 percent) than all subgroups of immigrant children. This result indicates that bullying is rather more of a problem for the native than for the immigrant children. These findings support results of a study conducted in the United States. Hanish and Guerra (2000b) showed that children of the host society (European American and African American) were at higher risk for peer victimization than Hispanic immigrant children.

Measuring Indirect Bullying in Immigrant Children

In this study, indirect bullying was defined under the terms of social exclusion (Olweus, 1989) and measured via self-ratings. Analyses of the psychometric properties of the Victim Scale of Indirect Bullying showed insufficient reliability estimates for all subsamples of immigrant children. Additional analyses revealed that the items of the scale do not build a homogeneous construct in immigrant children. Thus, we recommend not to investigate indirect aggression in immigrant children with scales that compound questions about feelings of loneliness and problematic social relationships. It seems to be more fruitful to focus on assessing social risk factors in immigrant children as defined by Hodges, Malone, and Perry (1997), that is, lack of supportive friends and rejection by the peer group.

Social Risk Factors in Immigrant Children

To measure social risk factors in this study, we investigated social acceptance, number of friends, and cross-cultural friendship patterns (e.g., Hodges, Malone, & Perry, 1997). Only Turkish/Kurdish children were shown to be at risk concerning their social relationships. They were less accepted by their peers, felt most lonely at school, and had fewer friends in class than native children and children from other immigrant groups. In the literature, the main causes for peer rejection (and low acceptance) are seen either in a higher aggression level (e.g., Parker & Asher, 1987) or in a social skill deficit (e.g., Putallaz & Gottmann, 1981) of the rejected child. Findings of Rost and Czeschlik (1994) and Vedder and O'Dowd (1999) emphasized the importance of verbal comprehension for peer acceptance. Because of the fact that Turkish and Kurdish immigrant children were less likely to be nominated as bullies in this study, we suggest that lack of "cultural skills" (e.g., lack of language proficiency, different behavior because of different cultural norms) could be an important factor that may contribute to higher social risk in immigrant children. This hypothesis is supported by the observation that Yugoslavian children, who were shown to be more similar to Austrians than the other immigrant children, had no problems with respect to their social relationships. Moreover, they established cross-cultural friendships more frequently than both native children and children from the other immigrant groups.

To prove this hypothesis and to explain the observed differences in interethnic interactions, further research is needed. As we found remarkable differences in peer acceptance and friendship patterns in children depending on their country of origin, we recommend distinguishing immigrant children in even more than three groups. As a consequence, however, large samples have to be collected.

Findings of this study suggest that social risk factors are not equally distributed in the four groups of children. Whereas native Austrians are more likely to be engaged in direct forms of bullying, Turkish/Kurdish children seem to have a lack in cooperative forms of interactions. These findings have to be taken into account when applying interventions in multicultural school classes. In any case, training of social skills, sensitization for differences in behavior of children depending on their country of origin, as well as activities promoting a common identity are recommended.

As this study is limited because of its cross-sectional design, longitudinal studies are recommended to get insights into the development of interethnic interactions in multicultural school classes. In future research, demographic and academic characteristics of immigrant children (e.g., duration of stay, language proficiency) as well as structural variables of the social environment (e.g., the ratio of immigrant children in the classrooms), should be investigated systematically.

NOTES

1. In Austria, compulsory schooling starts with a child's sixth birthday and lasts nine school years. In the first four years the attendance of a primary school is obligatory. After the primary school children can attend either a general secondary school (fifth to eighth grade) or an academic secondary school (fifth to twelfth grade).

2. "Here are some questions about bullying. We say a student is being bullied when another student, or a group of students, say nasty and unpleasant things to him or her. It is also bullying when a student is hit, kicked, threatened, locked inside a room, and things like that. These things may take place frequently and it is difficult for the student being bullied to defend himself or herself. It is also bullying when a student is teased repeatedly in a negative way. But it is not bullying when two students of about the same strength quarrel or fight" (p. 2).

3. In Austria, school grades range from 1 (excellent) to 5 (failed). Mother-tongue instruction is an additional voluntary lesson for immigrant children to learn their first language.

REFERENCES

Berry, J. W. (1980). Acculturation as varieties of adaptation. In A. Padilla (Ed.), *Acculturation, theory, models and some new findings* (pp. 9-25). Boulder, CO: Westview Press.

Berscheid, E. (1985). Interpersonal attraction. In G. Lindzey & E. Aronson (Eds.), *Handbook of social psychology* (pp. 413-484). New York: Random House.

Bjoerqvist, K., Lagerspetz, K. M. J., & Kaukiainen, A. (1992). Do girls manipulate and boys fight? Developmental trends in regard to direct and indirect aggression. *Aggressive Behavior, 18,* 117-127.

Boulton, M. J., & Smith, P. K. (1994). Bully/victim problems in middle-school children: Stability, self-perceived competence, peer-perceptions and peer acceptance. *British Journal of Developmental Psychology, 12,* 315-329.

Boulton, M. J., & Smith, P. K. (1996). Liking and peer perceptions among Asian and white British children. *Journal of Social and Personal Relationships, 13,* 163-177.

Bourhis, R. Y., Moise, C. L., Perreault, S., & Senecal, S. (1997). Towards an interactive acculturation model: A social psychological approach. *International Journal of Psychology, 32*(6), 369-386.

Brown, B. B. (1990). Peer groups and peer cultures. In S. Feldman & G. Elliott (Eds.), *At the threshold* (pp. 171-196). Cambridge, MA: Harvard University Press.

Brown, R. (1995). *Prejudice. Its Social Psychology.* Oxford: Blackwell.

Coie, J. D., & Dodge, K. A. (1983). Continuities and changes in children's sociometric status: A five-year longitudinal study. *Merrill-Palmer Quarterly, 29,* 261-282.

Coie, J. D., Dodge, K. A., & Coppotelli, H. (1982). Dimensions and types of social status: A cross age perspective. *Developmental Psychology, 18*(4), 557-570.

Crick, N., & Grotpeter, J. K. (1995). Relational aggression, gender, and social-psychological adjustment. *Child Development, 66,* 710-722.

Fuchs, M. (1999). Ausländische Schüler und Gewalt an Schulen. Ergebnisse einer Schüler- und Lehrerbefragung. [Foreign pupils and violence at school: Results of a pupil and teacher survey.] In Holtappels, H. G., Heitmeyer W., Melzer, W., & Tillmann, K. (Hrsg.) *Forschung über Gewalt an Schulen. Erscheinungsformen, Ursachen, Konzepte und Prävention.* [Research about violence in schools: Manifestations, causes, concepts and prevention.] (S. 119-136). Weinheim, München: Juventa Verlag.

Gasteiger-Klicpera, B., & Klicpera, C. (1997). Aggressivität und soziale Stellung in der Klassengemeinschaft. [Aggressiveness and social status in the classroom.] *Zeitschrift für Kinder- und Jugendpsychiatrie, 25,* 139-150.

Graham, J. A., & Cohen, R. (1997). Race and gender as factors in children's sociometric ratings and friendship choices. *Social Development, 6*(3), 355-372.

Graham, J. A., Cohen, R., Zbikowski, S. M., & Secrist, M. E. (1998). A longitudinal investigation of race and gender as factors in children's classroom friendship choices. *Child Study Journal, 28*(4), 245-266.

Hanish, L. D., & Guerra, N. G. (2000a). Predictors of peer victimization among urban youth. *Social Development, 9*(4), 521-543.

Hanish, L. D., & Guerra, N. G. (2000b). The roles of ethnicity and school context in predicting children's victimization by peers. *American Journal of Community Psychology, 28*(2), 201-223.

Hodges, E., Malone, M., & Perry, D. (1997). Individual risk and social risk as interacting determinants of victimization in the peer group. *Developmental Psychology, 33*(6), 1032-1039.

Kerschbaumer, G. (2000). *Schüler/innen nichtdeutscher Muttersprache an den allgemein bildenden Pflichtschulen der steirischen Schulbezirke. Daten zum Stichtag 30.9.1999. Offizielle Statistik des Grazer Stadtschulamtes, Schulberatungsstelle für Ausländer.* [Pupils with non-German mother-tongues in public schools in Styria. Due date: September, 30, 1999. Official statistics of the School Council of Graz, Information Center for Foreigners.]

Klicpera, C., & Gasteiger-Klicpera, B. (1996). Die Situation von "Tätern" und "Opfern" aggressiver Handlungen in der Schule. [The situation of "perpetrators" and "victims" of aggressive acts at school.] *Praxis Kinderpsychologie und Kinderpsychiatrie, 45*(1), 2-9.

Kupersmidt, J. B., DeRosier, M. E., & Patterson, C. P. (1995). Similarity as the basis for children's friendships: The roles of sociometric status, aggressive and withdrawn behavior, academic achievement, and demographic characteristics. *Journal of Social and Personal Relationships, 12,* 439-452.

Lagerspetz, K. M. J., Bjoerqvist, J., & Peltonen, T. (1988). Is indirect aggression typical of females? Gender differences in aggressiveness in 11- to 12-year-old children. *Aggressive Behavior, 14,* 403-414.

Lagerspetz, K. M. J., & Bjoerqvist, K. (1994). Indirect aggression in boys and girls. In L. R. Huesmann (Ed.), *Aggressive behavior: Current perspectives* (pp. 131-150). New York: Plenum.

Laireiter, A., & Baumann, U. (1992). Network structures and support functions: Theoretical and empirical analyses. In H. O. F. Veiel, & U. Baumann (Eds.), *The meaning and measurement of social support* (pp. 33-55). Washington: Hemisphere.

Loesel, F., Bliesener T., & Averbeck, M. (1999). Hat die Delinquenz von Schülern zugenommen? Ein Vergleich im Dunkelfeld. [Has delinquency risen in pupils?] In M. Schäfer, & D. Frey, (Hrsg.) *Aggression und Gewalt unter Kindern und Jugendlichen.* [Aggression and violence in children and adolescents.] (S. 65-90) Göttingen, Bern, Toronto, Seattle: Hogrefe, Verlag für Psychologie.

Maccoby, E. E. (1988). Gender as a social category. *Developmental Psychology, 24,* 755-765.

Maccoby, E. E. (1990). Gender and relationships: A developmental account. *American Psychologist, 45,* 513-520.

Maharaj, S. I., & Connolly, J. A. (1994). Peer network composition of acculturated and ethnoculturally affiliated adolescents in a multicultural setting. *Journal of Adolescent Research, 9*(2), 218-240.

Olweus, D. (1989). *The Olweus Bully/Victim Questionnaire.* Mimeograph. Bergen, Norway.

Olweus, D. (1993). *Bullying at School: What We Know and What We Can Do.* Oxford: Blackwell.

Parker, J. G., & Asher, S. R. (1987). Peer relations and later personal adjustment. Are low-accepted children at risk? *Psychological Bulletin, 102*(3), 357-389.

Peery, J. C. (1979). Popular, amiable, isolated, rejected: A reconceptualization of sociometric status in preschool children. *Child Development, 50,* 1231-1234.

Perry, D. G., Kusel, S. J., & Perry, L. C. (1988). Victims of peer aggression. *Developmental Psychology, 24,* 807-814.

Popp, U. (2000). Gewalt an Schulen als "Türkenproblem?" Gewaltniveau, Wahrnehmung von Klassenklima und sozialer Diskriminierung bei deutschen und türkischen Schülerinnen und Schülern. [Violence in schools as a problem of the Turkish pupils? Acts of violence, perception of the social climate in learning groups and social discrimination by German and Turkish pupils.] *Empirische Pädagogik, 14*(1), 59-91.

Putallaz, M., & Gottman, J. M. (1981). Social skills and group acceptance. In S. R. Asher & J. M. Gottman (Eds.), *The development of children's friendships* (pp. 116-149). New York: Cambridge University Press.

Robier, C. (1997). *Aggressionsbekämpfung in Hauptschulen. Zum Einfluss von Angst und Gewalt im Fernsehen.* [Tackling aggression in general secondary schools: On the influence of anxiety and violence at TV.] Unpublished master thesis, University of Graz, Austria.

Rost, D. H., & Czeschlik, T. (1994). Beliebt und intelligent? Abgelehnt und dumm? Eine soziometrische Studie an 6,500 Grundschulkindern [Popular and intelligent? Rejected and dumb? A sociometric study with 6,500 primary school pupils]. *Zeitschrift für Sozialpsychologie, 25,* S. 170-176.

Rys, G. S., & Bear, G. G. (1997). Relational aggression and peer relations: Gender and developmental issues. *Merrill-Palmer Quarterly, 43*(1), 87-106.

Salmivalli, C., Huttunen, A., & Lagerspetz, K. M. J. (1997). Peer networks and bullying in schools. *Scandinavian Journal of Psychology, 38,* 305-312.

Salmivalli, C., Lagerspetz, K., Bjoerkqvist, K., & Oestermann, K., (1996). Bullying as a group process: Participant roles and their relations to social status within the group. *Aggressive Behavior, 22*(1), 1-15.

Schuster, B. (1999). Outsiders at school: The prevalence of bullying and its relation with social status. *Group Processes and Intergroup Relations, 2*(2), 175-190.

Singer, M. (1998). *Anwendung des Anti-Aggressionsprogramms nach Dan Olweus an sterreichischen Schulen. Zusammenhänge zäwischen Aggression, Klassen- und Familienklima.* [Implementation of the anti-bullying program according to Dan Olweus at Austrian schools. Correlations between aggression, class-and family climate.] Unpublished master thesis, University of Graz, Austria.

Spiel, C. (2000). Gewalt in der Schule: Täter, Opfer, Prävention-Intervention. [Violence at school: Bullies, victims, prevention-intervention.] In E. Tatzer, S. Pflanzer, & K. Krisch, (Eds.), *Schlimm verletzt. Schwierige Kinder und Jugendliche in Theorie und Praxis* [Badly injured. Difficult children and adolescents in theory and praxis.] (pp. 41-53). Wien: Krammer.

Spiel, C., & Atria, M. (2001). *Tackling Violence in Schools: A Report from Austria.* Retrieved March, 30, 2002, from http://www.goldsmiths.ac.uk/connect/reportaustria.html.

Strohmeier, D., & Spiel, C. (2000, November). *Gewalterfahrungen von Kindern unterschiedlicher Muttersprachen–Eine Studie an Grazer Hauptschulen.* [Violence experiences of children with various mother-tongues–Preliminary results of a study conducted in general secondary schools in Graz.] Paper presented at the 5th workshop on "aggression" in Hannover, Germany.

Strohmeier, D., & Spiel, C. (2001, November). *Aussenseiter in der Schule. Bullying als Gruppenphänomen.* [Outsiders at school. Bullying as a group phenomenon.] Paper presented at the 6th workshop on "aggression" in Jena, Germany.

Sutton, J., & Smith, P. K. (1999). Bullying as a group process: An adaptation of the participant role approach. *Aggressive Behavior, 25*(2), 97-111.

Vedder, P., & O'Dowd (1999). Swedish primary school pupils' inter-ethnic relationships. *Scandinavian Journal of Psychology, 40,* 221-228.

Chapter 8

Peer Victimization in Middle School: When Self- and Peer Views Diverge

Sandra Graham
Amy Bellmore
Jaana Juvonen

A common theme underlying the articles on peer victimization in this volume is the vulnerability of those children and adolescents who are chronically picked on by others. Even more than their perpetrators, the targets of peer hostility face numerous mental health challenges and they are particularly at risk for social and emotional adjustment problems (see Nansel et al., 2001 for a recent review). Unfortunately, many cases of peer harassment go undetected because students are unwilling to talk about getting picked on at school. As a result, school professionals sometimes find themselves dealing with the symptoms of chronic harassment (e.g., feelings of anxiety and depression) before they learn about their cause. An important task for psychologists and other adults in the school setting is, therefore, to accurately identify those students whose adjustment difficulties are due to victimization by peers.

How do school personnel know which students are victims of peer harassment? Experience might suggest a simple answer to that question. Just ask the students. Survey their peers. Or simply observe for yourself. Yet accurate identification of children who are victims of peer harassment is more complex than simply asking, surveying, or observing. That is because each

This chapter was adapted from "Peer Victimization in Middle School: When Self- and Peer Views Diverge" by Sandra Graham, Amy Bellmore, and Jaana Juvonen, *Journal of Applied School Psychology, 19*(2), pp. 117-137.

Bullying, Victimization, and Peer Harassment
Published by The Haworth Press, Inc., 2007. All rights reserved.
doi:10.1300/5808_08

informant source produces a particular kind of data that has its own limitations. Self-reports of victimization are subjective experiences that are privately felt and are not necessarily verifiable by other informants. One particularly painful experience may have far-reaching effects on self-perceived victim status, just as multiple experiences with harassment may be discounted as a strategy to protect one's self-esteem. In other words, subjective disclosures of feeling like a victim are prone to all of the biases (e.g., underestimating, overestimating) that are associated with self-report data. Peer data produce reputational measures of victimization; they reflect agreement or consensus among peers about the relative standing of individuals compared to other members of the group. Because social reputations, once entrenched, are highly resistant to change, using peers as informants is subject to any of the biases or judgment errors that are associated with making inferences about others (Hymel, Wagner, & Butler, 1990). Observational data may be the least reliable source of information because much of peer harassment is covert. At least by middle school, the most common forms of harassment typically occur in "unowned" (and unseen) school spaces, such as bathrooms, hallways, and locker rooms where adult supervision is minimal (Astor, Meyer, & Behre, 1999).

In light of these reliability concerns, it is surprising that the issue of informant source has not received much attention in the peer harassment literature (but see Pelligrini, 2001 for a notable exception). Most studies have used either self-reports (e.g., "Are *you* someone who gets picked on by others?") or peer nominations (e.g., "Which kids in your class get picked on by others?"). Typically self-reports yield higher estimates of peer harassment than do peer reports (Schuster, 1996). Studies that use only one method may, therefore, be under- or over-identifying students who are truly victimized (Juvonen, Nishina, & Graham, 2001). Or they may overlook important differences between victimized youth for whom self- and peer views diverge. For example, might there be different concerns for victims who view themselves as harassed but have no such reputation among peers, compared to those who carry a reputation that they themselves do not endorse?

We documented some of these differences in a recent study that examined self-report and peer nomination victim data in a sample of middle school students (Graham & Juvonen, 1998). We identified four victim groups that took into account self- and peer views. Two groups enjoyed complete agreement between self and peers: those were nonvictims (low victim scores from both informants) and "true" victims (high scores from both). A third group was high on self-perceived victimization, but did not have that reputation based on peer reports. We labeled that group self-identified victims.

A fourth group, labeled peer-identified victims, did not perceive themselves as victims but had that reputation among their peers.

When comparing the victim groups across psychological and social adjustment indices, we found that particular patterns of adjustment were systematically related to different types of victims. Self-identified victims reported as much loneliness, anxiety, and low self-esteem as did true victims, but they were not more rejected by peers than nonvictims. Peer-identified victims, on the other hand, were just as rejected as true victims, but their self-views were no more negative than those of nonvictims. These findings suggested that self-views about victimization might be more predictive of psychological maladjustment, whereas peer views might be more predictive of social maladjustment. This distinction is important because most victimization studies describe a cluster of adjustment difficulties—including loneliness, anxiety, *and* peer rejection—without considering whether particular problems are more linked to particular types of identification methods.

In the research reported here, we further explored differences between victim subgroups based on self- and peer reports with a larger middle school sample and an expanded set of adjustment outcomes, including depression and physical symptoms. We also gathered data on teacher ratings of student academic and social behavior to determine whether the appraisals of third-party informants conform more closely to self-views or peer views. In addition, data on academic performance of students were collected from school records. A number of studies have reported a relationship between peer victimization and school problems (e.g., Juvonen, Nishina, & Graham, 2000; Kochenderfer & Ladd, 1996). However, it is unclear whether the peer harassment–low achievement linkage is the same or different for students who subjectively experience victimization versus those who only have that reputation among their peers. Examining different types of victims and their unique adjustment difficulties can provide useful information for professional staff as well as researchers working in school settings. That information relates to both identification (i.e., How do adults in the school know when someone is a victim of harassment?) and intervention (i.e., Should school personnel be tailoring specific types of intervention strategies to specific victim types?).

METHOD

Participants

Participants were 785 sixth-grade students (348 boys and 437 girls, Mean age = 11.5 years) recruited from eight middle schools in metropolitan

Los Angeles. The sample for this study was selected from a larger cohort of sixth graders ($n = 1,223$; 45 percent Latino, 39 percent African-American, 6 percent Caucasian, 5 percent Asian, 5 percent from other ethnic groups) who were taking part in a longitudinal investigation of peer relations during the middle school years. To examine the possibility of ethnic group differences in victim subtypes, we included participants from only the two largest ethnic groups; that is, Latinos ($n = 435$; 205 boys, 230 girls) and African Americans ($n = 350$; 143 boys, 207 girls). In terms of immigrant history, 90 percent of the Latino youth were at least second generation (U.S.-born children of immigrants) and all were sufficiently proficient in English to complete the surveys. The eight participating middle schools were randomly selected from those of comparable size in demographically similar communities of metropolitan Los Angeles. In terms of school-level indicators, student eligibility for free or reduced-price lunch programs ranged from 47 to 87 percent and all schools qualified for Title I compensatory education funds. Thus, by available indicators, the African-American and Latino students who participated in this study were primarily of low socioeconomic status (SES).

All of the data collected on this sample were gathered as part of a written questionnaire administered in classroom settings (see Procedure section). The measures are well-validated instruments that are used widely in school-based research on peer relations and in our own previous research with ethnic minority samples (e.g., Graham & Juvonen, 1998, 2002). For some instruments, subscales were used that most closely captured the constructs of interest.

Self-Report Measures

Self-Perceived Victimization

Four items from the Peer Victimization Scale (PVS; Neary & Joseph, 1994) and two new items written for this study were used to create a six-item measure of subjective feelings of victimization. Rather than directly asking students how frequently they get harassed by their peers, we utilized a response format that is designed to reduce social desirability effects (Harter, 1985). For each item, students were presented with two statements separated by the word *But*, with each statement reflecting high or low self-perceived victimization. An example item was as follows: "Some kids are *often* picked on by other kids BUT other kids are *not* picked on by other kids." Students chose one of the two alternatives and then indicated whether the selected alternative is *really true for me* or *sort of true for me*. That creates a 4-point scale for each item. The three other items from the PVS assessed being laughed at, pushed around, and called names. The new items measured whether participants felt that they were gossiped about by others (a form of indirect or relational victimization), and whether their possessions were damaged or stolen by others (direct victimization targeted toward property rather than person). Ratings for the six items were averaged to create a single measure of self-perceived victimization. The scale had good internal consistency ($\alpha = .79$).

Self-Esteem

Embedded in the self-perceived victimization measure was the six-item global self-worth subscale of the Harter Self-Perception Profile for Children (Harter, 1985). For each item, students chose between two statements separated by the word *But*, with each statement reflecting high or low self-worth. An example item was as follows: "Some kids are happy with themselves as a person BUT other kids are often *not* happy with themselves." By rating whether the chosen statement is *really true for me* or *sort of true for me*, a 4-point scale is created. Ratings for the six items were averaged ($\alpha = .77$ for this sample).

Social Anxiety

Two subscales from the Social Anxiety Scale for Adolescents (SAS-A, La Greca & Lopez, 1998) were used to measure fear of negative evaluation (e.g., "I worry about what others think of me") and social avoidance (e.g., "I'm afraid to invite others to do things with me because they might say no"). Each item is rated on a 5-point scale (1 = *not at all* and 5 = *all the time*). Combining the subscales yielded a twelve-item measure with good internal consistency ($\alpha = .82$).

Loneliness

A sixteen-item scale developed by Asher and Wheeler (1985) was used to measure loneliness. Students responded on 5-point scales (1 = *not true at all* through 5 = *always true*) to questions such as "I feel alone" and "I have nobody to talk to." Scores on the sixteen items were summed and averaged ($\alpha = .84$).

Depression

Ten items that make up the Short Form of the Children's Depression Inventory (CDI; Kovacs, 1985) were used to assess depressed affect. For each item, respondents were presented with three sentences that describe "how kids might feel" and they chose the sentence that best described how they had been feeling during the past two weeks. A sample item was as follows: "I do most things right"; "I do many things wrong"; "I do everything wrong." Item scores ranged from 0 to 2. Those ratings were summed and averaged ($\alpha = .79$).

Physical Symptoms

Students rated how much in the last two weeks they had been bothered by twelve somatic complaints that include headache, upset stomach, poor appetite, and trouble sleeping (1 = *not at all* and 4 = *almost every day*). The twelve items used here were selected from symptom clusters included in other well-established inventories for children and adolescents such as the Children's Somatization Inventory (CSI; Garber, Walker, & Zeman, 1991). Ratings on the twelve items were summed and averaged ($\alpha = .80$).

Peer-Reported Measures

Victim Reputation

We used peer-nomination procedures to determine which students had reputations as victims. Using a roster that contained the names of all the students in their homeroom, participants were instructed to name up to four students of either gender who fit each of three behavioral descriptions. By restricting the nominations to each homeroom (rather than the larger team or cluster that consisted of up to 120 students), the rosters were more manageable for youth. Two of the behavioral descriptions portrayed physical and verbal harassment *(gets pushed around, gets put down, or made fun of by others)*. A third description depicted indirect or relational victimization *(other kids spread nasty rumors about them)*. The number of nominations each participant received was summed and these scores were standardized within classroom to control for differences in class size.

Social Adjustment

Embedded in the peer-nomination measure were questions used to measure social adjustment. Respondents nominated up to four classmates whom they *liked to hang out with* and four whom they *did not like to hang out with*. Those nominations measured peer acceptance and rejection, respectively. Finally, participants nominated up to four classmates *who are the coolest kids*. Perceived coolness was judged to capture both popularity and possession of characteristics that are admired among early adolescents. Thus, being perceived as cool is not synonymous with acceptance, and in some cases the two measures could elicit disparate nomination patterns (e.g., adolescents might not want to hang out with classmates whom they perceive as most cool). Nomination totals were also summed for each student and standardized within classroom.

Teacher-Report Measure of Social Adjustment

Homeroom teachers rated the social behavior of participating students using eleven of the original eighteen items on the Interpersonal Competence Scale (ICT-T; Cairns, Leung, Gest, & Cairns, 1995). Those items yielded subscales on *internalizing* (three items, i.e., sad, worries, cries a lot, $\alpha = .59$); *externalizing* (three items, i.e., starts fights, argues, gets in trouble, $\alpha = .89$) and *popularity* (three items, i.e., popular with boys (girls), lots of friends, $\alpha = .85$). Each item was presented as a 7-point bipolar scale with anchors unique to that item (e.g., *never sad–always sad, never starts fights–always starts fights, lots of friends–no friends*).

Academic Performance

There were two measures of academic performance: homeroom teacher ratings of school engagement and grade point average (GPA). The degree to which students were perceived to be engaged versus disaffected from school activities was measured with six items from the eighteen-item Teacher Report of Engagement Questionnaire (TREQ; Wellborn & Connell, 1991). An example item was as follows: "In my class this student concentrates on doing his/her work." Ratings were elicited on 4-point scales (1 = *not at all characteristic of this student* and 4 = *very characteristic*). Item scores were summed and averaged ($\alpha = .86$). Data on semester GPA were collected from school records. Grades in academic classes were assigned scores of 0 to 4, with As, Bs, Cs, Ds, and Fs worth 4, 3, 2, 1, and 0 points, respectively. Students' scores were averaged across academic classes to create a single 5-point index of GPA.

Procedure

We recruited sixth grade students from fifty-four homerooms distributed across eight middle schools. Excluded in each school were self-contained special education classrooms and programs for gifted students. Initially, eligible homeroom teachers were informed about the study. In those classrooms where teachers expressed interest in the study, students took home letters and consent forms in both English and Spanish that explained the study. Only students who returned a signed consent form granting permission were allowed to participate. To increase return rate, students were informed that a raffle would be conducted on the day of data collection for everyone who returned their signed consent forms, with or without parental permission to participate (there was a place on the form to decline participation). In each classroom, two prizes with UCLA logos (e.g., tee-shirts, caps) were raffled at the end of data collection. We achieved an average return rate of 78 percent (range = 66 percent to 90 percent across the eight schools). Of those students who returned a signed consent form, 90 percent of their parents granted permission for them to participate.

Data were gathered in the fall of the academic year, once school had been in session for at least two months. Because all of the participating schools organized their sixth graders in teams or clusters, students spent several periods a day with the same classmates and a small number of teachers. Thus by the time of data collection, students knew one another well enough to complete the peer-nomination procedures and homeroom teachers knew students well enough to complete the ratings of social behavior and academic engagement.

Questionnaires containing all of the student measures were assembled in booklet form (titled *Middle School Survey*). Before beginning the survey, participants signed a Student Assent form that described our goal to better understand how middle school students feel about school. They were assured in writing that all responses would be kept confidential and they were encouraged to create "private spaces" at their desks, using their books as well as folders provided by the research team. Graduate student researchers working in pairs administered the questionnaires during an extended block period, since the survey usually required about one hour to complete. All instructions and questionnaire items were read aloud by one researcher as students followed along and responded on their own questionnaires. The other researcher circulated around the classroom, helping individual students as needed.

RESULTS

Creation of Victim Subgroups

The first step in the analysis was to create victim groups based on respondents' standardized self-perceived victim scores and peer-nominated victim scores. We followed the procedures used in Graham and Juvonen (1998) to create four groups. Students who were at or above the 70th percentile on both self-ratings and peer nominations were labeled as *true victims* (n = 81, 10 percent of the sample). *Nonvictims* (n = 431, 55 percent of the sample) were participants whose self- and peer scores fell below the 50th percentile. Students whose self-ratings were at or above the 70th percentile, but whose peer nominations were below the 50th percentile cutoff were classified as *self-identified victims* ($n = 192$, 25 percent of the sample). Lastly, students who had a reputation for being victims (peer nominations at or above the 70th percentile) but who did not perceive themselves as such (self-ratings below the 50th percentile) were labeled as *peer-identified victims* ($n = 81$, 10 percent of the sample). Note that more than twice as many participants were classified in the self-identified than in the peer-identified victim group (192 versus 81). Many youth report experiencing peer harassment in one form or another, whereas fewer individuals have public reputations that are widely endorsed.

Next we examined the victim subgroups by gender and ethnicity of participants. The association between victim status and gender was significant: $\chi^2 (3) = 42.28$, $p < .001$. More than twice as many boys as girls were classified as true victims (57 boys versus 24 girls), whereas the majority of nonvictims were girls (263 girls versus 168 boys). The gender pattern becomes more complex when we consider the groups where peer perceptions and self-perceptions diverged. More boys than girls were classified as peer-identified victims (51 boys versus 31 girls), but more girls than boys embodied the self-identified subgroup (120 girls versus 73 boys). The gender difference was significant in all four victim groups: true victims (z dif = 6.65), self-identified (z dif = 2.80), peer-identified victims (z dif = 4.75), and nonvictims (z dif = 3.07) (all $ps < .05$).

There also was a relationship between victim status and ethnicity, although it was not as strong as that for gender: $\chi^2 (3) = 14.23$, $p < .01$. Within group comparisons revealed that the only significant association involved peer-identified victims. Significantly more African Americans ($n = 52$) than Latinos ($n = 29$) had reputations as victims (64 percent versus 36 percent, z dif = 5.00, $p < .01$).

In the next set of analyses, we turned to the psychological and social consequences of victim status as defined by self-views and peer appraisals. The psychological adjustment variables (self-esteem, loneliness, anxiety, depression, and physical symptoms), social status variables (peer-nominated acceptance, rejection, and coolness), and teacher-rated adjustment variables (internalizing symptoms, externalizing, and popularity) were analyzed in a series of $4 \times 2 \times 2$ (victim group by gender by ethnicity) MANOVAs. Before the analyses, all of the variables were converted into standard scores with a mean of 0 and a standard deviation of 1 to facilitate the interpretation of group differences in measures from multiple informants and with different response scales. Hence, differences among the groups indicate their relative standing within the sample.

Because participants were recruited from eight different schools that varied in ethnic composition, preliminary analyses were conducted on all of the dependent variables with school type (majority Latino, majority African American, mixed ethnicity) as an independent factor. There were no significant main effects on interactions involving school type. The data were, therefore, combined across this variable for all analyses reported here.

Self-Reported Psychological Adjustment

For the five self-report adjustment variables, the multivariate main effect of group was significant, indicating that adjustment varied systematically by victim group status: $F(15, 1946) = 14.55, p < .001$. The top panel of Table 8.1

TABLE 8.1. Mean differences on the adjustment and achievement variables by victim group.

Variable	Victim group				$F(3, 777)$
	True victims	Self-Ident.	Peer-Ident.	Nonvictims	
Self					
Self-esteem	$-.63_a$	$-.40_a$	$.27_b$	$.34_b$	44.92**
Anxiety	$.64_a$	$.35_a$	$-.19_b$	$-.31_b$	39.14**
Loneliness	$.85_a$	$.20_b$	$.03_b$	$-.34_c$	47.83**
Depression	$.84_a$	$.18_b$	$-.28_c$	$-.29_c$	42.36**
Symptoms	$.38_a$	$.37_a$	$-.15_b$	$-.20_b$	19.22**
Peer					
Acceptance	$-.43_a$	$.07_b$	$-.30_a$	$.22_b$	15.12**
Rejection	$.97_a$	$-.28_b$	$.67_c$	$-.29_b$	76.24**
Coolness	$-.52_a$	$-.03_b$	$-.09_b$	$.19_b$	13.35**
Teacher					
Internalizing	$-.04_a$	$.09_a$	$.06_a$	$-.04_a$	<1
Popularity	$-.58_a$	$.06_b$	$-.30_a$	$.15_b$	16.46**
Externalizing	$.68_a$	$-.11_b$	$.74_a$	$-.26_b$	49.62**
Achievement					
Engagement	$-.67_a$	$.05_b$	$-.47_a$	$.26_b$	32.67**
GPA	$-.50_a$	$.09_b$	$-.48_a$	$.16_b$	16.29**

Note. Numbers in the table are standard scores. Row means with different subscripts are significantly different at $p < .05$. ** $p < .001$ for the univariate F-tests.

shows the means across the four victim groups for each psychological variable, as well as the univariate *F*-test for that variable. Turning first to the "pure" victim groups in the first and fourth columns, it is evident that true victims reported more psychological maladjustment than did nonvictims. Victims had lower self-esteem than nonvictims and they were more anxious, lonely, depressed, and bothered by physical symptoms. As standard scores ($M = 0$, $SD = 1$), the means in Table 8.1 also can be interpreted in terms of percentiles for this sample (i.e., these scores should not be viewed as clinical cut-offs). Values of 0 are at the 50th percentile; positive scores are above and negative scores are below the 50th percentile. Any score that approaches 1 is at about the 85 percent percentile and a score that approaches −1 hovers around the 15th percentile. Consider, for example, the loneliness scores of true victims compared to nonvictims. With $M = .85$, true victims lie at the 80th percentile; only about 20 percent of respondents in this sample would report more loneliness than would true victims. In contrast, with $M = -.34$, nonvictims are at about the 40th percentile; 60 percent of respondents are predicted to report more loneliness than nonvictims.

The pattern of (mal)adjustment for true victims compared to nonvictims is what we would expect based on previous research. But what about the two groups for whom self- and peer views diverged? For all variables, self-identified and peer-identified victims fell between the two "pure" groups in a systematic way that largely replicated our earlier findings (Graham & Juvonen, 1998). Self-identified victims were more similar to true victims, whereas peer-identified victims consistently resembled nonvictims. For example, students who perceived themselves as victims even when they have no such reputation among peers were just as low in self-esteem and just as anxious and symptomatic as true victims. On the other hand, those students who had reputations as victims were no more depressed, anxious, symptomatic, or low in self-esteem than their nonvictimized counterparts. In sum, the two groups who perceived themselves as victims (true victims and self-identified victims) reported similar levels of maladjustment, whereas the two groups who did not view themselves as victims (peer-identified victims and nonvictims) showed relatively better adjustment.

The pattern displayed in the top panel of Table 8.1 was not influenced by the gender or ethnicity of participants in the different victim groups (i.e., there were no interactions involving gender or ethnicity). However, there was a multivariate main effect of ethnicity, $F(5, 705) = 5.19$, $p < .001$. Independent of victim status and for each variable, Latinos reported more adjustment difficulties than their African-American counterparts.

Peer-Reported Social Adjustment

We turn next to social adjustment (acceptance, rejection, coolness) as defined by peer perceptions. Correlational analyses revealed that peer rejection was negatively related to both acceptance ($r = -.23$) and coolness ($r = -.11$). Although acceptance and coolness were positively correlated ($r = .56$), there was still sufficient nonoverlap in the meaning of these constructs to examine them separately.

The $4 \times 2 \times 2$ (victim group by gender by ethnicity) MANOVA on the three social adjustment variables documented a significant multivariate effect of victim group, $F(9, 1847) = 20.24, p < .001$. Those group effects are displayed in the second panel of Table 8.1. True victims were less accepted and more rejected than their nonvictimized counterparts. For these variables, however, it was peer-identified rather than self-identified victims who were more similar to true victims. Peer-identified victims were just as disliked as true victims, whereas self-identified victims were just as well liked as nonvictims. Thus, the two groups who had reputations as victims (true victims and peer-identified) had similar levels of social maladjustment, whereas the two groups who did not have such reputations (self-identified victims and nonvictims) showed relatively better social adjustment. For perceived coolness, the group effect was due to the fact that true victims were viewed as less cool than were the other three groups who did not differ significantly from one another.

There were more gender and ethnicity effects in these analyses, which highlights some of the determinants of social status among middle school students. Girls were more accepted than boys and they were less rejected: multivariate $F(3, 759) = 4.02, p < .01$. African-American students were more disliked than Latinos, but they were also perceived as more cool: multivariate $F(3, 759) = 5.68, p < .001$. Thus students tended to dislike some classmates whom they viewed as most cool. A three-way interaction for coolness indicated that African-American boys who peers considered to be victims were judged to be especially cool: $F(3, 761) = 2.84, p < .05$.

Teacher-Perceived Social Adjustment

Teachers provide an independent informant source because their perceptions did not enter into the creation of victim groups. For teacher perceptions, there was a multivariate main effect of victim group, $F(9, 1789) = 13.38, p < .001$ (see third panel of Table 8.1). Univariate ANOVAs revealed no effects of victim group for teacher-perceived internalizing symptoms. Teachers perceived nonvictims and self-identified victims to be more popular than true and peer-identified victims, but the opposite was true for the more negative externalizing (aggressive) behavior. In many ways, therefore, the teacher judgments were consistent with those of peers. Peer-identified victims were judged as poorly on these social outcomes as true victims, while self-identified victims fared as well as nonvictims.

There were also gender and ethnicity main effects for teacher judgments. The multivariate gender effect revealed that girls were viewed as more popular and less aggressive than boys: $F(3, 735) = 7.01$, $p < .001$. The multivariate ethnicity effect showed that African Americans were judged as more popular than Latinos, but also as more aggressive: $F(3, 735) = 11.98$, $p < .001$. The multivariate group × gender × ethnicity interaction was explained by the fact that the most aggressive students in the teacher's eyes were African-American boys who were identified by their peers as victims: $F(9, 1789) = 2.05$, $p < .05$.

Academic Achievement

To examine school outcomes, we analyzed teacher ratings of academic engagement and students' semester GPA in separate 4 × 2 × 2 ANOVAs (bottom panel of Table 8.1). For academic engagement there were main effects of victim group, $F(3, 733) = 32.67$, gender, $F(1, 733) = 9.57$; and ethnicity, $F(1, 733) = 32.13$ (all $ps < .01$). Consistent with the psychological and social variables, true victims were rated as less engaged than nonvictims. However, peer-identified victims resembled true victims in being relatively disengaged, whereas self-identified victims were akin to nonvictims in being perceived as relatively engaged. Furthermore, girls were rated more positively than boys and Latinos were judged more positively than African Americans. There was an identical pattern to the data for actual grades: $Fs = 16.29$, 15.84, and 29.49 for the victim group, gender, and ethnicity main effects (all $ps < .001$). The academic advantage that nonvictims enjoyed was shared by self-identified victims, while the relatively poor achievement of true victims also was characteristic of peer-identified victims. The gender and ethnicity main effects indicated that girls had better grades than boys and Latinos did significantly better than African Americans. None of the interactions were significant for either achievement variable.

Relations Between Variables: Predicting GPA

We know from the group analyses that being the victim of peer harassment was related to academic GPA. But what role might the psychological and social adjustment play in this relation? We hypothesized that the effect of self- and peer-perceived victimization on academic achievement would be largely explained by the adjustment outcomes. Thus, for example, perceiving oneself as a victim undermines school performance because of the psychological costs (e.g., depression, anxiety) that often accompany these self-views. Psychological maladjustment, in other words, was thought to be the more proximal determinant of poor grades. Similarly, having a reputation as a victim predicts low achievement because such children suffer the added burden of being rejected by their peers.

Path analysis was used to examine the hypothesized predictors of GPA. In path analysis the researcher can specify a set of relationships between variables and then test whether the specified model adequately fits the data. One index of model fit is the χ^2 statistic. A nonsignificant χ^2 (i.e., no difference between the tested model and the actual data) indicates a good fit.

The best fitting model of the relations between variables is shown in Figure 8.1: $\chi^2 (4) = 4.81$, *ns*. Note first that self- and peer-perceived victimization are only modestly correlated ($r = .19$), which means that there was little overlap between self-views and peer views, as we have emphasized in this chapter. Once these perceptions are activated, the model proposes two relatively independent sequences, with the upper pathway depicting the psychological processes affecting school achievement and the lower sequence portraying social mechanisms. The psychological adjustment variables were averaged to create a single index (average $r = .42$) and peer rejection was used as the social adjustment variable. In the first sequence, self-perceived victimization predicted psychological maladjustment ($\beta = .50$) and maladjustment, in turn, predicted low achievement ($\beta = -.18$). In the second sequence, victim reputation resulted in peer rejection ($\beta = .56$) and rejection was then related to diminished performance ($\beta = -.27$). Having a reputation as a victim was also moderately related to maladjustment ($\beta = .13$), which suggests that students are aware of how they are perceived in the eyes of others and that awareness influenced their own self-views.

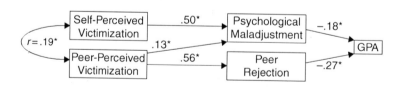

FIGURE 8.1. Path analysis of relations between victimization, adjustment, and academic achievement.

DISCUSSION

Being a victim of peer harassment places students at risk for many kinds of adjustment difficulties. Some of those adjustment challenges relate to self-appraisals, whereas others can be linked to the social context and one's reputation among teachers and peers. Still other consequences involve academic outcomes such as perceived engagement and grades. The findings presented here suggest that particular types of victims are vulnerable to specific kinds of maladjustment. Both self-reports of harassment experiences and peer reports of victim status are necessary to capture the full range of victim subgroups and the unique challenges of each.

"True" Victims: When Self- and Peer Views Converge

The best evidence for the negative consequences of peer harassment was seen in the group who felt like victims and had that reputation among peers. For every adjustment variable examined in this research, there were reliable differences between true victims and nonvictims, with the difference always favoring nonvictims. These findings replicate prior studies and underscore the fact that peer victimization cuts across race, SES, and different school contexts.

Self-Identified and Peer-Identified Victims: When Self- and Peer Views Diverge

For purposes of identification, the most challenging findings emerged for the victimized students for whom self- and peer perceptions were discrepant. On the self-report indexes (depression, anxiety, etc.) self-identified victims were consistently more similar to true victims, whereas peer-identified victims responded more like nonvictims. But on the peer-focused indexes (acceptance and rejection) peer-identified victims were just as rejected as true victims, whereas self-identified victims were as accepted as nonvictims. Had we relied only on self-reports we might wrongly have concluded that victimization is not associated with peer rejection. Had we relied only on peer reports, we might have been similarly misguided in concluding that victimization is not related to negative feelings about the self. In the path analysis, *both* maladjustment and peer rejection were risk factors for academic problems.

Because the two victim groups are linked to different risk factors, one might wonder whether there is any reason to think that one group is more vulnerable than the other. Concerning self-identified victims, a large body of clinical research has documented the short- and long-term effects of adolescent depression, anxiety, and low self-worth (Steinberg & Morris, 2001). That research reports greater mental health challenges for adolescent girls, which is consistent with our finding that the majority of self-identified victims were girls. Thus there is reason to be concerned about self-identified victims if they react to their plight by turning inward. In previous research, we found that self-identified victims, like true victims, were more likely to blame themselves for being picked on by others (Graham & Juvonen, 1998). They were more willing to endorse such statements as "It must be *me*" or "Why do *I* always get into these situations?" Self-blame then accounted for most of their negative feelings about themselves. Equally of concern is that disparaging self-views and depressed affect may go unnoticed by teachers. Recall that teachers in this study did not differentiate among victim groups (including nonvictims) when they rated the degree to which students were sad, worried, or tearful—the set of variables that we labeled as internalizing symptoms (see Table 8.1).

On the other hand, self-identified victims enjoyed widespread acceptance among their peers and their teachers perceived them to be popular and socially competent. As a group, they also were doing reasonably well in school. For some self-identified victims, it could be that the peer support and teacher approval were protective factors that lessened the impact of victim status.

Peer-identified victims, who were primarily boys and primarily African American, had quite a different risk profile. They did not view themselves as victims and they did not report disparaging self-views. Perhaps the incidents that peers perceive as harassment were not subjectively experienced in that way by these youth who may also be reluctant to report that they are victimized—an admission that implies that they are unable to defend themselves. Several studies have suggested that African-American adolescent boys sometimes exhibit exaggerated behavioral and emotional toughness, called male *bravado*, as a way of coping with negative experiences (e.g., Cunningham, 1999). Such coping styles may contribute to peer perceptions of this particular victim group as "cool" and an attraction to these boys who enjoy a particular kind of notoriety. Yet these peer-identified victims were also disliked by some of their classmates. The reputations of peer-identified victims were quite public in that teachers shared the negative views of peers. These students also were doing as poorly in school as true victims. Therefore, the benefits of positive self-views and some notoriety among peers did not offset the risks associated with victim reputation.

Limitations of the Current Study

Our sample of young Latino and African-American adolescents is a unique one and thus we do not know how well the findings regarding the two divergent victim groups will replicate across other samples. Our findings may have been influenced not only by the demographics of the participants (ethnicity, SES, community characteristics) but also the particular school contexts in which they reside. We did not uncover any school effects based on one contextual variable—the ethnic composition of schools—but other classroom and school effects warrant attention in future research. New statistical methods, such as hierarchical linear modeling (HLM), provide appropriate tools to examine such questions. Finally, we acknowledge that our cross-sectional data do not permit us to make causal inferences about the consequences of victimization. Yet the findings do provide a framework for testing the directionality of effects with longitudinal data from the larger project.

Implications for Assessment and Intervention

We believe that enriching the study of peer harassment to distinguish victims for whom self- and peer perceptions diverge has important implications for both assessment and intervention. If identification procedures rely primarily on reports of others, such as reputation among peers or teacher impressions, then we would have missed 192 students in our sample (self-identified victims) who felt vulnerable and victimized but did not have that reputation among their peers. Because youth in general are reluctant to seek help for peer harassment, and because these self-identified youth enjoyed a level of peer acceptance similar to nonvictims, it is unlikely that their adjustment problems would have been detected in the absence of self-report data.

What intervention strategies would be most helpful to self-identified victims given their particular vulnerabilities? One area of vulnerability might be their tendency to think that their own plight is unique (i.e., "I am the only one who gets picked on"). Preliminary evidence to support that assertion comes from a study in which children kept a daily diary of specific peer harassment incidents (Nishina & Juvonen, 2002). The analyses across a two-week period showed that the frequency of harassment incidents predicted negative self-views only for those children who never reported seeing other students getting picked on. Hence, the self-identified group might benefit from intervention approaches where the pervasiveness of the problem is acknowledged (i.e., "It's *not* just me"). But that strategy alone would not reduce anxiety or fear associated with repeated harassment. Teaching behavioral skills that allow youth to effectively respond to harassment episodes (e.g., leaving the situation before it escalates, staying with a group) would be likely to alleviate some of their anxieties. Both of these intervention strategies (changing perceptions of one's plight as unique and acquiring a behavioral repertoire to ward off victimization) can be accomplished by using a systemic, whole-school approach where all students are involved (Olweus, 1993).

Just as the self-identified victim group is likely to remain undiagnosed unless self-report instruments are used, the peer-identified victims would go undetected if the assessment relies only on self-reports. Because victims are highly likely to be rejected, the omission of the peer-identified group would constitute a serious oversight, given how much we know about peer rejection as a risk factor for many negative outcomes (e.g., Kupersmidt, Coie, & Dodge, 1990). Had we not included peer reports of victimization in the current sample, we would have missed the eighty-one students who had only social reputations as victims.

One of the challenges of intervention with peer-identified victims has to do with their level of awareness. It is not clear whether these youth knowingly refuse to admit that they get picked on by peers or whether they are simply unaware of their problems. Some degree of positive illusion may be adaptive (Taylor & Brown, 1988). But illusory beliefs are detrimental when they interfere with a person's ability to understand the effects of his or her behavior on others. In our study, some of the peer-identified victims (particularly African-American boys) were rated by their teachers as having externalizing problems. In those cases, it is likely that these youth get harassed because they (are perceived to) provoke others. Some of the known strategies for helping aggressive youth to better handle peer provocation might, therefore, be useful for children such as peer-identified victims. For example, teaching aggressive students to recognize when provocations are accidental rather than intended has proven to be an effective intervention (Graham, Taylor, & Hudley, 2002; Hudley & Graham, 1993). Conflict mediation as part of an antibullying prevention approach also is recommended. Such approaches typically involve analyses of specific incidents in terms of "who did what and when." These activities provide helpful feedback to youth about how they may have contributed to a particular harassment incident and what they could do differently in the future.

By comparing self-reports and peer reports of victimization, we have demonstrated that identifying the targets of peer harassment is complex. We are not advocating one method over another, nor are we proposing that school mental health professionals should conduct routine grade-wide screenings to identify victimized youth. Rather, we want to point out that different types of victims might be identified with each method and that findings of studies can vary depending on the type of assessment used. As long as the presence of peer harassment shapes the culture and climate of schools, it is important that professional staff be aware that the subjective experience of feeling victimized and the reputation as a victim in the eyes of others are distinct, albeit partly overlapping, phenomena. To our knowledge, whether agreement between different informants would change as a function of certain school-wide prevention programs has not been tested.

Beyond Victimization

With a large multiethnic sample, we would feel remiss if we did not call attention to some of the ethnicity main effects that emerged in the analysis independent of victim status. These findings remind us of the broader social context in which adolescents of color live and the multiple challenges that they often face. On the psychological adjustment variables, Latinos reported more negative feelings (e.g., depression, anxiety) than did African Americans. The majority of Latino students in our sample were children of immigrants and they attended schools that had large enrollments of Latinos with similar immigrant histories. Much has been written about the adjustment challenges of these second- generation youth and of the need for schools to be particularly sensitive to their psychosocial needs (Portes, 1996; Suarez-Orozco & Suarez-Orozco, 2001). On the social variables, African-American boys were judged in a more negative light (e.g., more rejected by peers, displaying externalizing problems) than were Latinos. Much also has been written about the adjustment challenges of African-American males and the stress of coping with negative evaluations of their group (e.g., Graham, Taylor, & Hudley, 1998; Spencer, Cunningham, & Swanson, 1995). Both sets of problems that we highlight—the psychological and the social—are risk factors for poor school achievement. Being an adolescent of color *and* a victim of peer harassment only magnifies that risk.

REFERENCES

Asher, S., & Wheeler, V. (1985). Children's loneliness: A comparison of neglected and rejected peer status. *Journal of Consulting and Clinical Psychology, 53,* 500-505.

Astor, R., Meyer, H., & Behre,W. (1999). Unowned places and times: Maps and interviews about violence in high schools. *American Educational Research Journal, 36,* 3-42.

Cairns, R., Leung, M., Gest, S., & Cairns, B. (1995). A brief method for assessing social development: Structure, reliability, stability, and developmental validity of the Interpersonal Competence Scale. *Behavioral Research and Therapy, 33,* 725-736.

Cunningham, M. (1999). African American adolescent males' perceptions of their community resources and constraints: A longitudinal analysis. *Journal of Community Psychology, 27,* 569-588.

Garber, J., Walker, L., & Zeman, J. (1991). Somatization symptoms in a community sample of children and adolescents: Further validation of the Children's Somatization Inventory. *Psychological Assessment, 3,* 588-595.

Graham, S., & Juvonen, J. (1998). Self-blame and peer victimization in middle school: An attributional analysis. *Developmental Psychology, 34,* 587-599.

Graham, S., & Juvonen, J. (2002). Ethnicity, peer harassment, and adjustment in middle school: An exploratory study. *Journal of Early Adolescence, 22,* 173-199.

Graham, S., Taylor, A., & Hudley, C. (1998). Exploring achievement values among ethnic minority early adolescents. *Journal of Educational Psychology, 90,* 606-620.

Graham, S., Taylor, A., & Hudley, C. (2002). *A social skills and academic motivation intervention for at-risk African American boys.* Manuscript submitted for publication.

Harter, S. (1985). *The self-perception scale profile for children: Revision of the Perceived Competence Scale for Children manual.* Denver, CO: University of Denver Press.

Hudley, C., & Graham, S. (1993). An attributional intervention to reduce peer-directed aggression among African American boys. *Child Development, 64,* 124-138.

Hymel, S., Wagner, E., & Butler, L. (1990). Reputational bias: View from the peer group. In S. Asher & J. Coie (Eds.), *Peer rejection in childhood* (pp. 156-186). New York: Cambridge University Press.

Juvonen, J., Nishina, A., & Graham, S. (2000). Peer harassment, psychological well-being, and school adjustment in early adolescence. *Journal of Educational Psychology, 92,* 349-359.

Juvonen, S., Nishina, A., & Graham, S. (2001). Self-views versus peer perceptions of victimization among early adolescents. In J. Juvonen & S. Graham (Eds.), *Peer harassment in school: The plight of the vulnerable and victimized* (pp. 105-124). New York: Guilford Press.

Kochenderfer, B., & Ladd, G. (1996). Peer victimization: Cause or consequence of children's school adjustment difficulties? *Child Development, 67,* 1305-1317.

Kovacs, M. (1985). The Children's Depression Inventory: A self-rated depression scale for school-aged youngsters. *Psychopharmacology Bulletin, 21,* 995-998.

Kupersmidt, J. B., Coie, J. D., & Dodge, K. A. (1990). The role of poor peer relationships in the development of disorder. In S. R. Asher & J. D. Coie (Eds.), *Peer rejection in childhood* (pp. 274-305). New York: Cambridge University Press.

La Greca, A., & Lopez, N. (1998). Social anxiety among adolescents: Linkages with peer relations and friendships. *Journal of Abnormal Child Psychology, 26,* 83-94.

Nansel, T., Overpeck, M., Pilla, R., Ruan, W., Simons-Morton, B., & Scheidt, P. (2001). Bullying behavior among US youth. Prevalence and association with psychological adjustment. *Journal of the American Medical Association, 285,* 2094-2100.

Neary, A., & Joseph, S. (1994). Peer victimization and its relationship to self-concept and depression among schoolgirls. *Personality and Individual Differences, 16,* 183-186.

Nishina, A., & Juvonen, J. (2002). *Daily reports of negative affect and peer harassment in middle school.* Manuscript submitted for publication.

Olweus, D. (1993). *Bullying at school: What we know and what we can do.* Oxford, UK: Blackwell.

Pelligrini, A. (2001). Sampling instances of victimization in middle school: A methodological comparison. In J. Juvonen and S. Graham (Eds.), *Peer harassment in school: The plight of the vulnerable and victimized* (pp. 124-144). New York: Guilford Press.

Portes, A. (Ed.). (1996). *The new second generation.* New York: The Russell Sage Foundation.

Schuster, B. (1996). Rejection, exclusion, and harassment at work and in schools: An integration of results from research on mobbing, bullying, and peer rejection. *European Psychologist, 1,* 293-317.

Spencer, M., Cunningham, M., & Swanson, D. (1995). Identity as coping: Adolescent African American males' adaptive responses to high-risk environments. In H. Blue, E. Griffith, & H. Harris (Eds.), *Racial and ethnic identity: Psychological development and creative expression* (pp. 31-52). New York: Routledge Publishers.

Steinberg, L., & Morris, A. (2001). Adolescent development. *Annual Review of Psychology, 52,* 83-110.

Suarez-Orozco, C., & Suarez-Orozco, M. (2001). *Children of immigration.* Cambridge, MA: Harvard University Press.

Taylor, S., & Brown, J. (1988). Illusion and well-being: A social psychological perspective on mental health. *Psychological Bulletin, 103,* 193-210.

Wellborn, J., & Connell, J. (1991). *Students' achievement relevant actions in the classroom: A self-report measure of student motivation.* Unpublished manuscript, University of Rochester.

Chapter 9

Developmental Trajectories of Victimization: Identifying Risk and Protective Factors

Suzanne Goldbaum
Wendy M. Craig
Debra Pepler
Jennifer Connolly

Peer bullying and victimization occur frequently among children. According to Olweus (1991), victims of bullying are exposed to repeated acts over time by someone in a position of more power, that cause them marked distress. Prevalence rates of victimization are consistent across different countries (Farrington, 1993). In Canada, researchers have found that 49 percent of students reported being bullied at least once or twice during the term, when different forms of bullying (e.g., verbal and physical) are considered together. Eight percent of children report being bullied regularly, at least once a week (Charach, Pepler, & Ziegler, 1995). Repeated victimization is an impediment to children's healthy social and emotional development. Adjustment problems such as depression and low self-esteem are associated with victimization (Craig, 1998). This form of harassment also is related to aggression; running away from home; alcohol and drug use; dropping out of school; and committing suicide (Olweus, 1993). Finally,

This chapter was adapted from "Developmental Trajectories of Victimization: Identifying Risk and Protective Factors" by Suzanne Goldbaum, Wendy M. Craig, Debra Pepler, and Jennifer Connolly, *Journal of Applied School Psychology, 19*(2), pp. 139-156.

Bullying, Victimization, and Peer Harassment
Published by The Haworth Press, Inc., 2007. All rights reserved.
doi:10.1300/5808_09

research suggests that childhood victimization strongly predicts later behavior adjustment and adult disturbance (Parker & Asher, 1987).

Despite the general consensus regarding prevalence rates of victimization, the predominant use of cross-sectional designs precludes investigations of the stability of victimization and how effects of victimization change over time. This study provides insight by using a longitudinal research design and a group-based approach that identifies victimization trajectories (Nagin, 1999). In addition, differences among participants in the victimization trajectories were investigated in order to identify risk and protective factors associated with different developmental patterns of victimization. Because of the cumulative effects of risk factors over time, it was predicted that the longer an individual is victimized, the more aversive the associated psychological outcomes. In addition to the duration of victimization, other individual and peer factors may act as risk or protection for the negative outcomes associated with victimization. Identification of these factors will provide direction for the development of prevention and intervention programs aimed at reducing victimization and promoting healthy development.

INTRAPERSONAL CHARACTERISTICS OF VICTIMS

Previous research identifies a number of risk factors that are associated with victimization, including internalizing problems such as anxiety, depression, loneliness, somatization, and low self-esteem (Boulton & Underwood, 1992; Craig, 1998). Since previous studies were primarily cross-sectional, the ways in which these variables changed relative to changes in victimization is not clear. Thus, investigations are needed to determine whether these intrapersonal problems preceded, are maintained, or were a consequence of victimization. Our longitudinal analysis and identification of trajectories may facilitate this understanding.

Interpersonal Factors Associated with Victimization

Aggressive behaviors also are commonly associated with victimization, though as with intrapersonal factors, the possible sequential relationship between aggression and victimization is only beginning to be investigated. Some children who are victimized are passive and do not overtly respond to their abuse, while others react to attacks in an aggressive manner (Pellegrini, 1998). This second category of victims is labeled victim/bullies, and these individuals are considered to be at increased risk for internalizing and externalizing disorders (Austin & Joseph, 1996), as well as the most severe rejection among peers (Pellegrini, 1998). Kochenderfer and Ladd (1997) found that children who "fought back" were more likely to have a stable pattern of victimization. Similarly, compared to bullies and victims, victim/bullies were particularly at risk for prolonged involvement in bullying interactions (Kumpulainen, Raesaenen, & Henttonen, 1999). These studies highlight the importance of understanding how aggression relates to victimization and how they change together over time. This study assessed changes in aggressive and bullying behavior across different trajectories of victimization.

In addition to aggressive behavior, interpersonal factors such as friendships and peer group status also are associated with victimization. Children in a mutual best friendship or popular children with more friends are less likely than rejected children with fewer friends to report internalizing and externalizing behaviors otherwise predicted by victimization (Hodges, Boivin, Vitaro, & Bukowski, 1999; Hodges, Malone, & Perry, 1997). The lack of a supportive network of friends puts children at considerably more risk than children with an adequate support system. Salmivalli, Huttunen, and Lagerspetz (1997) concluded that victims and defenders had the smallest peer networks and of the children who did not belong to any peer network, almost half were victims. If victims do not belong to a peer group, they may not benefit from peer group socialization experiences that are normally associated with the peer group (e.g., protection), and that are a requisite for healthy social development.

While previous research indicates that the number of friends children have, their popularity, as well as likeability, correlate with victim status (Hodges et al., 1997), it is possible that friendship quality also plays a role in victimization. Since victims do report having some friends, it may be that lower-quality relationships account for their lack of protection from friends. Friendship qualities such as trust and affection are important in developing intimate relationships. If high levels of these friendship qualities do not characterize victims' friendships, victims may not effectively communicate their distress and seek support and protection from their friends. This study examined the quality of participants' friendships as well as their social competence.

In summary, this study had three goals: To identify (1) the trajectories of victimization; (2) intra-and interpersonal risk and protective factors associated with victimization; and (3) the consequences associated with stable victimization.

METHOD

Participants

Participants were 635 boys and 606 girls enrolled in 7 schools in a large urban Canadian city. At the beginning of the study, participants were in Grade 5 ($N = 313$), Grade 6 ($N = 376$), and Grade 7 ($N = 552$). Previous research suggests that students in these grades report similar patterns of victimization over time (Goldbaum & Craig, 2001), and, therefore, grade differences were not examined. There were three test administrations (Time 1 = fall year 1; Time 2 = spring year 1; Time 3 = fall year 2), and participants' ages ranged between nine and fourteen. There was a 5 percent attrition rate. Schools represented diverse socioeconomic backgrounds. Both parent and child consent were obtained, with an overall participation rate of 84 percent. Seventy-seven percent and 72 percent of fathers and mothers, respectively, were university graduates; 17 percent and 22 percent, respectively, were high school or community college graduates; and 5 percent of fathers and mothers did not graduate from high school. The majority of participants identified themselves as European Canadian (74 percent); 4 percent as African or Caribbean Canadian; 10 percent as Native or Asian Canadian; and 11 percent identified their race in other ways. Seventy-five percent of participants lived with both parents; 13 percent lived with one natural parent; 12 percent of participants had other family configurations.

Measures

Victimization

A modified Bully/Victim Questionnaire (Olweus, 1993) derived victimization scores from two items, "About how many times have you been bullied in the last five days at school?" and "How often have you been bullied at school since the beginning of the school year?" Examples of bullying are provided (i.e., physical and verbal). Students responded on a 5-point scale, with "0" meaning "it hasn't happened," and "4" representing "several times a week" for the first question, and "five or more times" for the second question. Scores were standardized and used for group formation. Cronbach α for the three test administrations ranged from .80 to .85.

A modified version of the Conflict Tactics Scale (Straus, 1979) evaluated direct physical victimization. Respondents indicated on an 11-point scale how often each of six actions had occurred to them since the beginning of the school year, where higher numbers represent higher frequencies of events. Items were specific to close friends, peers, and romantic partners. Cronbach α ranged from .60 to .72.

Internalizing Problems

The Child Behavior Checklist-Youth Self-Report (CBCL-YSR) (Achenbach, 1991) assessed internalizing dimensions, including anxiety/depression, somatization, and withdrawal. Participants responded on a scale ranging from "0" to "2" ("Not true," "Somewhat or sometimes true," or "Very true or often true") indicating how frequently each item occurred in the past two months. Higher scores represented more internalizing problems. Fourteen items comprised the anxiety/depression subscale, which revealed alphas ranging from .86 to .88. Somatization was a reliable nine-item scale and alphas ranged from .77 to .80. The withdrawal subscale comprised seven items, and alphas ranged from .67 to .71.

Social Self-Competence

A modified version of Harter's Perceived Competence Scale for Children (1982) assessed participants' perceived social competence using a structured alternative format. Children indicated which description best described them and then chose whether it was "really" or "sort of" true. Each item was scored from 1 to 4, where a score of 1 reflects low perceived competence and 4 indicates high perceived competence. Only the five-item social competence subscale was used in this study. Alphas ranged from .77 to .80.

Peer Relations

A modification of the People in My Life Scale (Armsden & Greenberg, 1987; Furman & Buhrmester, 1995) assessed children's relationships with friends. Participants rated on a 5-point scale (ranging from "Almost never or never true" to "Almost always or always true"), high numbers representing higher levels of friendship qualities. Eleven items assessed trust (alphas from .89 to .93), four questions measured communication (alphas from .85 to .88), four items assessed alienation (alphas from .58 to .72), affection had two questions (alphas from .68 to .76), three items measured commitment (alphas from .75 to .79), and three items assessed intimacy (alphas from .80 to .87) in participants' friendships.

Aggression

Achenbach's YSR (1991) measured self-reported aggression. The nineteen questions demonstrated sufficient reliability (alphas ranged from .71 to .88).

Bullying

A modified Bully/Victim Questionnaire (Olweus, 1993), as described for victimization, was used to derive a bullying scale and demonstrated acceptable reliabilities (alphas ranged from .78 to .81). Bullying was measured with two items, each assessed on a 5-point scale, where higher numbers represented more bullying.

RESULTS

Group Formation

Previous studies categorizing children as victims employed arbitrary cutoff points in defining victimization group membership (Boulton & Underwood, 1992). While these classifications may be theoretically reasonable, they do not necessarily exist naturally, and may be based on potentially misleading categorizations. Advancements in methodology for examining individuals' developmental trajectories provide researchers with the ability to transcend the use of these traditional categorization procedures. Another advantage of the new techniques is that, in contrast to hierarchical and latent growth curve modeling, they make no assumptions regarding a continuous distribution of trajectories (Nagin & Tremblay, 1999) and are able to identify the existing differences among groups.

Results of the trajectory analyses indicated that a four-group model best represents how participants' levels of victimization change over time. Analyses comparing competing trajectories of victimization are described elsewhere (see Goldbaum & Craig, 2001). The following four groups were identified: nonvictims reported consistently low levels of victimization; desisters started with high levels of victimization that decreased over time; late onset victims reported increasing levels of victimization; and stable victims reported consistently high levels of victimization. Participants were assigned a probability for group membership for each trajectory that assessed how closely they represent each identified group (see Table 9.1). Whereas victimization changed over time for desisters and late onset victims

TABLE 9.1. Mean probabilities (and standard deviations) of group membership and number of participants in each group.

	Nonvictims	Desisters	Late onset victims	Stable victims
Probabilities	.99 (.04)	.95 (.11)	.95 (.11)	.96 (.10)
Males	546	44	33	12
Females	543	32	23	8

(and slightly for stable victims), nonvictims did not report changes in victimization over time (Figure 9.1).

A MANOVA testing an independent self-reported measure of physical victimization revealed a significant time by group interaction, multivariate $F(3, 966) = 13.33$, $p < .001$, attesting to the validity of the groups. Participants' changing levels of physical victimization corresponded to the shape of their respective groups' victimization trajectories: increases and decreases in physical victimization coincided with increases and decreases in the measure of victimization used to form the trajectories. The group of nonvictims consistently reported low levels of physical victimization, while stable victims consistently reported the highest levels.

GROUP DIFFERENCES

To investigate differences among the four groups over time, repeated measures MANCOVAs were performed. Because of the small number of participants classified as stable victims, desisters, and late onset victims, gender was entered as a covariate. A chi square analysis indicated that boys and girls were equally represented in the groups.

Intrapersonal Factors

Internalizing Problems

Results showed a significant time by group interaction, multivariate $F(18, 2511) = 2.65$, $p < .001$, with associated univariate effects of anxiety, $F(6, 1680) = 5.54$, $p < .001$, and withdrawal, $F(6, 1680) = 4.72$, $p < .001$ (see Table 9.2 for means and standard deviations). Post hoc analyses indicated that nonvictims always reported the lowest levels of anxiety. Late onset victims reported less anxiety than stable victims at Times 1 and 2,

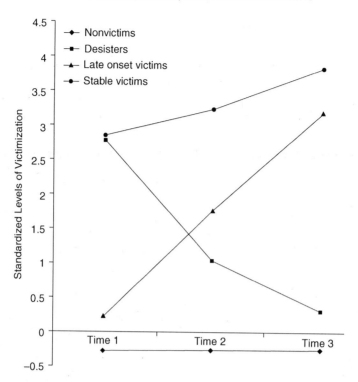

FIGURE 9.1. Trajectories of victimization.

though by Time 3, their anxiety was comparable to stable victims, and their anxiety was higher than that of the desisters. Desisters initially did not report less anxiety than stable victims, though by Times 2 and 3, desisters reported less anxiety than did stable and late onset victims. Late onset victims initially reported similar levels of anxiety to desisters (which was high at Time 1), suggesting that high levels of anxiety preceded increases in victimization. Planned contrasts examined whether any group reported significant changes in anxiety over time. Desisters reported decreasing levels of anxiety from Time 1 to Time 3, $F(1, 1680) = 24.92$, $p < .001$.

At Times 1 and 2 nonvictims reported less withdrawal than did all other participants. At Time 3, however, desisters reported similar levels of withdrawal to nonvictims. At Time 2, stable victims reported the highest levels of withdrawal, though by Time 3, late onset victims reported similar levels

TABLE 9.2. Means (and standard deviations) for internalizing problems.

Time of testing	Nonvictims	Desisters	Late onset victims	Stable victims
Anxiety				
1	.36 (0.31)[a]	.73 (0.36)[b]	.70 (0.47)[b]	.92 (0.59)[c]
2	.30 (0.33)[a]	.51 (0.36)[b]	.63 (0.52)[b]	1.00 (0.60)[c]
3	.29 (0.33)[a]	.44 (0.29)[b]	.76 (0.54)[c]	.94 (0.56)[c]
Withdrawal				
1	.37 (0.30)[a]	.61 (0.34)[b]	.55 (0.40)[b]	.73 (0.49)[b]
2	.32 (0.31)[a]	.44 (0.39)[b]	.47 (0.41)[b]	.87 (0.54)[c]
3	.30 (0.30)[a]	.34 (0.32)[a]	.56 (0.45)[b]	.62 (0.44)[b]

Note. Means in the same row that do not share superscripts differ at $p < .05$.

of withdrawal to stable victims. Desisters reported decreasing levels of withdrawal from Time 1 to Time 3, $F(1, 1680) = 22.00$, $p < .001$.

The MANCOVA also revealed a main effect of group, multivariate $F(9, 2520) = 14.80$, $p < .001$, with associated univariate effects for anxiety, $F(3, 840) = 43.71$, $p < .001$; withdrawal, $F(3, 840) = 17.36$, $p < .001$; and somatization, $F(3, 840) = 19.50$, $p < .001$. For all internalizing problems, nonvictims and stable victims were significantly different from each of the other groups, reporting the lowest and highest scores, respectively.

Interpersonal Factors

Social Self-Competence and Friendships

In the MANCOVA assessing group differences in social self-competence and friendship quality, there was a significant time by group interaction, multivariate $F(42, 2139) = 1.71$, $p < .01$, with associated univariate effects on social self-competence, $F(6, 1448) = 4.21$, $p < .001$; trust, $F(6, 1448) = 4.03$, $p < .01$; and affection, $F(6, 1448) = 3.65$, $p < .01$ (see Table 9.3). Nonvictims initially reported higher levels of social self-competence than did desisters or stable victims; and by Times 2 and 3, they reported the highest levels of social self-competence. At Times 1 and 2, stable victims reported the lowest levels of social self-competence, though by Time 3, late onset victims and desisters reported similarly low levels of social self-competence.

TABLE 9.3. Means (and standard deviations) for friendship variables.

Time of testing	Nonvictims	Desisters	Late onset victims	Stable victims
Social self-competence				
1	3.17 (.63)[a]	2.77 (.71)[b]	3.06 (.81)[b]	2.17 (.93)[c]
2	3.26 (.62)[a]	2.94 (.75)[b]	2.97 (.65)[b]	2.02 (1.03)[c]
3	3.30 (.61)[a]	3.04 (.79)[b]	2.87 (.74)[b]	2.78 (.92)[b]
Trust				
1	4.15 (.64)[a]	3.81 (.77)[b]	4.21 (.55)[a]	3.29 (1.45)[c]
2	4.24 (.65)	4.18 (.73)	4.12 (.65)	3.66 (1.47)
3	4.19 (.66)[a]	4.01 (.85)	3.84 (.88)[b]	4.00 (.90)
Affection				
1	4.35 (.75)[a]	3.95 (.83)[b]	4.30 (.67)[a]	3.44 (1.40)[c]
2	4.37 (.71)	4.29 (.78)	4.30 (.72)	3.72 (1.52)
3	4.29 (.71)[a]	4.17 (.91)[a]	3.87 (1.01)[b]	4.17 (.94)
Alienation				
1	2.21 (.83)	2.40 (.71)	2.48 (0.69)	3.03 (1.09)
2	1.97 (.74)	1.92 (.66)	2.13 (0.75)	2.24 (0.98)
3	1.98 (.77)	2.05 (.94)	2.23 (0.74)	2.53 (0.64)

Note. Means in the same row that do not share superscripts differ at $p < .05$.

Stable victims initially (Time 1) reported the lowest levels of trust in their friendships. At this time, nonvictims and late onset victims reported more trust in their friendships than stable victims or desisters. By Time 3, only late onset victims reported lower levels of trust in their friendships than nonvictims. Late onset victims reported decreasing levels of trust from Time 1 to Time 3, $F(1, 1448) = 6.40$, $p < .05$.

Stable victims reported the lowest levels of affection in their relationships at Time 1. At this time, desisters reported less affection than nonvictims, but similar levels of affection to late onset victims. Even before late onset victims' victimization increased, the level of affection in their friendships was similar to that of students who were reporting high levels of victimization. By Time 3, late onset victims reported less affection than nonvictims or desisters. Late onset victims reported decreasing affection over time, $F(1, 1448) = 6.17$, $p < .05$.

The MANCOVA analysis also revealed significant main effects of group, multivariate $F(21, 2160) = 3.07$, $p < .001$, with univariate effects for social self-competence, $F(3, 724) = 14.13, p < .001$; trust, $F(3, 724) = 4.26, p < .01$; alienation, $F(3, 724) = 3.77, p < .05$; and affection, $F(3, 724) = 4.33, p < .01$. Nonvictims and stable victims reported the highest and lowest levels of social self-competence, respectively. Stable victims reported lower trust and affection than either nonvictims or desisters. The reverse is true of alienation, for which stable victims reported higher levels.

Participants on different victimization trajectories reported differences in friendship quality with highly victimized adolescents reporting lower-quality relationships than participants with low levels of victimization. As well, there is some evidence that low levels of affection in friendships are associated with subsequent increases in victimization.

Self-Reported Aggression and Bullying

Results from the MANCOVA investigating the effects of group membership on aggression and bullying showed a significant time by group interaction, multivariate $F(12, 2865) = 4.80, p < .001$, with associated univariate effects for measures of aggression, $F(6, 1912) = 4.77, p < .001$; and bullying behavior, $F(6, 1912) = 7.64, p < .001$ (Table 9.4). At each time, nonvictims reported the lowest levels of aggression. By Time 2, desisters reported less aggressive behaviors than did stable victims. By Time 3, desisters reported less aggression than did late onset victims. Desisters and late onset victims reported decreasing, $F(1, 1912) = 12.86, p < .001$, and increasing, $F(1, 1912) = 4.49, p < .05$, levels of aggression, respectively.

Whereas stable victims reported the most bullying behavior at Times 1 and 2, by Time 3, late onset and stable victims had comparably high levels

TABLE 9.4. Means (and standard deviations) for aggression and bullying.

Time of testing	Nonvictims	Desisters	Late onset victims	Stable victims
Aggression				
1	.34 (.30)[a]	.52 (.33)[b]	.48 (.28)[b]	.52 (.27)[b]
2	.33 (.28)[a]	.43 (.28)[b]	.52 (.34)[b]	.67 (.40)[c]
3	.32 (.30)[a]	.42 (.28)[b]	.65 (.48)[c]	.56 (.42)[b,c]
Bullying				
1	.22 (.46)[a]	.68 (.90)[b]	.38 (.43)[c]	1.11 (1.42)[d]
2	.24 (.57)[a]	.44 (.54)[b]	.50 (.62)[b]	.86 (1.22)[c]
3	.30 (.62)[a]	.32 (.41)[a]	.93 (1.12)[c]	1.07 (1.41)[c]

Note. Means in the same row that do not share superscripts differ at $p < .05$.

of bullying. Similarly, desisters reported more bullying than late onset victims or nonvictims at Time 1, though by Time 3, they reported less bullying than late onset or stable victims, and similar levels of bullying to nonvictims. At Time 3, nonvictims reported less bullying behavior than late onset or stable victims. Desisters had decreasing levels of bullying, $F(1, 1912) = 9.81$, $p < .001$, and late onset victims' bullying behavior increased over time, $F(1, 1912) = 23.12$, $p < .001$.

The MANCOVA analysis also revealed significant main effects of group, multivariate $F(6, 1912) = 13.25$, $p < .001$, with univariate effects for aggression, $F(3, 956) = 16.23$, $p < .001$; and bullying, $F(3, 956) = 22.26$, $p < .001$. Nonvictims reported the lowest levels of aggression and bullying behavior. Stable victims reported the most bullying.

IMPLICATIONS AND INTERVENTION

The objectives of this study were to distinguish groups of children with unique profiles of victimization, to identify risk and protective factors associated with victimization, and to understand the consequences associated with stable victimization. Four groups were established: nonvictims were children who reported consistently low levels of victimization; desisters were children who started with high levels of victimization that decreased over time; late onset victims reported increasing levels of victimization; and stable victims reported consistently high levels of victimization. Examining intra- and interpersonal differences across these groups will facilitate the identification of risk and protective factors associated with victimization. Finally, there was evidence to support a sequential relationship between aggression and victimization.

Risk Factors for Subsequent Victimization

The late onset victims provide the opportunity to examine factors that preceded increases in victimization, thereby delineating risk factors for victimization. Late onset victims could be distinguished from the other groups at Time 1 by high levels of internalizing problems and low levels of affection in peer relationships. Children reporting high levels of internalizing problems (e.g., anxiety, withdrawal, somatization) may elicit behaviors or initiate interactions that place them at risk for peer victimization. Rubin, Bukowski, and Parker (1998) proposed that withdrawn children follow a distinct developmental course to peer rejection (a form of peer victimization) that begins in late childhood, when the peer group becomes aware of social withdrawal and judges it as atypical behavior. Observations of children indicate that bullying is more likely to occur when children are alone (Craig & Pepler, 1995). Anxious and withdrawn children may be hesitant to initiate social interactions and being isolated may suggest a lack of protection against bullying, and signal one's vulnerability. Bullies who harass anxious and withdrawn children may be reinforced if victims continue to be isolated. The harassment may intensify or become more frequent because the bullying may exacerbate victims' anxiety, thereby rewarding bullies who can observe their powerful effect. Furthermore, if victims are not supported by others or do not defend themselves, not only may the harassment continue, but there will likely be no consequences for the bully. Thus, internalizing problems may identify those at risk for victimization, as well as contribute to maintaining the victimization and exacerbating internalizing problems.

Individuals reporting lower-quality friendships also were at heightened risk for increasing victimization. Late onset victims rated affection similarly to desisters (when their victimization was high), indicating that prior to their victimization, late onset victims reported comparable levels of affection to those who were already experiencing significant harassment. The lack of quality relationships or supportive peers may increase late onset victims' vulnerability to victimization (Hodges et al., 1997), demonstrating the protective function of friends.

Late onset victims reported decreasing levels of trust and affection as their victimization increased. While it is likely that they are vulnerable because they lack protection provided by friends, it also is possible that lower affection in their friendships is a reflection of their victimization experiences. Adolescents who lack emotional support (i.e., intimacy and closeness) may lose trust in the friends they do have, who are ineffective at protecting them. Late onset victims likely did not engage in positive social interactions or experience companionship and support to help them practice social skills and develop a sense of interpersonal competence. Interestingly, despite experiencing less victimization, desisters did not report increasing levels of social competence over time. It is likely that although they were feeling less victimized by their peers, a sense of social competence would require more stable positive social interactions and experiences that perhaps were only emerging among the desisters.

Protective Factors Against Victimization

Examining the characteristics of desisters and nonvictims helps identify factors that protect children from peer victimization. Desisters were characterized by decreasing levels of internalizing problems, bullying, and aggressive behavior. Nonvictims reported the lowest levels of internalizing problems, bullying, aggressive behavior, and were the most socially competent. Low levels of aggression and anxiety may be the most robust protective factors, since nonvictims reported the lowest levels of these variables across time. Paralleling the results identifying low-quality friendships as a risk factor, high-quality friendships served a protective function. Friendships characterized by high levels of affection (representing warmth and intimacy) and trust buffered against victimization. Within these positive affective relationships a child may be more committed to a friend and, therefore, be inclined to intervene or protect him or her. Also, an intimate relationship may facilitate communication between friends and a supportive discussion can provide the opportunity to collectively solve the problem of bullying.

Friends can help children identify strategies to deal with their harassment. Children are most likely to use the least effective methods (verbal and physical aggression) when responding to bullying and these responses are associated with more prolonged and severe bullying interactions (Mahady-Wilton, Craig, & Pepler, 2000). In contrast, when children ask a peer for help with the bullying, it stops within ten seconds half the time (O'Connell, Pepler, & Craig, 1999). Because desisters report decreasing aggression over time, it is possible that they are coping in more effective ways (i.e., utilizing their friends or not responding aggressively) and these behaviors played a role in reducing victimization. The increase in aggression over time reported by late onset victims further supports this interpretation. Interventions designed to reduce aggressive behavior and to offer alternate coping strategies may prevent victimization, and the negative outcomes associated with it.

Stable Victimization Associated with Aversive Conditions

Stable victims reported the most severe intra- and interpersonal difficulties. High levels of anxiety, withdrawal, somatization, bullying, and low social competence characterize this group, suggesting that long-term exposure and cumulative effects of victimization place them at increased risk for long-term problems. Without intervention the cycle of victimization will intensify. Because stable victimization is associated with the most negative conditions, treatment aimed at decreasing risk or reducing victimization should occur early.

Relationship Between Aggression and Victimization

There was a sequential relationship between aggression and victimization. As victimization increased, late onset victims reported engaging in more aggressive and bullying behaviors. Children who are targets of victimization for prolonged periods may learn and model aggressive strategies from the bullies, whom they view as more powerful. Furthermore, they may aggress against those weaker than themselves as a way of coping with their anger and hostility associated with their own victimization experiences. Responding to bullying with aggression is not an effective strategy (Mahady-Wilton et al., 2000), even though it is the most frequent response. Interventions for victimized children should provide effective coping strategies.

Limitations

While the results of this study provide direction and implications for intervention, there are some limitations. Group membership and the dependent measures were both based on self-report, thus the results may be biased due to shared method variance. Previous research, however, indicates that self-reports are valid assessments of victimization (Farrington, 1993), particularly since adults and teachers tend to underestimate the problem. While results highlight the role of peer socialization in the development and maintenance of victimization, previous research acknowledges the importance of the family. This study did not evaluate parent–child relationships. Finally, participants came from highly educated, two-parent families; therefore, generalizations to other populations should be made with caution.

Implications for Research and Practice in Applied School Psychology

This study has implications for the prevention and intervention of peer victimization with respect to assessment and identification as well as specific program components. Since internalizing problems preceded victimization, children at risk for victimization can be identified with a screening tool that would assess levels of anxiety, withdrawal, and somatization, as well as victimization. Because of the cumulative effects of victimization, assessment and screening should occur early (i.e., in kindergarten) and at regular intervals. Once at-risk children are identified, school personnel and parents can intervene with individuals or peer group to decrease the risk factors and increase protective factors associated with victimization.

Targeted interventions for individual children should focus on reducing their internalizing problems, promoting interpersonal competence skills to enhance friendship initiation and maintenance, and reducing isolation and withdrawal (i.e., relaxation training, cognitive restructuring techniques to deal with anxiety provoking situations, social skills and assertiveness training). Victimized children also need to develop skills to communicate their distress in a way that promotes a positive response from peers and teachers. Teaching children specific strategies that are empirically demonstrated to be effective in stopping bullying, such as asking for help and positive conflict resolution, will reduce their risk for future victimization (O'Connell et al., 1999). Finally, education regarding the ineffectiveness of strategies such as aggression also is important.

In addition to working with individuals, programs should be directed at the peer group to encourage inclusion and foster supportive social networks. An example of a school-wide program for peers is "support circles," which offer children the opportunity to enhance their social competence through peer interaction and support. Small groups of students discuss regularly everyday events or personal concerns and problems. These opportunities help children to develop intimate and affectionate relationships that promote support and protection and may prevent future victimization. Through the creation of these groups, at-risk children and victimized children will have regular opportunities to interact with skilled peers, practice and develop their social skills, develop social competence, and acquire the peer support and protection they may lack. Another example of this type of intervention is mentoring programs whereby small groups of students meet with a teacher to address nonacademic concerns in a safe and nonjudgmental environment, creating a supportive context to discuss interpersonal matters. Finally, classroom discussions can identify prosocial strategies for intervening in bullying and emphasize the critical role and responsibility of the peer group in stopping the harassment by supporting and standing up for the victims. When bullying problems occur, teachers can focus on the nature of the peer involvement and identify the role that peers may play in exacerbating the problem. By encouraging the entire peer group to take responsibility for harassment, it should encourage individuals to intervene on behalf of victims.

In summary, the implications of this research are as follows: (1) victims should be identified early though regular screenings that assess internalizing problems and friendship quality; (2) interventions to reduce victimization should include specific elements that address intra- and interpersonal risk and protective factors (i.e., be systemic and include individuals as well as the peer group).

REFERENCES

Achenbach, T. M. (1991). *Manual for the Youth Self-Report and 1991 Profile.* Burlington, VT: University of Vermont Department of Psychiatry.
Armsden, G. C., & Greenberg, M. T. (1987). The inventory of parent and peer attachment: Individual differences and their relationship to psychological well-being in adolescence. *Journal of Youth and Adolescence, 16,* 427-454.

Austin, S., & Joseph, S. (1996). Assessment of bully/victim problems in 8- to 11-year-olds. *British Journal of Educational Psychology, 66*(4), 447-456.

Boulton, M. J., & Underwood, K. (1992). Bully/victim problems among middle school children. *British Journal of Educational Psychology, 62,* 73-87.

Charach, A., Pepler, D., & Ziegler, S. (1995). Bullying at school: A Canadian perspective. *Education Canada, 35*(1), 12-18.

Craig, W. M. (1998). The relationship among bullying, victimization, depression, anxiety, and aggression in elementary school children. *Journal of Personality and Individual Differences, 24*(1), 123-130.

Craig, W. M., & Pepler, D. J. (1995). Peer processes in bullying and victimization: An observational study. *Exceptionality Education in Canada, 5,* 81-95.

Farrington, D. P. (1993). Understanding and preventing bullying. *Crime and Justice, 17,* 381-458.

Furman, W., & Buhrmester, D. (1985). Children's perceptions of the personal relationships in their social networks. *Developmental Psychology, 21,* 1016-1024.

Goldbaum, S., & Craig, W. M. (2001, April). *Analyzing trajectories of victimization: A developmental perspective.* Poster session presented at the Society for Research on Child Development, Minneapolis, MN.

Harter, S. (1982). The Perceived Competence Scale for Children. *Child Development, 53,* 87-97.

Hodges, E. V., Boivin, M., Vitaro, F., & Bukowski, W. (1999). The power of friendship: Protection against an escalating cycle of peer victimization. *Developmental Psychology, 35*(1), 94-101.

Hodges, E. V., Malone, M. J., & Perry, D. G. (1997). Individual risk and social risk as interacting determinants of victimization in the peer group. *Developmental Psychopathology, 33*(6), 1032-1039.

Kochenderfer, B. J., & Ladd, G. W. (1997). Victimized children's responses to peers' aggression: Behaviors associated with reduced versus continued victimization. *Development and Psychopathology, 9,* 59-73.

Kumpulainen, K., Raesaenen, E., & Henttonen, I. (1999). Children involved in bullying: Psychological disturbance and the persistence of the involvement. *Child Abuse and Neglect, 23*(12), 1253-1262.

Mahady-Wilton, M. M., Craig, W. M., & Pepler, D. J. (2000). Emotional regulations and display in classroom victims of bullying: Characteristic expressions of affect, coping styles and relevant contextual factors. *Social Development, 9*(2), 226-244.

Nagin, D. (1999). Analyzing developmental trajectories: A semiparametric group-based approach. *Psychological Methods, 4*(2), 139-157.

Nagin, D., & Tremblay, R. E. (1999). Trajectories of boys' physical aggression, opposition, and hyperactivity on the path to physically violent and nonviolent juvenile delinquency. *Child Development, 70*(5), 1181-1196.

O'Connell, P., Pepler, D. J., & Craig, W. M. (1999). Peer involvement in bullying: Insights and challenges for intervention. *Journal of Adolescence, 22*(4), 437-452.

Olweus, D. (1991). Bully/victim problems among schoolchildren: Basic facts and effects of a school based intervention program. In Debra J. Pepler, &

Kenneth H. Rubin (Eds.), *The Development and Treatment of Childhood Aggression* (pp. 411-448). Hillsdale, NJ: Lawrence Erlbaum Associates, Inc.

Olweus, D. (1993). Victimization by peers: Antecedents and long-term outcomes. In K. H. Rubin & J. B. Asendorpf (Eds.), *Social Withdrawal, Inhibition, and Shyness in Childhood* (pp. 315-341). Hillsdale, NJ: Erlbaum.

Parker, J. G., & Asher, S. R. (1987). Peer relations and later personal adjustment: Are low-accepted children at risk? *Psychological Bulletin, 102*(3), 357-389.

Pellegrini, A. D. (1998). Bullies and victims in school: A review and call for research. *Journal of Applied Developmental Psychology, 19*(2), 165-176.

Rubin, K. H., Bukowski, W., & Parker, J. G. (1998). Peer interactions, relationships, and groups. In W. Damon & N. Eisenberg (Eds.), *Handbook of Child Psychology, 5th Edition: Social, Emotional, and Personality Development* (pp. 619-699). New York: John Wiley & Sons.

Salmivalli, C., Huttunen, A., & Lagerspetz, M. J. (1997). Peer networks and bullying in schools. *Scandinavian Journal of Psychology, 38*, 305-312.

Straus, M. A. (1979). Measuring intrafamily conflict and violence: The Conflict Tactics Scale. *Journal of Marriage and the Family, 41*, 75-88.

SECTION III:
EMPIRICALLY VALIDATED
AND PROMISING PREVENTIVE
AND SUPPORTIVE INTERVENTIONS

Chapter 10

Targeting Bystanders: Evaluating a Violence Prevention Program for "Nonviolent" Adolescents

Harry S. Freeman
Grace A. Mims

INTRODUCTION

According to a recent Surgeon General's report, numerous violence prevention programs have been initiated in schools and communities nationwide but few have been studied to the point of yielding confidence in their effectiveness (U.S. Department of Health and Human Services, 2001). The evaluation shortage is most notable among prevention programs targeting adolescent populations. Researchers, practitioners, and policymakers alike typically view adolescence as too late for prevention. For instance, in the Surgeon General's report (2001) not a single primary prevention program for high school populations was included in the document's comprehensive review. Adolescent programs are more likely to target at-risk youth or violent offenders in the form of secondary or tertiary programs, respectively. Unfortunately, these programs are unlikely to change violent norms that are supported by conventional youth. In this case, such norms represent attitudes and beliefs held by the majority of students that allow common forms of aggressive acts (e.g., bullying, threats, relational violence) to continue

This research was funded by a grant from the South Dakota Department of Education. The authors wish to thank the adolescents and school officials who participated in this research.

Bullying, Victimization, and Peer Harassment
doi:10.1300/5808_10

unchecked. Norms signal that aggression is not only to be accepted, but that the bystander who reports or intervenes may be subject to peer and adult sanctions. Contrary to most prevention programs that focus on the aggressor, the program reviewed in this study targeted conventional norms, which regulate bystander behavior. This chapter presents an empirical case for primary prevention during adolescence using evaluation data from a school-based program.

Contemporary approaches to treating and preventing youth violence recognize the importance of understanding peer norms that support aggressive behavior and cognitions (Pepler & Slaby, 1994). For instance, effective early intervention programs focus on healthy family functioning as a critical prerequisite to lessening childhood aggression, especially over the long term. In adolescence, peer groups are often considered a more powerful social context than family for promoting and maintaining individual violence among its members (Dishion, Patterson, & Griesler, 1994; Loeber & Stouthamer-Loeber, 1998). In this sense, interventions have targeted peer-group norms among delinquent youth (Elliot & Menard, 1996). Norms operate in conventional peer-group settings as well, and serve to regulate behavior among so called nonviolent youth. Conventional norms may perpetuate violence by condoning bystander behavior such as cheering a fight, laughing at a victim, circulating a rumor, or excluding or ignoring those in need of assistance (Slaby, Wilson-Brewer, & Dash, 1994). In this case, treatments must target the social norms that regulate, promote, and maintain overt and relational aggression among the general population, not just the individuals who perpetrate such behaviors and attitudes/beliefs.

Population-directed prevention programs are a good developmental fit for changing violent norms during adolescence (Guerra, Tolan, & Hammond, 1994). Compared to childhood, the adolescent period is recognized for accelerated growth in violent behavior and more extreme forms of violence (Loeber & Hay; 1997; Stanger, Achenbach, & Verhulst, 1997). In one study conducted in the United States, 75 percent of adolescents reported some form of victimization from a bully during their secondary school years (Oliver, Hoover, & Hazler, 1994). Although victims of aggression typically account for less than half of a school's population, its effects are not isolated to only perpetrator and victim. Aggressive acts commonly occur in classrooms, lunchrooms, and hallways, which expose the majority of the school's population to daily or weekly incidences of violence. From a bystander's perspective, many forms of aggression are the norm in schools rather than the exception. As a result, threats and intimidation associated with bully behaviors can create a negative atmosphere for all students (Oliver et al., 1994). When more students than not are experiencing aggressive acts, either directly or through witnessing, the aggression becomes an accepted part of school life. Adult and student acquiescence enables bullying and other forms of violence to continue under a cloak of normalcy (Olweus, 1978).

Ironically, adolescents more than children or adults may be at highest risk for conformity to population norms. As children's perspective taking abilities become more sophisticated during the middle school years, there is a corresponding increase in susceptibility to peer pressure. That is, students become acutely aware of group norms and are more likely to follow them compared to younger or older students (Berndt, 1979). This developmental trend, coupled with a rise in violent behavior during adolescence, suggests that violent norms are likely to emerge, which are practiced and supported by conventional or otherwise "nonviolent" youth. Early intervention programs that focus on family and community risk factors and at-risk programs that focus on marginalized adolescents are unlikely to impact conventional norms.

School-based programs focused on changing peer norms appear to be more effective than programs focusing on changing individuals (Gottfredson, Wilson, & Najaka, in press). Unfortunately, evaluation data on primary prevention programs are most wanting among those targeting adolescent populations. The current study provides needed empirical validation of a school-based violence prevention program for adolescents. The program is designed to help school service providers and teachers to change behavioral and attitudinal norms that support overt and relational forms of aggression among the schools' general populations. By creating a safer social climate, the program aims to reduce the incidence of violence and increase the responsibility of the bystander to take prosocial action or report violent acts to school adults.

PROGRAM DESCRIPTION

In the fall of 1998 the South Dakota Department of Health received block grant funding to implement a violence prevention program called Get Real About Violence (GRAV: Comprehensive Health Education Foundation, 1997). An extensive, two-day training seminar was conducted by GRAV trainers throughout the state with some twenty-eight schools participating. This chapter provides the results of a comprehensive program evaluation from one of the South Dakota high schools that implemented the GRAV prevention program.

GRAV is a K-12 primary prevention program; however, this evaluation focuses on Grades 9 through 12. Consequently, our discussion of the GRAV curriculum is limited to these grades. GRAV curriculum comprises three modules, each containing three to six fifty-minute lesson plans for infusion into most academic content areas. The first module is designed to increase students' awareness of violence inside and outside of their school. Ultimately, students are taught to recognize peer, media, and societal influences that foster violent norms. The second module focuses on the role of the bystander. This section examines how nonaction contributes to violence by enabling violent norms to continue. The final module focuses on skill building and teaches students strategies for changing violent norms.

The treatment group participated in four lesson units (approximately ninety minutes each, over two forty-five-minute class periods) designed to increase recognition of violence and the role of the bystander. Students participated in activities that ranged from placing themselves on a continuum to reflect their level of belief in violent norms to role-playing bystander behavior in a lunchroom fight scene. The curriculum provides engaging videos that portray bystander ability to stop violence and change school norms. The training also included teaching students appropriate responses to witnessing or experiencing a violent act.

METHOD

Sample

A total of 358 students participated in the GRAV evaluation, including 198 students (55 percent) in the treatment condition and 160 students (45 percent) in the control group. The sample was evenly distributed across the four grades; however, treatment and control groups were somewhat unbalanced (see Table 10.1). Few seniors qualified for the control group since the school wanted all seniors to participate in the violence prevention curriculum. Different sections of English and Health courses were targeted for the treatment and control groups. The curriculum was administered by a school counselor and two health instructors who attended the GRAV training.

Instrumentation

The School Safety Survey was created to tap students' beliefs, experiences, and behaviors related to aggressive acts that are a normal part of their

TABLE 10.1. Number of participants in the treatment and control group by grade.

	Freshman	Sophomore	Junior	Senior
Treatment	59	41	37	61
Control	36	50	61	13

school experience. As such, we were more interested in the degree to which students witnessed physical and relational forms of aggression than the degree to which they were perpetrators or victims of aggressive acts. Only aggressive acts that were reported by at least 50 percent of the sample were included as items in the scales. In this way, the scales were truly capturing relational and physical aggression norms in the school population.

Witnessing Relational Aggression

Five items of the School Safety Survey asked students to indicate the number of times they witnessed various types of relational aggression in the past four weeks. This scale was designed to assess the incidence of witnessing behavior; as such, it is a measure of the extent to which students experience aggressive acts as bystanders. The behaviors indexed included the following: tell others not to hang around with someone, criticizing someone behind their back, ignoring someone, gossiping about someone, and calling bad names behind their back. The five items were summed into a relational aggression scale, with higher scores indicating more violence witnessed. Scale scores ranged from 6 to 30 ($M = 14.87$). A Chronbach's internal consistency α was computed ($r = .85$).

Witnessing Physical Aggression

Two 4-point Likert items were used to index the degree to which physical violence against others was witnessed by students. The behaviors indexed included the following: physically hurt others and threaten others. The items were summed to make up the physical aggression scale, with higher scores indicating more witnessing of physical aggression. Scale scores ranged from 2 to 8 ($M = 3.98$). A Chronbach's α was computed to assess the internal consistency of the scale ($r = .83$).

Adult Norms

Six items were used to index student perceptions of what school adults would do if they were told that someone was getting hurt. Each item was measured on a 4-point Likert scale. Sample items include the following: "They would help; Make things worse for you; Tell you to mind your own business; and, Thank you for telling." Negative adult responses were reverse coded. The items were summed to compute the Adult Norm scale with higher scores indicating that adults would respond favorably to student reports of aggression. Scale scores ranged from 6 to 24, ($M = 17.4$). A

Chronbach's α was computed to assess the internal consistency of the scale ($r = .78$).

Peer Norms

Six items were used to index student perceptions of what their peers would do if they told a school adult that someone was getting hurt. Each item was measured on a 4-point Likert scale. Sample items include the following: "Think you did the right thing; Say good things about you; Think you did the wrong thing; and, Not like you." Negative peer responses were reverse coded. The items were summed to compute the Peer Norm scale with higher scores indicating that peers would respond favorably to students who reported aggressive acts to adults. Scale scores ranged from 6 to 24, ($M = 12.85$). A Chronbach's α was computed to assess the internal consistency of the scale ($r = .87$).

Behavioral Intent As Bystander

A scale was created to examine how students would respond to witnessing "someone hurting someone else." Students rated the following six response options on a 4-point Likert scale from "Very unlikely" to "Very likely": "Tell a school adult to stop it; Tell the student not to do it, Get the person who was hurt to a safe place, Cheer it on, Watch the fight, and, Join in." Negative peer responses were reverse coded. The items were summed to compute the Bystander Response Scale with higher scores indicating that students would respond favorably to witnessing an aggressive act. Scale scores ranged from 6 to 24, ($M = 16.25$). A Chronbach's α was computed to assess the internal consistency of the scale ($r = .74$).

Behavioral Intent As Victim

A scale was created to index student responses to two conflict resolution vignettes adapted from Slaby and Guerra (1988). Students were asked to choose one of five possible responses to being pushed out of line and being called a name. Response options were collapsed into three categories including: (1) aggressive response (sample items: say something rude or mean, push him or her away, join fight); (2) prosocial response (sample items: "Ask him or her why; Try to get them to calm down and stop fighting); and, (3) neutral response (sample items include: "Do nothing; Just walk away, Ignore the situation"). An internal consistency alpha was computed for the two items based on an aggressive response coded as 1, neutral as 2, and prosocial as 3. The resulting Chronbach's α was .65. The moderate internal consistency score is likely due to forcing categorical responses into an ordinal scale; however, the change from aggressive to neutral to prosocial should not be considered interval scaling.

RESULTS

Since this study lacks pretest information, it is necessary to establish that the treatment and control groups are similar on a number of key variables related to witnessing aggressive behavior. Treatment and control group scores on the relational and physical aggression scale were compared with independent sample *t*-tests.

Witnessing Relational and Physical Aggression

Results indicated that groups did not significantly differ in the degree of relational aggression witnessed ($t(333) = .881$), or physical aggression witnessed ($t(333) = 1.75$). These results suggest that students in the treatment and control groups experienced similar school environments and are likely exposed to the same adult and peer norms.

Over 50 percent of students in the treatment and control groups indicated that they witnessed, with a frequency of at least once per week, all of the relational and physical aggression behaviors identified in two scales. Relational aggression was the most frequently cited activity with over 80 percent of students reporting witnessing classmates do the following at least once per week: spread rumors, criticize others behind their back, ignore someone, and tell others not to hang around someone. In other words, relational aggression is a normal and ongoing part of most students' weekly, if not daily, school experience. Physical aggression was witnessed with less frequency. Less than 40 percent of students reported never seeing these acts within a thirty-day period. In summary, data from the scales indicate that the majority of students are exposed to relational and physical aggression on a routine basis and, consequently, must confront norms regulating the behavior of the bystander. Consistent with previous research a significant gender effect was found (Bjorkqvist, Lagerspetz, & Kaukiainen, 1992). Girls reported a higher incidence of witnessing relational aggression, while boys reported a higher incidence of physical aggression. The remainder of this section addresses whether the treatment group and control group report different peer and adult norms.

Adult Norms

The Adult Norm scale indexed the extent to which students perceive adults to respond positively to a student reporting an aggressive act. Results clearly revealed that students who participated in the GRAV curriculum were significantly more likely to view adult reactions positively ($t(333) = 2.26, p < .05$). Figure 10.1 indicates that over 75 percent of students in the treatment group believed that adults would help and appreciate being told, whereas these same beliefs were reported by less than two-thirds of the control group. In addition, the control group was more likely to perceive school adults as making it worse for the student reporter or as being unable to help. No significant differences were found by grade or gender; although girls, compared to boys, indicated a more positive view of adults, it was not a significant difference, $t(362) = 1.70, p < .10$.

Peer Norms

The difference between the control and treatment group was not significant when comparisons were made on the peer norm scale ($t(339) = 1.65, p < .10$). Figure 10.2 reveals that the treatment group reported in the expected direction across each of the items on the scale; however, these differences were small. Generally, both groups reported greater skepticism that peers would be helpful. Indeed, the majority of students indicated that they thought peers would either not be able to help, not care, and think that they

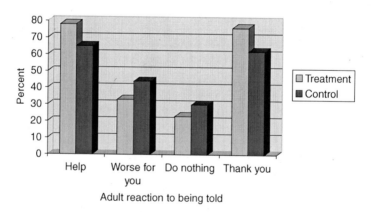

FIGURE 10.1. Perceptions of adult norms: adult response to being told of an aggressive act.

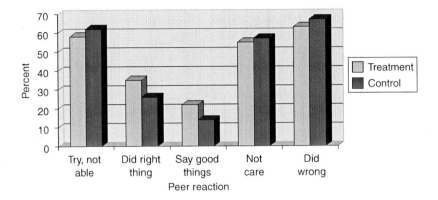

FIGURE 10.2. Perceptions of peer norms: peer response to reporting an aggressive act to an adult.

did the wrong thing by reporting to adults. In summary, these results suggest that peer norms are more resistant to change, at least as impacted by the GRAV curriculum. Although no grade effect was found, a significant gender main effect indicated that girls viewed peer responses more positively than boys, $t(362) = 2.26$, $p < .05$.

Behavioral Intent As Bystander and Victim

Students participating in the violence prevention program were more likely to choose prosocial responses as a witness to violence, based on the Bystander Behavioral Intent scale, $t(333) = 2.17$, $p < .05$. Figure 10.3 shows that the majority of the treatment group reported that they would try help the victim of a fight (58 percent), and a small minority (12 percent) reported that they would join the fight.

In regard to the two vignettes that asked students how they would respond to being the victim of an aggressive act, the treatment group was more likely to respond prosocially, $t(339) = 2.94$, $p < .01$. Figure 10.4 shows that those in the control group were more likely to retaliate to aggression with aggression. For example, if pushed out of line those in the control group were more likely to push back or use mean words. Students in the treatment group also indicated that they were less likely to do "nothing" in response to being pushed out of line. When asked what they would do if they were called a name, the control group was three times more likely than the treatment group to respond by hitting back and were less likely to ask why or walk away.

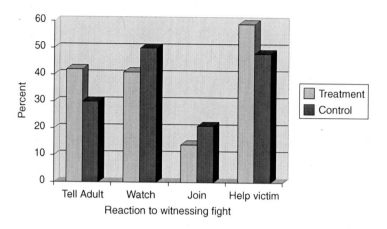

FIGURE 10.3. Behavioral intent as bystander.

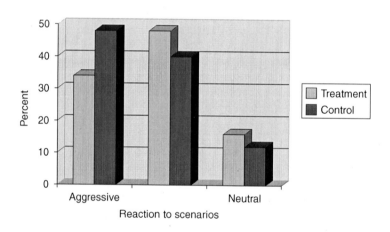

FIGURE 10.4. Behavioral intent as victim.

DISCUSSION

The importance of primary violence prevention efforts for conventional youth is not widely recognized or well understood, especially among adolescent populations. Yet, conventional norms may be a powerful force in shaping and maintaining overt and relational forms of aggression. The results of this study indicate that participation in a population-directed program helped change student perceptions of unfavorable norms that served to regulate how they responded to violence, both as a witness and a victim.

Findings suggest that students witnessed relational and physical forms of aggression on a consistent basis. Relational aggression, in the form of exclusion, name-calling, criticizing, and gossiping, was likely to occur on a daily basis; and, physical aggression in the form of threats and hurting another person were witnessed at least once per week. These findings clearly show that witnessing aggression can be a norm, even when the aggressive act itself may occur with less frequency. Said another way, perpetration of violent behaviors among a minority of students may be supported by norms held by conventional youth, which promote regulate bystander behavior. Our findings suggest that many bystanders take an active role in encouraging a fight or joke or interpersonal aggression through watching, nonreporting, or even encouraging the aggression. And, sanctions for not conforming or aiding such norms keep students from doing so.

Norms regulating peer and adult responses to reporting of an aggressive act were generated from two scales, which asked students to identify their perception of school-adult and peer responses to whistle blowers. Overall, the majority of students perceived positive responses from adults (65 percent) but not from peers (28 percent). More specifically, students viewed adults as supportive of reporting and likely to help. In contrast, peers were seen as not caring or likely to show negative responses to a reporter.

A significant difference was found between the treatment and control groups regarding adult norms, but not peer norms. That is, adolescents who participated in the GRAV curriculum were more likely to view adult responses favorably compared to the control group. This was not the case, however, for peer norms. Overall, student views of peer norms were less favorable to bystander reporting and appeared to be less malleable to the intervention. These qualities may point to how peer and adult norms are socially constructed and maintained. Since peer norms are constructed by the students themselves they may be viewed as in-group norms. If adult expectations are viewed as conflicting or separate from student norms, students would likely view them as out-group norms (Brown et al., 1994). In-group norms are more resistant to change, especially if the impetus for change is coming from the outside (adults) in the form of an intervention (Berndt, 1981; Brown et al., 1992). This issue is common to pull-out programs that attempt to change individual behaviors but fail to impact sustained change when the person reenters their peer group system and peer-group norms are reactivated (Dishion, Patterson, Stoolmiller, & Skinner, 1991). Even when these programs have demonstrated short-term success, follow-up assessments have failed to show sustained impact. The fade out has been attributed to individual relapse in the face of conventional norms, which are slower to change. In contrast, changing perceptions of adult norms may be more amenable to prevention programs since the school adults can teach what they expect of students. Yet, in the end, peer norms are likely to supercede adult norms if they conflict since students status among their peers is less tied to adult standards for interpersonal conduct.

Norms that support inaction among bystanders are also likely to stem from cultural mores. School norms reflect Western Cultural norms such as rugged individualism and causal attribution, which are institutionalized, covert, and stubborn to change. For example, common notions such as "mind your own business" and "you generally get what you deserve" pervade much of our society and inhibit people from helping others and actually encourage denial of victimization or a tendency to "blame the victim." Needless to say, changing these norms is likely to be a slow and difficult process.

Students who participated in the GRAV prevention program were far less likely (up to 50 percent) to respond to violence with violence. Indeed, the treatment group was significantly more likely to respond verbally rather than physically indicating that participation in the GRAV curriculum increased students' sense of efficacy to respond to violence in a prosocial manner. The results indicate that those who participated in violence prevention were more likely to choose prosocial or neutral reactions to violence while those who did not participate were far more likely to choose aggressive reactions. Together, the behavioral intent data indicates that the violence prevention program did in fact influence student's sense of efficacy or perceived ability to intervene or stop violence against self and others.

Real or Perceived Norms

At the conceptual level, it is important to note that student perceptions and not behaviors were assessed. Consequently, it is unclear whether student beliefs about how peers and adults would respond are accurate. All too often, perceptions are inaccurate and incorrect. Widespread misperceptions of norms can contribute to an increase in negative behavior. If people think harmful behavior is typical, they are more likely to engage in that type of behavior. If unhealthy behavior is perceived to be the standard in a social group, the social urge to conform will negatively affect overall behavior of group members. Perceptions of norms can be more powerful influences on behavior than actual norms (Slaby et al., 1994). According to social norms theory, correcting misperceptions fosters positive changes in attitudes and behavior. The goal is to change the perceptions that a group has about itself, thereby positively influencing individual behavior. Typically, the focus of prevention has been on problems and extreme behaviors (e.g., binge drinking, acquaintance rape).

The traditional social norms approach, however, may not be effective if the perceived norms are accurate. The norms targeted in this study do not identify extreme behaviors, but rather behaviors that are more likely to be true and accurate conventional norms, which are practiced by the majority of students. Unfortunately, due to social desirability factors, accurately measuring adult and peer behaviors (in response to whistleblowers) is not feasible using traditional self-report methods. Future studies that employ observation methods may be able to tease apart real and perceived norms. Nonetheless, whether the norms indexed in the current study are actual or perceived, they are real in their consequences.

Methodological Limitations

Although the study used a control group design, a few threats to internal validity remain. Of primary concern is the lack of pretest information, which presents a possible confound since it is impossible to know whether pretreatment differences existed between the treatment and control group. Nonetheless, students in each group did not differ in their reports of witnessing physical and relational aggression. These findings indicate that these groups are exposed to the same peer-group norms. In addition to pretest information, rigorous experimental designs should include follow-up posttests to examine the longevity of effects, especially in light of previous research that has shown consistent fade-out of short-term gains. The current sample was recruited from a rural area of the Midwest and, as such, poses strong limitations for extending the findings to more diverse student populations, both in geographic and cultural terms. An important next step is conducting the same study in urban settings with a culturally diverse sample.

Conclusion

This study offers new insight into the importance of a population-directed intervention for school-based violence prevention. In this sample, a majority of the students indicated that they witnessed relational and physical violence, thus suggesting that the impact of violence reaches far beyond the at-risk groups typically targeted in adolescent violence prevention programs. The findings offer some support for the unique focus of the GRAV program to successfully effect environmental or contextual change by targeting these bystanders of violence. That is, adolescents who participated in the GRAV program did indeed change their perceptions of the bystander role and subsequent actions. Furthermore, adolescents in the treatment group were more confident in adult responses and in their own ability to respond prosocially to violence. On the other hand, peer norms appeared more resistant to change. Overall, the majority of students viewed peers as hostile or unsupportive of the whistle blower. These perceptions of peer sanctions did not appear to be significantly impacted by participating in the intervention. It is possible that the attempt to replace conventional norms with prosocial norms is premature. The first step may be a comprehensive deconstruction of conventional norms such as social desirability, blaming the victim, rugged individualism, and casual attribution. These more subtle, yet widely held, norms may serve as a strong undercurrent that erodes intervention efforts to simply displace peer norms with adult-approved norms.

REFERENCES

Bjorkqvist, K, Lagerspetz, M. J., & Kaukiainen, A. (1992). Do girls manipulate and boys fight? Developmental trends in regard to direct and indirect aggression. *Aggressive Behavior, 18,* 117-127.

Berndt, T. (1979). Developmental changes in conformity to peers and parents. *Developmental Psychology, 15,* 608-616.

Berndt, T. (1981). Relations between social cognition, nonsocial cognition, and social behavior: The case of friendship. In J. Flavell & L. Ross (Eds.), *Social cognitive development: Frontiers and possible futures.* Cambridge, UK: Cambridge University Press.

Brown, B., Freeman, H., Huang, B., & Mounts, N. (1992). *"Crowd hopping": Incidence, correlates and consequences of change in crowd affiliation during adolescence.* Paper presented at the biennial meetings of the Society for Research on Adolescence, March, Washington.

Brown, B. B., Mory, M., & Kinney, D. (1994). Casting crowds in a relational perspective: Caricature, channel, and context. In R. Montemayor, G. Adams, & T. Gullotaa (Eds.), *Advances in adolescent development, Vol. 5: Personal relationships during adolescence.* Newbury Park, CA: Sage.

Dishion, T. J., Patterson, G. R., & Griesler, P. C. (1994). Peer adaptation in the development of antisocial behavior: A confluence model. In L. R. Huesmann (Ed.), *Aggressive behavior: Current perspectives* (pp. 61-95). New York: Plenum.

Dishion, T., Patterson, G., Stoolmiller, M., & Skinner, M. (1991). Family, school, and behavioral antecedents to early adolescent involvement with antisocial peers. *Developmental Psychology, 27,* 172-180.

Elliot, D. S., & Menard, S. (1996). Delinquent friends and delinquent behavior: Temporal and developmental patterns. In J. D. Hawkins (Ed.), *Current theories of crime and deviance* (pp. 28-67). Newbury, CA: Sage Publications.

Get Real About Violence (GRAV) (1997). Comprehensive Health Education Foundation, Seattle, Washington.

Gottfredson, D. C., Wilson, D. B., & Najaka, S. S. (in press). School-based crime prevention. In D. P. Farrington, L. W. Sherman, & B. Welsh (Eds.), *Evidence-based crime prevention*. London, UK: Harwood Academic Publishers.

Guerra, N., Tolan, P. H., & Hammond, W. R. (1994). Prevention and treatment of adolescent violence. In L. D. Eron, J. H. Gentry, & P. Schlegel (Eds.). *Reasons to hope: A psycholosocial perspective on violence & youth* (pp. 383-404). Washington, DC: American Psychological Association.

Loeber, R., & Hay, D. F. (1997). Key issues in the development of aggression and violence from childhood to early adulthood. *Annual Review of Psychology, 48,* 371-410.

Loeber R., & Stouthamer-Loeber, M. (1998). Development of juvenile aggression and violence: Some common misconceptions and controversies. *American Psychologist, 53,* 242-259.

Oliver, R., Hoover, J. H., & Hazler, R. (1994). The perceived roles of bullying in small-town midwestern schools. *Journal of Counseling and Development, 72*(4), 416-420.

Olweus, D. (1978). *Aggression in the schools.* New York: Wiley.

Pepler, D. J., & Slaby, R. G. (1994). Theoretical and developmental perspectives on youth and violence. In L. D. Eron, J. H. Gentry, & P. Schlegel (Eds.), *Reasons to hope: A psychosocial perspective on violence & youth* (pp. 27-58). Washington, DC: American Psychological Association.

Slaby, R. G., & Guerra, N. G. (1988). Cognitive mediators of aggression in adolescent offenders: I. Assessment. *Developmental Psychology, 24,* 580-588.

Slaby, R. G., Wilson-Brewer, R., & Dash, K. (1994). *Aggressors, victims, and Bystanders: Thinking and acting to prevent violence.* Newton, MA: Education Development Center, Inc.

Stanger, C., Achenbach, T., & Berhulst, F. (1997). Accelerated longitudinal comparisons of aggressive versus delinquent syndromes. *Development and Psychopathology, 9,* 43-58.

U. S. Department of Health and Human Services. (2001). *Youth Violence: A Report of the Surgeon General—Executive Summary.* Rockville, MD: U.S. Department of Health and Human Services, Centers for Disease Control and Prevention, National Center for Injury Prevention and Control; Substance Abuse and Mental Health Services Administration, Center for Mental Health Service; and National Institutes of Health, National Institute of Mental Health.

Chapter 11

Viennese Social Competence (ViSC) Training for Students: Program and Evaluation

Moira Atria
Christiane Spiel

This chapter describes a school-based intervention program designed to tackle bullying in school classes. In contrast to previous prevention programs, Viennese Social Competence (ViSC) training provides students with systematic theoretically based guidance in becoming responsible and competent actors in conflict situations. ViSC training has been especially designed for disadvantaged adolescents aged fifteen to nineteen who are considered at risk for eventual problems. This population has rarely been the target group of prevention programs. Until now in Austria, prevention programs have mostly been conducted in privileged schools like Gymnasiums (college prep) and not in schools with predominantly disadvantaged students (see also Atria & Spiel, 2003). Furthermore, these programs mostly target students below fifteen years of age. Thus a program like ViSC training might well be the last opportunity for youths to work on their social behavior, for example, to learn how to adequately deal with conflicts, before they have to manage their lives as adults in work or family.

This chapter gives an overview of the program's theoretical basis and its methods; some lesson examples are described for illustration. In addition, it sketches the evaluation design and presents some results of the program's first application in a pilot project. The program's conceptualization is based on social information-processing theory (e.g., Crick & Dodge, 1994) and

Bullying, Victimization, and Peer Harassment
© 2007 by The Haworth Press, Inc. All rights reserved.
doi:10.1300/5808_11

on empirical research into the nature of bullying as a group process (e.g., Salmivalli, Lagerspetz, Björkqvist, Österman, & Kaukiainen, 1996).

SCHOOL-BASED VIOLENCE PREVENTION

Many efforts to intervene against and prevent different forms of aggression have been undertaken within the past decade and a half (e.g., Cavell & Hughes, 2000; Naylor & Cowie, 1999; Olweus, 1994; Pepler & Rubin, 1991; Teglasi & Rothman, 2001). On a broad conceptual level, one can differentiate between two types of intervention: person-centered and environment-centered ("individual" versus "ecological") interventions. Person-centered programs try to reach the target person(s) directly without expecting any major environmental change. Treatment techniques drawn from the clinical and counseling literature, such as social learning and direct instructional approaches, are often used in this kind of program (e.g. Petermann, Jugert, Tänzer, & Verbeek, 1997). Environment-centered interventions try to change individuals by modifying their environment. Normally, these programs are integrated into a "whole school policy," or at least a "class policy." The main goal of these interventions is to establish an environment that supports healthy development. Obviously, a categorization using the terms "individual" and "ecological" intervention must be interpreted as the two ends of a continuum; many programs offer a combination of the two approaches while focusing on one or the other. Nevertheless, an awareness of different approaches can be useful in understanding a program's nature. Durlak and Wells (1997) stress an additional dimension characterizing a program's approach: the way populations are selected for intervention. Here they differentiate between three strategies: (1) a universal strategy, which includes all members of an available population (e.g., Olweus, 1994); (2) a strategy that includes groups considered to be at risk of developing problems, but who are not yet dysfunctional (e.g., Hudley & Graham, 1993); (3) a strategy that selects target groups of persons who are about to experience potentially stressful life events or transitions (e.g., Pepler, King, & Byrd, 1991).

Most programs, especially those in Europe, follow a universal strategy; programs targeting high-risk youths rarely exist (Smith, 2003). However, another aspect we found to be lacking in existing programs was the systematic guidance of students toward becoming responsible and competent actors in real problem situations. ViSC training has been developed to overcome this deficiency.

BULLYING AS A GROUP PROCESS

Bullying means aggression between peers in which there is an imbalance of power and that is repeated over time (Olweus, 1991). Originally, the bullying process was explained as an aggressive interaction between one "bully" (or more "bullies") and one "victim." There have been several efforts to establish a typology characterizing the "typical bully" and the "typical victim," some of them including a description of the child who is both, namely the "bully/victim." However, focusing on the main types "bully" and "victim" or "bully/victim" is clearly deficient on account of moderating contextual variables: within the bullying process, the group context in which students reinforce each other is very important (Salmivalli, Huttunen, & Lagerspetz, 1997; Salmivalli et al., 1996). Thus, bullying has collective aspects and is based on social relationships within the group (Lagerspetz, Björkqvist, Berts, & King, 1982). Olweus already listed the following group mechanisms that are at work in bullying situations: (1) "social contagion"; (2) "weakening of the control of or inhibitions against aggressive tendencies"; (3) "diffusion of responsibility"; and (4) "gradual cognitive changes in the perceptions of bullying and of the victim" (Olweus, 1994, p. 1182). A more systematic analysis of the group aspects of bullying has been initiated by Salmivalli and colleagues (1996). They showed that even those students who seem to be uninvolved play certain roles during the bullying process. In their survey, 87 percent of the students were assigned such a "participant role." Besides the directly involved "bullies" and "victims," a number of children acted as "reinforcers," who enjoyed watching the bullying situation, or as "defenders," who tried to support the "victim."[1] In terms of intervention, Salmivalli (1999) proposed utilizing this "peer group power" positively by systematically supporting the "natural" group that had already been conducting "anti-bullying policy" in their class, namely the "defenders."

Schwartz and colleagues (1993) have also shown how the peer group environment acts to foster chronic victimization by providing social reinforcement for aggressive acts directed toward victims. It is important to mention that most students tend to underestimate their aggressive behavior, even though the most aggressive children do seem to realize their central role within the process (Salmivalli et al., 1996).

In summary, bullying can be interpreted as a social interaction process that takes place in relatively permanent social groups (school classes) where most of the students are involved through playing different roles. What are the implications that can be drawn from these findings for the conceptualization of an intervention program?

1. When dealing with bullying, it is extremely important not to focus only on those students obviously involved in aggressive acts. Understanding bullying as a group process means that its prevention needs to take a whole-group approach (school and classroom).
2. Trainers have to be aware of the group processes activated during aggression: obviously, there are some children who enjoy the bullying process and others who would like to stop it.
3. Necessarily, intervention should focus on students' interactions and on the ongoing group mechanisms forming the basis for social responsibility within the group.

SOCIAL INFORMATION-PROCESSING THEORY

Models of social information have played an important role in developing an understanding between cognition and social behavior. These theories postulate that behavioral responses to complex stimuli occur as a function of a sequence of cognitive processes. Different models describing the linkage between cognitive processes and social behavior have been proposed (e.g., Dodge, 1986; Huesmann, 1988; McFall, 1982). All of these models understand competent performance in specific social situations as a function of several skillful steps in processing social cues, including encoding and interpretation of cues, response decision, and response enacting. Crick and Dodge (1994) reformulated former social information-processing (SIP) models by proposing a "theory of 'on-line' brain performance" (p. 77). They described SIP as a cyclic mental process in which five cognitive steps can be differentiated: (1) encoding of social cues; (2) interpretation of social information; (3) clarification of goals; (4) response access or construction; (5) response evaluation and decision making; and as a potential sixth step, behavioral enactment. These cognitive steps are always connected to a "database" of social knowledge, which is formed by the individual's social experiences and linked to memory, acquired rules, social schemas, and social knowledge (Crick & Dodge, 1994, p. 77). Thus, social behavior is interpreted as the cumulative product of these different mental operations activated during information processing. Deficits at one step could adversely affect later information-processing steps.

So far, the SIP model has served as a basis for conceptualizing various intervention programs (e.g., Pepler & Rubin, 1991), some of them focusing on certain steps of social information processing (e.g., Hudley & Graham, 1993). Social information-processing theory has been used as the theoretical basis for ViSC training because it provides relevant information at a variety of levels. It has indicated which processing steps have to be trained, suggesting a certain time structure for the intervention process. Initial exercises focusing on the encoding and interpretation of social situations are followed by response decision examples. The process ends with tasks related to students' enactment.

ViSC TRAINING

The integration of the empirical results of research concerning bullying as a group process and social information-processing theory yields the program's two main principles.

Participation

As shown earlier, bullying is a group process, and even those who seem to be uninvolved play certain roles. To put it succinctly: whoever is present when an aggressive action occurs is at the same time involved in it. He or she is a participant and not only a bystander. In terms of training, this principle means that an intervention program should include the whole group— here the school class—and should emphasize the social processes that occur (manifestly or latently) within the group. In addition to bullying, other negative social acts might be social exclusion, discrimination, peer pressure etc. The main idea is that adolescents who are aware of their involvement tend to take more responsibility for what is happening around them, starting to participate more consciously and actively.

Enrichment of the Behavioral Repertoire

Social information-processing theory interprets social behavior as the cumulative product of the different mental operations activated during social exchanges, with deficits at one step potentially yielding inappropriate reactions.

Although, it can be assumed that every single step plays an important role in forming social behavior, our program particularly focuses on step four—response access and construction—because of aggressive children's deficient ability to access responses that are nonaggressive (Crick & Dodge, 1994) and victims' tendency to react submissively (Schwartz et al., 1993). Response access and construction can be trained very successfully in adolescent groups, for example, by presenting a stimulus situation and asking them to produce different possible responses. While working at this processing stage it is possible to look forward, evaluating the suggested alternatives, and to look back, trying to reinterpret the stimulus situation because a better response was found. Due to the cyclic nature of information processing and the biased perception style of aggressive youths (e.g., hostile attribution), it might sometimes be more successful to start at a subsequent stage and "work back," reinterpreting the stimulus situation. In our opinion, an enrichment of the behavioral repertoire can help reduce aggression by showing that there are different ways of coping with one and the same social situation.

PROGRAM STRUCTURE
AND CURRICULUM COMPONENTS

Based on these principles, ViSC training was developed at the University of Vienna as a selective intervention program, which means that it was specially designed for adolescents "considered at risk for eventual problems, but who are not yet dysfunctional" (Durlak & Wells, 1997, p. 118). Its target group consists of school classes of adolescents from fifteen to nineteen years. The training combines an individual with an ecological approach by both training students' skills and working on ongoing group mechanisms.

ViSC training consists of thirteen lessons divided into three phases: (1) Impulses and Group Dynamics; (2) Reflection; (3) Action. The trainer should not be familiar with the training group before the training; that is, the training should be conducted by someone other than the classroom teacher. In a three-day workshop, trainers are familiarized with the ViSC program concept.[2] Ideally they should have experience working with young people in groups, for example, as a psychologist or teacher from another school. To maintain the necessary objectivity, it is essential to avoid any information about individual students being given to the trainer by teachers. The only necessary pre-information is provided by standardized diagnostic measurements. It is recommended that the training be conducted during regular class time and that the classroom teacher(s) be invited to assist in the ViSC lessons. The underlying idea for this classroom setting is to guarantee that the program will be taken seriously and provide appreciable relief to students and their teachers. In addition, participating teachers could also profit from the program without having to undergo special training.

Although the training lessons have to be well prepared and structured, the trainer's flexibility in modifying individual lessons is extremely important. During the first phase, the trainer should lead the group very actively, while in the second and particularly in the third phase he or she should yield control in favor of the group's increasing power and responsibility. Ideally, she or he should become more and more "unnecessary" during the training.

Phase 1: Impulses and Group Dynamics (What is Going on in Our Group? Do We Have Any Alternatives When Reacting to Critical Situations?)

The first part of the program consists of six lessons of one and a half hours each. Its principal aim is to strengthen the youths' competence in critical situations by looking at social situations from different perspectives and trying to find different ways of handling the situations. In addition, sensibility to ongoing group processes is an important intervention goal within this phase.

In the first lesson, the trainer introduces him- or herself and describes the program's goal (bullying prevention by focusing on social competence) and structure (three phases and their main issues). After a clarification of any questions regarding the trainer's person or the program, the students are asked whether they want to participate in the training. After the group's affirmation,[3] the main training rules are established in a group process and then visualized (e.g., "Each of us will speak about his or her own experience"; "Each of us will really try to listen to the others"; "We will not interrupt each other"). The students must accept these rules before the training can be started.

During the next five lessons, the training group works on practical exercises focusing on the group's norms and rules (group context) as well as on social information processing. The lessons consist of short presentations of the lesson's target aspects and psychological background,[4] group discussions, and work on examples and in real situations (role-plays). Concrete examples of a typical lesson and of work on "real situations" are given in the Appendix.

Phase 2: Reflection (What Has Been Learned?)

The one *Reflection* lesson (one and a half hours) gives the students and trainer an opportunity to reflect on what has been learned in the program's first part. When answering the question "How have you profited from the program?" each student must articulate and document her or his experiences (in written form). To gain deeper insight into the training processes, participants are also asked to write down a concrete example ("Which was the most important issue for you? Give a concrete example. Why was it so important?"). These answers include relevant information for further training implementation. After this individual work, all group participants (students, trainer, and teachers, if present) discuss how the group profited from the program and write this information on a placard.

Phase 3: Action (What Will the Group Do with What Has Been Learned?)

In the last phase, consisting of six one-and-a-half-hour lessons, the pupils and the trainer define together how they want to benefit from the remaining lessons. The pupils express goals and generate ideas to realize these aims. The trainer collects these ideas and they are evaluated together according to the program's global goal (social competence) and two main principles: *participation* and *behavioral enrichment*. Under the trainer's supervision, the group plans the last five lessons and executes the plans it has made. All planned activities must be realistic (resources) and aimed at helping the whole group. At this stage it is important for the trainer to turn over much of her or his responsibility to the group, yielding her or his dominant position and becoming the group's attendant/companion. In some cases the trainer may have to support the group in finding goals and appropriate activities, but the group must plan its activities by itself. Some groups plan a different activity for each remaining lesson; other groups plan projects of several units' duration. In any case, the last lesson should be reserved for parting from the trainer and developing future perspectives.

If a group is—in spite of strategies implemented by the trainer to support the group's goal-setting efforts—not able to specify realistic and prosocial activities, the trainer should first clarify the situation and stress its significance. Then she or he gives the pupils a further opportunity, for example, completing a task for the next unit ("How do you want to profit from the remaining lessons? Make a concrete and realistic suggestion that is aimed at helping our group"). In the case that the group is not able to fulfill this request, the trainer should stop the training.

EVALUATION OF ViSC TRAINING

The evaluation of the ViSC training program is part of an extended evaluation project. Using a cohort-sequence design, data was collected on various levels using different methods: (1) Self-rating questionnaires for students to investigate participants' perceived peer aggression and their perceived democracy level (individual level). (2) Problem-solving skills (individual level)—the students received a short written scenario (vignette) of a critical situation and were asked to write down how they would act in this situation. (3) Teacher ratings (class level)—teachers assessed the class's attitude toward work and the class's aggressive behavior. (4) Systematic observation (videotaped, class level)—before and after the training, students' behavior during subject lessons was filmed. (5) Program documentation— during ViSC training each lesson was systematically documented by the trainer, who described the lesson's goals, preparation, and activities as well as students' behavior during the lesson.

In this chapter, preliminary results of the evaluation of the ViSC training program based on the analyses of the questionnaire data covering students' perception of democracy and aggression (including bullying) are presented. Additionally, we present some examples from the program documentation to provide a deeper insight in the program's nature. The analysis of the entire evaluation design is part of an ongoing study. Considering ViSC training's goals and methods, we expected the following:

1. Compared to nontreatment groups, the trained students should have a higher perception of participation possibilities in school (democracy variables).
2. Compared to nontreatment groups, the trained students should show lower bullying and victimization rates (aggression variables).

Method

Two classes at a Viennese vocational school[5] (ninth and tenth grade) participated in ViSC training, while two other classes at the same school served as a control group. The four classes were randomly assigned either to the training or to the control group. Pretraining data collection took place in June 2000, before summer vacation, and in October 2000, at the beginning of the new school year. The intervention ran from November 2000 to June 2001. The two posttraining measurements were conducted in June 2001 and October 2001. Data collection was done by graduate students who did not know which classes were participating in the intervention and which were not (i.e., a blind study).

Instruments

As mentioned earlier, one of the program's goals was to enrich the adolescents' behavioral repertoire. Students' perceived *democracy* level within the school class was used as an outcome variable. Democracy was measured using a "Democracy Questionnaire" based on a version from Eder

(1998) consisting of the following subscales: (1) *equality* (8 items, $\alpha = .82$); (2) *information* (7 items, $\alpha = .76$); (3) *participation* (7 items, $\alpha = .72$); and (4) *diversity of opinions* (4 items, $\alpha = .79$). Here, students were asked to assess themselves on a 4-point Likert scale ranging from 1 (no agreement) to 4 (full agreement).

The students' perceived *aggression* was investigated using a modified version of Olweus's *Bully/Victim Questionnaire* (Olweus, 1989). The questionnaire includes four subscales: (1) *bullying against peers* (8 items, $\alpha = .80$); (2) *victimization by peers* (8 items, $\alpha = .85$); (3) *aggression against teachers* (4 items, $\alpha = .84$); and (4) *victimization by teachers* (3 items, $\alpha = .86$).

Sample Description

In total, 112 students (57 boys and 55 girls) participated in the evaluation study; 55 boys and girls participated in ViSC training; 57 belonged to the control group. The students' ages ranged between 15 and 21 years (median 17 years). Forty-seven percent spoke a language other than German at home—34 percent of the students spoke a former Yugoslavian language (e.g., Croatian or Serbian); 16 percent spoke Turkish, and 9 percent spoke another language. When asked about their parents' education, 20 percent of the students described their fathers as having had no secondary school education. Compared to Austrian education averages, these numbers indicate an unusually low level of parental education. Most of the students' mothers (67 percent) were described as "housewife."

RESULTS OF THE EVALUATION

For data analyses, MANOVAs were applied with group membership (training versus control) as the independent variable. Because of the sample sizes pre- and posttraining data were analyzed separately.

Pretraining Analyses

We compared the ViSC training group and the control group in students' sex, age, language, familial background (father's and mother's professional status and education), and in *bullying against peers* and *victimization by peers*. The other variables were only collected after the training using a MANOVA procedure at a one-tailed 5 percent α-level. Pretraining analyses at both time points (June 2000 and October 2000) did not show differences between groups in any of the variables investigated.

Posttraining Analyses

After the training we compared the two groups (ViSC training group and control group) in *democracy* (4 scales, see earlier) in June 2001 (for results see Table 11.1) and October 2001 (see Table 11.2) and in *aggression* (4 scales, see earlier) in June 2001 (see Table 11.3) and in October 2001 (see Table 11.4) to check for short-term training effects (June 2001) and medium-term effects (October 2001). Again MANOVA procedures at a one-tailed 5 percent α-level were applied.

As expected, results showed more *democracy* and less *aggression* in the training group than in the control group. However, not all differences be-

TABLE 11.1. Comparison between groups (MANOVA): *democracy*, June 2001.

Scale	Group	M	SD
Equality	Control	2.3739	.7015
	Training	2.7781	.5603
Information	Control	2.5789	.7437
	Training	2.9714	.4798
Participation	Control	2.4784	.5570
	Training	2.8952	.5661
Diversity	Control	2.5469	.8405
	Training	3.0286	.6580

Note. Multivariate tests—Wilks-Lambda = .866; F = 2. 394; df = 4 (62); p = .03.

TABLE 11.2. Comparison between groups (MANOVA): *democracy*, October 2001.

Scale	Group	M	SD
Equality	Control	2.5125	.7234
	Training	2.5283	.5453
Information	Control	2.5506	.7268
	Training	2.6373	.6217
Participation	Control	2.4851	.6529
	Training	2.5897	.5841
Diversity	Control	2.5469	.8278
	Training	2.8528	.5891

Note. Multivariate tests—Wilks-Lambda = .912; F = 1. 768; df = 4 (73); p = .07 (one-tailed).

TABLE 11.3. Comparison between groups (MANOVA): *aggression,* June 2001.

Scale	Group	M	SD
Victim. (peer)	Control	1.4800	.7228
	Training	1.4095	.6226
Bullying (peer)	Control	1.7396	.9282
	Training	1.4317	.5554
Victim. (teach)	Control	2.3958	1.4797
	Training	1.7810	.9833
Aggress. (teach)	Control	2.1328	1.2131
	Training	1.7000	.7736

Note. Multivariate tests—Wilks-Lambda = .077; F = 1.295; df = 4 (62); p = 0.14 (one-tailed).

TABLE 11.4. Comparison between groups (MANOVA): *aggression,* October 2001.

Scale	Group	M	SD
Victim. (peer)	Control	1.3299	.4518
	Training	1.2259	.2568
Bullying (peer)	Control	1.5182	.4968
	Training	1.4139	.4979
Victim. (teach)	Control	1.9792	.9612
	Training	1.6444	.6777
Aggress. (teach)	Control	2.0278	1.1302
	Training	1.6250	.6357

Note. Multivariate tests—Wilks-Lambda = .055; F = 1.067; df = 4 (73); p = .19 (one-tailed).

tween the groups were statistically significant: short-term training effects were observed in the *democracy* variables (see Table 11.1), in the *aggression* variables only a trend could be detected (see Table 11.3). Medium-term analysis showed a positive trend in both in the *democracy* variables (see Table 11.2) and in the *aggression* variables (see Table 11.4).[6]

Program Documentation

As mentioned earlier, each training lesson was documented by the trainer before and after implementation. This documentation was intended to monitor and guarantee implementation quality and also to gather detailed information that could serve as a basis for the program handbook, which is still in preparation.

Phase 1 (Impulses and Group Dynamics)

The training took place during the regular lesson time, so it was very easy to convince students to participate. In the first lesson, students were simply curious, but some of them were skeptical about the training (Is the trainer an enemy or maybe a friend?). In the next two lessons, students seemed to be testing the trainer's resilience, for example, by telling her very dramatic stories or by trying to provoke her. When the trainer "survived" all these acts, students began to cooperate very well and became more involved. After the fourth lesson, students began to bring their own current problems into the training and asked the trainer to work on these "real examples" (one example is presented in the Appendix).

Phase 2 (Reflection)

Here students had to reflect on how they had profited from the training. Most of the students' reports described a change of perspective in the sense of an increased ability to relativize their own interests and see situations through other people's eyes (e.g., "I learned in the training that you should also respect the teachers. For example, when you have a bad mark in math, you shouldn't just rant on about the teachers.").

Phase 3 (Action)

In this phase, students were to find their own activities. For example, they decided that they would like to know more about "youth laws" (juvenile law). During the training lessons they discussed how to get the information they were interested in. Some students used the Internet and contacted youth counseling agencies. They presented their results to the whole class and the laws were discussed (e.g., What do they mean?).

However, there was one severe problem that is typical for the school type where the training took place: a very high truancy rate. With time, as the students began to enjoy the program, some of them even participated in the training while skipping the regular lessons before and afterward. (Obviously, the program did not last long enough to motivate the students to generalize their "new behavior.")

DISCUSSION

ViSC training has been designed to prevent bullying in school classes. It differs from previous prevention programs in three aspects: First, the target group is adolescents between fifteen and nineteen years of age who are at risk of exhibiting bullying behavior. This group has been rather seldom targeted in school-based prevention programs. Second, the training tries to consistently combine an individual-centered approach with an ecological one. It is, therefore, theoretically based on two research traditions: (1) it uses the SIP model as an intervention pattern (individual approach), stressing the importance of mental processes related to the search for alternative responses during social exchange, and (2) it focuses on the school class as the crucial social unit (ecological approach) and not merely on aggressive and victimized youths. In ViSC training, students learn to cope better with conflicts and also to work on group processes and find new opportunities for participation in school (class) life. Third, ViSC training gives students the opportunity to work on real difficulties or problems and incites them to take responsibility for what is happening around them. As a consequence ViSC training provides students with systematic theoretically based guidance toward becoming responsible and competent actors in real situations.

The program's three phases allowed a successive development from appreciating psychosocial impulses to working on problem solving and—as the final goal—helping adolescents achieve social competence in their own actions. Generally, the training was aimed at devising a program with a strong structure as well as a maximum of flexibility. The program structure worked toward issues of increasing psychosocial complexity, turning over more responsibility to the adolescent group in its last phase.

In its initial application, the program was conducted by a trainer (psychologist) during regular lesson time, while teachers assisted in the program without undergoing special training. The underlying idea for using this classroom setting was to guarantee that the program would be taken seriously and provide appreciable relief to students and their teachers. Additionally, we hoped that the participating teachers would themselves also profit from the training.

To establish whether the goals of ViSC training had been attained, an extended evaluation project was conducted. Here, preliminary results of the evaluation focusing on democracy and aggressive behavior were presented. Additionally, insight into the program's documentation was provided. Short-term analysis showed training effects in the *democracy* variables and a trend in the *aggression* variables. Medium-term analysis (four months after training) could detect a tendency both in the *democracy* variables and the *aggression* variables. However, compared to the relatively modest training effects that have been demonstrated in the literature (Beelmann, Pfingsten, & Lösel, 1994; Durlak & Wells, 1997; Henrich, Brown, & Aber, 1999), we interpret the observed results as encouraging findings. The analysis of the overall evaluation project mentioned briefly here (scenarios, teachers' perceptions, observational data) is still going on. The program documentation gave insights into ViSC training's value implementation and its merits and limitations. It also provided some clues on how to implement the training in further applications.

With regard to the training's limitations, we conclude that a longer program duration might increase the sustainability of training effects. Therefore, we suggest starting ViSC training in ninth grade with the three-phase program described here and then offering brief "refreshers" in tenth and eleventh grade consisting of six units each year. Recently, the training has been applied at a school in Trier, Germany, showing positive training effects (Gollwitzer & Banse, 2005).

NOTES

1. In total, they enumerated seven types with the following prevalence rates: 11.7 percent "victims"; 8.2 percent "bullies"; 19.5 percent "reinforcers"; 6.8 percent "assistants"; 17.3 percent "defenders"; 23.7 percent "outsiders"; 12.7 percent "no role."

2. A training handbook is not yet available, but training seminars and supervision meetings have been held, where interested persons can be introduced to the training concept.

3. In the pilot study the training was implemented during lesson time; if students had not agreed, they would have been obliged to attend their subject lessons during the time reserved for the training lessons.

4. The presentation of psychological knowledge has to be adapted for specific age and intellectual capacity.

5. Due to certain factors such as the ethnically mixed population, the students' low academic level, and their families' low socioeconomic status, this school can be termed a high-risk school type.

6. The following information could be useful for comparison with other studies in which univariate analyses were applied. In the univariate comparisons used to check for short-term training effects, three variables showed lower scores in the training group than in the control group: *bullying against peers, victimization by teachers,* and *aggression against teachers.* No differences were observed in *victimization by peers.* Significant medium-term training effects were observed at the univariate level in *diversity of opinions* (democracy), *victimization by teachers,* and *aggression against teachers.*

APPENDIX

Example for working on a conflict situation (sample situation and idealized working structure)

How to cope with conflicts (time depends very much on the specific group, about sixty minutes)

A sample conflict situation that fits in well with the group's specific dynamics is presented. Themes could be as follows: social exclusion, group pressure, vandalism, truancy, etc. After the presentation, each student works quietly on the following questions (about five to ten minutes):

- How do you interpret this situation? *(Encoding and interpretation of cues)*
- How would you react in such a situation? *(Response access or construction)*
- What would probably happen if you reacted in this way? *(Response evaluation)*

Depending on the group's capacity, small groups of two to four students or the whole class discuss their "virtual" reactions and possible alternatives:

- Which reactions did you find?
- Do you see any alternative way of coping with this situation—this could also be a funny or surprising response? *(alternative response access or construction of alternatives)*

The whole class (or small groups) decides on one or more promising response alternative(s) *(decision making),* which is(are) enacted in a brief role-play.

Afterward, these alternatives are evaluated by the whole group. At the end of such a lesson it should be obvious that:

- There are different perceptions and interpretations of the same social situation.
- There are several different response alternatives, but some are better than others.
- Aggression and violence are poor strategies for coping with conflicts.

Ad Program Documentation (Phase 1)

Example—The Torn-Up Cards

When the trainer came into the class and as usual presented the lesson's specific goal (how to cope with conflicts), one boy (M.) told the trainer that he wanted to discuss what had just happened to him: M. liked to play cards during breaks, and that day he had brought a new deck of cards to school. He had briefly left the classroom, and when he came back he saw that some students had taken his cards and ripped them up. They were laughing and throwing them around the classroom.

Looking for a solution in the training lesson. The trainer proposed that the class work on this current incident even though some students thought it was insignificant and not worth dealing with. The trainer argued that it would be a good example of how to cope with conflicts. Small groups were formed and initially given the task of discussing the incident and finding a fair solution; the trainer also mentioned the possibility of restitution. After twenty minutes, the students presented their proposals: (1) find the students responsible and make them pay for a new deck of cards; (2) money for a new deck of cards should be collected from all the students in the class; (3) M. should not make such a big deal of the incident.

The solution chosen. During the discussion process, M. experienced a sense of unease. He stated that he wanted to give up and that the cards were not really so important to him. Here the trainer intervened, saying that the issue could serve as an important example and that a fair solution must be found. The class in the end agreed to collectively pay for a new deck of cards.

REFERENCES

Atria, M., & Spiel, C. (2003). The Austrian situation: Many initiatives, few evaluations. In P. Smith (Ed.), *Violence in schools: The response in Europe* (pp. 83-99). London: RoutledgeFalmer.

Beelmann, A., Pfingsten, U., & Lösel, F. (1994). Effects of training social competence in children: A meta-analysis of recent evaluation studies. *Journal of Clinical Psychology, 23*(3), 260-271.

Cavell, T. A., & Hughes, J. N. (2000). Secondary prevention as context for assessing change processes in aggressive children. *Journal of School Psychology, 38*(1), 199-235.

Crick, N. R., & Dodge, K. A. (1994). A review and reformulation of social information processing mechanisms in children's social adjustment. *Psychological Bulletin, 115,* 74-101.

Dodge, K. A. (1986). A social information processing model of social competence in children. In M. Perlmutter (Ed.), *The Minnesota Symposium on Child Psychology* (Vol. 18, pp. 77-125). Hillsdale, NJ: Erlbaum.

Durlak, J. A., & Wells, A. M. (1997). Primary prevention mental health programs for children and adolescents: A meta-analytic review. *American Journal of Community Psychology, 25,* 115-152.

Eder, F. (1998). *Linzer Fragebogen zum Schul- und Klassenklima für die 8. und 13. Klasse (LFSK 8-13).* [Linz school and classroom social climate questionnaire]. Göttingen: Hogrefe.

Gollwitzer, M., & Banse, R. (2005). Könnten Anti-Aggressions-Trainings in der Schule wirksamer sein, wenn sie weniger standardisiert wären? [Are anti aggression training more effective if they are less standardized?]. In A. Ittel & M. von Salisch (Eds.) *Lästern, Lügen, Leiden-Aggression bei Kindern und Jugendlichen.* Stuttgart: Kohlhammer.

Henrich, C. C., Brown, J. L., & Aber, J. L. (1999). Evaluating the effectiveness of school-based violence prevention: Developmental approaches. *Social Policy Report. Society for Research in Child Development, XIII*(3), 1-17.

Hudley, C., & Graham, S. (1993). An attributional intervention to reduce peer-directed aggression among African-American boys. *Child Development, 64*(1), 124-138.

Huesmann, L. R. (1988). An information processing model for the development of aggression. *Aggressive Behavior, 14,* 13-24.

Lagerspetz, K. M. J., Björkqvist, K., Berts, M., & King, E. (1982). Group aggression among school children in three schools. *Scandinavian Journal of Psychology,* (23), 45-52.

McFall, R. M. (1982). A review and reformulation of the concept of social skills. *Behavioral Assessment, 4*(1-33).

Naylor, P., & Cowie, H. (1999). The effectiveness of peer support systems in challenging school bullying: the perspectives and experiences of teachers and students. *Journal of Adolescence, 22,* 467-479.

Olweus, D. (1989). *Bully/Victim Questionnaire.* Bergen, Norway: Author.

Olweus, D. (1991). Bully/victim problems among schoolchildren: Basic facts and effects of a school based intervention program. In D. Pepler & K. Rubin (Eds.), *The development and treatment of childhood aggression* (pp. 411-448). Hillsdale, NJ: Erlbaum.

Olweus, D. (1994). Annotation: Bullying at school. Basic facts and effects of a school based intervention program. *Journal of Child Psychology and Psychiatry, 35*(7), 1171-1190.

Pepler, D. J., King, G., & Byrd, W. (1991). A social-cognitive based social skills training program for aggressive children. In D. J. Pepler & K. H. Rubin (Eds.), *The development and treatment of childhood aggression* (pp. 361-379). Hillsdale, NJ: Erlbaum.

Pepler, D. J., & Rubin, K. H. (Eds.). (1991). *The development and treatment of childhood aggression.* Hillsdale, NJ: Erlbaum.

Petermann, F., Jugert, G., Tänzer, U., & Verbeek, D. (1997). *Sozialtraining in der Schule.* [School-based social training]. Weinheim: Beltz.

Salmivalli, C. (1999). Participant role approach to school bullying: Implications for preventions. *Journal of Adolescence, 22,* 453-459.

Salmivalli, C., Huttunen, A., & Lagerspetz, K. M. J. (1997). Peer networks and bullying in schools. *Scandinavian Journal of Psychology, 38,* 305-312.

Salmivalli, C., Lagerspetz, K., Björkqvist, K., Österman, K., & Kaukiainen, A. (1996). Bullying as a group process: Participant roles and their relations to social status within the group. *Aggressive Behavior, 22,* 1-15.

Schwartz, D., Dodge, K. A., & Coie, J. D. (1993). The emergence of chronic peer victimization in boys' play groups. *Child Development, 64,* 1755-1772.

Smith, P. K. (Ed.). (2003). *Violence in schools: The response in Europe.* London: RoutledgeFalmer.

Teglasi, H., & Rothman, L. (2001). Stories: A classroom-based program to reduce aggressive behavior. *Journal of School Psychology, 39*(1), 71-94.

Chapter 12

Using a Participatory Action Research Model to Create a School-Based Intervention Program for Relationally Aggressive Girls—The Friend to Friend Program

Stephen S. Leff
Jennifer Angelucci
Amy B. Goldstein
LeeAnn Cardaciotto
Brooke Paskewich
Michael B. Grossman

INTRODUCTION

Although the majority of researchers and educators consider elementary schools to be safe places to promote children's academic and social competence (e.g., Pellegrini & Bjorklund, 1996), it is also recognized that peer harassment frequently occurs at school (Astor, Meyer, & Pitner, 2001). Low levels of peer bullying (e.g., hitting, pushing, shoving, and threatening) occur on a daily basis in schools across the nation (e.g., Leff, Kupersmidt, Patterson, & Power, 1999; Nansel et al., 2001). Further, some students avoid high-risk school settings, such as playgrounds, lunchrooms, and hallways (Astor

This research was supported by a NIMH grant to the first author, K23-MH01728. Portions of this chapter were presented at the American Psychological Association annual meeting (2004).

et al., 2001; Leff, Power, Costigan, & Manz, 2003) because these are unstructured school contexts in which students may be harassed and victimized outside of regular adult supervision (see Leff, Costigan, & Power, 2004).

Research documents the negative correlates of peer harassment in the schools. For example, children who are frequently aggressive toward their peers experience high rates of academic difficulties (Kazdin, 1994), social-cognitive processing deficits (Crick & Dodge, 1994; Dodge, 1986), emotional arousal deficits (Lochman & Dodge, 1994), and peer relationship difficulties (Pope & Bierman, 1999). As aggressive behaviors are relatively stable over time, some aggressors continue to experience difficulties in adolescence and adulthood (Loeber, Green, Lahey, & Kalb, 2000). Children who are victims of peer harassment experience depression, anxiety, and loneliness (Kochenderfer & Ladd, 1996), peer relationship difficulties (Hodges & Perry, 1999), and school avoidant behaviors over time (Kochenderfer & Ladd, 1996).

Recent research suggests that children express their anger toward others in multiple ways. In particular, boys are likely to harm others through physically aggressive behaviors, while girls are more likely to be relationally aggressive (i.e., harm another peer's social standing by using gossip, threatening to withdraw friendship, or excluding others from activities or games (Crick & Grotpeter, 1995). Given the wealth of research on aggression, it is not surprising that many programs help aggressors and/or bullies change their behaviors. However, these programs have focused primarily upon physical aggression (Leff, Power, Manz, Costigan, & Nabors, 2001), which are behaviors related to dominance, such as hitting, pushing, and threatening others (Crick & Grotpeter, 1995).

Research also demonstrates that children attending schools in urban, under-resourced areas are at increased risk for experiencing emotional and behavioral problems (Black & Krishnakumar, 1998; Wandersman & Nation, 1998). Many of these children and families are coping with an accumulation of chronic stressors, including high levels of poverty, single-parent homes, drug use and abuse, violence, and delinquency within their immediate neighborhoods (Black & Krishnakumar; Wandersman & Nation). Thus, school-and community-based intervention programs are sorely needed in the urban areas.

The goal of this chapter is to describe the Friend to Friend (F2F) Program, a school-based intervention program for relationally aggressive girls. This program was designed by combining prior empirical research and psychological theory with feedback from urban girls and teachers. The goals are to (1) decrease girls' levels of aggression and tendencies to make a hostile attributional bias (i.e., inferring hostile intentions to a peer that interacts with them in a negative situation), and (2) increase girls' range of prosocial behaviors and social-cognitive strategies.

REVIEW OF RELEVANT LITERATURE

Relevant Theories

The F2F Program combines several different theoretical models: a social information-processing theory of aggression (Crick & Dodge, 1994; Dodge, 1986), an ecological/systems model of development (Bronfenbrenner, 1986), a partnership-based model of program development (Nastasi et al., 2000), and a self-modeling application focused upon the image of future success (Dowrick, 1999). The authors posit that aggressive children's difficulties are best conceptualized by understanding their attributional and affective deficits (i.e., social information-processing theory) as well as the way in which peers, teachers, and parents respond to and perceive their behaviors and capabilities (i.e., ecological/systems theory). Intervention efforts are directed at retraining aggressive girls in their attributions and behaviors, while attempting to change the way in which they are viewed by the peer group and adults at school and home.

Social information-processing models propose that a child's ability to process a sequence of social cues within the environment (including their affective response) impacts whether he or she will respond to a situation in an aggressive or nonaggressive manner (Crick & Dodge, 1994; Dodge, 1986). The sequential processing steps include (1) encoding environmental cues, (2) interpreting cues accurately, (3) clarifying or selecting social goals, (4) generating potential behavioral responses, (5) evaluating potential responses, and (6) enacting a behavioral response (Dodge). It is thought that emotional arousal interacts with processing at each sequential step (e.g., Crick & Dodge). For example, at step two (interpretation of cues), angry feelings may influence one to interpret a behavior as hostile or non-hostile. It is thought that distorted or deficient processing during the early sequential processing stages contributes to impaired execution at later stages, such as aggressive behavior at step six (see Vasey, Dalgleish, & Silverman, 2003, for a review).

Across many studies physically aggressive boys and girls have been found to be deficient at each social processing step. A growing body of empirical research suggests that the SIP model is also applicable to relational aggression (see Crick et al., 1999). For instance, research has demonstrated that relational aggressors display a hostile attributional bias in relationally provocative social situations (SIP step 2; Crick, 1995; Leff, Kupersmidt, & Power, 2003), evaluate aggressive solutions more positively (SIP step 4; Crick & Werner, 1998), and respond more negatively in relationally provocative social situations (SIP step 6; Xie, Swift, Cairns, & Cairns, 2002) as compared to nonrelationally aggressive children. Although more research examining relational aggressors' social-cognitive processing style at the other steps in the model and with children of more diverse ethnic backgrounds is still needed, it appears that attribution-retraining programs may have merit for relationally aggressive youth. The Friend to Friend Program was based, in part, on two such programs, the Anger Coping Program (Lochman, 1992; Lochman, Burch, Curry, & Lampron, 1984) and the Brain Power Program (Hudley & Graham, 1993). These programs teach children to recognize signs of physiological arousal, and to more accurately evaluate others' intentions in social situations.

Principles from Bronfenbrenner's ecological/systems model (1986) also greatly influenced the design of the F2F Program. This paradigm suggests that an individual's development is shaped by his or her ongoing relationships with significant others in their social ecology (Kazak & Simms, 1996). This paradigm posits that individual–environmental interactions can occur at each of four levels: (1) microsystem, (2) mesosystem, (3) exosystem, and (4) macrosystem. The F2F Program primarily targets interactions at the microsystem and mesosystem levels. At the microsystems level, the childrens development is fostered by their immediate relationships and interactions with their parents, siblings, and extended family members. At the mesosystems level, relationships between the child and teacher, child and peers, and family and school are thought to have a large impact on the child's development. The F2F Program tries to improve participants' ability to interact and negotiate conflicts more successfully with peers (mesosystem), while also employing a number of strategies to foster improved parent–child relationships (microsystem).

The final paradigm that guided the design of the F2F Program was a participatory action research (PAR) framework. This paradigm is one in which the researchers form nonhierarchical relationships with research participants and include them as partners in the project (Leff, Costigan, et al., 2004: Leff, Power, et al., 2003; Nastasi et al., 1998). This approach blends empirical research with responsiveness to feedback from key stakeholders (see Leff, Costigan et al.). The authors used a PAR framework in designing the F2F Program by combining constructs from empirical research on aggressive children (Crick, 1995; Crick & Grotpeter, 1995) with intervention techniques from empirically supported interventions for physical aggressors (Hudley & Graham, 1993; Lochman, 1992) and extensive feedback from elementary schoolgirls and teachers. This combination allows for the design of empirically supported programs that are culturally sensitive. For example, key stakeholders (children and teachers) met with researchers to review the intervention manual, homework assignments, and projected role-plays to ensure that the procedures were feasible, acceptable, and engaging to African-American girls in the urban schools.

To increase children's ability to remember social-cognitive strategies taught in the F2F Program, a variation of self-modeling was included in the intervention. Self-modeling is defined as the use of images of oneself engaged in adaptive behaviors in order to foster desired behavior change (see Dowrick, 1999). Self-modeling techniques promote participants' emerging skills by serving as a powerful visual cue and by demonstrating that they have the ability to act appropriately in potential conflict situations. In the current program, our research team was careful not to videotape large portions of multiple sessions and/or to conduct extensive video-editing, as is done in some self-modeling applications (Dowrick). Instead, we videotaped several selected segments of sessions in which children are discussing anger management strategies or are performing brief role-plays demonstrating strategies. Thus, we balance employing aspects of self-modeling with procedures that could be easily replicated by clinicians and researchers.

DESCRIPTION OF APPLICATION

Target Population

The F2F Program was designed for third-, fourth-, and fifth-grade African-American girls attending urban elementary schools. Third through fifth graders were chosen for the program because they are at an age of important social–cognitive development as they begin to use more abstract psychological constructs (Aloise, 1993; Barenboim, 1981) and because they are at an age where peer reputations take on greater importance (Leff, Kupersmidt, et al., 2003). Only girls were included because relationally aggressive behavior is the type of aggression most prevalent among girls (Crick & Grotpeter, 1995). Furthermore, few interventions have been adopted specifically to be culturally sensitive and community-responsive for African-American girls residing in urban settings (Leff, Power, & Goldstein, 2004). Finally, we chose to include both relational aggressors and positive role models in the intervention because past research has shown that including only aggressive children within group interventions may not be effective in reducing aggression (Arnold & Hughes, 1999; Dishion, McCord, & Poulin, 1999).

Designing the Program

The use of a PAR approach allowed our research team to better understand the locations in which aggressive incidents typically occurred (e.g., the playground, lunchroom, and hallways), the way in which relational aggression often led to physically aggressive incidents at school, and the types of strategies girls used to negotiate these conflicts. Further, ongoing meetings with teachers helped to ensure that the resulting manual, cartoon handouts and homework sheets, and videotape illustrations of strategies presented in sessions were concrete, relevant, and culturally sensitive.

Brief Description of Program

Even though participants' main problems are related to relational aggression as opposed to not having or being able to make friends, we chose to name our program the Friend to Friend Program. This name is appropriate because participants' aggressive or disruptive behaviors often interfere with their ability to *maintain* friendships. We also wished to emphasize that the program supports a positive, productive environment in which group leaders strive to promote children's social skills and social problem-solving skills as opposed to solely decreasing problematic levels of aggression.

The F2F intervention is a twenty-session therapy group that meets twice per week for thirty to thirty-five minutes per session. Sessions typically occur during students' lunch-recess period in order to minimize disruption to classroom teaching. Groups consist of approximately eight to ten girls, including six to eight relational aggressors and two nonaggressive, positive role models. The group is generally coled by a Friend to Friend therapist (e.g., a graduate student) and a classroom teacher or teacher's assistant who is well known by many of the participating students. The teacher partners play a crucial role in the therapy process, as they are able to use their working relationships with the students and parents to foster a strong therapeutic alliance between group participants and the coleaders. After session 10, the facilitators collaborate with group participants to conduct 8 classroom sessions. The classroom sessions mirror the content covered in the group intervention, such that all students are taught the social-cognitive strategies. The classroom sessions serve several purposes. First, they help students and teachers view group participants as being more socially competent and confident. Second, the classroom sessions help teachers better understand the social-cognitive strategies and learn how to reinforce group members' developing anger management skills. And finally, the classroom sessions allow for more children to learn the social-cognitive strategies than just the eight to ten girls participating in the actual group intervention.

The F2F Program utilizes several innovative teaching modalities that have been tailored to African-American girls. For example, cartoon hand-outs are used to illustrate the main teaching points of each session, and cartoon homework assignments help girls to think about and practice new strategies between sessions. In order to be maximally sensitive to the ethnic background of the majority of the participants, the cartoons depict African-American girls. The cartoons were created by conducting extensive focus groups and pilot testing with third and fourth grade African-American girls attending public schools throughout the city in which the intervention was constructed. This allowed our cartoonist to ensure that the children depicted were age- and gender-appropriate (hair, clothes, and facial expressions) and that the school setting characteristics (e.g., classrooms, hallways, lunch-rooms, and playgrounds) were appropriately and sensitively portrayed (see Leff, Power, Grossman, Gill, & Blom-Hoffman, 2002). While the use of cartoons depicting African-American girls may limit the generalizability of the program to other ethnic groups, the intervention was designed to serve a specific population due to gaps in existing services.

A second innovation of the F2F Program is the use of short videotape illustrations of former group participants talking about, demonstrating, and role-playing various strategies. These videotaped clips are used in conjunction with cartoon handouts, and help participants become comfortable learning and practicing the strategies on their own. In addition to watching past group members demonstrating strategies, group leaders videotape current participants practicing and/or role-playing strategies that they are learning in group. This new videotape, which, when edited, emphasizes the emerging competencies of each group member, is shown to participants, parents, and teachers during the last two sessions of the group. Participants are also given a copy of the videotape to keep, which helps to remind them how to apply the different strategies.

Program Components

The following is a summary of the main components for the twenty-session group curriculum. See Table 12.1 for an outline of these components and for specific session topics.

TABLE 12.1. Main components and session outline for F2F program.

Component 1: Introduction

   Session 1: Discussing purpose, structure, and expectations for the group

   Session 2: Developing group rules and introducing detective analogy

   Session 3: Considering different types of friendship making problems

   Session 4: Determining settings in which "friendship problems" are most likely to occur

Component 2: Physiological Arousal and Calming Strategies

   Session 5: Understanding and identifying a range of feelings

   Session 6: Identifying body's warning signs when one is becoming angry (FBI-Self)

   Session 7: Identifying body's warning signs when one is becoming angry (FBI-Self) cont.

   Session 8: Developing strategies for coping with anger (CIA)

   Session 9: Practicing coping strategies cont. (CIA)

Component 3: Evaluating Intentions and Planning One's Response

   Session 10: Determining others' intentions (FBI-Other)

   Session 11: Practicing interpreting others' intentions (FBI-Other)

   Session 12: Exploring alternative ways of responding (CHOICES to MAP)

   Session 13: Exploring alternative ways of responding (CHOICES to MAP) cont.

   Session 14: Review of main strategies (FBI-Self, CIA, FBI-Other, CHOICES to MAP)

Component 4: Applying strategies to gossip and peer entry situations

   Session 15: Determining what gossip is, and learning the effects of gossip

   Session 16: Applying strategies for dealing with gossip

   Session 17: Understanding peer group entry and applying strategies

   Session 18: Practicing strategies for peer group entry

Component 5: Review

   Session 19: Wrap-up and review

   Session 20: Wrap-up and review cont.

Component 1: Introduction (Sessions 1-5)

The goal of the first component is to introduce girls to the group, and to help them learn to identify the range of friendship making problems that occur at school. In the first two sessions the basic structure, purpose, and rules for the groups are explained in detail. In session 2, a detective analogy is introduced and participants are given magnifying glasses to emphasize that the group will teach them to identify clues in themselves and in their social environment to help them get along better with classmates. In session 3, participants begin learning about different types of friendship-making problems. These include physical (i.e., hitting, pushing, and shoving), relational/social (i.e., gossiping, excluding someone from an activity), and verbal (i.e., making fun of someone or verbally insulting another) friendship-making problems. Finally, in session 4 participants begin to explore how friendship problems vary across school contexts, such as on the playground, and in the lunchroom and hallways.

Component 2: Physiological Arousal and Calming Strategies (Sessions 5-9)

The second component helps girls to identify signs of physiological arousal when they are experiencing a feeling (i.e., becoming mad) and to learn basic "cool-down"strategies. In session 5 girls are taught to identify a range of feelings that include feeling states of being mad, sad, happy, and anxious/confused. Then in sessions 6-7, participants are taught the acronym FBI-Self. FBI-Self teaches children that when they notice a physiological change in their face (F) and/or body (B), this should cue them that they may be experiencing a feeling state (e.g., mad or sad). The (I) stands for (other) Information, but is not utilized until the FBI-Other strategy is taught in the third component of the program. In sessions 8-9, participants are taught the acronym CIA, which stands for "Cool It (before) Action." They learn that once their face and body changes cue them to an underlying feeling (i.e., they are mad), they can take control and calm themselves down before deciding how to respond. Examples of CIA strategies include imagining yourself in a fun, faraway place, taking deep breaths, or talking to yourself in a calm and soothing manner. The last session (session 8) in this component allows participants to practice integrating FBI-Self and CIA strategies in potential conflict situations through role-play activities. Following session 9, a cartoon newsletter is sent to parents and teachers to help them understand the initial detective strategies that the girls have learned.

Component 3: Evaluating Intentions and Planning One's Response (Sessions 10-13)

The third component is modeled after procedures from the Brain Power Program (Hudley & Graham, 1993), and assists participants in more accurately assessing others' intentions in potential conflict situations, and in generating multiple alternative ways of responding. The acronym of FBI-

Other is introduced to illustrate that one can detect another's intentions by examining the other's Face (F), Body (B), or (other) Information (I) in the social environment. In a manner similar to Hudley and Graham (1993), if it is "too hard to tell" whether a situation was enacted on purpose or not, participants are encouraged to give others the benefit of the doubt. See Figure 12.1 for the cartoon handout for FBI-Other, and Figure 12.2 for an example of a portion of the cartoon newsletter that helps parents or teachers better understand how to apply FBI-Other.

Sessions 12 and 13 introduce the acronyms of CHOICES (Choose How Often I Can Exit Safely) to MAP (Make a Plan). Children are taught that once they have identified their own signs of physiological arousal and resulting feeling state (FBI-Self), used calming strategies (CIA), and examined the situation to determine the others' intentions (FBI-Other), they must then generate a range of potential CHOICES of how to respond, weigh the likely positive and negative consequence associated with each choice, and then enact a plan of action (e.g., MAP). For example, in the playground scenario illustrated in Figure 12.2, Erica may generate choices including the following: to walk away from the situation, to talk with a friend, to confront

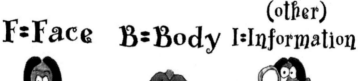

FBI-Other

**Use FBI-Other to figure out WHY Something Happened:
Was it On Purpose, By Accident, or is it Too Hard to Tell?**

**(other)
F=Face   B=Body   I=Information**

FIGURE 12.1. FBI-Other.

Here's an Exercise that we did with Group Members – "Using FBI CLUES"

Example : The girl in green bumps into the girl in blue while walking down the hall.
Question : Did she bump into her by mistake or on purpose (i.e., to be mean)?

Using FBI, we determined that it was **by mistake** (i.e., an accident)
Clues used when looking at the girl in green:
F (Face)
- Her face is turned away from the girl in blue in the first scene
- She says "Ooops sorry" after she bumps into her

B (Body)
- Her body is turned away from the girl in blue in the first scene
- Her body is relaxed in the second scene, as if she is surprised that she bumped into the other girl

I (other Information)
- The girl in green is thinking "oh no, the bell rang & I'm late." Thus, she may be rushing without looking where she is going.

FIGURE 12.2(a). Portion of a cartoon newsletter illustrating FBI-Other.

Here's another example of "Using FBI CLUES"

Example : The girl in red won't let the girl in purple play jump rope.
Question : Why? Is she not letting her play on purpose (i.e., to be mean)?

Using FBI, we determined that it was **on purpose** (i.e., to be mean)
Clues used when looking at the girl in red:
F (Face)
- Her face looks angry and she is gritting her teeth
- She says "You can't play with us!"

B (Body)
- Her body is tense (i.e., not relaxed)
- Her hand is in the other girl's face

I (other Information)
- There is no other relevant information in this picture

FIGURE 12.2(b)

Dominique, or to respond with physical or relational aggression. Participants are taught that there is never one "correct" way to MAP, but rather that they should consider the possible positive and negative consequence of several CHOICES before finalizing their MAP. Further, they are taught that they need to consider the particular situation or context that they are in (school, neighborhood, etc.) whenever finalizing their MAP. Finally, session 14 is a review session in which facilitators help participants summarize what they have learned in previous sessions and to think through ways in which they will continue to work on these detective strategies throughout the upcoming months.

Component 4: Using Strategies to Negotiate Gossip
and Peer Entry Situations (Sessions 15-18)

The fourth component teaches girls to apply the sequential social-cognitive strategies learned during earlier sessions to particular issues that have salience for girls in the urban schools, such as dealing with gossip and entering groups on the playground. In sessions 15 and 16, participants learn several facts about gossip, including (1) that it may be an exaggerated story, (2) that it can be a true statement that is embarrassing or upsetting to the victim, (3) that it often revolves around another's appearance, family members, or behaviors, and (4) that it is usually intended to be malicious or harmful. In addition, participants discuss why girls spread rumors, what the effects of gossip are, and how they can use the social-cognitive strategies (e.g., FBI-Self, CIA, FBI-Other, and CHOICES to MAP) to successfully resolve a gossip situation.

The focus of sessions 17 and 18 is to teach participants strategies for entering groups. First, participants apply their social-cognitive strategies to determine whether or not a particular group is a good one for them to try and join. For instance, participants learn to evaluate social groups to determine who the group members are (e.g., do they know and/or have good relationships with group members), how large the group is (e.g., children playing alone and groups of four or more members are generally easier to enter), and how receptive the group appears to be at including new members. If they determine that the group is likely to be challenging for them to successfully join in, then they are encouraged to find another child or group to play with. However, if they feel that the group would be receptive to their joining in, they are taught to use two additional strategies, termed WALL and TAG. Before entering a group, a girl should WALL. Wait And Look, & Listen, until there is a break in the activity (e.g., the girl who is jumping rope misses; a conversation appears to have paused) and then use TAG, to

Talk About (the) Game. These strategies are based upon prior literature suggesting that the sequencing, timing, and order of entry bids play a large role in whether an entry bid is accepted or not accepted by the group (Dodge, Schlundt, Schocken, & Delugach, 1983). A final cartoon newsletter is given to parents and teachers to explain that participants have learned strategies to decrease gossip and enter groups effectively.

Component Five: Review (Sessions 19-20)

The last component uses self-modeling techniques to help participants remember the strategies that they have learned. Participants view a brief videotape that depicts role-plays from earlier sessions, highlighting their new competencies in enacting the social-cognitive strategies. Teachers and parents are invited to view the videotape with participants in the last session, and participants are given their own copy of the tape.

Evaluation of the F2F Program

The initial effect size for the effectiveness of the F2F Program currently is being investigated as part of a grant from NIMH. Fifty-two relationally aggressive third- to fifth-grade girls attending three urban elementary schools are serving as participants in the initial effectiveness trial. Participating schools have predominately African-American students (i.e., between 85 and 100 percent of the student body depending upon the school) from lower SES families. All third through fifth graders (boys and girls) from the three schools who receive principal, teacher, and parental permission participate in an unlimited peer nomination-identification procedure (see Terry, 2000). Raw score nominations on the five peer-nomination items specific to relational aggression (adapted from Crick & Grotpeter, 1995) will be standardized within each grade, resulting in a final relational aggression z-score for each child. Girls with final relational aggression z-scores greater than .50 will be designated as being relationally aggressive for the purposes of this study.

Once peer-nomination procedures are completed, the prevalence rate of relationally aggressive girls within each is classroom is established. If a classroom has two or more relationally aggressive girls, then the classroom meets criteria for the study and is randomly assigned either to the intervention or control condition (i.e., standard school practice of referral to school counselor). This procedure is conducted for each grade. Relational aggressors are then randomly chosen within both experimental and control classrooms to participate in the study. Thus, relational aggressors participating in the intervention receive a twenty-session group intervention during lunch, and then work closely with group facilitators to conduct a parallel eight-session component for all students within their classroom. In contrast, relational aggressors randomly assigned to the control condition participate in several general discussions about friendships but receive no specific treatment strategies or group sessions. In the main analyses, relationally aggressive girls in the intervention group will be compared to relationally aggressive girls in the control condition on outcomes measures including: (1) rates of relational and physical aggression as assessed by teachers, parents, and self-report, (2) the percentage of hostile attributional biases as measured by a standard hypothetical vignette measure (Crick, 1995; Crick, Grotpeter, & Bigbee, 2002) adapted to cartoons (Leff et al., 2002), and (3) student self-reports of depression and loneliness. In addition, all group sessions are videotaped so that 15 percent of the sessions can be randomly selected and then coded for procedural integrity and therapist competency. Finally, treatment acceptability from the perspective of students, teachers, and parents is also being investigated.

CONCLUSION AND RECOMMENDATIONS

The F2F Program investigates whether an intensive twenty-session school-based group intervention is effective in decreasing relationally aggressive girls' aggression and tendency to make hostile attributional biases, while increasing their range of cooperative play behaviors and social problem-solving skills. The program is innovative in several different ways. First, a PAR framework is used to ensure that all procedures and activities are relevant and engaging to African-American girls in the urban schools. Second, cartoons and videotape illustrations of key strategies assist participants in relating to, remembering, and actively practicing these important strategies. Third, the F2F intervention is more comprehensive than many previous aggression-intervention programs that have focused primarily on physical aggression (see Leff et al., 2001), as the intervention addresses issues related to both relational and physical aggression. In addition, the curriculum takes into account the various school contexts in which aggression is most likely to occur. Fourth, the groups are conducted by both a research team member and by a teacher partner. Including a teacher partner makes it easier for the school to take ownership of the program as opposed to the intervention being viewed only as a university-based research project. Finally, by having group participants help teach the classroom sessions, we hope that the group participants will be viewed as confident leaders as opposed to being viewed as aggressive or bossy.

The F2F Program incorporates a number of aspects that are designed to improve generalizability across setting and context, including the following: (1) incorporating positive role models into the intervention; (2) disseminating cartoon newsletters to parents and teachers, (3) having group members co-teach eight class lessons in which they demonstrate socially competent strategies in role-play format in front of their classmates and teachers; (4) making, showing, and disseminating a videotape of participants successfully utilizing various social-cognitive strategies; and (5) working with teachers to help them learn how to cue group participants to use their strategies (e.g., FBI, CIA) when they see that the child is encountering a potential conflict or difficult situation. Teachers learn how to cue participants by reading the cartoon newsletters, by meeting with therapists on several occasions, and by having classroom lessons conducted within their classroom. In addition, although one could question the feasibility of conducting the F2F Program, we hope that reproduction of the cartoons, the manual, and videotape illustrations of key strategies will be available for dissemination in the future.

While the F2F Program has many strengths, there are also areas to improve upon. The program is still in its infancy, and cannot be considered effective until the initial effectiveness trial is completed. The F2F Program is also a relatively long intervention (twenty sessions plus eight class sessions) requiring strong school support and teacher input in order to be successful. As a result, clinicians and researchers hoping to implement the F2F Program in local schools need to devote considerable time to partnering and building relationships with diverse school staff and community members to ensure that the program best meets the needs of the school and community. Readers are referred to several examples of our earlier work, in which we discuss in detail the steps needed to accomplish this important task (Dowrick et al., 2001; Leff, Costigan, et al., 2004; Leff, Power, et al., 2003). As the F2F Program was designed for urban African-American girls, it is unclear how effective it would be if used with girls from other ethnic backgrounds or nonurban settings. In the future, it will also be important to consider how this program could be adapted to meet the needs of relationally aggressive boys. Finally, at this stage in the development of the program a research team member is still required to work with a teacher partner to implement the program. Over the coming years, we hope to work more closely with school psychologists and school counselors to take on this important role. These individuals would be in an ideal position to help both teacher partners and teachers who have students attending the group learn to better integrate the social-cognitive strategies into their everyday interactions with their students.

Programs such as F2F have implications for school practice. First, cocreating programs through partnerships between researchers and diverse school personnel allows schools to develop and adapt culturally specific and community-responsive intervention procedures for relationally aggressive girls. In addition, programs created through partnerships are more likely to be acceptable to key stakeholders and sustainable (Nastasi et al., 1998). Programs such as F2F also have implications for mental health professionals working within the schools. For example, these individuals, and especially school psychologists, can utilize their training in assessment, research design, and collaborative school consultation to assist schools in adapting, implementing, and evaluating intervention efforts. This prevention and early intervention emphasis is consistent with the priorities outlined in *School Psychology: A Blueprint for Training and Practice II* (Ysseldyke et al., 1997), and speak of the important role that mental health professionals may play in shaping educational and public policy initiatives in the coming years.

REFERENCES

Aloise, P. A. (1993). Children's use of psychological and behavioral traits: A forced-choice assessment. *Social Development, 2,* 36-47.

Arnold, M. E., & Hughes, J. N. (1999). First do no harm: Adverse effects of grouping deviant youth for skills training. *Journal of School Psychology, 37,* 99-115.

Astor, R. A., Meyer, H. A., & Pitner, R. O. (2001). Elementary and middle school students' perceptions of violence-prone school subcontexts. *Elementary School Journal, 101,* 511-528.

Barenboim, C. (1981). The development of person perception in childhood and adolescence: From behavioral comparisons to psychological constructs to psychological comparisons. *Child Development, 52,* 129-144.

Black, M. M., & Krishnakumar, A. (1998). Children in low-income urban settings: Interventions to promote mental health and well-being. *American Psychologist, 53,* 635-646.

Bronfenbrenner, U. (1986). Ecology of the family as a context for human development: Research perspectives. *Developmental Psychology, 22,* 723-742.

Crick, N. R. (1995). Relational aggression: The role of intent attributions, feelings of distress, and provocation type. *Development and Psychopathology, 7,* 313-322.

Crick, N. R., & Dodge, K. A. (1994). A review and reformulation of social information-processing mechanisms in children's social adjustment. *Psychological Bulletin, 115,* 74-101.

Crick, N. R., & Grotpeter, J. K. (1995). Relational aggression, gender, and social-psychological adjustment. *Child Development, 66,* 710-722.

Crick, N. R., Grotpeter, J. K., & Bigbee, M. (2002). Relationally and physically aggressive children's intent attributions and feelings of distress for relational and instrumental peer provocations. *Child Development, 73,* 1134-1142.

Crick, N. R., & Werner, N. E. (1998). Response decision processes in relational and overt aggression. *Child Development, 69,* 1630-1639.

Crick, N. R., Werner, N. E., Casas, J. F., O'Brien, K. M., Nelson, D. A., Grotpeter, J. K., et al. (1999). Childhood aggression and gender: A new look at an old problem. In D. Bernstein (Ed.), *Nebraska symposium on motivation.* Lincoln: University of Nebraska Press.

Dishion, T. J., McCord, J., & Poulin, F. (1999). When interventions harm: Peer groups and problem behaviors. *American Psychologist, 54,* 755-764.

Dodge, K. A. (1986). A social information processing model of social competence in children. In M. Perlmutter (Ed.), *Cognitive perspective on children's social and behavioral development* (pp. 77-125). Hillsdale, NJ: Erlbaum.

Dodge, K. A., Schlundt, D. C., Schocken, I., & Delugach, J. D. (1983). Social competence and children's sociometric status: The role of peer group entry strategies. *Merrill-Palmer Quarterly, 29,* 309-336.

Dowrick, P. W. (1999). A review of self modeling and related interventions. *Applied and Preventive Psychology, 8,* 23-39.

Dowrick, P. W., Power, T. J., Manz, P. H., Ginsburg-Block, M., Leff, Stephen, S., & Kim-Rupnow, S. (2001). Community responsiveness: Examples from under-resourced urban schools. *Journal of Prevention and Intervention in the Community, 21,* 71-90.

Hodges, E. V. E., & Perry, D. G. (1999). Personal and interpersonal antecedents and consequences of victimization by peers. *Journal of Personality and Social Psychology, 76,* 677-685.

Hudley, C., & Graham, S. (1993). An attributional intervention to reduce peer-directed aggression among African American boys. *Child Development, 64,* 124-138.

Kazak, A. E., & Simms, S. (1996). Children with life threatening illnesses: Psychological difficulties and interpersonal relationships. In F. W. Kaslow (Ed.) *Handbook of Relational Diagnosis and Dysfunctional Family Patterns* (pp. 225-238). New York: Wiley.

Kazdin, A. E. (1994). Interventions for aggressive and antisocial children. In L. D. Eron, J. H. Gentry, & P. Schlegel (Eds.), *Reason to hope: A psychosocial perspective on violence and youth* (pp. 341-382). Washington, DC: American Psychological Association.

Kochenderfer, B. J., & Ladd, G. W. (1996). Peer victimization: Cause or consequence of school maladjustment. *Child Development, 67,* 1305-1317.

Leff, S. S., Costigan, T. E., & Power, T. J. (2004). Using participatory-action research to develop a playground-based prevention program. *Journal of School Psychology, 42,* 3-21.

Leff, S. S., Kupersmidt, J. B., Patterson, C., & Power, T. J. (1999). Factors influencing teacher predictions of peer bullying and victimization. *School Psychology Review, 28,* 505-517.

Leff, S. S., Kupersmidt, J. B., & Power, T. J. (2003). An initial examination of girls' cognitions of their relationally aggressive peers as a function of their own social standing. *Merrill Palmer Quarterly, 49,* 28-53.

Leff, S. S., Power, T. J., Costigan, T. E., & Manz, P. H. (2003). Assessing the climate of the playground and lunchroom: Implications for bullying prevention programming. *School Psychology Review, 32,* 418-430.

Leff, S. S., Power, T. J., & Goldstein, A. (2004). Outcome measures to assess the effectiveness of bullying prevention programs in the schools. In. D. L. Espelage & S. S. Swearer (Eds.). *Bullying in American schools: A social-ecological perspective on prevention and intervention* (pp. 269-294). Mahwah, NJ: Lawrence Earlbaum Associates.

Leff, S. S., Power, T. J., Grossman, M., Gill, J., & Blom-Hoffman, J. (2002, August). Designing a cartoon-based attributional measure for use with urban African American females. In D. Nelson & W. Craig (Chairs), *Innovative approaches to understanding forms of aggression.* Symposium conducted at the International Society for the Study of Behavioral Development, Ottawa, Canada.

Leff, S. S., Power, T. J., Manz, P. H., Costigan, T. E., & Nabors, L. A. (2001). School-based aggression prevention programs for young children: Current status and implications for violence prevention. *School Psychology Review, 30,* 343-360.

Lochman, J. E. (1992). Cognitive-behavioral intervention with aggressive boys: Three year follow-up and preventive effects. *Journal of Consulting and Clinical Psychology, 60,* 426-432.

Lochman, J. E., Burch, P. R., Curry, J. F., & Lampron, L. B. (1984). Treatment and generalization effects of cognitive behavioral and goal setting interventions with aggressive boys. *Journal of Consulting and Clinical Psychology, 52,* 915-916.

Lochman, J. E., & Dodge, K. A. (1994). Social-cognitive processes of severely violent, moderately aggressive, and non-aggressive boys. *Journal of Consulting and Clinical Psychology, 62,* 366-374.

Loeber, R., Green, S. M., Lahey, B. B., & Kalb, L. (2000). Physical fighting in childhood as a risk factor for later mental health problems. *Journal of the American Academy of Child and Adolescent Psychiatry, 39,* 421-428.

Nansel, T. R., Overpeck, M., Pilla, R. S., Ruan, W. J., Simons-Morton, B., & Scheidt, P. (2001). Bullying behaviors among US youth: Prevalence and association with psychological adjustment. *Journal of the American Medical Association, 285,* 2094-2100.

Nastasi, B. K., Schensul, J. J., De Silva, M. W. A., Varjas, K., Silva, K. T., Priyani, R., & Schensul, S. (1998). Community-based sexual risk prevention program for Sri Lankan youth: Influencing sexual-risk decision-making. *International Quarterly of Community Health Education, 18,* 139-155.

Nastasi, B. K., Varjas, K., Schensul, S. L., Silva, K. T., Schensul, J. J., & Ratnayake, P. (2000). The participatory intervention model: A framework for conceptualizing and promoting intervention acceptability. *School Psychology Quarterly, 15,* 207-232.

Pellegrini, A. D., & Bjorklund, D. F. (1996). The place of recess in school: Issues in the role of recess in children's education and development. *Journal of Research in Childhood Education, 11,* 5-13.

Pope, A. W., & Bierman, K. L. (1999). Predicting adolescent peer problems and antisocial activities: The relative roles of aggression and dysregulation. *Developmental Psychology, 35,* 335-346.

Terry, R. (2000). Recent advances in measurement theory and the use of sociometric techniques. In A. Cillessen and W. Bukowski (Eds.), *Recent advances in the measurement of acceptance and rejection in the peer system: New directions in child and adolescent development* (pp. 27-53). San Francisco: Jossey-Bass.

Vasey, M. W., Dalgleish, T., & Silverman, W. K. (2003). Research on information-processing factors in child and adolescent psychopathology: A critical commentary. *Journal of Clinical Child and Adolescent Psychology, 32,* 81-93.

Wandersman, A., & Nation, M. (1998). Urban neighborhoods and mental health: Psychological contributions to understanding toxicity, resilience, and interventions. *American Psychologist, 53,* 647-656.

Xie, H., Swift, D. J., Cairns, B., & Cairns, R. B. (2002). Aggressive behaviors in social interaction and developmental adaptation: A narrative analysis of interpersonal conflicts during early adolescence. *Social Development, 11,* 205-224.

Ysseldyke, J., Dawson, P., Lehr, C., Reschly, D., Reynolds, M., & Telzrow, C. (1997). *School psychology: A blueprint for training and practice II.* Bethesda, MD: National Association of School Psychologists.

Chapter 13

A Story-Guided Peer Group Intervention for Reducing Bullying and Victimization in Schools

Hedwig Teglasi
Stephanie Rahill
Lee Rothman

INTRODUCTION

Acts of violence, vandalism, assault, bullying, and hostile communication occur in a social context and affect all participants of the interaction including the aggressor, the victim, and the bystander (Pepler & Slaby, 1994); both bullies and victims are at risk for subsequent maladjustment. Manifestations of aggressive or destructive behaviors in early childhood are relatively stable (Shaw, Owens, Vondra, Keenan, & Winslow, 1996) and predict subsequent antisocial behaviors during school age and into adulthood (Farrington, 2000; Tremblay, Pihl, Viataro, & Dobkin, 1994). Likewise, victim status is stable among frequently harassed children (Boulton & Smith, 1994) and is associated with adjustment problems (for reviews, see Egan & Perry, 1998; Hodges & Perry, 1996), that include peer rejection (Graham & Juvonen, 1998) and academic failure (Austin & Joseph, 1996). Early onset and stability of problems with aggression and victimization underscore the need for prevention or early intervention programs to address the associated risk and protective factors. The STORIES program (Rahill & Teglasi, 2003; Teglasi & Rothman, 2001) uses the peer group process and the story form to enhance the complexity and organization of social problem-

Bullying, Victimization, and Peer Harassment
© 2007 by The Haworth Press, Inc. All rights reserved.
doi:10.1300/5808_13

solving for aggressors, victims, and bystanders to reduce disruptive and hostile peer interactions in schools through two mechanisms: (1) experiential learning as the process by which temperamental risk or protective variables characterizing bullies and victims become translated into social cognitions that also function as risk/protective variables; and (2) the synergy between the "story" form and the peer group influence as tools for harnessing the experiential process of learning to improve social information processing.

Risk Factors, Experiential Learning, and the Story Form

All variables that promote individual differences in exchanges with the environment or in the interpretation of these exchanges also contribute to individuality in what persons learn from their surroundings (see Teglasi & Epstein, 1998). According to the "gradual consolidation hypothesis," repeated experiences become structured into schemas that organize subsequent perceptions about the self, others, and the world (Alsaker & Olweus, 1992) and, ordinarily, earlier experiences are more powerful than subsequent experiences. If, as suggested, the individual's social problem-solving resources are built on the organized representation of the flow of events in the internal and external environments (Stein, Trabasso, & Liwag, 1993), then interventions may target the processes by which individuals learn and revise their schemas.

Risk Factors

Three types of risk factors are associated with peer status as bully or victim: temperamental reactivity and self-regulation, social cognition, and responses of others in the social context.

Temperament

Behaviors of bullies and victims reflect temperamentally rooted difficulties with negative emotionality and problems with self-regulation of emotion, behavior, and attention (Eisenberg et al., 1995; Schwartz et al., 1998). However, subtypes of bullies and victims present somewhat different risk factors. Temperamentally, the proactive bully is not emotionally reactive (low anxiety, low empathy, and little emotion) whereas the reactive bully is easily provoked emotionally. Two distinct types of victims of peer harassment identified as "passive" and "provocative" (Olweus, 1978) also present with different temperamental risk factors. The majority of those repeatedly targeted for harassment comprise the "passive" subtype because they are submissive, fearful, inhibited, or socially withdrawn (Olweus, 1994; Perry, Perry & Kennedy, 1992), and these characteristics mark them as easy targets (Boulton, 1999; Egan & Perry, 1998; Hodges & Perry, 1996). Fearful withdrawal may be a more salient risk factor for peer harassment for boys than for girls (Boulton). The "provocative" victims resemble the passive victims except that they respond to others' taunting by reactive expressions of anger or aggression (Schwartz et al., 1998) that often invite further victimization (Perry et al., 1992). Aggressive victims are more likely to experience peer rejection and general maladjustment than "passive" victims, bullies, or normative peers (Schwartz, 2000).

Social Cognitions

Whereas the research on aggressive children has examined the role of social cognitions as risk factors, the literature characterizing victims has emphasized the role of behaviors that unwittingly reinforce the bully (Perry et al., 1992). Again, cognitive risk factors of bullies may be specific to their subtype as proactive (planned and controlled pursuit of social or material rewards) or reactive (unreflective response to perceived provocation; see Crick & Dodge, 1996; Dodge, Lochman, Harnish, Bates & Pettit, 1997). Reactive bullies tend to misinterpret the situation by focusing on hostile cues whereas proactive bullies may accurately interpret the social cues but use the information deliberately to manipulate others (Sutton, Smith, & Swettenham, 1999). In their belief that aggression is an effective means to attain their goals (Crick & Dodge, 1999), proactive bullies neglect the possible drawbacks of such actions.

Context

Children who are repeatedly victimized by peers rarely receive support from bystanders because they are generally disliked (Perry, Kusel, & Perry, 1988; Hodges, Malone, & Perry, 1997), elicit little empathy from onlookers (Perry, Williard & Perry, 1990), and are viewed as responsible for their plight (see, Schuster, 2001). Having friends protects against peer harassment (Hodges et al., 1997) particularly if the friend speaks up during a bullying episode (Hodges & Perry, 1999).

Experiential Learning and the Story Form

The dual process learning theories account for individuality in schemas about the self and the world by positing two different, though related modes of processing information (Epstein, 1994; Sloman, 1996). Schemas that organize knowledge produced by two different modes of learning have distinct properties (Horowitz, 1991; Wozniak, 1985). Through the *experiential process,* the individual consolidates emotion-laden experiences from daily encounters into knowledge structures or schemas that are subjective and reflect unique perceptions about the regularities of experience that tend to be validated by others who share similar perspectives but not by logical analysis. In contrast, through the *rational process,* individuals organize information into schemas that are relatively independent of emotions and amenable to public scrutiny and change by direct instruction. Such rational schemas include widely accepted social scripts or mathematical formulas that are publicly verifiable and independent of the experiences of the knower. Both types of schemas are tools for problem solving because they allow prior learning to inform the current predicament.

The experiential schemas develop through the capacity of human beings to detect, process, and use information about covariations of stimuli and events in their surroundings without conscious effort (Lewicki, Hill, & Czyewska, 1992). The automatic use of perceived covariations to guide subsequent responding demonstrated in the laboratory is observable in daily life. Young children speak according to the encountered regularities in language patterns but without awareness that they are using nouns and verbs according to the rules of grammar. Likewise, from the earliest months, children act according to implicit rules gleaned from their social encounters without being directly instructed to do so (e.g., Dunn, 1991). With experience, individuals notice links between their actions and outcomes, thereby forming expectations about what actions can or cannot bring about desired effects in specific situations. In this way individuals also develop beliefs regarding sources of distress and about their own efficacy to regulate uncomfortable states. The story form provides a cognitive context for emotional experiences by situating them into a network of justifying conditions and action plans as well as expected outcomes.

STORIES: THEORETICAL AND EMPIRICAL CONSIDERATIONS

The story structure weaves together all components of social information processing including external events, emotions, cognitions, action plans, and outcomes and thereby functions as the "schema" that reflects their organization. Researchers taking social information processing (SIP) perspectives on aggressive behavior invoke schema-based explanations.

Examples are the tendencies of aggressive children in comparison to their peers to base their interpretations on their schemas acquired from past experience without fully processing the available situational cues (Dodge & Tomlin, 1987) and to repeatedly retrieve and use scripts that call for aggressive responding (Huesmann, 1988). Despite their step-like designation in reference to a sequence of social problem-solving cognitions, the various components of social information processing are interrelated components of schemas that cohere within the story form (Table 13.1), often operate outside of awareness in day-to-day interactions (Rabiner, Lenhart, & Lochman,

TABLE 13.1. The story as a context for social information processing.

Social information processing	Story
Identify the Problem:	
1. *External—size up the cues in the context*	*What is happening* to the characters on the outside and inside? How do the different characters view the problem?
2. *Internal—size up tensions, emotions, intentions, relationships*	
Goal of intervention: Coordinate inner and outer sources of tension	
Delineate Causal Sequences:	
1. *External—organize the stream of events, including time frame and cause-effect connections*	*What happened before?* What caused what to happen to whom? What is the role of emotions and intentions? What could be done given a character's resources, intentions, feelings?
2. *Internal—organize motives, feelings, or intentions driving the sequence of events*	
Goal of intervention: Coordinate inner world (intentions, feelings, thoughts) with the logical unfolding of external cues and events.	
Integrate Sources of Emotion:	
1. *External only—emotions or thoughts are reactive to events or external considerations*	*What are characters' thoughts and feelings as well as their intentions?* What are the sources of their feelings? What, if any, changes occur? How do characters link intentions, emotions, and behaviors to short- and long-term aims?
2. *Internal only—actions and reactions are short-term responses to emotional promptings*	
Goal of intervention: Coordinate emotions, intentions and thoughts with one another, the external context, and with *proactive* actions or decisions that consider self and other.	
Coordinate Means—Ends Sequences:	
Goal of intervention: Derive the moral or lesson of the scene or story by working backward from an outcome to understand how the inner and outer worlds shaped the decisions or actions that contributed to the outcome (i.e., did actions address the problem in the short or long run, reflect characters' true intentions, and were they realistic in light of characters' resources or available help)?	*How does the story end?* What did plans, actions, decisions, events or other factors contribute to the outcome? What did each character learn? What is the lesson or moral of the story?

1990), and are influenced by emotional traits and states (Lemerise & Arsenio, 2000).

The meaningful organization of stressful experience into narrative form makes the emotional impact of that experience more manageable (K. J. Gergen, & M. M. Gergen, 1988). Accordingly, writing about one's own traumatic experiences has health benefits for college students (Pennebaker & Seagal, 1999) and, for healthy students, these benefits are comparable to talking with a therapist (Donnelly & Murray, 1991; Murray, Lamnin, & Carver, 1989). Writing about someone else's trauma as if it were one's own produced effects that were similar to writing about one's own traumatic experience (Greenberg, Wortman, & Stone, 1996). Research on the effects of emotional venting does not support the value of emotional expression in the absence of cognitive processing (Lewis & Bucher, 1992). Such findings support the use of the story as a structure to improve children's social reasoning (e.g., Gardner, 1971; Gray, 1998; Russell & van den Broek, 1988).

The peer group processes in STORIES provide the two ingredients of relationships that promote constructive changes in schemas: the "corrective experience" of new patterns of interactions and an "alliance" that enables the exploration of the experiential world (Shirk & Russell, 1996). The exchanges provide "corrective" opportunities to disconfirm problematic assumptions and to change expectations about others' responses. As an "alliance" the therapeutic relationship provides a secure base for the child to explore his or her experiences to reappraise and revise schemas or "working models" of relationships (Bowlby, 1988).

The remainder of this chapter compares an implementation of a story-guided intervention, STORIES (Teglasi & Rothman, 2001), which was adapted to the needs of children identified with emotional disability (see Rahill & Teglasi, 2003 for more detail) with the Skillstreaming Curriculum (McGinnis & Goldstein, 1997). Research has shown less favorable progress resulting from social competency training among students with more serious or longer-lasting emotional or behavioral difficulties (Kamps, Kravitz, Stolze, & Swaggart, 1999). Given general trends toward deterioration of children exhibiting maladjusted behaviors (four years later) regardless of participation in a social competency enhancement program (Skroban, Gottfredson, & Gottfredson, 1999), pre- and posttest comparison may not be sufficient to demonstrate treatment efficacy with children identified with Emotional Disability (ED). Therefore, the evaluation strategy compared two different types of group interventions in ways that linked process variables to changes in outcomes.

DESCRIPTION OF THE APPLICATION

Target Population, Educational Needs of the Children, and Relevant Context of the Application

The interventions were delivered to children identified with an ED and served in one of four self-contained Special Educational Centers. Given that the Centers have a therapeutic mission to serve all students, everyone in Grades 2 through 6 participated in one of three types of groups: Skill-streaming, STORIES and nonspecific counseling. The latter groups, typically provided at the centers, were not a focus of this study. A total of 63 students participated either in STORIES (7 groups, $n = 35$; 31 males, 4 females) or Skillstreaming (5 groups, $n = 28$; 24 males, 4 females). The mean numbers of participants per group for the STORIES and Skillstreaming, respectively, were 5.0 and 5.6. The mean age of the children was 10.09 ($SD = 1.16$). The sample was ethnically diverse: 25 percent African American, 10 percent Hispanic American, and 65 percent European American.

Methods

The groups met once a week for forty-five to forty-five minutes for twenty-five sessions. Following a pilot study undertaken to adapt STORIES to the needs of children served at the centers and to train the group leaders, several changes were made: (1) the number of sessions was increased from fifteen to twenty-five to compensate for the children's lower level of "readiness" in understanding emotions and relationships; (2) selection of different books to allow for a more basic level of discussion of emotions and relationships; (3) greater reliance on visual aids such as emotion thermometer to quantify feelings and more frequent use of picture displays to illustrate characters' relationships; and (4) more active role for the coleader to help children regulate their behaviors.

Relevant Activities Constituting STORIES

The first session, devoted to promoting cohesion and to setting the parameters for how the group would function, included several activities: choosing a group name, generating the rules by which the group will operate (including confidentiality), and cooperatively making a poster to illustrate the group name. As set out in the Manual, pre-reading, reading, discussing, and sharing stories proceed according to a predetermined plan for when to stop, what topics to discuss, what themes to emphasize, and what activities to introduce. Before starting to read a book or when moving on to a new chapter, section, or scene, relevant ideas are introduced, and children examine the pictures to identify the cast of characters, their feelings, and the likely themes. Scrutinizing the pictures is intended to refine the process of encoding emotional cues as part of building frameworks for understanding characters' emotions. When the stage has been set, the group leader reads segments of the book with drama and animation, stopping to elaborate, ask questions, or define concepts such as what is a bully, victim, or bystander. As the story progresses, information about each character is added to a character web, displayed on poster paper for continuing revision and reference. Group members are guided to examine the plight of each character in terms of what is happening in the outer world (circumstances, events) and in the inner world (motives, intentions, feelings, goals), predicting what will happen next, and drawing lessons from the characters' experiences. This process is mirrored by group members respectfully sharing ideas and becoming aware of each others' feelings, thoughts, and reasons for actions (intentions). Activities are introduced to increase understanding and promote the application of the "lessons" learned to children's lives. Generally, about one-quarter of the session is spent on reading and the rest of the time on discussion, application of the learning, and group activities.

Relevant Activities Constituting Skillstreaming

The Skillstreaming (McGinnis & Goldstein, 1997) curriculum emphasizes the planned and systematic instruction of acceptable social skills and uses behaviorally oriented teaching procedures comprising identifying a skill, followed by modeling, role-playing, performance feedback, and transfer of training (Merrell & Gimpel, 1998). The competencies that most closely matched the STORIES themes were selected from the Skillstreaming curriculum.

Treatment Integrity

Leaders of Skillstreaming and STORIES groups received training during the pilot phase of the project or had previous familiarity with the intervention. STORIES group leaders were given the step-by-step working manual of the story-based program, and Skillstreaming group leaders were given the published manual (McGinnis & Goldstein, 1997). To assure consistency in treatment implementation (1) the Skillstreaming and STORIES group leaders met separately approximately once per month to discuss the progress of the groups; (2) several informal discussions between group leaders occurred throughout the programs as questions were asked or advice was sought on implementation; (3) process notes written by group leaders and coleaders following each session were reviewed periodically; and (4) on a selected basis, taped sessions were transcribed and reviewed.

Budget, Personnel, and Staff Involved

External funding was not needed as group counseling is part of the therapeutic mission of the setting and the Center-based school psychologists, assisted by a coleader, conducted the STORIES and Skillstreaming groups as part of their ongoing activities. Coleaders were either school psychology doctoral student volunteers or interested pupil personnel staff. The role of the coleader was to maintain order nonverbally by making eye contact, sitting between students or the like as well as to add to the discussion or help with the posters and art projects.

Plan for the Evaluation of the Application

Two interventions designed to promote social competence in different ways were compared on group process and outcome variables (see Rahill & Teglasi, 2003). Although all students in one class were assigned to the same type of group, in some cases, more than one group was conducted within each classroom due to the number of students in the class. Both types of groups were conducted at each of the four centers and students at each Center were assigned in equal proportions to respective groups to control for potential differences between students who attended the different centers.

Measures

Outcome Variables

Two teacher rating scales with well-documented psychometric properties were completed immediately before and after the interventions: The Behavioral Symptoms Index (BSI) of the Behavioral Assessment System for Children (BASC; Reynolds & Kamphaus, 1992) and the Social Competence and Antisocial Behavior Scales of the School Social Behavior Scales (SSBS; Merrell, 1993). The BSI score of the BASC reflects an overall level of problem behavior (aggression, hyperactivity, anxiety, depression, and atypicality).

Peer- and teacher-rated sociometric information was obtained with eight items that used 5-point Likert scales with test–retest reliability established during a pilot phase. Principal Components factor analyses with varimax rotations of the pre- and post test teacher ($n = 14$) and peer ratings ($n = 82$) in the current investigation indicated that the "bully" factor (fights with others; teases others) was stable over time and informant and that factor was retained for subsequent analyses. The bivariate correlation between peer and teacher rated "bully" score was .44 ($p < .01$).

Process Variables

Cognitive and behavioral responses during the group sessions comprised the process variables.

Transcript Coding. All sessions were audio-taped and three sessions for each group were transcribed: One session for the Early phase (3-7), one session for the Middle phase (11-15), and one session from the Later phase (19-23). The earliest session within each time block was selected based on maximum attendance and intelligibility of all student verbalizations. Mean cognitive levels were calculated for each individual for each phase and across all phases. Procedures for coding the transcripts were similar to those in a previous study (Teglasi & Rothman, 2001). In the current study, the interrater reliability was 90 percent for Skillstreaming and 86 percent for STORIES. The coding categories were: 1 = negative, uncooperative, or disrespectful; 2 = off task, out of context, or personalized (intended to be cooperative but shows significant misunderstanding of the situation in the story or in the group); 3 = tangential or loosely connected to the topic at hand or mildly inappropriate (e.g., interrupts, or repeat what has just been said); 4 = on target, responsive (answers factual questions), constructive engagement in the group process; and 5 = interpretive or integrative, showing insight about the psychological world of the characters, self, others (uses information learned to formulate a moral, apply a moral, predict actions or reactions, or suggest appropriate problem-solving).

Group Leader Ratings

Immediately following each session, the group leaders and coleaders independently rated each child in the group (from 0 to 3) on cognition and behavior.

Behavior Process Coding Categories. Zero = disruptive to the conduct of the group: aggressive, destructive of materials, leaving the room, consistently inappropriate language, and talking out of turn. When redirected, the child does not respond beyond a few moments; 1 = disruptive behavior interferes with group activity but the student responds to redirection—rejoins the group activity only to be problematic again; 2 = variable loss of control but resumes participation upon redirection: distracted by others, off-task behaviors, silliness, promoting a different agenda for a short time; 3 = appropriate level of self-control—spontaneously redirects self back to group activity when distractions occur, resists off-task behaviors of others, encourages resolution of problems within the group, or helps others resume on-task behavior without disrupting the group activity.

Cognitive Process Coding Categories. Zero = no apparent cognitive response: overt attention or response is not directed toward group activity, preoccupied with other interests; 1 = minimal cognitive response—attention may be divided between group activity and preoccupation with unrelated activity. When cued to respond to direct questions, the child does not demonstrate awareness or understanding of content or ideas. During discussion about affective concepts, the child either does not contribute or expresses unrelated, disorganized content; 2 = some cognitive response: active participation by attending visually, listening, response to direct questions or spontaneous factual statements or recollection of concepts presented earlier; 3 = cognitive growth—relating information or concepts from earlier sessions or segments of the current session, spontaneously or when prompted by offering pertinent ideas or information or interpretive statements or concepts, or connecting concepts, skills, events, or emotions to relevant personal experiences. Agreement of two group leaders on students' cognitive and behavioral codes was over 90 percent when the criterion was an exact match between the two raters. Mean cognitive and behavioral process scores were calculated for each participant for each of thee phases: Early (sessions 1-8), Middle (sessions 9-16), and Late (sessions 17-24).

RESULTS

Preliminary Analyses

Groups did not differ on the following variables: attendance, proportion of participants from the four schools, proportion of males and females. There were significant age differences, $F(2, 79) = 16.119$, ($p < .01$) with participants in STORIES being about one year younger than students in the Skillstreaming and the nonspecific counseling groups. However, age was not correlated with any of the outcome variables in this study. Pretest scores on outcome measures did not differ significantly across groups. Nevertheless, subsequent analyses controlled for initial scores.

Outcome Variables

A multivariate analysis of covariance (MANCOVA) comparing the groups on the three teacher-rated behavior scales, the BASC BSI, SSBS Social Competence, and SSBS Antisocial Behavior, with pretests as covariates, revealed that on the BSI Index but not on the other variables, STORIES participants had significantly more favorable scores than Skillstreaming participants (BSI Index Adjusted Posttest Means: STORIES: 64.05; Skillstreaming: 69.20). Groups did not differ on teacher- and peer-rated "bully" behaviors and this variable did not yield significant differences between the intervention types.

Process Variables

Separate repeated measures multivariate analyses of variance were conducted to compare groups on each of three process variables at three designated phases of the intervention. Phase was the within subject variable and group was the between subjects variable.

Transcript Codes

The repeated measures MANOVA comparing STORIES and Skillstreaming groups on transcript codes on the three phases of the intervention (Early, Middle, and Late) indicated that phase and its interaction with group did not emerge as significant. However, a significant linear effect emerged for group, $F(1, 46) = 13.71, p < .001$ (Eta squared for group effects = .230). Follow-up tests showed higher scores for STORIES than Skillstreaming at each phase (Early: $F(1, 54) = 7.33, p < .001$; Middle: $F(1, 53) = 7.16, p < .01$; Late: $F(1, 52) = 17.06, p < .001$). To further examine these findings, separate ANCOVAs were conducted to compare the two groups on Middle and Late phases on the transcript-coded cognitive level after controlling for scores in the Early phase. Results indicated that after covarying out differences in the initial phase, STORIES participants had higher scores by the Late, $F(1, 48) = 9.16, p < .01$, but not Middle, $F(1, 48) = 2.51$, phase.

Group Leader Ratings of Cognition

The repeated measures MANOVA comparing the two interventions on group leader-rated cognitions during each of three phases (Early, Middle, Late) indicated two significant findings: phase by group interaction, $F(2, 45) = 7.59 \, p < .01$, and main effect of phase, $F(2, 33) = 8.70, p < .01$. Eta squared values were as follows: interaction effect = .474; linear effect of phase = .103, and group effect =.162. Follow-up paired samples t-tests showed significant differences within STORIES when comparing the Early with the Late phase ($t = -2.63$, $p < .05$) suggesting higher cognitive level with increasing sessions. No phase differences emerged within Skillstreaming. Results of ANOVAs comparing the groups on each of the three phases showed that STORIES participants received higher cognitive ratings than did Skillstreaming participants for the Middle, $F(1, 53) = 6.23$, $p < .05$) and Late, $F(1, 52) = 6.60$, $p < .05$), but not the Early sessions. One way ANCOVAs controlling for scores in the Early phase indicated a significant difference in group leader-rated cognitive processing with STORIES participants scoring higher than Skillstreaming participants by the Late phase, $F(1, 48) = 6.76$, $p < .05$), although not by the Middle one.

Group Leader Ratings of Behavior

A repeated measures MANCOVA comparing STORIES and Skillstreaming on group leader behavior ratings on the three phases of the intervention (Early, Middle, and Late phases) indicated no significant findings.

Process ("In-Group") Variables As Predictors of Outcome ("Outside Group") Variables

Hierarchical multiple regression analyses were utilized to determine whether children's "in-session" cognitive and behavioral responses predicted posttest outcome scores after controlling for the pretests. For each multiple regression analysis, the pretest score was entered at the first step, followed by the mean score of the particular "in-session" variable (transcript mean, group leader cognition mean, and group leader behavior mean) and then by the interaction of the two. Collinearity statistics indicated that all variables in the regression equations were well within the tolerance range and residual diagnostics showed no evidence of heteroscedasticity. Whereas none of the interactions emerged as significant, cognitive and behavioral responses during the sessions predicted favorable changes in outcome variables as follows: (1) *BASC BSI*—the transcript cognitive processing code and group leader cognitive ratings (but not behavioral ratings), made significant contribution to the prediction beyond the pretest score; (2) *Social Competency Index of the SSBS*—all three "in-session" responses (transcript code, group leader cognitive and behavior codes) contributed to the prediction beyond the pretest score; (3) *Antisocial Behavior Index of the SSBS:* group leader-rated cognitive processing and behavioral codes (but not transcript code) were predictive beyond the pretest score; (4) *Peer-Rated Bullying:* all three "in-session" variables predicted peer-rated bullying beyond the pretest; (5) *Teacher-Rated Bullying*: only group leader behavior ratings were predictive beyond the pretest.

CONCLUSIONS

Group Differences in Process and Outcome Variables

Consistent with the goals of STORIES, two different measures of cognitive process, transcript codes, and group leader ratings, indicated higher levels for STORIES than Skillstreaming. Moreover, the groups changed differentially in cognitive level from the initial to the final set of sessions in ways that favored STORIES. In contrast, behaviors did not change across sessions and did not differ across groups probably because the small size and structured nature of both types of groups promote behavioral self-regulation. When the two types of groups were compared on the outcome variables, only the BASC BSI reached significance indicating less favorable scores for Skillstreaming than STORIES.

Outcomes Predicted by Process Variables

Group differences in process variables are important given their connections with the outcomes. Both cognitive process measures were higher among STORIES participants and leader-rated cognitive level increased from Early to Late sessions within STORIES. Cognitive process variables predicted changes in several outcome measures beyond the pretests including peer-rated bullying, SSBS Social Competency, and BASC BSI but not teacher-rated bullying and teacher-rated Anti-Social Behavior. Behavioral ratings during the sessions did not change as a function of number of sessions or type of intervention but were, nevertheless, linked to outcomes including teacher- and peer-rated bullying, SSBS Antisocial and Social Competence scores, but not BASC BSI ratings. One explanation for process-outcome links in the absence of change with increasing sessions or type of treatment is that the process measures may reflect student characteristics (i.e., risk/protective variables reviewed earlier) that influence not only their responses to the intervention but also shape their interactions outside the sessions. Thus, behavioral self-regulation during the sessions reflects the same tendencies that are measured in ratings of bullying and antisocial behaviors outside the sessions. Increasing cognitive level with more treatment sessions may reflect engagement with the content of the intervention in ways that forecast a more favorable trajectory. Thus the risk and protective variables characterizing children at the onset of the intervention may influence both the process and outcome variables.

Caveats and Future Directions

The assignment of children in the same class to the same treatment condition raises the possibility that the influence of the teachers and the impact of the treatment may be confounded. Arguing against this interpretation is the pattern of relationships whereby changes in the BSI, the only outcome variable on which the groups differed, were predicted only by the two process variables that distinguished the groups, cognitive level as coded from transcripts and as rated by group leaders. Whereas the two cognitive measures contributed to the prediction of the BSI beyond the pretest, group leader behavior ratings did not. This link between cognitive process and outcome variables also argues against discounting group differences in these process variables as mere products of the demand characteristics of the respective programs. Separate multiple regression analyses for each treatment group would clarify possible differences between programs in how "in-session" process responses predict changes in outcomes, but the number of participants was not sufficient to conduct such analyses.

Given that cognitive process predicted change in a variety of meaningful outcome measures and, given the improvement in cognition with increasing STORIES sessions, it may be reasonable to anticipate further improvement with continued programming, both within the group setting and in the classroom. Effect sizes were modest and in light of the severity of deficits and prolonged nature of many behavioral problems demonstrated by children with ED, it may be necessary to increase the length, comprehensiveness, and "in-session" engaged time of intervention programs to overcome the typical barriers to generalization of social skills in this population.

REFERENCES

Alsaker, F. D., & Olweus, D. (1992). Stability of global self-evaluations in early adolescence. A cohort longitudinal study. *Journal of Research on Adolescence, 2,* 123-145.

Austin, S., & Joseph, S. (1996). Assessment of bully/victim problems in 8 to 11 year-olds. *British Journal of Educational Psychology, 66,* 447-456.

Boulton, M. J. (1999). Concurrent and longitudinal relations between children's playground behavior and social preference, victimization, and bullying. *Child Development, 70,* 944-954.

Boulton, M. J., & Smith, P. K. (1994). Bully/victim problems in middle-school children: Stability, self-perceived competence, peer perceptions, and peer acceptance. *British Journal of Developmental Psychology, 12,* 315-329.

Bowlby, J. (1988). *A secure base: Parent-child attachment and healthy human development.* New York: Basic Books.

Crick, N. R., & Dodge, K. A. (1996). Social information-processing mechanisms on reactive and proactive aggression. *Child Development, 67*(3), 993-1002.

Crick, N. R., & Dodge, K. A. (1999). "Superiority" is in the eye of the beholder: A comment of Sutton, Smith and Swettenham. *Social Development, 8*(1), 128-131.

Dodge, K. A., Lochman, J. E., Harnish, J. D., Bates, J. E., & Pettit, G. S. (1997). Reactive and proactive aggression in school children and psychiatrically-impaired chronically assaultive youth. *Journal of Abnormal Psychology, 106,* 37-51.

Dodge, K. A., & Tomlin, A. (1987). Cue utilization as a mechanism of attributional bias in aggressive children. *Social Cognition, 5,* 280-300.

Donnelly, D. A., & Murray, E. J. (1991). Cognitive and emotional changes in written essays and therapy interviews. *Journal of Social and Clinical Psychology, 10,* 334-350.

Dunn, J. (1991). Young children's understanding of other people: Evidence from observations within the family. In D. Frye & C. Moore (Eds.), *Children's theories of mind: Mental states and social understanding* (pp. 97-114). Hillsdale, NJ: Erlbaum.

Egan, S. K., & Perry, D. G. (1998). Does low self-regard invite victimization? *Developmental Psychology, 34*(2), 299-309.

Eisenberg, N., Fabes, R., Murphy, B., Mask, P., Smith, M., & Karbon, M. (1995). The role of emotionality and regulation in children's social functioning: A longitudinal study. *Child Development, 66,* 1360-1384.

Epstein, S. (1994). Integration of the cognitive and psychodynamic unconscious. *American Psychologist, 49,* 709-724.

Farrington, D. P. (2000). Explaining and preventing crime: The globalization of knowledge—The American Society of Criminology 1999 presidential address. *Criminology, 38*(1),1-24.

Gardner, R. A. (1971). *Therapeutic communication with children: The mutual story telling technique.* New York: Science House

Gergen, K. J., & Gergen, M. M. (1988). Narrative and the self as relationship. In L. Berkowitz (Ed.), *Advances in experimental social psychology* (Vol. 21) (pp. 17-56). New York: Academic.

Graham, S., & Juvonen, J. (1998). Self-blame and peer victimization in middle school: An attributional analysis. *Developmental Psychology, 34,* 587-599.

Gray, C. A. (1998). Social stories and comic strip conversations with students with Asperger's Syndrome and high functioning autism. In E. Schopler, G. B. Mesibov, & L. J. Kunce (Eds.), *Asperger Syndrome or high-functioning autism?* (pp. 167-198). New York: Plenum.

Greenberg, M. A., Wortman, C. B., & Stone, A. A. (1996). Emotional expression and physical health: Revising traumatic memories or fostering self-regulation? *Journal of Personality and Social Psychology, 71*, 588-602.

Hodges, E. V. E., Malone, M. J., & Perry, D. G. (1997). Individual risk and social risk as interacting determinants of victimization in the peer group. *Developmental Psychology, 33*, 1032-1039.

Hodges, E. V. E., & Perry, D. G. (1996). Victims of peer abuse: An overview. *Journal of Emotional and Behavioral Problems, 5*, 23-28.

Hodges, E. V. E., & Perry, D. G. (1999). Personal and interpersonal antecedents and consequences of victimization by peers. *Journal of Personality and Social Psychology, 76*, 677-685.

Horowitz, M. J. (1991). States, schemas, and control: General theories for psychotherapy integration. *Journal of Psychotherapy Integration, 1*, 85-102.

Huesmann, L. (1988). An information processing model for the development of aggression. *Aggressive Behavior, 14*(1), 13-24.

Kamps, D., Kravits, T., Stolze, J., & Swaggart, B. (1999). Prevention strategies for students at risk and identified as serious emotionally disturbed in urban, elementary school settings. *Journal of Emotional and Behavioral Disorders, 7*, 178-188.

Lemerise, E. A., & Arsenio, W. F. (2000). An integrated model of emotion processes and cognition in social information processing. *Child Development, 71*, 107-118.

Lewicki, P., Hill, T., & Czyewska, M. (1992). Nonconscious acquisition of information. *American Psychologist, 47*, 792-801.

Lewis, W. A., & Bucher, A. M. (1992). Anger, catharsis, the reformulated frustration-aggression hypothesis, and health consequences. *Psychotherapy, 29*, 385-392.

McGinnis, E., & Goldstein, A. (1997). *Skillstreaming the elementary school child* (School manual). Champaign, IL: Research Press.

Merrell, K. W. (1993). Using behavior rating scales to assess social skills and antisocial behavior in school settings: Development of the School Social Behavior Scales. *School Psychology Review, 22*, 115-133.

Merrell, K. W., & Gimpel, G. A. (1998). *Social skills of children and adolescents: Conceptualization, assessment, treatment.* Mahwah, NJ: Lawrence Erlbaum Associates.

Murray, E. J., Lamnin, A. D., & Carver, C. S. (1989). Emotional expression in written essays and psychotherapy. *Journal of Social and Clinical Psychology, 8*, 414-429.

Olweus, D. (1978). *Aggression in the schools: Bullies and whipping boys.* Washington, DC: Hemisphere.

Olweus, D. (1994). Bullying at school: Long-Term outcomes for the victims and an effective school-based intervention program. In L. R Huesmann (Ed.), *Aggressive behaviour: Current perspectives* (pp. 97-1300). New York: Plenum Press.

Pennebaker, J. W., & Seagal, J. D. (1999). Forming a story: The health benefits of narrative. *Journal of Clinical Psychology, 55*, 1243-1254.

Pepler, D. J., & Slaby, R. (1994). A development perspective on aggression. In L. D. Eron, J. H. Gentry, & P. Schlegel (Eds.) *A reason to hope: A psychosocial perspective on violence and youth* (pp. 44-50). Washington, DC: American Psychological Association.

Perry, D. G., Kusel, S. J., & Perry, L. C. (1988). Victims of peer aggression. *Developmental Psychology, 24*, 807-814.

Perry, D. G., Perry, L. C., & Kennedy, E. (1992). Conflict and the development of antisocial behavior. In C. Shantz & W. W. Hartup (Eds.) *Conflict in child and adolescent development* (pp. 301-329). Cambridge: Cambridge University Press.

Perry, D. G., Williard, J. C., & Perry, L. C. (1990). Peers' perceptions of the consequences that victimized children provide aggressors. *Child Development, 61*, 1310-1325.

Rabiner, D. L., Lenhart, L., & Lochman, J. E. (1990). Automatic *vs.* reflective social problem solving in relation to children's sociometric status. *Developmental Psychology, 26*, 1010-1026.

Rahill, S. A., & Teglasi, H. (2003). Processes and outcomes of story-based and skill-based social competency programs for children with emotional disabilities. *Journal of School Psychology, 41*, 413-429.

Reynolds, C. R., & Kamphaus, R. W. (1992). *The Behavior Assessment System for Children.* Circle Pines, MN: American Guidance Service.

Russell, R. L., & van den Broek, P. (1988). A cognitive-developmental account of storytelling in child psychotherapy. In S. R. Shirk (Ed.), *Cognitive development and Child Psychotherapy* (pp. 19-52). New York: Plenum.

Schuster, B. (2001). Rejection and victimization by peers: Social perception and social behavior mechanisms. In J. Juvonen & S. Graham (Eds.), *Peer harassment in school* (pp. 290-309). New York: Guilford.

Schwartz, D. (2000). Subtypes of victims and aggressors in children's peer groups. *Journal of Abnormal Child Psychology, 28*(2), 181-192.

Schwartz, D., Dodge, K. A., Coie, J. D., Hubbard, J. A., Antonius, H. N., Cillessen, E. A., et al. (1998). Social-cognitive and behavioral correlates of aggression and victimization in boys' play groups. *Journal of Abnormal Child Psychology, 26*, 431-440.

Shaw, D. S., Owens, E. B., Vondra, J. I., Keenan, K., & Winslow, E. B. (1996). Early risk factors and pathways in the development of early disruptive behavior problems. *Development and Psychopathology, 8*, 679-699.

Shirk, S. R., & Russell, R. L. (1996). *Change processes in child psychotherapy: Revitalizing treatment and research.* New York: Guilford Press.

Skroban, S. B., Gottfredson, D. C., & Gottfredson, G. D. (1999). A school-based social competency promotion demonstration. *Evaluation Review, 23*, 3-27.

Sloman, S. A. (1996). The empirical case for two systems of reasoning. *Psychological Bulletin, 119*, 3-22.

Stein, N., Trabasso, T., & Liwag, M. (1993). The representation and organization of emotional experience: Unfolding the emotion episode. In M. Lewis & J. M. Haviland (Eds.), *Handbook of emotions* (pp. 279-300). New York: Guilford.

Sutton, J., Smith, P. K., & Swettenham, J. (1999). Social cognition and bullying: Social inadequacy or skilled manipulation? *British Journal of Developmental Psychology, 17,* 435-450.

Teglasi, H., & Epstein, S. (1998). Temperament and personality theory: The perspective of cognitive-experiential self-theory. *School Psychology Review, 27,* 534-550.

Teglasi, H., & Rothman, L. (2001). STORIES: A classroom-based program to reduce aggressive behavior. *Journal of School Psychology, 39,* 71-94.

Tremblay, R. E., Pihl, R. O., Viataro, F., & Dobkin, P. L. (1994). Predicting early onset of male antisocial behavior from preschool behavior. *Archives of General Psychiatry, 51,* 732-739.

Wozniak, R. H. (1985). Notes toward a co-constructive theory of the emotion/cognition relationship. In D. Bearison & H. Zimiles (Eds.), *Thought and emotion: Developmental issues* (pp. 39-64). Hillsdale, NJ: Erlbaum.

Chapter 14

Empowering the Victim: Interventions for Children Victimized by Bullies

Maury Nation

Several studies have suggested that bullying is a significant problem in American schools (Hoover, Oliver, & Hazler, 1992; Nansel et al., 2001). In response to this problem, most interventions have been focused on bullies and have promoted systemic change throughout the targeted schools (e.g., Limber, Flerx, Nation, & Melton, 1998; Olweus, 1993; Pepler, Craig, Ziegler, & Charach, 1994). These "whole school" programs have appropriately emphasized holding bullies responsible for their behavior and have successfully reduced overall bullying rates. However, in general, these interventions have failed to recognize the acute problems faced by victims of bullying that often leave professionals, parents, and the victimized children themselves wondering about the proper response to a bully.

A casual review of the popular literature has suggested some anecdotal recommendations for victims of bullying and their parents. A cover story of *Psychology Today* (Marano, 1995), for example, provided a list of suggestions for victimized children that included avoidance (i.e., walking or running away), recruiting a friend, acting assertively, and using humor. The juvenile literature is full of similar, and sometimes contradictory, suggestions. In their review of twenty-two children's books, Oliver, Young, and LaSalle (1994) found that the recommendations for bullied children ranged from active strategies such as attempting to embarrass the bully to passive strategies such as imagining someone else in greater misery. Although some of these suggestions may have face validity, research suggests that

Bullying, Victimization, and Peer Harassment
© 2007 by The Haworth Press, Inc. All rights reserved.
doi:10.1300/5808_14

these recommendations may be of little use to victimized children, and could be counterproductive (Smith, Shu, & Madsen, 2001). Therefore, the purpose of this chapter is to provide a summary of the research on interventions for children who have been victimized by bullies, and to use this review to provide recommendations for researchers and practitioners who work with these children.

WHY ARE INTERVENTIONS FOR VICTIMS NEEDED?

Although bullies should be held accountable for their behaviors, the existing research on the victims of bullying suggests several reasons for developing effective victim-focused interventions. These reasons include the following:

- Psychological correlates and consequences of victimization

The poor outcomes of chronically bullied children (e.g., suicides, low self-esteem, academic failure) suggest the need for intensive intervention, beyond that which is provided in most systemic interventions. Olweus (1993) indicated that victims tend to be passive, timid, and isolated. Hodges and Perry (1999) reported that victims were rejected by peers and tended to be plagued with internalizing problems (e.g., anxiety and depression). In a review of the research on the victims of bullying, Bernstein and Watson (1997) found that victimized children were different in personality, behavior, and social/cognitive skills from other children. These differences included the tendency to be submissive in relationships, to use passive coping techniques, and to repeat behaviors that result in victimization. Some studies suggest that these differences may precede the onset of victimization (Schwartz, Dodge, & Coie, 1993), may be reciprocally reinforced by victimization (Goldbaum, Craig, Pepler, & Connolly, 2003), and that the psychological difficulties that are associated with victimization persist into adulthood (Olweus).

Also, research has suggested that for a subgroup of victims, aggressive victims, chronic victimization may result in acts of violence toward peers. Leary, Kowalski, Smith and Phillips (2003) analyzed the youth who perpetrated fifteen recent school shootings and found that teasing, bullying, and rejection by peers played a key role in almost all of the cases. Similarly, Holmes and Holmes (2000) reviewed school shootings resulting in deaths and found that among the common characteristics was a sense of isolation, alienation, and anger toward individuals or groups of students. In both studies, the authors noted that in some cases teachers and other school representatives were aware of the plight of the perpetrator but ignored or were ineffective in ameliorating the situation.

- The need to respond to specific request by victimized children

Teachers and counselors are sometimes confronted with a request for help from victims after a specific act of bullying. However, the lack of victim-focused interventions may limit a teacher's ability to respond effectively. In their analysis of comments made by middle- and high school students, Hazler, Hoover, and Oliver (1992) found that they believed that the adults at their schools (1) were not as informed about the bullying as they should have been, (2) were reluctant to act when they were aware of bullying, (3) knew about bullying but did not care enough to intervene, or (4) intervened with the victim in a way that might target them for further bullying. While systemic interventions are good at changing the environment to prevent victimization, they are limited in providing support for the victimized individuals who may consult a counselor or teacher, leaving these students to conclude that adults do not care.

- Effective individual-level intervention can be an important adjunct to systemic level interventions.

Olweus (1993), for example, suggested interventions at the school, classroom, and individual level. Proposed interventions for victims included support groups for parents and serious talks with the victimized child. However, Olweus provides few suggestions for specific content of these serious talks and provides no practical guidelines for determining which students are in need of this type of intervention. Also, Olweus's evaluations of the program do not include an evaluation of the effectiveness of these conversations independent of the overall results of the systemic program, and none of these evaluations have checked for changes in the psychosocial functioning of the victims of bullying. Although a decrease in bullying is a desirable outcome for many reasons, there is no evidence that lowering the rates of bullying result in a corresponding improvement in the social and psychological adjustment of children already impacted by bullying.

Despite the evidence suggesting that victims of bullying are a neglected group, relatively little of the intervention research has addressed the needs of this group. To the degree that intervention with victims has been suggested, the attention has largely focused on aggressive victims who are targeted for treatment because of their disruptive behaviors and not their victimization (e.g., Hanish & Guerra, 2000). A review of the scholarly literature that did recognize the needs of the victims of bullying provided a wide range of recommended interventions. Smith, Cowie, and Sharp (1994), for example, described the interventions involving victims that were practiced in European schools: The Shared Concern Method, the No-Blame Approach, and bully courts. Other reviewers, Ross (1996a) for example, suggest that school-based programs designed to deal with other behavioral or disciplinary problems such as conflict resolution, peer mediation, and assertiveness training might be useful in resolving bullying situations. Finally, a search of online databases indicated that a variety of therapy-focused interventions have been employed with victimized children. In the next section, we provide a detailed description of these interventions and review the empirical research related to their effectiveness in addressing the needs of children involved in bullying.

REVIEW OF RELEVANT LITERATURE

The suggested interventions that involve victims of bullying can be organized around two distinct models of the problem. One model suggests that victimization is a by-product of the dynamics of the relationship between the bully (or group of bullies) and the victim. Consequently, victimization can be halted and/or prevented by changing the dynamics of that relationship. Conversely, a second model suggests that victimization is, in part, the product of poor social, cognitive, or behavioral skills of the victimized child. Therefore, victimization can be prevented or ameliorated by helping the victimized child to attain the skills needed to form adaptive relationships with his or her peers. These models have resulted in contrasting intervention techniques that can be divided into two groups: (1) victim-inclusive interventions (i.e., interventions that include both perpetrator and the victim), and (2) victim-focused interventions (i.e., interventions that are directed only at the victimized child).

Victim-Inclusive Interventions

These interventions operate by enlisting the support of the bullies and the victim in identifying a solution and implementing a solution to the bullying. Although the victim is included, the amount of involvement may vary from a cursory to a central role. Also, these programs are united by their emphasis on interpersonal problem-solving (through a variety of techniques).

The Shared Concern Method/No-Blame Approach

The Shared Concern Method provides a structure approach for bringing bullies and victims together. This approach dictates that once bullying has taken place, the teacher meets individually with all of the students involved in the event (Pikas, 1989). The interviews start with the most powerful student (the ring leader) and ends with the least powerful (the victim). Each bully is asked to identify the problem and behaviors he or she can engage in to help the victim. The bully is asked to engage in the behaviors for a week, with the promise that the teacher will check back with him or her in a week to see how it is working. For the victim, the intervention is mostly focused on supportive listening but may include information on how to avoid being bullied. Follow-up meetings are continued until the bullying has ended. The process culminates in a group meeting in which the bullies share positive feedback with the victim and discuss how the positive relationship can be maintained.

The No-Blame Approach focuses on a similar process. This approach, developed by Maines and Robinson (1998), differs from the Shared Concern Method in three ways. First, the bullied child is the first to be consulted. By starting the process with the victim, they argue that the adult can serve as the voice for the victim during the remainder of the process. Second, the students involved in bullying meet as a group throughout the process. Finally, the group (as compared to its individual members) is given the responsibility of implementing the solution. As with the Shared Concern Method, these meetings would continue until the bullying has ended.

There are few published evaluations of the effectiveness of these approaches. Pikas (1989) provides anecdotal examples of the effectiveness of the Shared Concern Method. These reports suggest that the procedure was overwhelmingly successful; however, they did not provide much detail of the implementation or evaluation procedures. Although he has recently clarified the procedures of this method (Pikas, 2003), he still fails to provide an empirical evaluation of the program. Smith, Cowie, and Sharp (1994) reported that more than half of the twenty-one teachers they trained were able to use the method successfully, and that teachers who used it felt it was effective. They concluded that it was useful as short-term intervention, but might need to be paired with other interventions to achieve long-term results. There is less published evidence of the effectiveness of the No-Blame approach. Maines and Robinson (cited in Smith et al., 1994) presented case study evidence supporting the effectiveness of the No-Blame Approach, including a 100 percent success rate among primary school students and a 96 percent success rate among secondary school students. However, these results are based on a relatively small number of cases ($N = 57$).

Bully Courts

Bully courts are a strategy in which students are allowed to review behavioral problems and mete out punishment, ideally within the context of a larger antibullying policy (Elliott, 1991). The courts are organized around student councils that consist of four students. One adult attends the meetings, but decisions are made by the students and are binding. They meet once per week and hear presentations by the victim, bully, and witnesses. This approach requires active involvement from the victim by making the victim responsible for presenting his or her case before the council.

Kidscape did establish thirty bully courts in primary and secondary schools and have generally reported positive results (Elliott, 1991). They monitored the intervention in eight schools and found a profound drop in the amount of bullying reported (a drop from 70 to 6 percent). However, their report was not a systematic evaluation, and subsequent attempts to followup on those results have been unsuccessful (Smith, Cowie, & Sharp, 1994). Mahdavi and Smith (2002) evaluated a bully court program implemented with 1,800 secondary school students. They found strong support for the effectiveness of the bully court as perceived by both students and staff. For example, 77 percent of victims reported that the bully courts resulted in better outcomes than when individual teachers attempted to deal with bullying. However, they did not provide much information on the program's impact on the overall rates of bullying in the school.

Conflict Resolution and Peer Mediation

Most often conflict resolution programs are curricula-based programs that are designed to train students and school staff in formal methods of resolving interpersonal conflict. The skills aspect of the training may focus on practical skills (e.g., effective communication, negotiation, and anger management), or understanding of conflict (e.g., attitudes toward conflict). These programs can be adult or child focused. In the case of child-focused programs, frequently a set of peer mediators receive intensive training in conflict-resolution skills and are then responsible for helping their peers resolve conflict. For most programs the process is similar. First, the students experiencing the conflict present their stories. Then, the mediator helps the plaintiffs to recognize commonalities in their perception of the problem and leads them in discussing potential solutions to the problem. Finally, the mediator uses the solutions generated by the plaintiffs to help identify a mutually agreeable resolution to the problem.

Although these programs have been growing in popularity as a potential solution to school violence, they have rarely been implemented specifically for bullying. Their presence in schools makes it likely that they are being used to resolve bullying situations. The small literature evaluating these programs has provided limited support for their effectiveness. In support of peer mediation, Cunningham and colleagues (1998) implemented a peer-focused conflict-resolution curriculum in three primary schools. They found that the program resulted in dramatic reductions in physical aggression as measured by mediator reports and direct observation. Also, they found that teachers and mediators felt positive about the program and desired to continue it.

In contrast, Orpinas and colleagues (2000) evaluated a program designed to reduce aggressive behaviors that included (among other interventions) conflict-resolution training for teachers, and peer-mediation training for students. They found that the intervention had virtually no effect on aggressive behaviors (including fight, fight-related injuries, threats of harm), or on the rate of students missing school out of fear of being harmed. Smith and colleagues (Smith, Daunic, Miller, & Robinson, 2002) conducted a combination conflict resolution–peer mediation program in three middle schools. After up to four years of intervention (the dosage per year was small), their evaluation found no changes in the school environment as perceived by teachers and students, no differences in student conflict-related attitudes, and only a downward trend in the number of disciplinary problems.

Summary

Although this review is not comprehensive, it is sufficient to illustrate some concerns about the state of what is known about this approach. First among these concerns is that there were few published evaluations of the programs, and frequently the evaluation information that was available was not from controlled studies. Second, these interventions require teachers (an in some cases other youth) to accomplish complex tasks that are made even more complex by the power differentials that are found in bullying relationships. It seems risky and potentially dangerous to engage in these interventions without extensive training and supervised practice, and the involvement of school counselors or psychologists. Unfortunately, the published descriptions of these programs do not provide many details on training and supervision required for successful implementation of these programs.

Also, the application of the existing research may be limited by the fact that the published evaluations were almost exclusively done in Great Britain. Cross-cultural differences in the prevalence, stability, and dynamics of bullying (e.g., Smith, et al., 1999; Watts, 1998) suggest that these interventions will need to be tested in other cultures.

Although there was more research on peer mediation and conflict resolution, there is limited support for effectiveness of this approach. Williams (2001) argued that the success of these programs might be affected by several implementation issues, including the selection of the mediators, the quality of the training and feedback, and the types of cases that are referred to mediation. For peer mediation and bully courts, interventions that require the victim to publicly defend themselves, referrals for victimized children, may be inappropriate given what is known about their difficulties with assertion. In fact, Rigby (1996) suggested that peer mediation works best when the participants are roughly of equal power. By definition victims of bullying are subordinate, so they may be at risk of being unable to mediate a solution that is equitable. At this point there is no way to evaluate the validity of this claim, since the effectiveness of peer mediation in bullying situations has not been directly tested.

Furthermore, most of the programs that have been evaluated are evaluated relative to outcomes for aggressive children. In fact, the descriptions of these interventions suggest that they are conceptually more similar to perpetrator-focused interventions than victim-focused interventions. To the degree that they are effective, they were effective with aggressive children. The one study (Orpinas et al., 2000) that did measure outcomes related to victimization found that the program had no effect on children's perception of their risk of being harmed.

Victim-Focused Interventions

In general, these interventions are focused on providing the victimized children with the skills needed to prevent victimization, to stop existing victimization, or to improve the psychological well-being of children who have been victimized. Although there are some conceptual differences among the interventions, the programs in this category are focused on the needs of the victim and provide little, if any, direct intervention with bullies. Examples include the following:

- Social skills training/assertiveness training,
- Miscellaneous therapies (e.g., peer counseling, art therapy, martial arts training).

Social Skills Training/Assertiveness Training

Social Skills. Social skills training refers to a variety of programs and curricula that focus on helping youth establish and/or maintain appropriate relationships. To enhance social competency, curricula such as Skillstreaming (e.g., McGinnis & Goldstein, 1997) employ a variety of interventions ranging from teaching interpersonal skills (e.g., the ability to communicate with adults and peers, social rules such as giving and receiving feedback, and social manners) to enhancing cognitive and behavioral self-management skills (e.g., the ability to appraise social situations, awareness of the impact of one's behavior on others). Within the social skills research, there is a distinct literature that focuses on assertiveness training. These programs seek to help victimized students stand up for themselves without becoming aggressive or violating the rights of others, by helping them to develop new responses to bullying situations and by giving them a forum in which to rehearse and receive feedback on these strategies (Sharp & Cowie, 1994).

Social skills training programs have rarely been used as a primary intervention for bullying, but they have been implemented successfully with school-aged children for a variety of behavioral problems (e.g., Rotheram-Boris, 1988). In a review of twenty-five social skills programs, Moote, Smythe, and Woodarski (1999) found some positive results reported in twenty-three programs. Positive changes were found on several characteristics relevant to victims of bullying, including improved self-perception, greater likeability among peers, and greater social support from peers. Arora (1991) implemented a social skills intervention that included modules on maintaining friendships and managing anger. She found decreases in bullying and increases in self-esteem as reported by students and teachers. Schneider's (1999) meta-analysis of seventy-nine studies found that social skills training was only moderately effective, but showed its largest effects for withdrawn or socially isolated children.

One of the few evaluations of a social skills training as an intervention for victims of bullying reported mixed results. Fox and Boulton (2003) studied the effects of an eight-week social skills intervention on fifteen children identified as chronic victims of bullying. The intervention included sessions on problem solving, relationship skills (e.g., listening), and assertiveness. The results indicated that the program had significant positive effects on self worth, and marginal improvement in social acceptance. However, there were no changes in several other outcome measures, including measures of psychological symptoms and victimization.

Fox and Boulton's findings are consistent with meta-analyses of social skills training interventions with children who have emotional or behavioral disorders. Quinn and colleagues (Quinn, Kavale, Mathur, Ruterford, & Forness, 1999), for example, found relatively small effect sizes for group interventions. These interventions were not enhanced by the length of the intervention or the age at which intervention was provided. Topping and colleagues' (Topping, Holmes, & Bremmer, 2000) review of 700 outcome evaluations found similar results and concluded that the overall effects of social skills training were mixed.

Sharpe and Cowie (1994) described an assertiveness training program that was included as an adjunct of their bullying prevention program, the Sheffield Project. The program, which included small groups of students from three schools, consisted of lessons in how to be assertive, how to respond to specific bullying situations, and how to request help from others. Their evaluations of the program (both Childs, 1993 and Tonge, 1992 are referenced in Sharpe & Cowie, 1994) indicated significant improvement in self-esteem, and more adaptive coping strategies. Also, 68 percent of the participants reported being bullied less frequently. A follow-up study showed that the decline in bullying and the gains in self-esteem were maintained into the next school year.

Miscellaneous Therapies

Research on effective interventions for victims of bullying contains many idiopathic interventions that can best be summed up as miscellaneous therapies. There is growing sentiment among school counselors and psychologists that this approach should be among the options offered to students involved in bullying. Sandhu (2000), for example, recommended that school counselors expand their roles beyond traditional activities to include developing counseling and therapeutic relationships, and organizing individual and group sessions to provide support to alienated students. In general, interventions in this category treat victimized children individually or in small groups, and at times conceptualize the intervention more as supportive therapy than as a skills-based intervention.

Ross (1996a) proposed a support group format that would involve meeting with six to twelve child or adolescent victims of bullying. The intervention consisted of twelve to twenty weekly sessions that last approximately one hour. The group would initially focus on sharing experiences and emotional catharsis in the context of a safe and supportive environment. However, the ultimate goal is to help the students increase their social skills and decrease the likelihood of continued victimization. Although she recommends that group members be evaluated in terms of self-esteem and behavior change, she does not provide an outcome evaluation of an existing program.

Ross (1996b) described an art therapy that was used with seven primary school children who were traumatized by bullies. Drawings were used to help group members share their feelings and as a way of introducing discussions regarding their relationships with their peers. The artwork was based on relevant topics such as how it feels to be bullied, and facilitated the transition to more complex issues including role-plays that allowed them to gain a deeper understanding of their interactions with the bullies. There was no systematic evaluation of the intervention; however, she did note more confidence and improved social skills in six of seven students.

Peer counseling involves providing a supportive peer-staffed network for the victims of bullying. The interventions range from an anonymous telephone hotline that is staffed by students, to in-person counseling. Carr (1988) provides the most complete description of a peer-counseling training program. The program consisted of more than 100 hours of training including 45 hours of supervision. Sharp and Cowie (1994) described the Bully Line, a peer-counseling center that was used in conjunction with their whole school intervention. The peer counselors provided support for bullied children and, when appropriate, acted as advocates by connecting them with adults. The evaluation, which included sixty randomly selected students, indicated that nearly one-third of the seventh-grade students had used the service, and nearly all students thought it was a good idea.

Twemlow and colleagues (Twemlow, Fonagy, & Sacco, 2001) intervened in the bully/victim problem with a martial arts intervention called the Gentle Warriors Program. The program, which was part of their whole school program, consisted of twenty-four sessions that were tailored to the grade level of the students. Activities included a question-and-answer period, role-playing, reading stories that emphasize ethical principles, and practicing martial arts techniques. All of these activities are provided within a context that emphasized the traditional martial arts values of self-respect, self-control, and virtuous behavior. In this case, it was also provided in the context of a program that emphasized zero tolerance of being a bully or victim. Although they did not include the details of the analysis, Twemlow et al. (2001) reported decreases in disciplinary problems and an increase in academic achievement. In relationship to victims of bullying, they reported less victim behavior such as withdrawal and externalized self-esteem.

Summary

Theoretically, there is a compelling case to be made for interventions like peer counseling. In their study of the stress experienced by secondary school students, Sharp and Thompson (1992) found that students were more likely to talk to peers than to adults. Rigby (1996) reported that, in general, students are sympathetic toward the victim and feel some obligation to help stop bullying. However, Ross (1996a) cautioned that dependence upon peer counselors may decrease students' willingness to consult with adults even when it is indicated. Also, she argues that there is a risk that peer counselors will assume responsibilities far beyond their expertise, thereby placing everyone at greater risk. Existing research suggests that peers can be great assets for preventing bullying, but they are not a panacea and should not substitute for adult advocacy for victimized children.

With therapy interventions, there is a risk (depending on how the program is conceptualized) that the interventions may be seen as blaming the victim. Ross (1996b) showed some sensitivity to this issue by making it a special opportunity afforded to participants. Sharp and Cowie (1994) addressed the issue by setting up strategies to protect the anonymity and confidentiality of students who used peer-counseling services. There is no disputing that the responsibility for bullying lies with the perpetrator. However, the zeal to hold bullies accountable does not necessitate leaving victimized children to their own devices to cope with and recover from their experiences. The risk of blaming the victim is real and requires that extra effort be made to communicate the purpose of victim-focused interventions. This also provides another rationale for pairing these interventions with interventions designed to hold the bully accountable.

The research on interventions that focus on building social skills as a solution to bullying is meager and limited by a variety of methodological and conceptual issues. Most of these studies depend on case study or narrative description (e.g., Ross, 1996b) to validate their effectiveness. These anecdotes are effective in communicating the plight of victims, but are limited when it comes to providing a rationale for widespread adoption of these interventions. Although the outcomes for assertiveness training were impressive, we could find information on only one evaluation of that intervention and that evaluation had a relatively small sample size. The overall lack of information on victim-focused interventions leads us to conclude that it is a promising but still exploratory approach.

CONCLUSIONS AND RECOMMENDATIONS

This survey of the prevention literature does support the argument that victims are a forgotten group. The lack of sufficient evaluation of many of the victim-related interventions is particularly troubling given the distress that is experienced by victimized children. The bullying literature is full of stories and studies that describe the impact of victimization, including severe emotional distress, suicide, and homicide (e.g., Glover, Cartwright, & Gleeson, 1998; Harold, 2002; Head, 1996; Marano, 1995). Also, the occasional violent acting out by victims may grow out of a perceived lack of awareness and/or lack of concern among parents and school staff about the emotional pain and alienation experienced by the victimized child (Hazler & Carney, 2000). The characteristics that put children at risk of victimization also put them at risk for a variety of other poor outcomes, including a variety of internalizing disorders, low self-esteem, and low academic achievement (Durlak, 1995). This makes it all the more important to find ways to intervene directly as a way of changing the developmental trajectory of the victimized child. Toward that goal, this review has two implications/recommendations for school staff or others involved in program implementation, and three recommendations for researchers and others involved in designing and evaluating programs.

Given a dearth of empirically validated intervention programs, the models of the bullying problem and the anecdotal research findings suggest some ways in which teachers, counselors, and other school personnel can assist these youth. First, support appears to be a critical issue for chronically bullied children. As noted earlier, victims of bullying are often isolated, and may believe that adults are unconcerned about their situation (Hazler et al., 1992). If schools adopt an approach that includes bullies and victims, the support may focus on validating their experiences, and protecting them in situations or structuring the environment to minimize situations in which they have to confront bullies. If the focus is only on the victim, the support may be more in the form of listening and giving feedback. The results of Ross (1996b), and Sharp and Thompson (1992) suggest that other victimized children may be an important resource for helping a child improve her or his quality of life.

The information on interventions also suggests a need for school personnel to work on the social skills of victimized children. The interventions that involve victims and bullies assume a requisite set of social skills that may not be natural for victimized children. Consequently, a great deal of preparation may be necessary to ethically and successfully use these interventions. For victim-only interventions, the initial outcomes of assertiveness training are promising (Sharp & Cowie, 1994). More general social skills interventions may help with decreasing the isolation and alienation that is often reported by victimized children (Hodges & Perry, 1999). Whichever intervention approach that is chosen, should not be implemented in a way that results in further stigmatization or blame.

This review of interventions also suggests some next steps for researchers. First, there are several programs that may be effective in improving outcomes for victims, but more research is needed to validate them. In particular, more evaluations are needed for social skills and therapy-focused interventions. For interventions that involve mediation, evaluations need to be expanded to a variety of contexts, and the programs need to be tested in bullying situations. Second, future research of antibullying programs of all types should include measures that are sensitive to victim characteristics and should expand their evaluation of the effectiveness of programs to include these measures. In most of the intervention research, there is a largely unacknowledged assumption that if acting out among bullies is decreased, victim outcomes will automatically improve. The outcomes from studies included in this review and most of the outcomes from evaluations of whole school programs indicate that this assumption is largely untested and may be incorrect.

Finally, greater effort should be made to include victim-focused intervention as a part of whole school bullying prevention interventions. The dearth of research on interventions for victims appears to be, at least in part, the result of an emphasis on interventions focused on bullies. There is consensus that victim-focused programs should not replace interventions for bullies, but in fact operate best within the context of these programs (Smith & Sharp, 1994). Therefore, with each implementation of a whole school program, the implementers should be required to provide details on how the program will provide support, enhance skills, or otherwise address the needs of victimized children and their families.

REFERENCES

Arora, T. (1991). The use of victim support groups. In P. K. Smith & D. Thompson (Eds.), *Practical approaches to bullying* (pp. 37-47). London: David Fulton.

Bernstein, J. Y., & Watson, M. W. (1997). Children who are targets of bullying: A victim pattern. *Journal of Interpersonal Violence, 12,* 483-498.

Carr, R. A. (1988). The city-wide peer counseling program. *Children and Youth Services Review, 10,* 217-232.

Cunningham, C. E., Cunningham, L. J., Martorelli, V., Tran, A., Young, J., & Zacharias, R. (1998). The effects of primary division, student-mediated conflict resolution programs on playground aggression. *Journal of Child Psychology and Psychiatry & Allied Disciplines, 39,* 653-662.

Durlak, J. (1995). *School-based prevention programs for children and adolescents.* Thousand Oaks, CA: Sage.

Elliott, M. (1991). *Bullying: A practical guide to coping for schools*. Harlow: Longman.

Fox, C. L., & Boulton, M. J. (2003). Evaluating the effectiveness of a social skills training programme for victims of bullying. *Educational Research, 45*, 231-247.

Glover, D., Cartwright, N., & Gleeson, D. (1998). *Towards bully-free schools: Interventions in action*. Philadelphia: Open University Press.

Goldbaum, S., Craig, W. M., Pepler, D., & Connolly, J. (2003). Developmental Trajectories of victimization: Identifying risk and protective factors. *Journal of Applied School Psychology, 19*, 139-156.

Harold, E. (2002). Preventing youth violence and bullying: Respect yourself, protect yourself. Retrieved August 17, 2006, from www.ncjrs.gov/html/ojjdp/news_at_glance/2002_11_6/other.html]

Hazler, R. J., & Carney, J. V. (2000). When victims turn aggressors: Factors in the development of deadly school violence. *Professional School Counseling, 4*, 105-112.

Hazler, R. J., Hoover, J. H., & Oliver, R. (1992). What kids say about bullying. *Executive Educator, 14*, 20-22.

Head, R. (1996). Remembering Brian. *Journal of Emotional and Behavioral Problems, 5*, 6-9.

Hodges, E. V., & Perry, D. G. (1999). Personal and interpersonal antecedents and consequences of victimization by peers. *Journal of Personality and Social Psychology, 76*, 677-685.

Holmes, R. M., & Holmes, S. T. (2000). *Mass murder in the United States*. Upper Saddle River, NJ: Prentice Hall.

Hoover, J. H., Oliver, R., & Hazler, R. J. (1992). Bullying: Perceptions of adolescent victims in the mid-western USA. *School Psychology International, 13*, 5-16.

Leary, M. R., Kowalski, R. M., Smith, L., & Phillips, S. (2003). Teasing, rejection, and violence: Case studies of the school shootings. *Aggressive Behavior, 29*, 202-214.

Limber, S. P., Flerx, V. C., Nation, M. A., & Melton, G. B. (1998). Bullying among school children in the United States. In M. W. Watts (Ed.), *Cross-cultural perspectives on youth and violence* (pp. 159-173). Stamford, CT: JAI Press.

Mahdavi, J., & Smith, P. K. (2002). The operation of a bully court and perceptions of its success: A case study. *School Psychology International, 23*, 327-341.

Maines, B., & Robinson, G. (1998). The no blame approach to bullying. In D. Shorrocks-Taylor (Ed.), *Directions in educational psychology* (pp. 281-295). London: Whurr Publishers.

Marano, H. E. (1995, September/October). Big, bad, bully. *Psychology Today, 50-56, 62-69, 72-82.

McGinnis, E., & Goldstein, A. P. (1997). *Skillstreaming the elementary school child: New strategies and perspectives for teaching prosocial skills*. Champaign, IL: Research Press.

Moote, G. T., Smythe, N. J., & Woodarski, J. S. (1999). Social skills training with youth in school settings: A review. *Research on Social Work Practice, 9*, 427-465.

Nansel, T. R., Overpeck, M., Pilla, R. S., Ruan, W. J., Simons-Morton, B., & Scheidt, P. (2001). Bullying behaviors among US youth: Prevalence and association with psychosocial adjustment. *Journal of the American Medical Association, 285,* 2094-2100.

Oliver, R. L., Young, T. A., & LaSalle, S. M. (1994). Early lessons in bullying and victimization: The help and hindrance of children's literature. *School Counselor, 42,* 137-146.

Olweus, D. (1993). *Bullying at school: What we know, what we can do.* Oxford, UK: Blackwell.

Orpinas, P., Kelder, S., Franlowski, R., Murray, N., Zhang, Q., & McAlister, A. (2000). Outcome evaluation of a multi-component violence-prevention program for middle schools: The students for peace project. *Health Education Research, 15,* 45-58.

Pepler, D. J., Craig, W. M., Ziegler, S., & Charach, A. (1994). An evaluation of anti-bullying intervention in Toronto schools. *Canadian Journal of Community Mental Health, 13,* 95-110.

Pikas, A. (1989). A pure concept of mobbing give the best results for treatment. *School Psychology International, 10,* 95-104.

Pikas, A. (2002). New developments of the Shared Concern Method. *School Psychology International, 23,* 307-326.

Quinn, M. M., Kavale, K. A., Mathur, S. R., Rutherford, R. B., Jr., & Forness, S. R. (1999). A meta-analysis of social skill interventions for students with emotional or behavioral disorders. *Journal of Emotional and Behavioral Disorders, 7,* 54-64.

Rigby, K. (1996). *Bullying in schools and what to do about it.* Melbourne: Council for Educational Research.

Ross, D. M. (1996a). *Childhood bullying and teasing: What school personnel, other professionals, and parents can do.* Alexandria, VA: American Counseling Association.

Ross, C. (1996b). Conflict at school: The use of an art therapy approach to support children who are bullied. In M. Liebman (Ed.), *Arts approaches to conflict* (pp. 131-151). Bristol, PA: Jessica Kingsley.

Rotheram-Boris, M. J. (1988). Assertiveness training with children. In R. H. Price and E. L. Cowen's (Eds.), *Fourteen ounces of prevention: A casebook for practitioners* (pp. 83-97). Washington, DC: American Psychological Association.

Sandhu, D. S. (2000). Alienated students: Counseling strategies to curb school violence. *Professional School Counseling, 4,* 81-85.

Schneider, B. H. (1992). Didactic methods for enhancing children's peer relations: A quantitative review. *Clinical Psychology Review, 12,* 363-382.

Schwartz, D., Dodge, K. A., & Coie, J. D. (1993). The emergence of chronic peer victimization in boys' play groups. *Child Development, 64,* 1755-1772.

Sharp, S., & Cowie, H. (1994). Empowering pupils to take positive action against bullying. In P. K. Smith & S. Sharp (Eds.), *School bullying: Insights and perspectives* (pp. 108-131). New York: Routledge.

Sharp, S., & Thompson, D. (1992). Sources of stress: A contrast between pupil perspective and pastoral teachers' perceptions. *School Psychology International, 13,* 229-242.

Smith, P. K., Cowie, H., & Sharp, S. (1994). Working directly with pupils involved in bullying situations. In P. K. Smith & S. Sharp (Eds.), *School bullying: Insights and perspectives* (pp. 193-212). New York: Routledge.

Smith, P. K., Morita, Y., Junger-Tas, J., Olweus, D., Catalano, R., & Slee, P. (Eds.) (1999). *The nature of school bullying: A cross-national perspective.* New York: Routledge.

Smith, P. K., & Sharp, S. (Eds.) (1994). *School bullying: Insights and perspectives.* New York: Routledge.

Smith, P. K., Shu, S., & Madsen, K. (2001). Characteristics of victims of school bullying: Developmental changes in coping strategies and skills. In J. Juvonen & S. Graham (Eds.), *Peer harassment in school: The plight of the vulnerable and victimized* (pp. 332-351). New York: Guilford.

Smith, S. W., Daunic, A. P., Miller, M. D., & Robinson, T. R. (2002). Conflict resolution and peer mediation in middle schools: Extending the process and outcome knowledge base. *Journal of Social Psychology, 142,* 567-586.

Topping, K., Holmes, E. A., & Bremner, W. (2000). The effectiveness of school-based programs for the promotion of social competence. In R. Baron & J. Parker (Eds.), *The handbook of emotional intelligence: Theory development, assessment, and application at home, school, and in the workplace* (pp. 411-432). San Francisco: Jossey-Bass.

Twemlow, S. W., Fonagy, P., & Sacco, F. C. (2001). A social systems-power dynamics approach to preventing school violence. In M. Shafii, E. Shafii, & S. Lee (Eds.), *School violence: Assessment, management, prevention* (pp. 273-289). Washington: American Psychiatric Press.

Watts, M. W. (Ed.). (1998). *Cross-cultural perspectives on youth and violence.* Stamford, CT: JAI Press.

Williams, K. M. (2001). What derails peer mediation? In J. N. Burstyn, G. Bender, R. Casella, H. W. Gordon, D. P. Guerra, K. V. Luschen, R. Stephens, & K. M. Williams (Eds.), *Preventing Violence in Schools: A Challenge to American Democracy* (pp. 199-208). Mahwah, NJ: Erlbaum.

Chapter 15

Peer-Rejected and Bullied Children: A Safe Schools Initiative for Elementary School Students

Melissa E. DeRosier

PEER RELATIONSHIPS

Children's social relationships with other children are critically important for their adjustment and sense of well-being (see Parker, Rubin, Price, & DeRosier, 1995, for review). Children are highly motivated to get along with and be accepted by peers (DeRosier, 1995). From the time children enter school, peers take on an increasingly meaningful and influential role, becoming key providers of support, companionship, advice, and affirmation as children mature through the elementary school years and adolescence (Furman & Burhmester, 1992).

Children who experience difficulties in their peer relationships exhibit a number of concurrent behavioral, psychological, and academic problems and are at heightened risk for a wide variety of later maladjustment (Kupersmidt, Coie, & Dodge, 1990; Parker et al., 1995). Research supports the influential role of peer problems in the development of numerous negative outcomes, including suicide (Carney, 2000), drug abuse (Spooner, 1999), educational underachievement (Woodward & Fergusson, 2000), delinquency and antisocial behavior (Brendgen, Vitaro, & Bukowski, 1998), and depression (Boivin & Hymel, 1997). The predictive strength of peer problems is not simply an artifact of other associated problems, such as aggression or low socioeconomic status (SES). Rather, rejection and victimization have been repeatedly supported as independent and unique contributors to

Bullying, Victimization, and Peer Harassment
© 2007 by The Haworth Press, Inc. All rights reserved.
doi:10.1300/5808_15

future adjustment problems (DeRosier, Kupersmidt, & Patterson, 1994; Hugh-Jones & Smith, 1999; Olweus, 1993). As peer problems become more chronic or severe, the risk for negative outcomes significantly increases (DeRosier et al., 1994).

Peer relationship problems typically fall within two broad categories: rejection and bullying. Peer rejection involves the active dislike, avoidance, and exclusion of a child by many other peers. Other children actively avoid interacting with this child and he lacks social support within the peer group. Bullying includes a wide variety of peer behaviors, including verbal and physical assault, intimidation, humiliation, damaging another's property, rumor spreading, and organizing exclusion. While experiencing either rejection or bullying places children at risk for adjustment problems, experiencing both rejection and bullying makes the risk for maladjustment even greater. Unfortunately, when children experience one of these peer problems, they are more likely to experience the other (DeRosier & Thomas, 2003). For example, when rejection is more extreme (disliked by a large majority of peers), it is more likely that a child will experience bullying by peers (DeRosier & Thomas). Bullies may see a rejected child as an easy target because he or she clearly lacks potential defenders within the peer group.

There are many reasons why a particular child might develop peer problems (Coie, 1990, provides a review of enduring value). Social immaturity, mean behavior, intrusiveness, and shyness have all been linked to the development of poor peer relationships. However, regardless of the cause(s), social difficulties with peers are extremely stressful for children (Zakriski, Jacobs, & Coie, 1997). It is traumatic for children to be picked on, bullied, and teased by peers and this stressful life event has been found to greatly impact on children's psychological adjustment and development (Beane, 1998; Repetti, McGrath, & Ishikawa, 1999).

PEER PROBLEMS AND SCHOOL VIOLENCE

A great number of children experience rejection and bullying by peers within their school environment. Research examining children's social status within the peer group through peer nominations for liking and disliking have consistently found that approximately 10 percent to 12 percent of students experience significant levels of peer rejection (Coie, Dodge, & Coppotelli, 1982; Parker et al., 1995). Most students (approximately 80 percent) report being bullied at some time during their school years with approximately 15 percent being bullied on a regular basis (National Center for Education Statistics [NCES], 2000; Olweus, 1993). Nearly one in every five students (20 percent) reports being physically threatened by another student (Gottfredson Associates, Inc., 2000). Over 43 percent of students fear harassment at school (U.S. Bureau of Justice [USBJ], 2000). School violence typically escalates over the late elementary and middle school years (USBJ, 2000) with middle school students reporting the highest frequency of bullying and interpersonal threats (22 percent). Expressions of aggression, however, tend to intensify as children become older. Students aged twelve to nineteen experience actual violent assaults (e.g., physical attacks, taking property by force, use of weapons) at a rate of 4.2 percent (U.S. Department of Justice, 1998), up from 3.1 percent in just three years.

When bullied, rejected, or harassed, most children do not confide in adults. This secrecy is partly due to embarrassment, but primarily, children do not believe that adult intervention will be effective (Olweus, 1993). In fact, most children believe that telling an adult will result in retribution by the bully. Therefore, adults are often unaware of the extent of children's peer problems. When bullying becomes more chronic and severe, children attempt to escape or avoid the bullies. For example, 15 percent of all school absenteeism is directly related to fears of being bullied at school (USBJ, 2000). When avoidance is unsuccessful, victims may engage in spontaneous reactive aggression toward bullies in an attempt to escape or thwart the bullying (Schwartz, Proctor, & Chien, 2001). The anger and resentment that result from being bullied also promote reactive aggression in the form of revenge or retribution (Schwartz, Dodge, Pettit, & Bates, 1997). Observations and student reports indicate that over 50 percent of fights at school are initiated as retaliation against teasing or bullying (Boulton, 1993). Seeing adults as ineffective, victims of bullying believe that they must take matters into their own hands through vengeful aggression (Cintron, 2000).

Targeted school shootings exemplify extreme examples of this phenomenon. The United States Secret Service (USSS) and U.S. Department of Education recently investigated all examples of targeted school violence (i.e., school shootings by students on school grounds) in America between 1974 and 2000 (thirty-seven shootings, forty-one attackers; Vossekuil, Fein, Reddy, Borum, & Modzeleski, 2002). The USSS found that, in the majority of cases, the shooters had experienced chronic, severe rejection and bullying by peers and their primary motivation for violence was revenge. In multiple case histories, school shooters had experienced peer problems of social ostracism and peer victimization that they experienced as harassment. These peer experiences contributed significantly to the planning and actualization of violence (Vossekuil et al., 2002).

SAFE SCHOOLS INITIATIVES

In the aftermath of tragic incidents of school violence in the United States, increased emphasis and attention have been placed on the quality of the social climate in our nation's schools. Numerous national and local initiatives have been started to address school violence concerns and to intervene with youth who experience peer problems. In 1998, the U.S. Department of Education set forth a major national initiative to combat school violence. Legislation was passed by Congress to provide substantial monies to school systems through the Safe Schools/Healthy Students (SS/HS) Initiative Grant Awards. Since that date, millions of federal dollars have been awarded to over 100 school districts across the country. Each school district proposed a unique set of interventions and services aimed at promoting healthy childhood development and preventing school violence. Collaboration among educational, mental health, social service, law enforcement, and, as appropriate, juvenile justice systems was set out as an integral part of each SS/HS award.

In 1999, the Wake County Public School System (WCPSS) of North Carolina was awarded a three-year SS/HS grant. A primary goal of Wake County's initiative was to infuse multiple levels of intervention and prevention efforts for K-12 students and to promote an infrastructure that would sustain these efforts beyond the end of the granting period. Community involvement and the establishment of safe and secure facilities were also primary goals of the grant. Peer Connections was selected by Wake County as one if its three safe schools initiatives with elementary school students. Peer Connections combines accurate assessment of peer problems with an effective social skills group intervention for children experiencing significant peer problems of rejection and bullying. Through Peer Connections, forty elementary school counselors were trained, social climate and peer relations was assessed for each school, and social skills small group interventions were implemented within the school setting. This chapter is devoted to describing each component of Peer Connections and examining its impact on the school-based adjustment for elementary students who participated in the program.

ASSESSMENT

The first component of Peer Connections is accurate assessment of the school social climate in order to identify students who are experiencing a significant level of peer rejection or bullying by peers. For this purpose, sociometric methodology is used (i.e., SCAN; DeRosier & Thomas, 2003) through which trained staff administer a peer-nomination technique so that a set of children (typically a class or grade at school) can nominate peers who match specific descriptions (e.g., children who are teased or bullied) in an anonymous, confidential manner. By comparing scores across the entire grade, a child's social functioning in a particular area can be evaluated relative to that of his or her broader peer group. Since the 1930s, the use of sociometric peer-nomination methods to evaluate peer relationships has been repeatedly supported through hundreds of studies with children (see Cillessen & Bukowski, 2000 for review). Abundant support has been provided for the predictive and concurrent validity of the sociometric classification system as well as for its stability over time and across settings (e.g., Cillessen, Bukowski, & Haselager, 2000). Given that peer problems are underreported by children to adults, sociometrics are the most accurate means of identifying children who experience elevated levels of bullying and rejection by peers at school.

SOCIAL SKILLS GROUP INTERVENTION (SSGRIN)

The second component of Peer Connections is a small group social skills intervention entitled SSGRIN (i.e., *S*ocial *S*kills *GR*oup *IN*tervention; DeRosier, 2002a) for children experiencing rejection and bullying at school. SSGRIN was originally developed and refined through years of evaluation research and clinical experience implementing the intervention in the WCPSS. Beginning in 1994, the author worked with school principals and counselors to develop a program that was not only effective, but also feasible for use within the school setting. For the SS/HS grant, students who were identified through SCAN's sociometric methodology as experiencing significant peer problems of rejection or bullying participated in SSGRIN through small groups at school. Trained school counselors and psychologists headed the program at their school, leading the SSGRIN groups with identified students.

By definition, peer problems are social in nature. Understandably, group interventions are often the treatment of choice for youth experiencing rejection or bullying by peers (Gresham, 1997). In a group, youth learn and practice in vivo with other same-aged peers. Peer interactions in the group occur in real time so that group leaders can directly intervene with problem situations and reinforce positive changes as they occur. A group setting is more structured and safe than real-life peer settings, so willingness to try new social behaviors is increased. Also, youth can receive immediate, constructive feedback from peers, which has significant weight.

In general, the research on social skills training groups has a long history and documents a large number of programs with differing populations, ages, and skill sets targeted for investigation. While this literature is too extensive to review here, recent comprehensive reviews of empirically rigorous studies of social skills training with children clearly support their use for improving children's social relations and functioning across a diverse set of problematic behaviors and psychopathology (for reviews, see Asher, Parker, & Walker, 1996; Consortium on the School-based Promotion of Social Competence, 1994; Gresham, 1997).

The SSGRIN protocol combines multiple empirically validated social learning and cognitive–behavioral techniques in order to (1) build basic behavioral and cognitive social skills, (2) reinforce prosocial attitudes and behavior, and (3) build adaptive coping strategies for social problems, such as teasing. SSGRIN is designed to be a *generic* social skills training intervention that can be applied to a wide variety of social problems. To this end, SSGRIN incorporates skills and techniques that have been empirically supported through different types of intervention programs. Successful social skills programs for children with peer problems (see Asher et al., 1996 for review) typically focus on building *prosocial skills* (e.g., communication, initiation, cooperation). Successful preventive interventions with aggressive, antisocial youth typically focus on *inhibition skills* (e.g., anger management, impulse control) to decrease negative behaviors (Greenberg, Domitrovich, & Bumbarger, 2001). Successful interventions for internalizing disorders often focus on *coping skills* (e.g., cognitive restructuring, emotion management, positive assertion) (Greenberg et al., 2001). Therefore, SSGRIN incorporates each of the aforementioned skill areas into its training so as to be as generally applicable to different types of peer problems (e.g., rejected, socially isolated, bullies and victims) as possible.

During SSGRIN, elementary-aged children attend ten small group sessions, typically one time per week for fifty minutes. For Peer Connections, groups take place within the school; however, the curriculum can be used within clinic, camp, or after-school programs as well. Six to eight children is the recommended size for the groups. Within the sessions, skills and concepts are taught through didactic instruction, practice (games, activities), modeling, role-playing, positive reinforcement, and cognitive reframing. Each session's content builds upon that of previous sessions so that new information is integrated with acquired information in a step-wise fashion. Similar to the acquisition of academic skills, training of more complicated social skills (e.g., negotiation) builds on the training of more basic skills (e.g., impulse control) in prior sessions. SSGRIN places all skill training within a conceptual framework of achieving social goals. Stressing not only what to do (i.e., behavior), but also why to do it (i.e., cognition) helps increase children's perceptions of the importance or meaningfulness of the skills, so that they may be more motivated to attempt these skills outside of the group (Weist, Borden, Finney, & Ollendick, 1991). Behavior management is accomplished through use of a combined short- (end of each session) and long-term (end of all sessions) token economy. Table 15.1 provides a detailed list of each skill and concept taught in each session.

PRIOR EFFECTIVENESS RESEARCH ON SSGRIN

Since 1994, yearly pre–post evaluations have been conducted on the efficacy of SSGRIN for improving children's peer relationships and social behavior. Early results in combination with experience working in schools and constructive feedback were used to modify SSGRIN's content and procedures. The intervention's current form was finalized in 1996. Pre–post control group evaluations with third through fifth graders have been conducted and bore similar results.

For example, in a study of third graders (DeRosier, 2004), students with specific peer relationship problems (i.e., elevated peer dislike, victimization, or social anxiety) were identified in the fall and randomly assigned to treatment ($N = 187$) or no-treatment control ($N = 194$) conditions. Trained school counselors and their interns administered SSGRIN within the school setting between January and April. Identical pre–post measures (peer nominations, teacher-report, self-report) were administered approximately six months apart.

An examination of the magnitude and direction of change (standardized with mean $= 0$, $SD = 1$) in functioning for each group revealed multiple significant group differences. For example, children who participated in SSGRIN showed (1) improvement in peer liking, whereas control children showed a decline; (2) improvement in self-esteem and self-efficacy for social situations, whereas control children showed declines in these areas; and (3) a decrease in antisocial affiliations, whereas control children affiliated more with antisocial peers at follow-up. Further evaluation, one-year following completion of SSGRIN, revealed that these benefits were not only sustained, but enhanced. Additional benefits of fewer negative nominations by peers, lower depressed affect, and more positive outcome expectancy for social situations were evident one year post intervention (DeRosier & Marcus, 2005). Overall, evaluation results support the effectiveness of

TABLE 15.1. Skills and concepts taught during each session of SSGRIN.

Session 1: Getting acquainted
Purpose, goals of group
Group rules, confidentiality, and token economy
Getting acquainted, Group cohesion building
Session 2: Showing respect for yourself and others
Self-esteem, respect for self and others
Motto #1: "I am special and important"
Motto #2: "I respect myself and others"
Respect versus fear distinction
Teasing, integrated with self-esteem and respect
Session 3: Looking toward the future
Role models
Goals, short- and long-term
Action plans, developing action plans for social situations
Consequences, positive and negative, short- and long-term
Session 4: Taking responsibility
Motto #3: "I am responsible for what I do and say"
Stop and think, tie to goals and consequences
Session 5: Communicating your thoughts and feelings
Verbal versus nonverbal communication
Listening skills
Coping with rumors

Session 6: Changing your Point of View
Assumptions
Check-it-out
Perspective taking, empathy
Session 7: Building friendships
Friendship qualities, personal strengths and weaknesses
Initiation of play and conversation
Coping with peer rejection
Perseverance, social motivation
Session 8: Cooperating with others
Cooperation
Compromise and negotiation
Coping with peer pressure
Session 9: Knowing how you feel
Emotional interference
Self-awareness of emotions, physiological signs
Motto #4: "I know how I feel"
Managing emotions, taking a break
Session 10: Reviewing what you've learned
Comprehensive review
Role-play review
Social goal setting

SSGRIN not only for enhancing children's relationships, but also for improving social-cognitive and behavioral skills, both at immediate and one-year follow-up.

SS/HS IMPLEMENTATION OF SSGRIN

Pretest data were collected in the fall of the school year. A total of 943 fourth-grade students across 10 elementary schools participated in the study at both time points. The sample was evenly distributed across genders with a mean age of 9.6 years. The racial distribution was: 71 percent white, 20 percent African American, 3 percent Hispanic, 2 percent Asian, and 4 percent mixed race or other minorities. This distribution mirrors that of the broader community. The SES of the sample ranged from lower to upper middle-class families.

Children with significant peer relationship difficulties in the fall were identified through SCAN. Specifically, children were eligible to participate in SSGRIN if they were highly disliked by peers *or* if they experienced a significant level of bullying by peers (i.e., the number of peer nominations a child received was greater than or equal to one standard deviation above the mean for either item). Out of the total, 200 students were identified as experiencing one (46 percent were disliked only and 21 percent were bullied only) or both (33 percent) of these peer problems. The racial and gender distributions of this subsample were equivalent to those of the total sample.

Then, school counselors attended a one-day training workshop during which the author reviewed all SSGRIN treatment procedures and materials. Training involved didactic instruction, extensive role-playing, and modeling to master the treatment. Each school was also assigned an intern to work with the school counselor as a coleader for the SSGRIN groups. Following training, counselors attended three follow-up supervision meetings and interns attended weekly supervision meetings.

Parental consent for participation in the intervention was sought in early January. Of the 200 eligible students, 139 received parental consent to participate. Analyses revealed that those students who received parental consent were significantly more disliked and had fewer friends in their grade compared to those who did not receive parental consent ($F(5,195) = 6.94$, $p < .0001$). These groups did not differ on demographic characteristics or any other adjustment areas. For subsequent analyses, eligible students without consent were dropped from the sample.

The SSGRIN groups began in January and continued for ten weeks. Groups included five to six students and were of mixed gender with no fewer than two members of either gender per group. Based on the size of the school, two to three groups were conducted. Sessions ran for fifty minutes, one time per week, and were conducted during school hours. To sustain the integrity of treatment, (1) group leaders were blind as to which eligibility criteria led to a child's inclusion in treatment; (2) group leaders followed the SSGRIN treatment manual in which each session was clearly structured and scripted; (3) all needed materials were provided, including worksheets, poster boards, and prizes; and (4) standardized progress notes were completed by both group leaders after each session to document what transpired and the progress made for the group and each child. Following the ten sessions, the posttest data collection took place.

Data Collection Procedures

Identical measures were collected from students at both pre- and posttest. At each time point, pencil-and-paper questionnaires were group administered to students by classroom. For the sociometric nominations, students were asked to nominate all the peers in their grade who matched each of the following descriptions: (1) children they like the most (LM), (2) children they like the least (LL), (3) children who fight a lot (aggression), (4) children who get picked on or called names a lot (victimization), and (5) children who are their friends (friendship). To make a nomination, students were presented with a roster for each item that included all the students in the fourth grade at their school. Students were asked to circle the number next to the name of all students who met each description.

Four self-report questionnaires were also completed by students. First, children's social self-perceptions were assessed via the Social Interactions Survey (SIS; DeRosier, 1995, 2002b). The SIS provides several short vignettes describing a social situation (e.g., rejection by peers) and children indicate, on a 100-point analog scale, the degree to which they fit each description. Six specific areas were assessed: peer acceptance, peer rejection, bullying behavior, victimization by peers, social withdrawal, and affiliating with antisocial peers (hanging out with children who get in trouble a lot or engage in antisocial activities). Next, the Social Anxiety Scale for Children-Revised (La Greca & Stone, 1993) was used to assess children's social anxiety with peers. This measure includes statements reflecting anxiety about interacting with peers, such as "I feel shy even with kids I know well" and "I worry about what other kids think of me." Scale scores for anxiety in general and fear of negative evaluation were generated from these items.

Third, children's depressive symptoms were assessed using the Mood and Feelings Questionnaire-Short form (Angold, Costello, Messer, & Pickles, 1995). This measure consists of items describing depressive symptoms, such as "I felt miserable or unhappy" and "I didn't enjoy anything at all." Items are averaged to form a scale with higher scores indicating greater levels of depressive symptoms. Last, the Motivation Assessment (DeRosier, 1998) was used to assess students' level of motivation to be successful socially (e.g., importance of getting along well with other children) and academically (e.g., importance of getting good grades).

EVALUATION RESULTS

There were four primary research questions to be addressed through the statistical analyses. First, did the treatment group show significant change in adjustment over time? If so, what was the magnitude and direction of change? Second, did the pattern of change for the treatment group differ from that of the broader peer group (i.e., students who were not identified as having peer problems in the fall). Third, did the pattern of change for the treatment group vary according to specific subgroups of participants (i.e., disliked versus bullied versus both)? And, fourth, did pattern of change in adjustment differ by gender or baseline level of aggression?

Change by Group Type

The first step in the analytic process was to conduct an omnibus repeated measures multivariate analysis of variance (MANOVA) across all adjustment measures with group type as the between-subjects factor (treatment group versus nonidentified students). Results indicated that both groups showed significant change in adjustment over time ($F(15, 536) = 26.91, p < .0001$). (Follow-up analyses revealed that this effect held for each group when examined separately.) However, the pattern of change differed significantly for the treatment and nonidentified groups ($F(15, 536) = 3.49, p < .0001$). In other words, the magnitude and direction of change in adjustment was different for students who participated in the intervention compared to change evidenced in the broader peer group. Therefore, follow-up repeated measures analyses of variance (ANOVAs) were then used to determine which area(s) of adjustment evidenced significant change for each group.

In order to aid interpretation of the findings, change scores were calculated by subtracting pretreatment from posttreatment scores for each area of adjustment. Then, these change scores were standardized with a mean of zero and standard deviation of one. Table 15.2 displays the standardized change scores for each area of adjustment for each group. Overall, the treatment group's level of adjustment changed significantly over the course of the school year for multiple areas: peer-rated acceptance, rejection, aggression, and victimization and self-reported levels of peer acceptance, rejection, and social withdrawal. Peers reported that they liked the children who participated in the treatment significantly more in the spring than in the fall. Peers also reported that treatment children were less aggressive to peers and were less picked on or bullied by peers. These same areas showed a significant worsening pattern for the broader peer group. Interestingly, the social self-perceptions of the treatment children revealed worsening views of their peer acceptance, seeing themselves as less accepted and more rejected in the spring than in the fall. Treatment children reported less social withdrawal over the course of the school year.

TABLE 15.2. Standardized change scores (standard deviations) for patterns of adjustment over time.

Area of adjustment	Change (SD)	
	Treatment (N = 139)	Non Identified (N = 743)
Peer noms acceptance	.27* (.93)	−.03 (1.01)
Peer noms rejection	.34* (1.14)	−.10* (.89)
Peer noms aggressive	.21* (1.11)	−.08* (.87)
Peer noms bullied	.33* (1.59)	−.09* (.87)
Peer noms friendship	.07 (.99)	.01 (.99)
Self-report peer acceptance	−.17* (1.17)	.01 (.99)
Self-report peer rejection	−.28* (1.51)	.03 (1.05)
Self-report bully peers	.02 (1.31)	−.01 (.98)
Self-report bullied by peers	.00 (1.20)	−.01 (.94)
Self-report antisocial affiliations	.02 (1.25)	.00 (1.03)
Self-report social withdrawal	.11* (1.28)	.03 (1.11)
Self-report social motivation	.08 (1.24)	.04 (1.14)
Self-report academic motivation	.03 (1.05)	.03 (1.03)
Self-report generalized social anxiety	−.03 (1.04)	.04 (.92)
Self-report fear of negative evaluation	−.07 (1.00)	.04 (.94)
Self-report depression	.08 (1.22)	.01 (1.08)

Note. Standardized change scores have a mean of zero and a SD of one. A positive sign represents improvement in functioning whereas a negative sign represents worsening functioning for that area. Starred areas denote change significantly different from zero.

Subgroup Differences in Change

A repeated measures MANOVA was run across all adjustment measures for the treatment group to examine whether the observed pattern of change varied according to the three different subgroups of participants. Change for students who were disliked only, who were bullied only, and who were both disliked and bullied were compared. Results indicated no significant differences in the pattern of change for these three subgroups. Therefore, the observed pattern of change was the same regardless of the specific type of peer problem that made a student eligible to participate in the intervention.

Gender and Baseline Aggression Differences in Change

Repeated measures MANOVAs were conducted to examine differences in the pattern of change according to gender and baseline aggression. Baseline aggression was defined according to sociometric nominations at pretest. Students who were nominated as highly aggressive by peers (i.e., >1 SD above the mean) were classified as aggressive at baseline ($n = 40$ treatment students and $n = 24$ nonidentified students).

An omnibus analysis with follow-up ANOVA analyses was conducted. Results indicated that there were no differences in the patterns of change by gender. However, the pattern of change did differ by baseline aggression ($F(15, 536) = 2.48$, $p < .01$) and there was a significant difference in this pattern for the treatment group versus the broader peer group ($F(15, 536) = 2.12$, $p < .01$). Follow-up analyses revealed that change for the treatment group by baseline aggression was significantly different from change in the broader peer group by baseline aggression for six areas of adjustment: peer-rated aggression ($F(1, 763) = 7.03$, $p < .01$), self-reported bullying behavior ($F(1, 763) = 5.50$, $p < .05$), self-reported antisocial affiliations ($F(1, 763) = 4.43$, $p < .05$), social motivation ($F(1, 763) = 13.09$, $p < .001$), social anxiety ($F(1, 763) = 2.56$, $p < .05$), and depression ($F(1,763) = 5.94$, $p < .05$). Across these six areas, no significant group differences in change were present for nonaggressive children. All group differences held only for aggressive children.

Figure 15.1 graphically displays the pattern of results for each of these significant areas of adjustment. For externalizing problems, both peers and students themselves reported that the aggressive, bullying behavior of aggressive treatment children decreased significantly over the course of the school year. This was not the case for aggressive children in the broader peer group. Also, aggressive children did not report the escalation in affiliations with antisocial peers that aggressive nonidentified children reported.

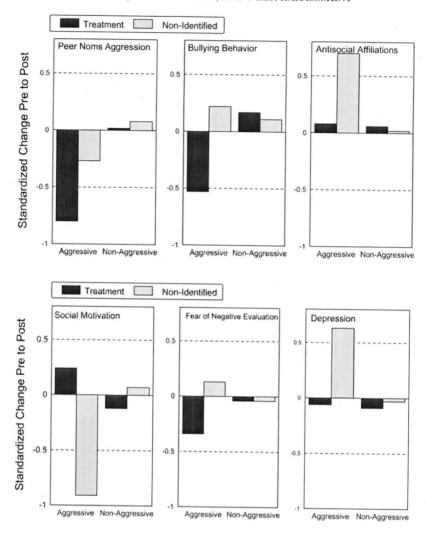

FIGURE 15.1. Patterns of change as a function of group type and aggression.

Aggressive nonidentified children showed a significant drop in social motivation between the fall and spring whereas aggressive treatment children showed a slight increase. Aggressive children who participated in SSGRIN also reported declines for the internalizing problems of social anxiety and depression while aggressive children within the broader peer group reported higher levels of anxiety and depression in the spring.

CONCLUSION

Peer problems have been repeatedly related to a myriad of concurrent adjustment problems (e.g., disruptiveness, loneliness, academic failure) and later negative outcomes (e.g., suicide, dropping out of school, criminality, drug use, and mental health problems) each of which exacts a significant toll both on individuals and society. In the aftermath of the tragic incidents of school violence in America, increased emphasis and attention have been placed on the quality of students' peer relations in our nation's schools. Safe Schools/Healthy Students (SS/HS) represents a major, national initiative to improve the social climate of schools and prevent school violence.

In this chapter, the SS/HS initiative entitled Peer Connections was presented along with research evaluating this program with fourth-grade students. A primary component of Peer Connections is accurate assessment. Given the tremendous impact of peer relations on children's school functioning, it is crucial that we be able to identify peer problems when they occur and as early as possible so that interventions can be most effectively applied. Teachers and other adults are rarely privy to the social interactions among students, particularly those related to bullying and rejection. Children who experience these social difficulties are unlikely to turn to adults for help. The most accurate and reliable means of assessing peer problems and the social climate at school is to ask the children themselves, that is, SCAN. Children are the best informants regarding their social interactions with one another. And, accurate assessment means more effective intervention as well as more efficient use of limited school resources (personnel, time, money).

Once children experiencing significant bullying and rejection by peers are identified, intervention can take place. For Peer Connections, SSGRIN helps children with peer problems to learn basic social and cognitive skills with the goals of enhancing the quality of social relationships, confidence in dealing with social situations, and social behavior. Overall, this study supports the efficacy of SSGRIN for achieving these goals.

The patterns of findings reported in this chapter are similar to that of past research (DeRosier, 2004; DeRosier & Marcus, 2005). Specifically, participation in SSGRIN was associated with greater social acceptance by peers, less aggressive behavior toward peers, and less bullying by peers over the course of the school year. Children's social self-perceptions regarding their peer relations also became more accurate over time. Helping children build their social acceptance is key to promoting more positive school-based adjustment across multiple areas (Parker et al., 1995).

Similar to past findings, no subgroup differences for gender or social problem type were found. The generic and broad-based nature of SSGRIN is applicable to a broad array of social difficulties for both boys and girls. Given the high comorbidity of psychopathology and peer problems (Kupersmidt et al., 1990), it may be that application of a generic intervention can meet the needs of a diverse set of social difficulties. However, also consistent with past research (DeRosier, 2004; DeRosier & Marcus, 2005), particular benefits of SSGRIN for aggressive children was supported through this study. Aggressive children who participated in the intervention showed a marked decline in aggressive and bullying behavior. Aggressive children in the broader peer group reported a marked increase in antisocial affiliations across the school year whereas aggressive children who participated in SSGRIN did not. This finding was mirrored in the pattern for social motivation where aggressive children in the broader peer group reported a significant drop in their desire to have positive social relationships while aggressive treatment children reported more social motivation. Social skills training that promotes peer acceptance may serve to prevent the development of more negative and antisocial affiliations over time. Combining different sets of skills (inhibitory and prosocial) may also be particularly helpful for aggressive children who tend to be less able to generate nonaggressive alternatives for dealing with social situations (Lochman & Dodge, 1994).

Peer relationship problems are prevalent in schools and significantly influence children's school-based adjustment and increase risk for future negative outcomes. Without intervention, peer problems typically continue over time resulting in escalating adjustment problems (DeRosier et al., 1994). Overall, this study lends additional support to SSGRIN as a promising program for promoting positive benefits through a relatively short, inexpensive treatment design. Schools can use SSGRIN to aid students with support, social skills, and coping mechanisms to combat the negative influences of bullying, social isolation, and rejection. Multiple problem areas can also be addressed through the application of a single intervention, promoting both greater efficacy of the intervention and more effective use of school resources.

Safe schools initiatives, such as Peer Connections, play a crucial role in promoting positive social environments for all students and for decreasing the risk for school violence. Early intervention, in the elementary years when bullying and rejection emerge and escalate, will be most effective for breaking the cycle of violence in our nation's schools (Greenberg et al., 2001). Schools need low-cost, time-efficient means of effecting positive change in student behavior and school social climate. Peer Connections suggests that social skills intervention is a feasible option for school staff who wish to implement an effective school-based program for students.

Whereas prior work investigating the effectiveness of SSGRIN utilized a randomized control group for comparison (DeRosier, 2004; DeRosier & Marcus, 2005), the current study lacked such a control group due to the design of the SS/HS project. However, the patterns of change for the treatment group in this study largely mirrored those of past treatment groups. Continued investigation of SSGRIN is warranted to further evaluate its effectiveness for helping children build positive social relations. Further longitudinal research is needed in order to understand the durability of evidenced gains and the utility of multiple applications of SSGRIN. Assessment of the fidelity and maintenance of the intervention by schools over time is also needed in order to more fully evaluate the long-term viability of *Peer Connections* within the school setting.

REFERENCES

Angold, A., Costello, E. J., Messer, S., & Pickles, A. (1995). Development of a short questionnaire for use in epidemiological studies of depression in children and adolescents. *International Journal of Methods in Psychiatric Research, 5*(4), 237-249.

Asher, S. R., Parker, J. G., & Walker, D. L. (1996). Distinguishing friendship from acceptance: Implications for intervention and assessment. In W. Bukowski, A. Newcomb, & W. Hartup (Eds.), *The company they keep: Friendship in childhood and adolescence* (pp. 366-405). New York: Cambridge University Press.

Beane, A. (1998). The trauma of peer victimization. In T. Miller (Ed.), *Children of trauma: Stressful life events and their effects on children and adolescents* (pp. 205-218). Madison, CT: International Universities Press.

Boulton, M. J. (1993). Proximate causes of aggressive fighting in middle school children. *British Journal of Educational Psychology, 63,* 231-244.

Boivin, M., & Hymel, S. (1997). Peer experiences and social self-perceptions: A sequential model. *Developmental Psychology, 33,* 135-145.

Brendgen, M. Vitaro, F., & Bukowski, W. M. (1998). Affiliation with delinquent friends: Contributions of parents, self-esteem, delinquent behavior, and rejection by peers. *Journal of Early Adolescence, 18,* 244-265.

Carney, J. V. (2000). Bullied to death: Perceptions of peer abuse and suicidal behavior during adolescence. *School Psychology International, 21,* 213-223.

Cillessen, A. H., & Bukowski, W. M. (2000). *Recent advances in measurement of acceptance and rejection in the peer system.* San Francisco, CA: Jossey-Bass.

Cillessen, A. H., Bukowski, W. M., Haselager, G. J. (2000). Stability of sociometric categories. In A. H. Cillessen & W. M. Bukowski (Eds.), *Recent advances in measurement of acceptance and rejection in the peer system* (pp. 75-93). San Francisco, CA: Jossey-Bass.

Cintron, R. (2000). Listening to what the streets say: Vengeance as an ideology. *Annals, AAPSS, 567,* 42-53.

Coie, J. D. (1990). Toward a theory of peer rejection. In S. R. Asher & J. D. Coie (Eds.), *Peer rejection in childhood* (pp. 365-402). New York: Cambridge University Press.

Coie, J. D., Dodge, K. A., & Coppotelli, H. (1982). Dimensions and types of social status: A cross-age perspective. *Developmental Psychology, 18,* 557-570.

Consortium on the School-based Promotion of Social Competence (1994). The school-based promotion of social competence. In R. J. Haggerty & L. R. Sherrod (Eds.), *Stress, resilience in children and adolescents: Processes, mechanisms, and interventions* (pp. 268-316). Cambridge, England: Cambridge University Press.

DeRosier, M. E. (1995, March). *Actual and perceived peer relationships: Implications for children's academic, behavioral, and emotional adjustment problems.* In M. E. DeRosier, & A. H. Cillessen, (Chairs), *Children's social self-perceptions: Developmental links to social, behavioral, and emotional adjustment.* Paper presented at the Biennial Meeting of the Society for Research in Child Development, Indianapolis, IN.

DeRosier, M. E. (1998). The Motivation Assessment. Manuscript submitted for publication.

DeRosier, M. E. (2002a). *Group interventions and exercises for enhancing children's communication, cooperation, and confidence.* Professional Resources Press.

DeRosier, M. E. (2002b). The Social Interaction Survey. Manuscript submitted for publication.

DeRosier, M. E. (2004). Building relationships and combating bullying: Effectiveness of a school-based social skills group intervention. *Journal of Clinical Child and Adolescent Psychology, 33*(1), 196-201.

DeRosier, M. E., Kupersmidt, J. B., & Patterson, C. P. (1994). Children's academic and behavioral adjustment as a function of the chronicity and proximity of peer rejection. *Child Development, 65,* 1799-1813.

DeRosier, M. E. & Marcus, S. (2005). Building relationships and combating bullying: Effectiveness of a school-based social skills group intervention at one-year follow-up. *Journal of Clinical Child and Adolescent Psychology, 34*(1), 140-150.

DeRosier, M. E., & Thomas, J. (2003). Strengthening sociometric prediction: Scientific advances in the assessment of children's peer relation. *Child Development, 75,* 1379-1392.

Furman, W., & Buhrmester, D. (1992). Age and sex differences in perceptions of networks of personal relationships. *Child Development, 63,* 103-115.

Gottfredson Associates, Inc. (2000). *A national study of school environment and problem behavior: The national study of delinquency prevention in schools.* Retrieved August 17, 2006, from http://www.gottfredson.com/Delinquency%20Prevention%20in%20Schools/titlepgs.pdf.

Greenberg, M. T., Domitrovich, C., & Bumbarger, B. (2001). Prevention of mental disorders in school-aged children: Current state of the field. *Prevention & Treatment, 4*, 1-67.

Gresham, F. M. (1997). Social competence and students with behavior disorders: Where we've been, we are, and we should go. *Education and Treatment of Children, 20*, 233-249.

Hugh-Jones, S., & Smith, P. K. (1999). Self-reports of short- and long-term effects of bullying on children who stammer. *British Journal of Educational Psychology, 69*, 141-158.

Kupersmidt, J. B., Coie, J. D., & Dodge, K. A. (1990). Predicting disorder from peer social problems. In S. R. Asher & J. D. Coie (Eds.), *Peer rejection in childhood* (pp. 274-305). New York: Cambridge University Press.

La Greca, A. M., & Stone, W. L. (1993). Social anxiety scale for children-revised: Factor structure and concurrent validity. *Journal of Clinical Child Psychology, 22*, 17-27.

Lochman, J., & Dodge, K. (1994). Social-cognitive processes of severely violent, moderately aggressive, and nonaggressive boys. *Journal of Consulting and Clinical Psychology, 62*(2), 366-374.

National Center for Educational Statistics (October, 2000). *Indicators of school crime and safety*. US Department of Education, Office of Educational Research and Improvement (NCES 2001-017), and US Department of Justice, Office of Justice Programs (NCJ-184176).

Olweus, D. (1993). Victimization by peers: Antecedents and long-term consequences. In K. H. Rubin & J. B. Asendorpf, (Eds.), *Social withdrawal, inhibition, and shyness in childhood* (pp. 315-341). Hillsdale, NJ: Lawrence Erlbaum.

Parker, J. G., Rubin, K. H., Price, J. M., & DeRosier, M. E. (1995). Peer relationships, child development and adjustment: A developmental psychopathology perspective. In D. Cicchetti & D. J. Cohen (Eds.), *Developmental psychopathology: Risk, disorder, and adaptation* (pp. 96-161). New York: Wiley.

Repetti, R., McGrath, E., & Ishikawa, S. (1999). Daily stress and coping in childhood and adolescence. In A. Goreczny & M. Hersen (Eds.), *Handbook of pediatric and adolescent health psychology* (pp. 343-360). Boston, MA: Allyn & Bacon.

Schwartz, D., Dodge, K. A., Pettit, G. S., & Bates, J. E. (1997). The early socialization of aggressive victims of bullying. *Child Development, 68*, 665-675.

Schwartz, D., Proctor, L. J., & Chien, D. H. (2001). The aggressive victim of bullying: Emotional and behavioral dysregulation as a pathway to victimization by peers. In J. Juvonen & S. Graham (Eds.), *Peer harassment in school: Plight of the vulnerable and victimized* (pp. 147-174). New York: Guilford.

Spooner, C. (1999). Causes and correlates of adolescent drug abuse and implications for treatment. *Drug & Alcohol Review, 18*, 453-475.

US Bureau of Justice (2000). *School Crime and Safety Report*. Washington, DC: Bureau of Justice Statistics.

US Department of Justice (1998). *Students' reports of school crime: 1989 and 1995/ Student Victimization*. Washington, DC: Bureau of Justice Statistics.

Vossekuil, B., Reddy, M., & Fein, R. (2002). *Safe school initiative: Final report on the prevention of targeted violence in schools.* US Secret Service National Threat Assessment Center, US Department of Education, & National Institute of Justice.

Weist, M. D., Borden, C. M., Finney, J. W., & Ollendick, T. H. (1991). Social skills for children: Training empirically derived target behaviors. *Behaviour Change, 8*(4), 174-182.

Woodward, L. J., & Fergusson, D. M. (2000). Childhood peer relationship problems and later risks of educational underachievement and unemployment. *Journal of Child Psychology and Psychiatry, 41,* 191-201.

Zakriski, A., Jacobs, M., & Coie, J. (1997). Coping with childhood peer rejection. In S. Wolchik & I. Sandler (Eds), *Handbook of children's coping: Linking theory and intevention* (pp. 423-452). New York: Plenum Press.

SECTION IV:
GUIDELINES FOR PRACTICE:
PROFESSIONAL ISSUES
AND LEGAL CONSIDERATIONS

Chapter 16

Sexual Harassment
and the Cultures of Childhood:
Developmental, Domestic Violence,
and Legal Perspectives

Philip C. Rodkin
Karla Fischer

Communities of children both reflect and transform into communities of adults, so it should come as little surprise when the pathologies of one generation are also manifested in the other. Sexual harassment, once thought to be a social problem exclusive to women in the workplace, is now recognized as a common experience for both girls and boys in school. As revealed by the AAUW's well-known *Hostile Hallways* surveys, four out of five students in eighth through eleventh grades have experienced some form of sexual harassment in their school lives (American Association of University Women [AAUW], 1993, 2001). Sexual harassment is an intimidating challenge for school service providers, who have just begun to scratch the surface of the too often aggressive, coercive, destructive behavior patterns between boys and girls in the early adolescent years. The reper-

---

This chapter was adapted from "Sexual Harassment and the Cultures of Childhood: Developmental, Domestic Violence, and Legal Perspectives" by Philip C. Rodkin, and Karla Fischer, *Journal of Applied School Psychology*, *19*(2), pp. 177-196. This work was supported by a Faculty Fellows grant from the Bureau of Educational Research, College of Education, University of Illinois at Urbana-Champaign to Philip C. Rodkin.

Bullying, Victimization, and Peer Harassment
Published by The Haworth Press, Inc., 2007. All rights reserved.
doi:10.1300/5808_16

cussions of school-based harassment are severe: harassment leads to children staying home from school, not talking as much in class, and decreasing their attention to their classwork (AAUW, 1993). For girls, harassment has additional detriments, most prominently to their self-esteem (Murnen & Smolak, 2001).

Despite the serious effects of sexual harassment, teachers and school officials often downplay its significance: sometimes by looking the other way, other times by standing by as girls are harassed in front of them in the school corridors and even the classrooms (Phillips, 1998). This "head in the sand" approach has earned school districts wide condemnation in the courts as well as legal liability (Romano, 2001). Threatened with large, punitive consequences, school service providers have promoted quick, sometimes drastic, and not necessarily optimal educational responses to the larger issue of how boys and girls relate to one another.

According to the AAUW report, sexual harassment is: "unwanted and unwelcome sexual behavior that interferes with your life. Sexual harassment is not behaviors that you like or want (for example, wanted kissing, touching, or flirting)" (2001, p.2). At its core, peer sexual harassment is about aggressive and power-based social interactions between boys and girls. Because aggression and power are conjoined in many situations, we look to two arenas closely related to peer sexual harassment that help illuminate common issues and their solutions. First, we describe how aggression can sometimes fit naturally into elementary and middle school societies, an ecology where interactions between boys and girls are typically negative. Second, we examine the psychological reactions of adult victims to domestic violence and track the institutional responses to reporting. In each case, we attend to the implications of the research for peer sexual harassment. Our larger aim is to objectify social forces that, because they fade invisibly into the normal workings of social ecologies, are easy to overlook (Milgram, 1977; Ross & Nisbett, 1991). Indeed, we feel that adults who deal with peer sexual harassment issues may sometimes fail to recognize critical relational and cultural dynamics that enable harassment to flourish. We attempt to help foster appropriate responses to peer-based sexual harassment that are legally sensitive, responsive to the reality of children's gendered social development, and cognizant of the social supports that promote a culture of negativity between boys and girls in childhood and early adolescence. Our primary concern here is with the phenomenon of boys harassing girls, as this is not only the most common form of harassment, but also the most severe in terms of psychological consequences (Romano, 2001).

DEVELOPMENTAL PERSPECTIVES:
GENDER, AGGRESSION, AND STATUS
IN CHILDREN'S SCHOOL SOCIETIES

Our interpretation of research on children's social development is that peer-based sexual harassment (1) has its origins in the gendered peer cultures of early and middle childhood, and (2) is propelled forward by peer culture norms, to which both boys and girls may contribute, which legitimizes at least some kinds of aggression for some boys. Could boys' harassment of girls be a peer-sanctioned form of aggression? The question is unanswered in current research, but the hypothesis needs to be explored. We hope that our review can give some guidance to those interested in how the interpersonal dynamic of peer sexual harassment might be conceptualized, and in how to focus prevention and intervention attempts.

Developmental Origins: The School Societies of Middle Childhood

We begin with a conceptual heuristic called the *school society*. The school society framework is a structuralist-agentic form of a more general class of contextual-holistic theories (e.g., Cairns, Elder, & Costello, 1996; Farmer, 2000) that view social behavior as a joint product of a person acting within his or her subjective social environment (Coleman, 1961; Lewin, 1943). A social environment is not a unitary place, nor can it be assessed with a single measure. Rather, social environments are multileveled and characterized by hierarchical micro- to macrosocial structures (e.g., peer social network, classroom, school, community, national culture) that Bronfenbrenner "conceived as a set of nested structures, each inside the next, like a set of Russian dolls" (1979, p. 3). The strongest contextual elicitors of behavior are the proximal, microsocial situations in which behavior unfolds. The right proximal contexts to examine depend upon the kind of behavior under study and the setting (e.g., school, home) in which it occurs. For example, as children make the transition from elementary to middle or junior high school the classroom (but not the peer group or school) often (but not always) loses its coherence as a meaningful social unit.

The school society heuristic focuses specifically on peer interaction in school-based settings. Other, larger social contexts, such as media influences on society or national policy, can frame the culture of the school society from a top-down perspective but are often removed from children's day-to-day interactions with one another. The most prominent social structures in the school society organize children's behavior—and here we focus on children's gendered and/or aggressive behavior—horizontally and vertically. By *horizontally*, we mean that even simple grade school classrooms are contoured social environments featuring multiple *peer groups* (i.e., cliques) and hence multiple avenues for children to find a niche and mobilize social support. Peer groups are microsocial structures. They include a small number of children (e.g., two or three to seven or eight) and are often the most immediate context of children's perceptions and behaviors (Allen, 1981; Cairns, Xie, & Leung, 1998). Children inevitably construct distinct (but also dynamic and overlapping) peer groups that are segregated by gender, race, and ethnicity (see Graham & Juvonen, 2002), and other demographic and behavioral attributes. Our emphasis on the group as the seminal unit of the school society falls closely in line with Kurt Lewin, who wrote that "all education is group work" (1943, p. 115).

By *vertical structure*, we mean that children and their peer groups vary in *social status and influence*. The vertical structure of the school society corresponds to a dimension of social power (Lippitt, Polansky, Redl, & Rosen, 1952) and is usually accepted by children as a source of legitimate peer authority even when it is personally disliked. One important consequence of social status differences is that some children have more of a say than others in determining what their peers value and devalue, support and stigmatize. When considering aggressive behavior, particularly boys' aggression toward girls, this perspective broadens the focus from the well-established connection between aggression and low social status (e.g., peer rejection) to include recent findings showing that aggression and social status can be positively related (e.g., Rodkin, Farmer, Pearl, & van Acker, 2000). For the school psychologist, this boils down to a question of whether the underlying dynamics of a harassment episode(s) lies in the margins or nearer to the heart of the dominant peer cultures.

Structuralist accounts of social environments like the school society can often seem static, but descriptions and explanations of peer sexual harassment need to be developmentally oriented. Developmental trajectories are important to examine over both the short term and the long term. By *short-term trajectories*, we focus on events that occur over the course of a school year or two that can yield insight into the formation, stabilization—and sometimes alteration—of a school society. The most elegant analyses of short-term developmental changes have involved studies of children's social interaction at summer camp (Lippitt et al., 1952; Parker & Seal, 1996; Sherif, 1956). For example, in the Robbers Cave experiments with white, eleven- and twelve-year-olds, Sherif (1956) tracked in fascinating detail the natural formation of peer groups and social hierarchies, their later consolidation into deeply entrenched, intensely negative intergroup dynamics, and finally their radical alteration from aggression to collaboration by outside intervention. Developments over the short term are essential for explaining the norms and interpersonal dynamics that arise within a school society, but they have been largely overlooked in recent literature. Instead, researchers have focused on *long-term trajectories* where focus is on how behavior patterns that are established during one stage of the life course (e.g., middle childhood) set children on paths toward adjustment or maladjustment in adolescence and beyond. For example, researchers whose interest lies primarily in predicting which boys will go on to become serious abusers as men would concentrate on long-term developmental trajectories.

What are the implications of a school society framework for sexual harassment? Peer groups and social status are critical elements of the interpersonal context between harassers and victims. AAUW (2001, p. 41) reports that four in ten self-reported harassers defend their actions by saying that "a lot of people do it" and one-quarter "say their friends encouraged or pushed them to do it" (multiple responses were possible so percentages are not exclusive). These answers implicate others in the harasser's environment and call for a framework where we know how harassers are socially connected to their peers. Harassment is often a group activity (AAUW, 2001, p. 26) and as the literature on children's bullying suggests (reviewed later), it often occurs under group influence. Thanks to the presence of multiple social groups (i.e., centers of influence), school societies like most societies tolerate multiple, dissonant messages. Many children may be in prominent peer groups that promote and accept dominant societal values. But other children may be in equally prominent peer groups (prominent, at least, to other children) that promote subversive messages of aggression and harassment. As we describe later in this chapter, in many sexual harassment cases school officials seemed to fail to recognize these subversive groups, with adults intentionally or unintentionally supporting negative peer group attitudes about gender. Childhood social status is closely aligned with the values of peer culture, where those with more status have a greater say in generating the values of the group. Neither childhood nor adult sexual harassment could ever be understood without a concept of power in the equation. The dominant framework for childhood social status in the developmental literature focuses on likeability, not power or prominence, and so the possibility that popular leaders in peer cultures could engage in sexual harassment has not been a focus.

Gender Boundaries and Borderwork in School Societies

Even though peer sexual harassment may take on more recognizable (i.e., adult) forms during the dramatic transition to adolescence (e.g., AAUW,

1993, 2001; Craig, Pepler, Connolly, & Henderson, 2001), dysfunctional interaction patterns between boys and girls take root in middle childhood. The 2001 AAUW survey (p. 25) reports that 38 percent of girls who experience sexual harassment "say they first experienced it in elementary school: sixth grade or before." Eleanor Maccoby's (1998) book, *The Two Sexes,* makes three critical points on the origins of negative boy–girl interactions. First, children's preference for same-sex peers emerges between two to three years of age (with girls exhibiting same-sex preferences somewhat before boys) and consolidates during the grade school years. Second, gender differentiation requires the continued presence of children's peer groups, the horizontal structure of school societies. Third, Maccoby points out that the active ingredient in children's gendered social development is the children themselves. Children actively construct separate cultures of male and female peer groups in which interaction with opposite-sex peers (henceforth *opposite-sex interaction*) becomes uneasy and tense. Parents and educators may validate negative opposite-sex interactions, going along with children's constructions of gender rather than resisting its negative excesses, or trying to alter (as difficult as it may be) normative developmental trajectories of behavior toward opposite-sex peers.

Recent research supports the Maccoby thesis. Gender segregation is quite possibly the signature phenomenon of middle childhood social development. A number of studies have found that the internal structure of boys' and girls' groups differ from one another, with boys' groups being larger, more cohesive, and more stratified on the basis of power and status (Benenson, Apostoleris, & Parnass, 1998). Boy and girl peer groups can also diverge on the behavioral and social characteristics that children support and emulate. Groups of boys tend to value toughness and competition, while for girls material possessions, cooperation, and intimacy, and physical appearance may have the strongest links to social status (Adler & Adler, 1998; Maccoby, 1998).

The portrait drawn so far suggests that boys and girls choose to affiliate in starkly gender-segregated peer groups. Boys and girls in middle childhood, despite being in the same classroom, live in psychologically "separate" (Thorne, 1993) or "special" (Bernard, 1979) worlds with few opportunities for voluntary interaction. But even strong boundaries are permeable. As two cultures living in close proximity within the confines of a larger social unit (i.e., the classroom or school), intergroup dynamics inevitably develop. Maccoby (1998) suggests that groups of boys and girls do not merely differ in a separate-but-equal fashion, but that there also exists an entrenched power asymmetry in favor of boys. Social development research increasingly indicates that opposite-sex interaction, called "borderwork" by Thorne

(1993), too often constitutes a zone of danger for female students—a highly charged, uncomfortable, unbalanced, ill-defined affiliative zone (Adler & Adler, 1998; Eder, Evans, & Parker, 1995; Maccoby, 1998).

The study of children's enemies is a newly emerging body of work that has potential to shed significant light on social relationships between boys and girls (Hodges & Card, in press). Enemy relationships have typically been measured by asking children to nominate peers whom they "like least" or "would least like as a play or work partner" and identifying reciprocated, mutual nominations of dislike (i.e., A nominates B as "liked least" and B returns the favor). Rodkin, Pearl, Farmer, and van Acker (2003) examined the nature of children's enemy relationships in a mostly suburban sample of approximately 500 children followed from the spring of third grade to the spring of fourth grade. They examined the proportion of enemy dyads that were composed of a boy and a girl, two boys, and two girls. One possibility, following from a strong form of the "separate worlds" hypothesis was that boys and girls would rarely name one another as enemies for the same reason that they rarely nominate one another as friends—that a buffer zone of neutrality, ignorance, and lack of awareness exists between the sexes. Instead, 52 percent of enemy dyads in the spring of third grade were between boys and girls, with only a slightly smaller rate of opposite-sex enemies (41 to 42 percent) during the two fourth-grade assessments.

Other studies also show that opposite-sex enmities are common in middle childhood and early adolescence (Abecassis, Hartup, Haselager, Scholte, & van Lieshout, 2002; Hodges & Card, 2003). Sometimes, enmity between a boy and a girl may be the only legitimate way to express any feelings toward a member of the opposite sex, including feelings of sexual tension or interest (Adler & Adler, 1998, p. 166; Maccoby, 1998, p. 69). Other times, opposite-sex enmities may reflect a polluted social dynamic between the sexes. For example, Underwood, Schockner, and Hurley (2001) placed eight-, ten-, and twelve-year-olds from urban areas of the Pacific Northwest in an experimental scenario where they were teased by either a same- or opposite-sex confederate while losing at a computer game. Observational data indicated that children who were teased by an opposite- as compared to same-sex peer showed more negative facial expressions, made more negative remarks, and displayed more negative gestures. Postexperimental interviews revealed that children liked and wanted to be friends with the provocateur less when they were of the opposite sex.

In sum, we propose that boys' harassment of girls emerges from and can be elicited by a climate of tense, unequal social relations between groups of boys and groups of girls beginning in middle childhood. Indeed, mutual antipathy may be one of the only kinds of relationships that indexes borderwork between boys and girls at school. Of course, social environments do not, in and of themselves, cause any one boy to sexually harass any one girl. We turn now to the vertical structure of school societies, focusing on prevailing social norms toward at least some forms of male aggression (e.g., proactive, instrumental) and the characteristics of boys held in high status among their peers. Our review will speculate that at least some high-status boys and/or their affiliates may be particularly effective at sexually harassing opposite-sex peers. More generally, norms that support aggressive behavior can be pervasive and need to be an important area in future peer relations and peer sexual harassment research.

Relations Between Social Status and Aggression Among Boys

More than one school psychologist have told us that their professional training led them to expect that popular children would be prosocial and aggressive children would be rejected, until their professional experiences proved otherwise. Ethnographers of children's peer culture were among the first to conclude that popular elementary (Adler & Adler, 1998) and middle school (Eder et al., 1995; Merten, 1997) children, whether male or female, could be rebellious, ruthless, and Machiavellian in establishing and maintaining their high social positions (see Rodkin et al. (2000) for a more extensive review). Rodkin et al. (2000) examined subtypes of popular fourth to sixth-grade boys in a diverse sample of urban and rural children. Popular-prosocial ("model") boys were perceived as cool, athletic, leaders, cooperative, studious, not shy, and nonaggressive, while popular-antisocial ("tough") boys were perceived as cool, athletic, and antisocial. Rodkin et al.'s (2000) findings suggested that highly aggressive boys (if they are also attractive and/or athletic) can be among the most popular and socially connected children in elementary classrooms. In fact, educators should know that aggressive children vary widely in social status (see Farmer, 2000). Rodkin et al.'s (2000) basic finding has been replicated in a variety of samples, including tough, popular-aggressive boys in third grade, suburban communities (Estell, Farmer, van Acker, Pearl, & Rodkin, 2003) and older adolescent children, where the connection between popularity and aggression seems to become even stronger (e.g., Gorman, Kim, & Schimmelbusch, 2002; LaFontana & Cillessen, 2002; Prinstein & Cillessen, 2003).

Tough children rely on a network of supporters, subordinates, and scapegoats to establish and exercise influence (Salmivalli, Huttunen, & Lagerspetz, 1997). Recent work suggests that aggressive boys, but less so aggressive girls, are well established in school societies. Far from being relegated to a low status, deviant group, fourth- to sixth-grade aggressive boys affiliate with a wide range of aggressive and nonaggressive peers (Farmer et al., 2002). Rodkin (2002) examined whether popular-aggressive boys tended to be nominated as "cool" by a broad or narrow cross-section of their classmates. Results indicated that popular-aggressive boys were peer group leaders, perceived as cool by their fellow group members, by groups of unpopular boys—and also by girls (see also Bukowski, Sippola, & Newcomb, 2000). The only children not likely to name popular-aggressive boys as cool were boys in groups with mostly nonaggressive children. This suggests that popular-aggressive boys have a broad (though not universal) base of support in the elementary classroom to which girls, regardless of their liking for popular-aggressive boys, may contribute.

An emerging literature on bullying and victimization converges closely with research on the popularity of aggression and a school society framework stressing the importance of peer groups and social status. Current research indicates that the relationship between bullies and victims involves much of the elementary classroom (O'Connell, Peplar, & Craig, 1999). In a rural sample of fifth graders, bullies tended to be friends with other bullies (Pellegrini, Bartini, & Brooks, 1999). Many children who are not themselves aggressive validate bullies with applause, or play supporting roles in bully-led peer groups (O'Connor et al., 1999; Salmivalli et al., 1997). Bullies are often popular within their groups (Pellegrini et al., 1999). Boulton (1999) reported that bullies' cliques tended to be larger than those of nonbullies in an English urban middle school sample of eight- to twelve-year-olds. In a third- to seventh-grade mostly white university school sample, Hodges, Malone, and Perry (1997) found that potential victims also rely on a network of supporters that can thwart bullies, but support is only effective if friends are not themselves unpopular or physically weak. These findings have led some to question the traditional view that bullies, as aggressive children, lack social skills and sophistication (Sutton, Smith, & Swettenham, 1999). Indeed, bullies may successfully form a number of distinct relationships with their peers (including the victim him- or herself) in order to attain their social goals.

Summary

Children's school societies provide fertile soil for peer sexual harassment. Boys and girls occupy segregated peer groups that promote negative gender stereotypes and relationships of dislike. The leading edge of peer sexual harassment may reside with popular, high-status boys, although such a linkage has not been established empirically. One possibility is that popular boys are themselves most likely to indulge in, or are at least most effective in, sexually harassing girls. Another possibility is that less popular and/or nonaggressive children in groups dominated by aggressive boys come to believe that harassment is acceptable and status enhancing. Although our discussion has emphasized conflict between the sexes, middle childhood gender relations can be characterized on multiple dimensions. The agreement between boys and girls on sex-specific aspects of coolness suggests that both boy and girl peer cultures, and the borderwork between them, can work together to contribute to gender socialization. For example, Rodkin's (2002) findings are consistent with Bukowski et al.'s (2000) conclusion that early adolescent girls can become attracted to aggressive boys. Indeed, girls' nominations of tough boys as cool may be the early origins of later attraction to aggressive boys. As Nisbett and Cohen (1996) found in adult, white southern culture, women validate men who aggress over issues of honor to the same extent that men do. Cultural values about aggression may be transmitted to girls even before issues of sexual attraction surface. Any intervention strategy would be wise to attend to these cross-currents of collaboration and competition, enmity and admiration, that flow between boys and girls during childhood and early adolescence.

GENDER AND AGGRESSION IN DOMESTIC VIOLENCE: APPLICATIONS TO PEER SEXUAL HARASSMENT

From our perspective, the most important similarity between peer sexual harassment and domestic violence is that each occurs in complex interpersonal environments marked by the construction of social norms and influence processes that can be difficult for outsiders to appreciate. The school society research sketched out here is a framework for understanding the peer environments within which relationships of abuse can emerge. Youth culture, increasingly from middle childhood to adolescence, houses small ecologies that can too easily engender relationships of abuse. We now turn to an examination of the psychological reality of dyadic relationships of abuse, using research on the dynamics of adult domestic violence as a guide. Once formed, the relationship of abuse becomes yet another, distinct social context embedded within the school society, even harder for an outsider to penetrate but critical for understanding the phenomenology of peer sexual harassment and its anchors. As in the social development literature, the literature in domestic violence underscores the importance of power in gendered social interactions. By attending to issues of power, the domestic violence paradigm offers a relational social context that complements the school society.

We focus on three ways that domestic violence research may help inform the problem of sexual harassment between children. First, like adults who are dating or married to each other, children in classrooms share physical space, a social environment, and have ongoing relationships. Second, similar to adults in abusive relationships, sexual harassment between children entails exercises of control implicating the vertical, power-based structure of classroom societies. Consequently, we might expect to see the same kinds of dynamics between child sexual harassers and their victims as we do between adult batterers and their victims. Third, legal responses to domestic violence increasingly build on the psychological reality of abusive relationships, providing a useful guide for remedies to childhood sexual harassment. We will identify the sexual harassment dynamics that seem applicable from the domestic violence literature and illustrate these themes from narratives from child sexual harassment victims derived from interviews and legal cases. We suggest that identifying these dynamics may assist educators in understanding the nature and seriousness of sexual harassment and, ultimately, in the resolution of disputes in the school system. Finally, we examine institutional (legal) responses to domestic violence and their parallels in the response to sexual harassment by school authorities. We close by offering solutions to peer sexual harassment that school officials can utilize to avoid the problems identified in the domestic violence literature.

The research on domestic violence that analyzes the dyadic interactions between abuser and abused implicates several common contextual themes that may apply to sexual harassment between school children in early and mid-adolescence. First, domestic violence abuse is nested within a broader relationship context of rules and rule making, where batterers enforce explicit as well as implicit rules about what victims are and are not allowed to do (Fischer, Vidmar, & Ellis, 1993). As described in the first part of this chapter, a comparable norm-governed context can sometimes be constructed by children in school concerning how girls should and should not be.

Examining the narratives of girls who have been sexually harassed appears to amply support an ongoing rule-based culture in schools, with a power asymmetry in favor of boys. This culture sets up a hierarchy of boys controlling girls, and also reinforces a structure in which girls are punished for responding to sexual harassment in active (rather than passive) ways. Similar to domestic violence victims who can explain their relationship rules, girls seem able to articulate the unwritten yet enforced rules in their school. One common rule may be some variation of "the guys would want you to let them touch you all over" (Stein, 1999, p. 15). Girls who refuse to accept this may be threatened or physically assaulted, which serves only to reinforce the rule:

> I could never stand up to him because if I told him to stop he'd threaten me . . . he'd hit me (hard enough to bruise me twice) and then pin my arms behind my back till it hurt and push against a wall and tell me all the awful things he would do to me if I ever hit him again, so I quit standing up to him again.

Some boys who sexually harass girls openly acknowledge power-based reasons for engaging in sexually harassing behavior: because they want dates or something else from their victims (43 percent) or because they are encouraged or pushed by their friends (20 percent) (AAUW, 1993). A small percentage of boys (5 percent) admit that they explicitly wanted their victim to feel less powerful. As with the case of domestic violence, part of the power dynamics between boys and girls in schools may be based on physical size differentials: one of the effects of "antibullying" programs may be that boys treat girls differently in terms of global teasing, chasing, and insulting, while girls stop teasing and bullying "shrimpy or short boys" (Stein, 1999, p. 63).

A rule-based school culture, therefore, is more than just the content of the rules (that boys control girls). It is a culture in which sexual harassment is an accepted tool for achieving that control. As Nan Stein (1999) has observed, sexual harassment in schools is public in nature: many incidents of sexual harassment, like the more general instances of bullying described earlier, are not simply between harasser(s) and victim(s), but consist of bystanders and observers—including adult employees of the school. The physical locations of sexual harassment are contained overwhelmingly in the public spaces of schools, the spaces that victims cannot avoid: 65 percent of sexual harassment takes place in the hallways of the school, while 55 percent occurs in the classrooms (AAUW, 1993). More than half of all girls who have been harassed report being harassed by a group of boys (AAUW, 1993). The fact that more sexual harassment happens in the public rather than private spaces of schools and in groups rather than in dyads suggests that sexual harassment can become integral to the culture of schools.

Other factors suggest that sexual harassment is well integrated into school culture. Almost half of boys who admit sexually harassing someone (41 percent) say that they did it because "it's just part of school life" and/or "lots of people do it" (AAUW, 1993); and victims report that experiencing sexual harassment is "normal" and "just one of those things that I have to put up with" (Stein, 1999, p. 146). Many legal cases involving peer harassment, even before *Davis v. Monroe* (giving rise to a cause of action for peer harassment, if school officials know of the conduct but fail to act to stop it) suggest that teachers and principals tend to normalize sexual harassment.

For example, in *Bruneau v. South Kortright Central School District* (1996), several girls were verbally harassed in demeaning ways, including being called "lesbian," "whore," and "ugly dog faced bitch." These girls were also physically harassed by these same boys, who snapped their bras, stuffed paper down their blouses, cut their hair, grabbed their breasts, and spit, shoved, hit, and kicked them. When they told one of their teachers about the harassment, he responded that the boys were engaging in "normal flirting and teasing" and that one of the girls "was so beautiful that the boys would be all over her in a couple of years."

If sexual harassment arises from the rule-based cultures of schools, then it is also likely that other domestic violence dynamics are operating in this context. Victims of domestic violence seem to internalize their relationship rules over time by self-censoring their own behavior—altering what they say and what they do. The fact that victims of sexual harassment in schools speak less in class (AAUW, 1993) suggests that self-censoring may be a part of the ongoing power dynamic of the harassment. As the girl in the narrative quoted earlier expressed, she began to react passively rather than "tell him to stop" to avoid being further harassed. Last, domestic violence victims react in predictable ways to the abuse: because of the shame and embarrassment abuse generates, they hide from others, deny that it is occurring, and minimize its effect. Given that few students tell their teachers (7 percent) or families (23 percent) (AAUW, 1993) about the harassment that they have experienced, victims of school-based harassment appear to share the psychological reactions of adult women who have been abused. An important direction for research is to examine these possibilities empirically, elaborating how the domestic violence paradigm aligns with girls' reaction to sexual harassment at school.

Institutional (Legal) Responses to Domestic Violence: Avoiding Their Pitfalls in Sexual Harassment School Policy

Perhaps it is not surprising that the parallels in the dynamics between peer sexual harassment and domestic violence are similar. A review of the case law in peer sexual harassment suggests striking parallels between institutional responses to domestic violence by legal authorities and institutional responses to sexual harassment by school authorities. Both kinds of authorities have made similar mistakes and fallen into similar pitfalls. In both cases, one avenue for progress is to devise institutional/legal responses that recognize the operating social contexts that support abusive relationships.

As noted earlier, school officials typically respond to victims' complaints of sexual harassment by dismissing it as "normal teasing and flirting" or by failing to react altogether. Now that the Monroe case has opened up the potential for liability by engaging in "head in the sand" approaches to peer harassment, we would expect to see fewer cases of inaction in the future. When school officials do act, however, they often do so in ways that punish victims and fail to punish perpetrators appropriately.

Girls who physically fight back may be punished not only by the boys who attack them, but also by school authorities unfairly and unevenly. The narratives of girls who are harassed and who respond actively to that harassment are filled with stories of unjust punishment. One girl who was backed into a corner and physically touched by two or three boys in her classroom was punished by her teacher for running out of the room, while her harassers went unpunished (Stein, 1999, pp. 13-14). The same teachers and principals who observe multiple incidents of harassment of girls and fail to respond at all seem to quickly notice as well as discipline girls for striking back at their harassers. Girls report being caught hitting their attackers, who typically deny any provocation—and it is the girls, not the boys, whose stories are disbelieved (Stein, 1999). This dynamic appeared in a recent legal case for peer sexual harassment from Indiana: a "more physically developed" eighth-grade girl, the frequent target of harassment and sexual remarks from boys in her class, jabbed one of these boys with a pen after he "threatened to poke her breast and made a lewd, offensive remark" (*B.A.L. v. Apple,* 2001). Both students were sent to the principal's office, where the boy was sent back without any punishment, while the girl was given a choice between two days' suspension or three swats of a paddle. Perhaps the most egregious example of punishing and blaming the victim hails from a 1999 case from Colorado in which a school janitor found a male student who had been awarded privileges as a "janitor's assistant" raping a female student with cerebral palsy and told him to "clean up the mess" (*Murrell v. School District,* 1999). In a later meeting between the female student's mother and the school principal, the principal declined to investigate the incident or punish the attacker in any way, even though he admitted engaging in the assault. Instead, the principal responded by suspending the victim for "behavior which is detrimental to the welfare, safety or morals of other pupils or school personnel." These and other cases illustrate how school personnel can acquiesce or support the excesses of a gendered peer culture. To punish girls who engage in resistance to the sexual harassment culture of schools, whether that resistance is in the form of trying to hold their harassers accountable or in the form of physical resistance, implicates school officials in the reinforcement of the cultural dynamics that they would like to extinguish.

Finally, another common approach to dealing with sexual harassment between children in the same classroom is to move the perpetrator to another class. This reflects the approach of restraining order laws that enforce "no contact" between domestic violence offenders and their victims, and the appeal of other solutions that require the victim to leave her abusive mate. The unfortunate fact is that battered women are often attacked and killed after they leave, a phenomenon which is well known as "separation assault" (Mahoney, 1991). It has long been recognized by battered women's advocates that leaving the relationship may solve the immediate problem for the victim (if it does not create greater ones), but it leaves the perpetrator free to move on to a new victim—which happens in the vast majority of cases.

A similar principle applies to children involved in peer harassment. In one recent case, a sixth-grade girl in Georgia was repeatedly touched during class in front of her teacher and classmates by a boy in her class before any action was taken by the school principal (*Clark v. Bibb County Board of Education,* 2001). After he was moved to another class, he continued to harass her in the hallways and other public spaces of the school. When the victim's parents asked that he be transferred to another school, their request was declined—although they did offer to transfer their daughter to another school. Perhaps even more startling is a case from Virginia involving a kindergarten boy who exhibited acts of sexual aggression toward his classmates, including "humping" them, fondling their genitals, and initiating acts of sexual intimacy. After several children and their parents complained, the boy was simply moved to another class and a folder about his behavior placed on his teacher's desk (*Doe v. Sabine Parish Board,* 1998). Not surprisingly, he began to assault his new classmates shortly after his arrival in his new classroom.

Whatever the stereotype that moves school officials to simply change the physical location of the sexual harasser and think they have solved the problem, it is likely to be ineffective. Although it is a punishment to remove a child from his familiar classroom and that action will keep the immediate victim safe during classtime, the Clark case, which is consistent with the AAUW statistics, reminds us that harassment can and often does occur in the hallways and other public spaces of a school. Failing to guard against victims' vulnerabilities outside the classroom is a mistake that may incur liability for a school under Monroe. In addition, a change of location creates new opportunities for the harasser to find new victims. Clearly, school officials may use removal of a child who is sexually harassing his classmates in their repertoire of appropriate responses, but they must also address the harassing conduct itself and take steps to insure that it is not simply recreated in a new classroom environment that, despite having different children, operates according to the basic principles of most school societies.

CONCLUSION

Peer sexual harassment occurs in a context that sometimes may be hard for school service providers to see, or before they expect to see it. Sexual harassment is aggressive behavior, not "normal flirting and teasing," although its perceived normality can be part of the problem. We have suggested that aggressive and/or gendered behavior in school is best viewed within a contextualist framework like the school society where peer groups and social status are recognized as key organizing factors. As our narrative cases suggest, even well-meaning school service providers can unintentionally collaborate with peer culture dynamics that normalize or reinforce behaviors that to the rest of us clearly suggest harassment. They can also dismiss the challenges made by girls in protest of unwanted sexual behavior. Among researchers and educators alike, attention needs to be paid to the peer groups of the victim and the harasser, their behavioral characteristics and ties to the larger peer culture. School authorities need to ask questions about who else was present (as bystander, encourager, co-harasser, co-victim, or victim protector) before, during, and after harassment, and they should assess to what degree the students involved seem to be leaders or otherwise have social status among their peers (Farmer, 2000). In particular, school service providers should not assume that the instigators of harassment (whether out in-front or behind the scenes) are rejected, unpopular, children on the periphery of school social life. Even popular leaders may engage in sexually harassing behavior.

We are also suggesting that the sexual harassment experienced in school by girls contains many of the same dynamics as domestic violence between adults. Understanding that victims may respond in active, aggressive ways to such harassment or retaliate for earlier harassment should be useful to officials when deciding how to punish that aggressive behavior. The way that school officials typically respond to harassment also has parallels in domestic violence intervention. By avoiding the pitfalls and errors that have plagued police and other legal personnel in domestic violence calls, school officials will be better equipped to recognize the nature of sexual harassment between children in their schools and respond in a manner that sends the appropriate messages to both victims and perpetrators. Specifically, school officials should hesitate before assuming that girls, who may be afraid to speak out against their harassers, have initiated physical aggression against a bigger, more powerful boy, as it would be a reasonable hypothesis that her aggression might be a response to ongoing or past harassment, to that boy or to his peers. The other common mistake that school officials appear to make that bears correcting is to solve the problem of harassment by moving the perpetrator to another classroom, leaving him to freely harass his victim(s) at recess, lunch, and before and after school as well as providing him with a naïve environment in which to find new victims.

We do think that a framework that encourages school officials to think more broadly about relational and societal contexts when responding to sexual harassment will make those responses more effective. If school officials are able to significantly intervene in aggression between boys and girls in grade school, the stage for how men and women treat each other as adults may be set in a very different place than it is now.

REFERENCES

Abecassis, M., Hartup, W. W., Haselager, G. J. T., Scholte, R., & van Lieshout, C. F. M. (2002). Mutual antipathies and their significance in middle childhood and early adolescence. *Child Development, 73,* 1543-1556.

Adler, P. A., & Adler, P. (1998). *Peer power: Preadolescent culture and identity.* New Brunswick, NJ: Rutgers University Press.

Allen, V. L. (1981). Self, social group, and social structure: Surmises about the study of children's friendships. In S. R. Asher & J. M. Gottman (Eds.), *The development of children's friendships* (pp. 182-203). New York: Cambridge University Press.

American Association for University Women Educational Foundation. (1993). *Hostile hallways: The AAUW survey on sexual harassment in America's schools.* Washington, DC: Author.

American Association of University Women Educational Foundation (2001). *Hostile hallways: Bullying, teasing, and sexual harassment in school.* Washington, DC: Author.

B.A.L. v. Apple, 2001 WL 1135024 (not reported), S.D. Indiana (2001).

Benenson, J., Apostoleris, N., & Parnass, J. (1998). The organization of children's same-sex peer relations. In W. M. Bukowski & A. H. N. Cillessen (Eds.), *Sociometry then and now: Building on six decades of measuring children's experiences with the peer group* (pp. 5-23). San Francisco: Jossey-Bass.

Bernard, J. (1979). *The female world.* New York: Basic Books.

Boulton, M. J. (1999). Concurrent and longitudinal relations between children's playground behavior and social preference, victimization, and bullying. *Child Development, 70,* 944-954.

Bronfenbrenner, U. (1979). *The ecology of human development: Experiments by nature and design.* Cambridge, MA: Harvard University Press.

Bruneau v. South Kortright Central School District, 935 F. Supp. 162 (N.D.N.Y. 1996).

Bukowski, W. M., Sippola, L. K., & Newcomb, A. F. (2000). Variations in patterns of attraction to same- and other-sex peers during early adolescence. *Developmental Psychology, 36,* 147-154.

Cairns, R. B., Elder, G. H., Jr., & Costello, E. J. (Eds.). (1996). *Developmental science.* New York: Cambridge University Press.

Cairns, R. B., Xie, H., & Leung, M-C. (1998). The popularity of friendship and the neglect of social networks: Toward a new balance. In W. M. Bukowski & A. H. Cillessen (Eds.), *Sociometry then and now: Building on six decades of measuring children's experiences with the peer group* (pp. 25-53). San Francisco: Jossey-Bass.

Clark v. Bibb County Board of Education, 174 f. Supp. 2d 1369 (M.D. Ga. 2001)

Coleman, J. (1961). *The adolescent society.* Glencoe, IL: Free Press.

Craig, W. M., Pepler, D., Connolly, J., & Henderson, K. (2001). Developmental context of peer harassment in early adolescence: the role of puberty and the peer group. In J. Juvonen & S. Graham (Eds.), *Peer harassment in school: The plight of the vulnerable and victimized* (pp. 242-261). New York: Guilford.

Davis. v. Monroe County Board of Education, 526 U.S. 629 (1999).

Doe v. Sabine Parish Board, 24 F. Supp. 2d 655 (W.D. La. 1998).

Eder, D., Evans, C. C., & Parker, S. (1995). *School talk: Gender and adolescent culture.* New Brunswick, NJ: Rutgers University Press.

Estell, D. B., Farmer, T. W., Van Acker, R., Pearl, R., & Rodkin, P. C. (2003). Heterogeneity in the relationship between popularity and aggression: Individual, group, and classroom influences. In S. C. Peck & R. W. Roeser (Eds.), *Use of person-centered approaches in the study of human development in context.* San Francisco: Jossey Bass.

Farmer, T. W. (2000). Social dynamics of aggressive and disruptive behavior in school: Implications for behavior consultation. *Journal of Educational and Psychological Consultation, 11,* 299-322.

Farmer, T. W., Leung, M.-C., Pearl, R., Rodkin, P. C., Cadwallader, T. W., & Van Acker, R. (2002). Deviant or diverse peer groups? The peer affiliations of aggressive elementary students. *Journal of Educational Psychology, 94,* 611-620.

Fischer, K., Vidmar, N., & Ellis, R. (1993). The culture of battering and the role of mediation in domestic violence cases. *Southern Methodist University Law Review* (Special Issue on Alternative Dispute Resolution), *46,* 2117-2173.

Gorman, A. H., Kim, J., & Schimmelbusch, A. (2002). The attributes adolescents associate with peer popularity and teacher preference. *Journal of School Psychology, 40,* 143-165.

Graham, S., & Juvonen, J. (2002). Ethnicity, peer harassment, and adjustment in middle school: An exploratory study. *Journal of Early Adolescence, 22,* 173-199.

Hodges, E. V. E., & Card, N. (Eds.). (2003). *The (unwanted) company they keep: Enemy relationships in childhood and adolescence.* San Francisco: Jossey Bass.

Hodges, E. V. E., Malone, M. J., & Perry, D. G. (1997). Individual risk and social risk as interacting determinants of victimization in the peer group. *Developmental Psychology, 33,* 1032-1039.

LaFontana, K. M., & Cillessen, A. H. N. (2002). Children's perceptions of popular and unpopular peers: A multi-method assessment. *Developmental Psychology, 38,* 635-647.

Lewin, K. (1943). Psychology and the process of group living. *Journal of Social Psychology, 17,* 113-131.

Lippitt, R., Polansky, N., Redl, F., & Rosen, S. (1952). The dynamics of power: A field study of social influence in groups of children. In G. E. Swanson, T. M. Newcomb, & E. L. Hartley (Eds.), *Readings in social psychology* (Rev. ed., pp. 623-636). New York: Holt.

Maccoby, E. E. (1998). *The two sexes: Growing up apart, coming together.* Cambridge, MA: Harvard University Press.

Mahoney, M. R. (1991). Legal images of battered women: Redefining the issue of separation. *Michigan Law Review, 90,* 1-94.

Merten, D. E. (1997). The meaning of meanness: Popularity, competition, and conflict among junior high school girls. *Sociology of Education, 70,* 175-191.

Milgram, S. (1977). *The individual in a social world: Essays and experiments.* New York: McGraw Hill.

Murnen, S. K., & Smolak, L. (2000). The experience of sexual harassment among grade-school students: Early socialization of female subordination. *Sex Roles: A Journal of Research, 43,* 17-25.

Murrell v. School Dist. No. 1, Denver, Colo., 186 F.3d 1238 (Colo. 1999).

Nisbett, R. E., & Cohen, D. (1996). *Culture of honor: The psychology of violence in the South.* Boulder, CO: Westview Press.

O'Connell, P., Pepler, D., & Craig, W. (1999). Peer involvement in bullying: Insights and challenges for intervention. *Journal of Adolescence, 22,* 437-452.

Parker, J. G., & Seal, J. (1996). Forming, losing, renewing, and replacing friendships: Applying temporal parameters to the assessment of children's friendship experiences. *Child Development, 67,* 2248-2268.

Pellegrini, A. D., Bartini, M., & Brooks, F. (1999). School bullies, victims, and aggressive victims: Factors relating to group affiliation and victimization in early adolescence. *Journal of Educational Psychology, 91,* 216-224.

Phillips, L. (1998). *The girls report and what we need to know about growing up female.* New York: National Council for Research on Women.

Prinstein, M. J., & Cillessen, A. H. N. (2003). Forms and functions of adolescent peer aggression associated with high levels of peer status. *Merrill Palmer Quarterly, 49,* 310-342.

Rodkin, P. C. (2002). *I think you're cool: Social status and group support for aggressive boys and girls.* Invited address to the 8th Triennial Meeting of the Northeast Social Development Consortium, New York.

Rodkin, P. C., Farmer, T. W., Pearl, R., & van Acker, R. (2000). Heterogeneity of popular boys: Antisocial and prosocial configurations. *Developmental Psychology, 36,* 14-24.

Rodkin, P. C., Pearl, R., Farmer, T. W., & van Acker, R. (2003). Enemies in the gendered societies of middle childhood: Prevalence, stability, associations with social status and aggression. In E. V. E. Hodges & N. Card (Eds.), *The (unwanted) company they keep: Enemy relationships in childhood and adolescence.* San Francisco: Jossey Bass.

Romano, P. (2001). *Davis v. Monroe County Board of Education:* Title IX recipients' 'head in the sand' approach to peer sexual harassment may incur liability. *Journal of Law and Education, 30,* 63-84.

Ross, L., & Nisbett, R. E. (1991). *The person and the situation: Perspectives of social psychology.* New York: McGraw Hill.

Salmivalli, C., Huttunen, A., & Lagerspetz, K. M. J. (1997). Peer networks and bullying in schools. *Scandinavian Journal of Psychology, 38,* 305-312.

Sherif, M. (1956). Experiments in group conflict. *Scientific American, 195,* 54-58.

Stein, N. (1999). *Classrooms and courtrooms: Facing sexual harassment in K-12 schools.* New York: Teachers College Press.

Sutton, J., Smith, P. K., & Swettenham, J. (1999). Bullying and "theory of mind": A critique of the "social skills deficit' view of anti-social behaviour. *Social Development, 8,* 117-127.

Thorne, B. (1993). *Gender play: Girls and boys in school.* New Brunswick, NJ: Rutgers University Press.

Underwood, M. K., Schockner, A. E., & Hurley, J. C. (2001). Children's responses to same- and other-gender peers: An experimental investigation with 8-, 10-, and 12-year-olds. *Developmental Psychology, 37,* 362-372.

Chapter 17

The Mental Health Professional's Role in Understanding, Preventing, and Responding to Student Sexual Harassment

Ellie L. Young
Linda M. Raffaele Mendez

Sexual harassment is unwanted and unwelcome behavior that interferes with a student's participation in an educational program. Sexual harassment can include verbal comments, nonverbal communication, or physical contact. Unwanted sexual advances or requests for sexual favors are considered sexual harassment. To be identified as sexual harassment, the behavior must be either implicitly or explicitly sexual and be perceived by the recipient as undesirable (Paludi, 1997; Stein, 1999).

Sexual harassment is a common experience for the majority of today's secondary school students in the United States. Recently, 81 percent of secondary students reported experiencing sexual harassment during their educational careers (American Association of University Women [AAUW], 2001). Approximately one-third of students reported first experiencing sexual harassment before sixth grade. Sexual harassment is not something that happens just to girls: 79 percent of boys and 83 percent of girls reported being sexually harassed at school, although boys and girls experience sexual ha-

---

This chapter was adapted from "The Mental Health Professional's Role in Understanding, Preventing, and Responding to Student Sexual Harassment" by Ellie L. Young and Linda M. Raffaele Mendez, *Journal of Applied School Psychology, 19*(2), pp. 7-23.

Bullying, Victimization, and Peer Harassment
Published by The Haworth Press, Inc., 2007. All rights reserved.
doi:10.1300/5808_17

rassment quite differently. Most incidents of sexual harassment occur in public places in schools, such as classrooms, hallways, and cafeterias (AAUW, 2001). Sexual harassment has become pervasive to the extent that it is considered part of adolescent culture (Lee, Croninger, Linn, & Chen, 1996).

Mental health professionals' understanding of human development and behavior, emotional health, and school organization provides a foundation to respond effectively and proactively in addressing sexual harassment issues. Their training and work assignments facilitate their role as advocates and leaders for antiharassment efforts. They easily can become the point person for antiharassment efforts. This chapter first presents a working definition, including specific examples of sexual harassment. A brief section clarifies the distinctions between sexual and gender harassment. Next, current research about prevalence, gender, and ethnicity issues is reviewed. In addition, a brief integration of developmental and sexual harassment is discussed. A legal history is included to assist mental health professionals when they are asked to consult with school administrators on these issues. Finally, several levels of effective prevention and intervention strategies are presented. With this foundational knowledge, psychologists, counselors, and social workers will be better equipped to be advocates for and participants in successful intervention and prevention of sexual harassment.

DEFINING SEXUAL HARASSMENT

The legal definition of sexual harassment is "unwelcome sexual advances, requests for sexual favors, sexually motivated physical conduct or other verbal or physical conduct" that limits a student's participation in an educational program (U.S. Department of Education, Office for Civil Rights and National Association of Attorneys General, 1999, p. 17). The context of the behavior, the difference in status and power of the victim and perpetrator, as well as the impact of the behavior must be considered. Although this definition of sexual harassment is quite succinct, in practice, defining and identifying sexual harassment can be quite challenging, especially for students.

In contrast to sexual harassment, good-natured teasing and flirting tend to be mutually acceptable, enjoyable, and pleasant, and both parties participate willingly. When sexual harassment occurs the targets may feel threatened, embarrassed, fearful, or self-conscious. Power and intimidation are inherent in sexual harassment. Victims of sexual harassment experience an absence of choice and control, and perpetrators communicate a sense of hostility (AAUW, 2001, Levy & Paludi, 2002; Stein & Sjostrom, 1994). Distinguishing between normal teasing and unwanted harassment is a social skill that requires accurately perceiving others' feelings and intentions (Elias et al., 1997; Goldstein, 1999). At the other end of the continuum, sexual assault and rape would be extreme forms of sexual harassment, if the context is in the workplace or an educational setting. Legally, sexual harassment does not occur in personal or private relationships, the context is an employment or school environment where a person with power abuses that power to coerce some one because of his or her sex. The most common forms of sexual harassment, such as sexist comments or gestures, do not have legal consequences when they are experienced to lesser extents. However, rape is a criminal offense, which has distinctly different legal implications (Levy & Paludi, 2002; Paludi & Barickman, 1998).

Quid pro quo and hostile environment have been the most commonly discussed forms of sexual harassment (Shoop & Edwards, 1994). Quid pro quo literally means "you do something for me and I'll do something for you." It also can include threats to avoid harm rather than achieving any gain. This type of harassment happens when a person with authority, such as a teacher or a coach, demands a sexual favor in return for some educational benefit or avoidance of harm. He or she may request a sexual favor in return for a higher grade or a position on the varsity soccer team (Paludi, 1997). Quid pro quo harassment also can occur among students. A student editor might threaten a student reporter to perform sexual acts in order to keep her or his coveted assignments (see Stein, 1999).

A hostile environment exists when sexual teasing, insulting, touching, or other unwanted sexual behavior is pervasive, persistent, and severe to the extent that students' ability to participate in or benefit from an educational program is denied (U.S. Department of Education, 2001). A single incident of teasing or similar behavior generally will not constitute legally significant sexual harassment. The behavior may violate the school's policy, be offensive and insulting, and require school discipline, but not have legal consequences. Legal action is a result of significant and severe harassment that impedes a student's participation in an educational program (Paludi, 1997).

Sexual harassment can take many forms. The most common types reported by secondary school students include both sexual comments and jokes and physical actions, such as being touched, grabbed, pinched, or brushed against in a sexual way (AAUW, 2001). Sexually harassing comments can include being persistently called "babe" or "sweetheart," sexual or gender insults, or remarks about specific body parts. Leering, displaying pornography, writing sexual graffiti, and rumor mongering have been legally identified as sexual harassment (Shoop & Hayhow, 1994; U.S. Department of Education, 2002).

The impact of the behavior rather than the intent of the behavior determines whether sexual harassment has occurred (Paludi, 1997). For example, if a girl repeatedly blows kisses at a boy or pinches his buttocks several times to the extent that the young man is uncomfortable or irritated, her behavior has created a hostile environment, even though her intention was to develop a dating relationship. Perpetrators and their targets often have different perspectives about the intent of the harassing behavior. Those who harass may perceive their behavior as flattering, inoffensive teasing, or harmless touching, while the target finds it unpleasant, awkward, or humiliating (Layman, 1994). Using the impact rather than the intent standard of determining whether sexual harassment has occurred can be problematic because the rights of the accused may not be considered. To address this issue, those investigating the claim determine whether a "reasonable woman" or "reasonable man" experiencing the alleged harassment would find the behavior offensive. Using the same gender perspective as the victim is imperative because males and females tend to have different perceptions of harassing behavior (Levy & Paludi, 2002).

Some have expressed concern that the well-intentioned hug from a teacher to a student will be construed as sexual harassment. The U.S. Department of Education's Office for Civil Rights (OCR) guidelines clearly indicate that not all physical contact between teachers and students or between students is sexual harassment. For example, comforting a child with a skinned knee is not sexual harassment, and neither is a coach hugging a player after the player has made a goal. Physical contact between students that is nonsexual, such as practicing a sports maneuver, also does not constitute sexual harassment. However, nonsexual contact may be interpreted as sexual harassment if it occurs repeatedly and under inappropriate circumstances (U.S. Department of Education, 2001).

GAY AND LESBIAN ISSUES

The harsh and cruel incidents of harassment and bullying reported by gay, lesbian, bisexual, transgender, or questioning students are more likely to be gender harassment rather than sexual harassment (Human Rights Watch, 2001). Gender harassment includes behaviors that are verbally or physically aggressive, intimidating, or hostile but are not sexual or a sexual proposition (Stein, 1999). In contrast to sexual harassment, gender harassment focuses on behaviors that target a person because of his or her sexual orientation or behaviors that do not fit sociocultural norms for the victim's gender (U.S. Department of Education, 2001). The OCR has provided two examples to clarify sexual and gender harassment. If a female student who is a lesbian sexually propositions another female student to the extent that a hostile environment is created, a legally significant occurrence of sexual harassment has occurred. If a female student harasses another female student about her sexual orientation, gender harassment has occurred.

When students are harassed or bullied because of their sexual orientation, the Equal Protection Clause of the Fourteenth Amendment of the U.S. Constitution provides a safeguard. Generally, legal issues arise when harassment of sexual minority students has been ignored by school authority figures. In 1996, a federal court awarded a Wisconsin student, Jamie Nabozny, over $900,000 for the harassment he endured when school administrators repeatedly ignored his complaints of severe harassment based on his sexual identity. One administrator allegedly told Jamie that he should get used to the torment because he was so openly gay. In this case, cause is not the issue; harassment in any form, for any reason is unacceptable (Henning-Stout, James, & Macintosh, 2000; Stein, 1999; U.S. Department of Education, Office for Civil Rights and National Association of Attorneys General, 1999).

PREVALENCE OF SEXUAL HARASSMENT

One of the most comprehensive investigations of the prevalence of sexual harassment in schools was commissioned by the American Association of University Women in 1993 (AAUW, 1993) and then repeated in 2001. The questions on the survey related only to sexual harassment at school or school-related activities, and sexual harassment was defined as "unwanted and unwelcome sexual behavior that interferes with your life. Sexual harassment is not behaviors that you like or want" (AAUW, 2001, p. 2). The percentage of students reporting sexual harassment at school did not change from 1993 to 2001. The most dramatic change occurred in the students' awareness of their schools' sexual harassment policy: there was a 40 percent increase in students reporting their awareness of a school sexual harassment policy. Although it appears that students are more aware of school policies against sexual harassment, this alone does not seem to be decreasing the prevalence of sexual harassment. In fact, educating students about policy may actually increase the reports of harassment because it normalizes reporting offensive behavior (Brooks & Perot, 1991). Increasing awareness of sexual harassment policies may be a necessary but insufficient condition for decreasing sexual harassment. Although boys (79 percent) and girls (83 percent) reported experiencing comparable frequencies of sexual harassment, these data can be misleading. Girls reported experiencing harassment somewhat more frequently, experiencing more severe types of harassment, and having more negative emotional reactions to harassment than boys. When girls experienced harassment, they were more likely than boys to report being upset by it and feeling self-conscious, embarrassed, afraid, and less self-assured. Girls indicated that sexual harassment contributes to feelings of shame: "dirty-like a piece of trash," "like a second-class citizen," and "sick to my stomach" (AAUW, 2001, p. 36). Girls also were more likely than boys to be harassed by a school-related adult, which tends to be more severe than student-to-student harassment. Girls were more likely to report sexual harassment to authority figures (AAUW, 2001; Stein, 1999). In contrast, when boys report sexual harassment, Stein (1999) suggested that boys may experience a second victimization because attention from girls generally is viewed as an honor or rite of passage. Boys who complain about inappropriate sexual attention from girls go against cultural norms. Ethnicity also plays a role in what types of harassment students experience and how students report feeling about it. White males are more likely to be called gay or to have their clothes pulled at or down in a sexual way. Hispanic males are more likely to be the brunt of sexual jokes, comments, gestures, or looks. When young black females and males experience harassment, they report being less affected than either white or Hispanic students. White females are more likely to be the targets of rumors and are more likely to be called a lesbian. Black females are more likely to report being touched, grabbed, or pinched in a sexual way or to have their clothing pulled at in a sexual manner (AAUW, 2001). Although these statements are quite general, they illustrate how ethnicity may play a role in how an individual experiences and responds to sexual harassment. In addition, it encourages the use of a multicultural perspective in understanding sexual harassment or developing interventions.

Further analysis of the data from the AAUW (1993) survey on sexual harassment revealed that almost 75 percent of students who indicated that they were victims of sexual harassment also claimed that they had been a perpetrator of sexual harassment at least once, which is comparable to the 53 percent of students reporting being both a victim and a bully in the bullying literature (Haynie et al., 2001). However, because the sexual harassment data are not longitudinal, determining whether victimization or perpetration came first is not possible. These findings have important implications for preventing and responding to sexual harassment. When schools adopt only a punish-the-perpetrator model of responding to sexual harassment, the cultural context of sexual harassment is not integrated into the conceptualization of the problem. Effective interventions will be aimed at creating an inclusive and respectful school climate (Lee et al., 1996).

DEVELOPMENTAL ISSUES

When sexual harassment policies are applied rigidly and student developmental issues are disregarded, the children involved are not well served. For example, in 1996, a six-year-old boy kissed a girl in his class and was accused of sexual harassment. Common sense and understanding of human development would lead most educators to the conclusion that young students or students with developmental delays may not understand the complexities and sexual content of adolescent and adult sexual harassment. However, caution is warranted in interpreting not only the teasing or harassing behaviors but the impact of these behaviors among young children. Sexual harassment in early elementary school frequently is viewed as just teasing, bullying, or normal childhood play. However, this perception can be at odds with federal mandates. Sexual harassment can occur among elementary students, but the victim's perceptions about the interaction and the context of the behavior need to be considered (Stein, 1999).

As students move from elementary school to junior high or middle school, several factors contribute to increased incidence of sexual harassment. As early adolescents experience the physical changes of puberty, move from same-sex to mixed-sex peer groups, and begin to experience sexual feelings, sexually harassing behavior may be an attempt to explore their sexuality and to realize new ways of interacting with their peers. Within this age group, the distinction between flirting and sexual harassment may not be evident to many students (Craig, Pepler, Connolly, & Henderson, 2001). Other developmental issues associated with sexual harassment include the increased likelihood that either males or females who experience puberty earlier than their peers may be more likely to be targets of sexual harassment because early maturation is a highly salient characteristic during early adolescence and is typically an effective means of creating distress for students in this age group. Early developers and their peers may not have attained the cognitive and emotional resources to deal with these complicated issues. Their still-developing social skills may not correspond to their physical development (Craig et al., 2001).

Mental health professionals' understanding of child and adolescent development can help administrators develop reasonable responses to sexual harassment claims. Through assessment, observations, and interviews, psychologists, counselors, and social workers can assist in determining developmentally appropriate interventions and disciplinary actions. Professionals need to attend not only to developmental issues but also to a child's disability, especially if that child has been identified with an emotional or behavioral disability.

PROCEDURAL AND LEGAL ISSUES

The legal mandate that addresses sexual harassment of students is Title IX of the Educational Amendments of 1972, which applies to all educational institutions receiving federal funding. Title IX prohibits discrimination in educational programs based on sex; and sexual harassment has been determined by courts to be a form of sex discrimination (Stein, 1999). Under Title IX, lawsuits are brought against educational institutions rather than individuals. However, a student may have recourse against the individual perpetrator on the basis of other federal or state law (Layman, 1994). Both females and males are protected by Title IX (U.S. Department of Education, 2002).

Title IX mandates that schools take three actions to address sexual discrimination and, therefore, sexual harassment. First, school districts must have a policy stating that they do not discriminate on the basis of sex in determining participation in any of their educational programs (Stone, 2000). Schools are not required to have a sexual harassment policy that is separate from their sexual discrimination policy, but this is recommended (Webb, Hunnicutt, & Metha, 1997). Second, school districts must have published guidelines on sex discrimination and inform employees and students of this policy. Third, this policy must include a grievance procedure to address complaints. If a school district fails to meet these three stipulations, the district may be found in violation of Title IX, and its federal funding could be threatened (Layman, 1994). While there are approximately two dozen court cases that have influenced sexual harassment policy, there are several that merit the attention of school-based professionals. The first case that held a school monetarily liable for sexual harassment was *Franklin v. Gwinnett County (GA) Public Schools*. In the twenty-year existence of Title IX, this was the first time that a school district was held liable for compensatory damages because of failure to provide an educational setting free from sexual discrimination. In this case, a male teacher had sexual intercourse with a female student three times on campus. The administration arranged the resignation of the teacher, and no further action against the teacher was taken. The courts decided that the young woman had experienced sexual discrimination, and she was granted compensatory damages (Layman, 1994; Stein, 1999).

Some school districts have questioned their liability to protect students from other sexually harassing students. In May 1999, the Supreme Court clarified that school districts can be held liable for student-to-student harassment if the school knew about it but did not take reasonable steps to stop it. In the case of *Davis v. Monroe County Board of Education*, a male classmate seated next to a fifth-grade girl harassed her over a period of five months by grabbing her breasts and crotch, using sexual and crude language, and rubbing his body against hers (Stein, 1999). Incidents were reported by the child to her mother, who in turn reported the incidents to her daughter's teacher and the building principal. Only after three months were the children's desks moved. The young woman's grades dropped significantly, and a suicide note was discovered by her father. The sexual harassment did not stop until the parents filed a complaint with the sheriff's office and charged the young man with sexual battery, to which he pleaded guilty. Mrs. Davis then filed a sexual discrimination suit against the school under Title IX. The Supreme Court favored Mrs. Davis, explaining that its decision was influenced by the school's intentional lack of concern for the welfare of the young woman (Stein, 1999).

The Davis ruling clarified that liability for student-to-student harassment can be claimed only when the school has been "deliberately indifferent to sexual harassment, of which the recipient [of federal funding] has actual knowledge" (Biskupic, 1999, p. A.1). The guidance given by OCR (U.S. Department of Education, 2001) succinctly states, "If harassment has occurred, doing nothing is always the wrong response" (p. iii). OCR recognizes that schools cannot micromanage students' behavior or propensity toward sexual harassment. However, OCR does expect school districts to respond to sexual harassment when they know about it or when they reasonably should have known about it. A response indicating that the student "asked for it" or that "it was just a joke" has been considered blatantly insufficient by OCR (Layman, 1994; U.S. Department of Education, 2001).

PRIMARY, SECONDARY, AND TERTIARY PREVENTION STRATEGIES

This section examines three levels of prevention aimed at decreasing sexual harassment: (1) primary prevention (e.g., initiatives targeted at all students and faculty to prevent or decrease occurrences of sexual harassment); (2) secondary prevention (e.g., initiatives targeted toward those who are at risk for engaging in sexual harassment of others or who are at risk of being the target of sexual harassment); and (3) tertiary prevention (e.g., initiatives and interventions that focus on perpetrators and their targets after repeated harassment already has occurred, and that aim to prevent its further recurrence and to minimize the negative impact).

Primary Prevention

Educators are recognizing that primary prevention of sexual harassment in schools is rooted in a school's overall culture and climate (Stein, 1995; U.S. Department of Education, Office for Civil Rights and National Association of Attorneys General, 1999). A recent government publication focusing on protecting students from harassment and hate crimes noted "a growing consensus among educators that the best way to protect students from harassment is to establish a secure environment that expects appropriate behavior and promotes tolerance, sensitivity to others' views, and cooperative interactions among students" (U.S. Department of Education, Office for Civil Rights and National Association of Attorneys General, 1999, p. 8). Mental health professionals in the schools are key players in assisting administrators to understand the importance of school climate in sexual harassment prevention, to identify the most effective ways to measure school climate, and to develop interventions to improve school climate.

Some of the most important climate-related questions that school personnel can ask themselves are as follows: Do staff, students, and parents perceive an atmosphere of mutual respect and understanding at their school? Does the school climate reflect an appreciation for differences and diversity? What is the level of support among administrators and staff in implementing the sexual harassment policy? A school climate survey can be an effective way to answer these and similar questions, and several are available for use in the schools (Lehr & Christenson, 2002). Overall school climate is key to sexual harassment prevention efforts because in schools where there is little caring, respect, or trust between teachers and students, it is doubtful that students will approach school adults for help in resolving problems. Excellent suggestions for improving overall school climate with regard to appreciation of racial, cultural, and other forms of diversity can be accessed at http://www.ed.gov/pubs/Harassment/climate1.html and http://www.CASEL.org.

In addition to considering overall school climate, mental health professionals can directly assess the perceptions of sexual harassment at their schools by using separate teacher, parent, and student surveys targeted at sexual harassment (see AAUW [2002] and United States Department of Education, Office for Civil Rights and National Association of Attorneys General [1999], Appendix B, p. 111). Publicly observed or survey-reported sexual harassment is likely to be just the tip of the iceberg. In many schools, the majority of sexual harassment will go unreported and unidentified. These surveys can identify "hot spots" or create environmental maps to determine places in schools that are most troublesome.

Parents have many roles to play in addressing sexual harassment. They can and should be included in the school climate survey or other surveys about sexual harassment. Including parents in sexual harassment educational activities increases their awareness of the issues, which in turn helps them to be better advocates for their children and ensure that schools are safe places for children. Parents can help their children practice assertiveness skills and report harassing behaviors. Creating and maintaining effective communication between students and parents may be one of the most effective measures of dealing with sexual harassment (AAUW, 2002). Mental health professionals can refer parents to the materials from AAUW(2002) that identify specific activities to help parents to take the initiative in addressing these issues with their children and the schools.

As stated earlier, Title IX requires only that a school district have a published sex discrimination policy and a grievance procedure. However, best practices dictate that the policy contains a range of actions that could be taken when sexual harassment is substantiated. Mental health professionals should provide guidance to administrators in selecting targeted, age-appropriate responses for violating the policy. Depending on the severity, responses can range from providing education about sexual harassment and its effects on victims to more punitive responses, such as suspension or expulsion (Kopels & Dupper, 1999). Rather than touting a "zero tolerance" policy, the administrative response to sexual harassment should consider the age of the perpetrator and the target, as well as the nature and severity of the behavior. Using functional behavioral assessment strategies will ensure that positive behavioral interventions are designed to meet the student's specific needs.

Mental health professionals also can assist administrators to address the needs of the victim in the school's sexual harassment policy (Kopels & Dupper, 1999). A statement assuring the confidentiality of complaints should be included in the policy (Webb et al., 1997). The policy also should include preestablished guidelines for providing assistance to targets of sexual harassment, such as meeting with a peer support group or counselor at school. Finally, students should be assured that retaliation for making a complaint is not acceptable. If changes to a student's schedule are necessary, changes to the perpetrator's (rather than the victim's) schedule should be considered in addition to increased supervision where the harassment occurred (Shoop & Edwards, 1994). To help targets of sexual harassment feel more comfortable when making a complaint, the policy should stipulate that sexual harassment reports can be made to either a male or female official. Sexual harassment complaints should include written documentation of what happened, when, and who witnessed the events. Excellent examples of complaint forms are found in the new AAUW (2002) publication.

To ensure that the policy is effectively implemented, school personnel need training to identify sexual harassment and to intervene when they observe sexual harassment or when sexual harassment is reported to them. This training must be concrete and detailed; case studies may be useful. Role-plays may be especially effective in helping school adults become more comfortable in this role (Stein, 1993). This training also should include descriptions of the legal and emotional consequences of sexual harassment. All school adults (including paraprofessionals, bus drivers, cafeteria workers, and custodians) need to have the opportunity to clarify their own values, attitudes, and experiences about sexual harassment (Strauss, 1988). During the training school adults must be encouraged to model behavior at school that avoids sexual references, innuendoes, and jokes (AAUW, 2002). Notably, even with adequate training in how the policy is to be implemented, if there is insufficient staff buy-in or administrative support, it is unlikely the policy will be enforced and incorporated into the school culture.

When conducting training programs with students, their cognitive and emotional maturity must be carefully considered (e.g., elementary school students will need more concrete examples than high school students), and the trainer must be able to establish an atmosphere of trust among the students so that their feelings can be dealt with openly and honestly (Paludi & Barickman, 1998). Additionally, inviting others (e.g., parents, school board members) to participate in the training can help to ensure support outside of the classroom for students and teachers (Paludi & Barickman, 1998). Keeping males and females together ensures that all students receive consistent messages and communicates that both boys and girls can be targets of sexual harassment (Shoop & Edwards, 1994).

Notably, many professionals are already involved in building-level or district-wide primary prevention activities focused on increasing cultural sensitivity, tolerance of individual differences, and the development of prosocial behaviors. Consultants often train teachers, who then implement the curriculum in the classroom (e.g., Knoff and Batsche, 1995). In conjunction with these existing programs, folding in a sexual harassment curriculum may be a reasonable approach. Incorporating sexual harassment training into already existing social skills or character education initiatives may help to reduce the ecological intrusiveness of the training and increase teacher acceptance of the intervention (see Witt, 1986). Elias et al. (1997) offer specific guidelines for social and emotional learning programs that can be applied to sexual harassment prevention programs.

Because little empirical research exists on the efficacy of sexual harassment education in the schools, school personnel are left to choose a curriculum that appears educationally sound and that meets the needs of their students and teachers. Those choosing or developing the curriculum should be aware that students' perceptions of using assemblies or classroom videos were not positive (AAUW, 2001). Students want adults to *talk* to them about these issues. A discussion-oriented curriculum titled *Flirting or Hurting* was developed for Grades 6-12 (Stein and Sjostrom, 1994). In addition, fairly concrete curriculum, with different lesson plans for elementary and secondary students, can be found in the appendix of Paludi and Barickman (1998). A program developed by the Minnesota Department of Education (1993) for Grades K-3 and 4-6 also provides an excellent approach to teaching respect and tolerance to younger age groups.

Secondary Prevention

Secondary prevention of sexual harassment targets those who are at risk for experiencing sexual harassment as either a victim or a perpetrator. Although predicting with accuracy who is at risk for engaging in sexual harassment is difficult, it is known that students who may be at greater risk include early maturing students and gay, lesbian, bisexual, or transgender students (Craig et al., 2001; Human Rights Watch, 2001). Other students targeted for intervention may be students who make inappropriate comments or gestures. For example, if a student makes offensive comments about girls' or boys' bodies during an in-class discussion (which often are humorous to other students but may be ignored by the teacher), the student is likely expressing an underlying attitude about others that also is reflected in other inappropriate behaviors outside the classroom. Teachers often know who these students are but are not aware of how to respond to them. Targeting these students for intervention and not just disciplinary action is key.

Teachers who notice students being teased, bullied, or harassed (even if the student does not report the behavior) should guide these students to school resources so that they can increase their skills in responding to harassment. Perpetrators also should be referred for intervention. Another important component includes training students who observe harassing behaviors not just to ignore what they see but to report the behavior to someone who can provide assistance. Shoop and Edwards (1994) offer a number of suggestions for teaching students how to be assertive and to document when they experience harassment. Readers are referred to Goldstein (1999) for ideas on intervening specifically with perpetrators of sexual harassment.

Tertiary Prevention

The primary difference between tertiary prevention and secondary prevention entails initiatives that are focused on the most serious and chronic incidences of harassment. In this case, school personnel must know how to respond when a student engages in serious acts of sexual harassment or demonstrates a chronic pattern of such behavior. Additionally, they must know how to respond to and assist students with a pattern of victimization at school. Chronic perpetration of sexual harassment should be handled using a combination of disciplinary and educational interventions. Disciplinary actions may include exclusionary responses, such as suspension or expulsion in severe situations.

Exclusionary discipline techniques serve to protect other students from inappropriate behavior and send a message that such behaviors will not be tolerated, but they do not address the underlying issues that led to the behavior in the first place (Raffaele Mendez, Knoff, & Ferron, 2002). In the case of sexual harassment, students who show repeated disregard for the rights of others should have opportunities to learn skills for treating others with respect and for appreciating diversity. Mental health professionals can provide assistance to these students and their families by gathering additional information to determine which community and school resources may best meet their needs.

When sexual harassment is reported to a school adult, a critical first step is for the adult to listen and be responsive to the student's concerns and emotions. Title IX requires that school adults who have knowledge of sexual harassment report it to school officials who have the responsibility to investigate the claim and take corrective action. In addition, Stone (2000) notes that OCR promotes protection of the confidentiality of the target of sexual harassment. The name of the victim need not be revealed if she or he would prefer to remain anonymous. This is true even if failure to identify the target would significantly impair the investigation of the alleged harassment. If the target does not wish to be identified, others who witnessed the harassment may be interviewed. It may, however, be necessary in cases where the victim's physical safety is threatened to reveal his or her identity so that the investigation can be pursued expediently. In addition, staff should inform students that information about sexual harassment may need to be reported to the student's parents (Stone, 2000).

Finally, students who have experienced sexual harassment need to regain a sense of security and trust. This may be accomplished in a variety of ways, including peer support groups at school, individual counseling either at school or in the community, and opportunities for students who have experienced harassment to help other students understand its impact or assist with their recovery. Protection from retaliation is a part of regaining a sense of security. When working with groups of victims in a peer support group, group leaders should be aware of inadvertently reinforcing the victim role. Group leaders can help students who have experienced repeated victimization develop skills in assertion and personal power rather than focusing exclusively on the students' experiences as victims.

CONCLUSION

Mental health professionals working in the schools can do much to address sexual harassment. We have examined a working definition of sexual harassment, gender and ethnicity issues, developmental factors, and special concerns related to gay and lesbian students. We also have offered an overview of legislation and case law related to sexual harassment in schools. Additionally, we have discussed specific primary, secondary, and tertiary prevention strategies to be considered. We consider the area of primary prevention to be particularly important. Greater emphasis must be placed on developing respect and appreciation for diversity. Within this realm, school psychologists, counselors, and social workers can assist other educators in assessing school climate; developing comprehensive, developmentally sensitive sexual harassment policies; and designing effective training for students and staff in this area. Such efforts are likely to substantially reduce sexual harassment and lead to a safer, more comfortable, and more respectful learning environment for all students.

REFERENCES

American Association of University Women. (1993). *Hostile hallways: The AAUW survey on sexual harassment in America's schools.* Washington, DC: Author.

American Association of University Women. (2001). *Hostile hallways: Bullying, teasing, and sexual harassment in school.* Washington, DC: Author.

American Association of University Women. (2002). *Harassment-free hallways: How to stop sexual harassment in schools.* Washington, DC: Author.

Biskupic, K. (1999, May 25). *Davis v. Monroe County Board of Education et al. The Washington Post,* pp. A1:1.

Brooks, L., & Perot, A. R. (1991). Reporting sexual harassment: Exploring a predictive model. *Psychology of Women, 15,* 31-47.

Craig, W. M., Pepler, D., Connolly, J., & Henderson, K. (2001). Developmental context of peer harassment in early adolescence: The role of puberty and the peer group. In J. Juvonen & S. Graham (Eds.), *Peer harassment in school: The plight of the vulnerable and victimized* (pp. 242-261). New York: Guilford Press.

Elias, M. J., Zins, J. E., Weissberg, R. P., Frey, K. S., Greenberg, M. T., Haynes, N. M., et al. (1997). Promoting social and emotional learning: Guidelines for educators. Alexandria, VA: Association for Supervision and Curriculum Development.

Goldstein, A. P. (1999). *The prepare curriculum: Teaching prosocial competencies* (Rev. ed.). Champaign, IL: Research Press.

Haynie, D. L., Nansel, T., Eitel, P., Crump, A. D., Saylor, K., Yu, K., et al. (2001). Bullies, victims, and bully/victims: Distinct groups of at-risk youth. *Journal of Early Adolescence, 2,* 29-49.

Henning-Stout, M., James, S., & Macintosh, S. (2000). Reducing harassment of lesbian, gay, bisexual, transgender, and questioning youth in schools. *School Psychology Review, 29,* 180-192.

Human Rights Watch. (2001). *Hatred in the hallways.* New York: Author.

Knoff, H. M., & Batsche, G. M. (1995). Project ACHIEVE: Analyzing a school reform process for at-risk and underachieving students. *School Psychology Review, 24*(4), 579-603.

Kopels, S., & Dupper, D. R. (1999). School-based peer sexual harassment. *Child Welfare, 78*(4), 435-460.

Layman, N. S. (1994). *Sexual harassment in American secondary schools.* Dallas, TX: Contemporary Research Press.

Lee, V. E., Croninger, R. G., Linn, E., & Chen, X. (1996). The culture of sexual harassment in secondary schools. *American Educational Research Journal, 33,* 383-417.

Lehr, C. A., & Christenson, S. L. (2002). Best practices in promoting a positive school climate. In A. Thomas & J. Grimes (Eds.), *Best practices in school psychology IV-Volume 2* (pp. 929-947). Bethesda, MD: National Association of School Psychologists.

Levy, A. C., & Paludi, M. A. (2002). *Workplace sexual harassment* (2nd ed.). Upper Saddle River, NJ: Prentice Hall.

Minnesota Department of Education. (1993). *Girls and boys getting along. Sexual harassment prevention in the elementary grades.* St. Paul, MN: Author.

Paludi, M. A. (1997). Sexual harassment in schools. In W. O'Donohue (Ed.), *Sexual harassment: Theory, research, and treatment* (pp. 225-240). Needham Heights, MA: Allyn and Bacon, Inc.

Paludi, M. A., & Barickman, R. B. (1998). *Sexual harassment, work, and education: A resource manual for prevention.* Albany, NY: State University of New York Press.

Raffaele Mendez, L. M., Knoff, H. M., & Ferron, J. (2002). School demographic variables and out-of-school suspension rates: A quantitative and qualitative analysis of a large, ethnically diverse school district. *Psychology in the Schools, 30*(3), 259-277.

Shoop, R. J., & Edwards, D. L. (1994). *How to stop sexual harassment in our schools: A handbook and curriculum guide for administrators and teachers.* Boston: Allyn & Bacon.

Shoop, R. J., & Hayhow, J. W. (1994). *Sexual harassment in our schools: What parents and teachers need to know to spot it and stop it.* Needham Heights, MA.

Stein, N. (1993). Breaking through casual attitudes on sexual harassment. *Education Digest, 58*(9), 7-10.

Stein, N. (1995). Sexual harassment in school: The public performance of gendered violence. *Harvard Educational Review, 65*(2), 145-162.

Stein, N. (1999). *Classrooms & courtrooms: Facing sexual harassment in K-12 schools.* New York: Teachers College Press.

Stein, N., & Sjostrom, L. (1994). *Flirting or hurting? A teachers' guide on student-to-student sexual harassment in schools (grades 6-12).* Washington, DC: National Education Association.

Stone, C. B. (2000). Advocacy for sexual harassment victims: Legal support and ethical aspects. *Professional School Counseling, 4,* 23-30.

Strauss, S. (1988). Sexual harassment in the school: Legal implications for principals. *National Association of Secondary School Principals Bulletin, 72*(506), 93-97.

United States Department of Education, Office for Civil Rights. (2001). *Sexual harassment policy guidance: Harassment of students by school employees, other students, or third parties.* Washington, DC: Author. Retrieved January 14, 2002, from http://www.ed.gov/office/OCR/shguide/index.html

United States Department of Education, Office for Civil Rights. (2002). *Sexual harassment: It's not academic.* [Pamphlet]. Washington, DC: Author. Retrieved January 14, 2002, from http://www.ed.gov/office/OCR/docs/ocrshpam.html

United States Department of Education, Office for Civil Rights and National Association of Attorneys General. (1999). *Protecting students from harassment and hate crime: A guide for schools.* Washington, DC: Author. Retrieved March 1, 2002, from http://www.ed.gov/pubs/Harassment/

Webb, L. D., Hunnicutt, K. H., & Metha, A. (1997). What schools can do to combat student-to-student sexual harassment. *National Association of Secondary School Principals Bulletin, 81*(585), 72-79.

Witt, J. C. (1986). Teachers' resistance to the use of school-based interventions. *Journal of School Psychology, 24,* 37-44.

Chapter 18

Bullying Is Power:
Implications for School-Based
Intervention Strategies

Tracy Vaillancourt
Shelley Hymel
Patricia McDougall

Much of what is known about bullies and bullying behavior comes from Olweus's (1973, 1978, 1993, 1996) large-scale studies of Scandinavian children in which he distinguished bullies from noninvolved students or victims in terms of their positive views of violence and of themselves (high rather than low self-esteem), their impulsivity and physical strength, and their lack of insecurity, anxiety and empathy for victims. More recent studies have focused on the mental health functioning of children identified as bullies. Like victims, bullies are at risk for internalizing difficulties including depression, suicidal ideation (Kaltiala-Heino, Rimpela, Marttunen, Rimpela, & Rantanen, 1999), and loneliness (Forero & McLellan, 1999), and like aggressive children, bullies are at risk for externalizing disorders (Kumpulainen et al., 1998), delinquency and criminality (Olweus, 1993), as well as poor academic achievement, smoking, and substance abuse (Nansel et al., 2001). These findings are consistent with traditional, intuitive notions of bullies as poorly accepted, marginal members of the peer group who are psychologically unfit. We question this stereotypic portrayal

This chapter was adapted from "Bullying Is Power: Implications for School-Based Intervention Strategies" by Tracy Vaillancourt, Shelley Hymel, and Patricia McDougall, *Journal of Applied School Psychology, 19*(2), pp. 157-176.

Bullying, Victimization, and Peer Harassment
Published by The Haworth Press, Inc., 2007. All rights reserved.
doi:10.1300/5808_18

of bullies, and suggest that there are distinct subtypes of bullies, differentiated in terms of their social power and status.

Issues of social power are critical to understanding the complex nature of bullying. Despite the fact that current definitions of bullying emphasize the power differential that exists within bully-victim relationships as a key characteristic of bullying (Besag, 1989; Olweus, 1993, 1996), there has been little, if any, systematic investigation of the links between bullying and power, and little appreciation of the fact that social power reflects an interaction between the characteristics of the individual and the social context in which he or she operates. Accordingly, this study distinguishes different subtypes of bullies on the basis of their perceived power within the group. Our hypotheses regarding bullying subtypes are based on a distinction between implicit and explicit social power made by LaFreniere and Charlesworth (1983). Explicit social power "is expressed explicitly and forcefully and thereby elicits fear, submission, or compliance"; implicit social power "stems from a recognition of status or competence and thereby depends upon acceptance by subordinates" (p. 66). We believe that all bullies rely on explicit social power to some degree, using such things as greater size and strength and various forms of aggressive behavior to coerce peers who, in turn, are submissive as a result of fear. However, some bullies also possess characteristics and assets that are valued by the peer group and, as a result, these bullies are afforded a high degree of status within the group, giving them implicit social power. In both cases, bullies may be granted a certain degree of dominance and influence within the peer group, but for different reasons. Moreover, relative reliance on implicit versus explicit social power may contribute to social status within the peer group, with implicit social power associated with greater status.

Critical to understanding the relationship between bullying and status is the distinction made by Parkhurst and Hopmeyer (1998) between sociometric acceptance/rejection (operationalized as the degree to which one is generally liked versus disliked by peers) and peer perceptions of "popularity" or status within the group. In their study of early adolescents, Parkhurst and Hopmeyer found that these two status indicators, both derived from peer assessments, were significantly but modestly related ($r = .28$), with only 36 percent of sociometrically accepted or well-liked students actually being perceived as "popular." Moreover, some disliked or rejected students (11 percent) and nearly half of the "controversial" students (liked by some, disliked by others) were perceived as "popular." Thus, sociometric liking/disliking is not necessarily synonymous with perceived status or popularity; being rejected is not the same as being viewed by peers as unpopular or low in status.

With regard to the social status of bullies, early studies by Olweus (1973, 1978, 1993) found bullies to be average in terms of peer liking, although this "acceptance" was rather short lived, as the majority of bullies were disliked by their peers once they reached the later elementary and high school years. Other studies generally have found bullies to be disliked or rejected by their peers (Boulton, 1999; Boulton & Smith, 1994; Pelligrini, Bartini, & Brooks, 1999). Similar associations have been documented between aggression and peer rejection (see Rubin, Bukowski, & Parker, 1998), although the magnitude of this relationship is modest, with only about 50 percent of aggressive children actually being rejected by peers (e.g., Rubin et al., 1998). At least some aggressive children and adolescents are actually solid and central members of their social clique (e.g., Farmer & Rodkin, 1996), are liked by their peers (e.g., Hess & Aiken, 1998), and are perceived as popular or highly visible and prominent within the peer group (e.g., Estell, Cairns, Farmer, & Cairns, 2002; Vaillancourt & Hymel, 2002). Recent ethnographic studies (e.g., Adler & Adler, 1998; Merten, 1997) also demonstrate links between cruel and aggressive behavior and high levels of status and popularity within the peer group.

In light of this research, we hypothesized that, like aggressive children and adolescents, bullies are generally disliked by their peers, owing primarily to the fact that all bullies rely to some degree on explicit social power (i.e., aggression). However, some bullies are also perceived as popular and powerful as a function of their access to implicit social power. Following from the argument that possession of peer-valued characteristics provides the basis for implicit social power, we hypothesized that bullies who wield implicit social power would differ from those who do not in terms of their level of perceived social status and their possession of certain competencies and assets that are valued by the peer group. Of additional interest was whether subtypes of bullies would also differ in terms of their own social self-perceptions and indices of mental well-being, with more favorable perceptions and outcomes expected for those bullies who enjoy high levels of power. Understanding these relationships between power, status, and bullying is critical to informing intervention efforts aimed at reducing bullying in schools.

METHOD

Participants

As part of a larger longitudinal project, students in Grades 6-10 (age range = eleven to seventeen years) were recruited from all five elementary schools (Grades K-7) and the only secondary school (Grades 8-12) that serviced a moderate-sized, western Canadian city (population approx. 9,000). All participants received parental consent (270 girls, 285 boys; M age = 13.3 years, SD = 1.49 years), with approximately equal numbers across grades and an overall participation rate of 95 percent. The sample was predominantly white (93 percent), with a small percentage of First Nations, Asian Canadian, Indo Canadian, and Latin Canadian students, reflecting the makeup of the community.

Procedures

Students participated in a single group-testing session (fifty minutes) during which they completed both self-report and peer assessment measures, as described later. Participants were assured of the confidentiality of their individual responses to all measures.

Peer Assessment Measures

Students were asked to nominate an unlimited[1] number of grade-mates of either gender who best fit each of forty sociometric, behavioral, and nonbehavioral descriptors, as described in Table 18.1. For each item, nominations received from grade-mates were summed and standardized within grade to yield a continuous measure of the characteristic assessed. In some cases (see Table 18.1), conceptually related items were averaged to create composite indices, computed as the sum of standardized items divided by the number of items in the composite. For each construct, higher scores reflected greater peer perceptions of the characteristic described.

Peer nominations were used to assess perceptions of bullying behavior, with higher scores indicating that a greater number of peers viewed that person as a bully. Although self-report data are often used to identify bullies (e.g., Olweus, 1994; Rigby, 1999), peer nominations represent a more time-consuming, but face-valid alternative (Perry, Kusel, & Perry, 1988) that avoids potential self-reporting biases (e.g., denial, exaggeration) and reflects the perspective of multiple informants within students' primary social context. Peer nominations were also used to assess perceived power using a composite of two items, and to assess three different indices of social status: perceived popularity (succeeding Parkhurst & Hopmeyer, 1998) and the more traditional sociometric indices of peer liking (acceptance) and disliking (rejection). Following previous research (Coie & Dodge, 1983; Crick & Grotpeter, 1995; Galen & Underwood, 1997), peer nomination composites were also used to assess both physical aggression (i.e., hitting), and rela-

TABLE 18.1. Peer assessment measure.

Construct	Item(s)	Internal consistency	Range of scores (unstandardized proportion scores)*
Bullying	Who is a bully?		0-91% of peers
Power	Who seems to have a lot of power over others? + Who can pressure others into doing things?	Alpha = .83	0-83% of peers
Social status			
Perceived popularity	Who are the most popular people in your grade?		0-96% of peers
Liking/acceptance	Who are the people you like most in your grade?		0-63% of peers
Disliking/rejection	Who are the people you like least in your grade?		0-65% of peers
Aggressive behavior			
Physical aggression	Who starts fights and arguments with others? + Who hits, pushes others?	Alpha = .86	0-76% of peers
Relational aggression	Who spreads rumors about someone to get others to stop liking the person? + Who tries to control or dominate a person by excluding him or her from the peer group? +Who tells others to stop liking a person to get even with him or her? + Who ignores people when they are mad at them (gives people the silent treatment)? + Who will make someone feel bad or look bad by making a face, turning away, or rolling their eyes?	Alpha = .86	0-35% of peers
Competencies and assets			
Prosocial behavior	Who always gets along well with other people? + Who is able to understand other people's point of view? + Who is helpful and cooperative? + Who is kind and nice to others? + Who helps others when they have a problem?	Alpha = .89	0-38% of peers

TABLE 18.1 *(continued)*

Construct	Item(s)	Internal consistency	Range of scores (unstandardized proportion scores)*
Leadership	Who is a good leader?		0-70% of peers
Wealth	Who seems to be rich?		0-92% of peers
Appearance	Who is good looking or attractive? + Who dresses well and is in style?	Alpha = .86	0-63% of peers
Athletic competence	Who does well in sports?		0-88% of peers
Academic competence	Who does well in their schoolwork?		0-91% of peers

Note.* Unstandardized proportion scores reflect the extent to which individuals were perceived by their peers to possess the behavioral or nonbehavioral characteristics in question. For example, the range of scores of 0-91 percent obtained for the bullying item indicates that at least one participant was nominated as a bully by 91 percent of her or his grade-mates.

tional aggression, defined as social manipulation that is intended to harm (i.e., spreading rumors; Crick & Grotpeter). Finally, peer nomination data were used to assess six assets or competencies: prosocial behavior, leadership, appearance, wealth, academic and athletic competence, with higher scores reflecting peer perceptions of greater levels of competence or assets in each case.

Self-Report Measures

Self-report questionnaires were used to assess both social self-perceptions and internalizing difficulties. Specifically, social self-efficacy, or the degree to which a person believes he or she can evoke change within a social context, was measured using a 5-item scale adapted for adolescents (Sletta, 1998) from Wheeler and Ladd's (1982) *Social Self-Efficacy Scale* ($\alpha = .74$; $M = 17.67$, $SD = 3.85$). Perceptions of peer social support were assessed using two seven-item subscales of the *Relational ProvisionsLoneliness Questionnaire* developed by Hayden (1989), see Terrell-Deutsch, 1999), one assessing perceived intimacy (having others to confide in; $\alpha = .85$; $M = 28.92$, $SD = 5.93$) and one assessing perceived integration or belonging (having others to hang out and do things with; $\alpha = .89$; $M = 28.62$, $SD = 5.57$). The eight-item social self-concept subscale of the

Self-Description Questionnaire I (SDQI; Marsh, 1988) was used to assess the extent to which students held positive opinions of their peer interactions (e.g., "Most other kids like me"; $\alpha = .90$; $M = 31.18$, $SD = 6.40$). Depression was assessed using a twenty-six-item adaptation (one item on suicide deleted at the request of the schools) of the *Child Depression Inventory* (Kovacs, 1991,1992; $\alpha = .89$; $M = 35.74$, $SD = 8.58$), while students' feelings of loneliness were assessed using the sixteen-item, *Loneliness and Social Dissatisfaction Scale* (Asher, Hymel, & Renshaw, 1984; $\alpha = .88$; $M = 28.41$, $SD = 9.67$). Finally, the extent to which students held global, positive perceptions of self was assessed using the general self-worth subscale of the *SDQ I* ($\alpha = .86$; $M = 33.28$, $SD = 5.15$).

RESULTS

Characteristics Associated with Bullying and Power

Zero-order correlational analyses were first conducted to examine the relationships among bullying, power, and various indices of *status* (popularity, liking, disliking), *aggressive behavior* (relational, physical), *competencies and assets* (appearance, wealth, athletic and academic competence, prosocial behavior, leadership), *social self-perceptions* (social self-efficacy, peer intimacy, peer integration, social self-concept) and *internalizing difficulties* (depression, loneliness, general self-worth) across the entire sample. Results indicated that peer perceptions of bullying were significantly related to a broad range of peer-assessed characteristics (degrees of freedom range from 524 to 553; all p levels <.001 unless otherwise indicated, although the magnitude of these correlations varied considerably. As expected, children identified as bullies were generally viewed by peers as more powerful ($r = .67$) and, to a lesser extent, as more popular ($r = .29$), although they were also generally disliked ($r = .32$). Not surprisingly, bullies were viewed by peers as more physically ($r = .79$) and relationally aggressive ($r = .50$). With regard to positive competencies and assets, bullying was significantly, but only minimally associated with peer perceptions of greater leadership ($r = .21$), athletic competence ($r = .14$) and appearance ($r = .18$), as well as less prosocial behavior ($r = -.17$) and lower academic competence ($r = -.12$; $p = .006$). The low magnitude of these correlations suggests that each of these positive characteristics is not evident across all students identified as bullies. With regard to self-perceptions and internalizing difficulties, peer-identified bullies reported feeling more socially competent ($r = .13$, $p = .004$) and efficacious ($r = .23$). Bullying was not significantly related to depression ($r = .06$), general self-worth ($r = .05$), loneliness ($r = -.08$), *liking* ($r = .03$), wealth ($r = .04$), or perceptions of peer social support in the form of intimacy ($r = .03$) or integration ($r = .08$).

A similar pattern of correlations was observed when peer ratings of power were considered. On the positive side, greater power was associated with being popular ($r = .58$), frequently liked ($r = .22$), and less disliked by peers ($r = -.19$). Similarly, perceived power was associated with better appearance ($r = .46$), wealth ($r = .19$), athleticism ($r = .27$), and leadership ($r = .42$). Higher power, however, was also linked to more aggressive behavior in both physical ($r = .57$) and relational forms ($r = .57$). Like the self-perceptions of bullies, students with higher power reported greater social self-efficacy ($r = .26$) and competence with peers ($r = .22$). But unlike bullies, students viewed by peers as powerful saw themselves as better integrated within the peer group ($r = .16$), less lonely ($r = -.17$), and were higher in general self-worth ($r = .14$). Power was not significantly related to peer nominations of academic competence ($r = -.07$), prosocial behavior ($r = -.04$), perceptions of peer intimacy ($r = .08$), or reports of depression ($r = .02$).

Given our interest in demonstrating a link between bullying and power, we wanted to ensure that power was not synonymous with other peer-nominated characteristics or behaviors (e.g., aggression). Specifically, we sought to examine whether power would continue to be predictive of bullying even when the effects of other related peer nominations were partialled out. In a simultaneous regression analysis with indices of peer status, aggressive behavior, and competencies as predictors, we were able to account for 69 percent of the variability in peer nominations of bullying ($F(12, 522) = 96.76$, $p < .001$). After controlling for the effects of other peer nominations, power ($p = .297$; semi-partial (sr) $= .18$, $p < .001$), relational aggression ($p = .089$; $sr = .07$, $p = .008$), physical aggression ($p = .579$; $sr = .43$, $p < .001$), and leadership ($p = .066$, $sr = .05$, $p = .042$) remained uniquely predictive (all $ps < .001$) of bullying. Thus, despite the fact that both leadership and aggressive behavior appear to be important correlates of bullying, power makes a unique contribution and is not simply redundant with aggression and leadership qualities.

Creating Subtypes of Bullies

Of primary interest here was consideration of the characteristics associated with bullying. To this end, a subsample of students identified as bullies by their peers was selected, operationally defined as those who scored at or above 1/2 standard deviation of the mean for their grade on the item, "Who is a bully?" Our use of the 1/2 standard deviation as a cutoff criterion follows from the work of Schwartz (2000). Of these bullies, forty-four were in elementary school, fifty-eight were in secondary school, and thirty-three were girls, sixty-nine were boys. Subsequent analyses examined whether the characteristics associated with bullying varied as a function of sex (girls versus boys) and school context (elementary versus secondary school). Specifically, for the subsample of 102 peer-identified bullies, a series of 2 (sex) × 2 (school context) MANOVAs were conducted using the following dependent variables: (1) peer nominations of bullying, (2) aggressive behaviors (intercorrelation $r = .48$), (3) social status (intercorrelations among variables ranged from $-.01$ to .44), (4) competencies and assets (intercorrelations ranged from .06 to .46), (5) social self-perceptions (intercorrelations ranged from .27 to .80) and (6) internalizing difficulties (intercorrelations ranged from .35 to $-.46$).

Results of these analyses revealed one significant multivariate interaction between sex and school context for *aggressive behaviors* (Wilks's $\lambda = .88$, $F(2,91) = 6.07$, $p = .003$, $\eta^2 = 12$) and one significant main effect at the multivariate level, also for *aggressive behaviors* (Wilks's $\lambda = .88$, $F(2, 91) = 5.95$, $p = .004$, $\eta^2 = 12$), along with significant main effects of sex in the domains of *aggressive behaviors* (Wilks's $\lambda = .66$, $F(2, 91) = 23.29$, $p < .001$, $\eta^2 = .34$), *competencies and assets* (Wilks's $\lambda = .73$, $F(6, 88) = 5.35$, $p < .01$, $\eta^2 = .27$), and *social self-perceptions* (Wilks's $\lambda = .84$, $F(4, 85) = 3.94$, $p = .006$, $\eta^2 = .16$). Follow-up ANOVAs indicated that the sex by school context interaction was significant for *physical aggression* ($F(1,92) = 6.03$, $p = .016$, $\eta^2 = .06$). Although peer reports of physical aggression declined from elementary to secondary school for boys ($M = 1.80$, $SD = 1.15$; $M = .76$, $SD = 1.25$, respectively), this shift was not significant for girls ($M = .57$, $SD = .72$ elementary; $M = 1.10$, $SD = 1.38$ secondary). In contrast, the main effect of context for *relational aggression* ($F(1, 92) = 11.82$, $p = .001$, $\eta^2 = .11$) revealed a decrease in the use of this type of aggression for both girls and boys from elementary ($M = .85$, $SD = .90$) to high school ($M = .37$, $SD = .63$). Finally, follow-up ANOVAs showed sex differences for relational aggression ($F(1, 96) = 24.89$, $p < .001$, $\eta^2 = .21$), *athletic competence* ($F(1, 93) = 5.35$, $p = .023$, $\eta^2 = .05$), *appearance* ($F(1, 93) = 4.92$, $p = .029$, $\eta^2 = .05$) and *peer intimacy* ($F(1, 88) = 10.71$, $p = .002$, $\eta^2 = .11$). Female bullies were seen as more relationally aggressive ($M = 5.44$, $SD = 4.52$), yet reported higher peer intimacy ($M = 31.81$, $SD = 5.49$) as compared to male bullies ($M = 1.78$, $SD = 3.00$, and $M = 27.74$, $SD = 5.68$, respectively). Further, male bullies were viewed as more athletic ($M = .23$, $SD = 1.01$) but less attractive ($M = .15$, $SD = 1.94$) than female bullies ($M = -.15$, $SD = .67$ and $M = 1.16$, $SD = 2.2$, respectively).

Differences in Power: Subtypes of Bullies

As mentioned previously, our central interest was in the identification of subtypes of bullies who were expected to vary in terms of a number of characteristics. Accordingly, the 102 peer-identified bullies were classified into one of three subgroups, based on peer reports of power. Bullies who scored at or above standard deviation of the mean for their grade on perceived power were categorized as highly powerful, whereas bullies who scored at or below 1/2 standard deviation of the mean were categorized as having low power. Bullies with perceived power scores within ±1/2 standard deviation of the mean were categorized as moderate in power. Using these criteria, we identified ten low power bullies (one girl, nine boys), forty-one moderately powerful bullies (fifteen girls, twenty-six boys), and fifty-one highly powerful bullies (seventeen girls, thirty-four boys). Of interest was whether these subgroups differed in terms of behavioral and nonbehavioral characteristics.

Subgroup differences for both relational and physical aggression were assessed using a one-way MANOVA. Results (see Table 18.2) revealed significant differences in *aggressive behavior* (Wilks's $\lambda = .84$, $F(4, 182) = 4.33$, $p = .002$, $\eta^2 = .09$), with follow-up univariate ANOVAs and post hoc LSD tests showing that highly powerful bullies were viewed as more relationally aggressive ($F(2, 93) = 7.70$, $p = .001$, $\eta^2 = .14$) as compared to moderate- and low-power bullies. Powerful bullies also demonstrated a tendency toward being seen as more physically aggressive ($F(2, 93) = 2.73$, $p = .071$, $\eta^2 = .06$) as compared to bullies with low power.

Given the strong zero-order associations observed between bullying, power, and aggressive behavior and the fact that relational and physical aggression emerged as uniquely predictive of bullying in our regression analysis, efforts to control for aggressive behavior were undertaken in subsequent analyses examining variations across bullying subgroups. Our goal was to examine characteristics of various subtypes of bullies that reflect variations in implicit power, not explicit power exerted through aggressive behavior. A series of one-way MANCOVAs were conducted examining differences across the three bullying subgroups in terms of (1) social status, (2) competencies and assets, (3) social self-perceptions, and (4) self-reported internalizing difficulties, after covarying out the effects of relational and physical aggression. Results (see Table 18.2) indicated significant differences in *social status*, Wilks's $\lambda = .71$, $F(6, 176) = 5.39$, $p < .001$, $\eta^2 = .16$, and *competencies and assets*, Wilks's $\lambda = .74$, $F(12, 162) = 2.16$, $p = .016$, $\eta^2 = .14$. No statistically significant differences were observed across subtypes for social self-perceptions or internalizing difficulties.

TABLE 18.2. Differences across bullying subgroups (unadjusted means).

	High-power bully (n = 51) *Average proportion = 16%		Moderate-power bully (n = 41) Average proportion = 3%		Low-power bully (n = 10) Average proportion = 0%		†Post hoc comparisons
	M	(SD)	M	(SD)	M	(SD)	
Aggressive behavior							
Physical aggression	1.27	(1.24)	.94	(1.20)	.34	(.88)	Trend HI > LO
Relational aggression	.87	(.82)	.42	(.72)	.04	(.34)	HI > MOD, LO
Social status							
Perceived popularity	1.32	(1.58)	-0.16	(.58)	-0.29	(0.29)	HI > MOD, LO
Liked most	.40	(1.03)	-.29	(.81)	-.08	(1.14)	HI > MOD
Liked least	.46	(.79)	.51	(1.18)	.18	(.92)	
Competencies and assets							
Appearance	.69	(1.32)	-.17	(.48)	-.32	(.17)	HI > MOD, LO
Wealth	.18	(1.13)	-.10	(.72)	.07	(.55)	
Athleticism	.33	(1.11)	.01	(.80)	-.43	(.06)	
Prosocial behavior	-0.22	(.41)	-.42	(.37)	-.20	(.57)	
Leadership	.93	(1.52)	-.28	(.47)	-.47	(.47)	
Aademic	-.25	(.57)	-.35	(.22)	-.26	(.42)	HI > MOD, LO
Social self-perceptions							
Self-efficacy	20.00	(3.08)	18.89	(4.41)	18.11	(3.92)	
Intimacy	29.42	(5.84)	29.23	(5.48)	24.78	(7.16)	

327

TABLE 18.2 (continued)

	High-power bully (n = 51) *Average proportion = 16%		Moderate-power bully (n = 41) Average proportion = 3%		Low-power bully (n = 10) Average proportion = 0%		†Post hoc comparisons
	M	(SD)	M	(SD)	M	(SD)	
Integration	28.93	(7.03)	28.69	(5.28)	26.44	(5.10)	
Peer self-concept	33.67	(6.42)	31.14	(7.40)	28.44	(2.79)	
Internalizing difficulties							
Depression	38.79	(8.79)	37.69	(10.69)	36.44	(8.47)	
Loneliness	26.23	(8.91)	29.75	(10.42)	30.67	(14.20)	
General self-worth	33.36	(6.18)	33.44	(5.51)	30.11	(4.11)	

Note. *Average proportion scores represent the percentage of students in the nominating network who perceived the individual as powerful. For example, students in the moderate-power group were, on average, viewed as powerful by 5 percent of their peer network. †HI = high power, MOD = moderate power, LO = low-power bully.

Follow-up univariate tests for *social status* revealed that variations in peer liking and perceived popularity were both statistically significant ($F(2, 90) = 5.53$, $p = .005$, $\eta^2 = .11$ and $F(2, 90) = 16.82$, $p < .001$, $\eta^2 = .27$, respectively), with LSD post hoc tests on adjusted means indicating that powerful bullies were perceived as more popular than moderate- or low-power bullies. Similarly, bullies with high power were better liked than moderate-power bullies. For *competencies and assets*, follow-up ANCOVAs revealed significant variations across bullying subtypes for leadership ($F(2, 86) = 11.84$, $p < .001$, $\eta^2 = .22$) and appearance ($F(2, 86) = 6.56$, $p = .002$, $\eta^2 = .13$). Results of LSD post hoc tests on adjusted means showed that powerful bullies were viewed more favorably by their peers, who saw them as more attractive (e.g., stylish) and as better leaders compared to moderate- and low-power bullies.

DISCUSSION

Definitions of bullying emphasize the power differential that exists between bullies and their victims. In this study, we verify the link between bullying and perceived power within the adolescent peer group. Although not synonymous, bullying and power are linked in significant and complex ways. In this sample, many (if not most) of the bullies identified by peers did not fit the stereotype of a psychologically maladjusted, marginalized individual. Rather, correlational results indicated that bullies in this study were considered both popular and powerful, even if they were generally disliked. Given their apparent high status within the peer group, it is not surprising that, overall, bullies reported a positive sense of social self-efficacy, and a positive social self-concept. Further, peer-nominated bullies also reported feeling well integrated with the peer group and less lonely. Consistent with Olweus (1993, 1996), peer-identified bullies in this study did not report lower self-esteem. However, in contrast to previous research suggesting that bullies may be at risk for depression (e.g., Roland, 2002), peer-identified bullies in this study did not report greater levels of depression.

When the sex of the bully was considered, an interesting yet predictable pattern of results emerged. Specifically, consistent with what has been found with aggressive children (e.g., Crick & Grotpeter, 1995), female bullies in this study were viewed by peers as being more relationally aggressive and less physically aggressive than male bullies. Moreover, female bullies reported greater peer intimacy than male bullies, a sex difference that has been demonstrated for children in general (Hayden, 1989). Finally, female bullies were perceived by peers to be more attractive than male bullies, whereas male bullies were perceived to be more athletic than female bullies—a finding that is not surprising considering prevailing gender-role stereotypes. The characteristics associated with bullying were also found to differ significantly across the elementary and secondary school contexts. Consistent with research on the development of aggression (see Bjorkqvist, Lagerspetz, & Kaukiainen, 1992), a decrease in the use of physical aggression (for male bullies) with increased age was noted, as was a decrease in the use of relational aggression (for female and male bullies) with increased age.

In this study, we saw that bullying was associated with both explicit and implicit forms of social power (LaFreniere & Charlesworth, 1983). Bullies were generally perceived to be physically and relationally aggressive, both of which are classic forms of explicit power over others and at least some bullies were also perceived to be leaders and to possess certain nonbehavioral competencies and assets that are valued in the peer group, including wealth, attractiveness, and/or athletic competence, which more aptly suggests implicit power. These generally positive correlates of bullying were not enjoyed by all bullies, however. Three subgroups of bullies were distinguished on the basis of their relative power within the group, as perceived by peers. The fact that over half of the students who were identified as bullies were categorized as *powerful* bullies, and only a few (14 percent) were categorized as relatively powerless is indeed noteworthy. Powerful bullies, in contrast to moderate-power bullies and low-power bullies, were perceived by peers to possess a mixture of both positive and negative characteristics that, as predicted, reflect both explicit and implicit sources of social power (LaFreniere & Charlesworth, 1983). Powerful bullies were viewed as more popular and more liked as well as more physically and relationally aggressive than less powerful bullies. Additionally, consistent with the notion of implicit power, powerful bullies were perceived to possess more competencies and assets than less powerful bullies, including such things as being physically attractive, wearing stylish clothing, and being better leaders. Although we believe that leadership and peer-valued characteristics are at the core of implicit social power, we also recognize the need for more direct measures of this form of power. For example, future research on implicit power would benefit from asking students questions such as, "Who do you look up to?" or "Who do you want to be like?" that would also reflect a recognition of status and competence.

Contrary to expectations, no statistically significant differences across bully subtypes were found on social self-perceptions or self-reported internalizing difficulties. Why might this be the case? It is possible that, generally speaking, oppressing others feels good and this positive feeling is not dependent upon one's level of peer-perceived power. Interestingly, the growing consensus in the self-esteem literature is that individuals with high self-esteem are the ones who aggress when there is a threat to ego as opposed to those with low self-esteem (see Baumeister, Smart, & Boden, 1996 for a review). It is also possible that differences were not found across bully subtypes because bullies (and power) were identified using peer nominations as opposed to self-reports. As such, it could be that bullies are not even aware of their level of power within the peer group, nor may they be aware that they are perceived as bullies by their peers. This lack of awareness of how the peer group views them may be why their social self-perceptions and self-reported internalizing difficulties did not differ across varying levels of perceived power. These points notwithstanding, it is important to consider that the correlation patterns obtained in this study suggest that both powerful students and bullies by and large feel good about themselves and their social interactions.

These results replicate previous findings that bullies are generally rejected/disliked (e.g., Boulton, 1999; Boulton & Smith, 1994; Pelligrini et al., 1999), but also confirm our expectations that, for a significant number of bullies, bullying behavior is associated with a high degree of social status. As hypothesized, greater power was evident among bullies who utilized both "explicit power" and "implicit power." Perhaps as a result of these characteristics, powerful bullies were more likely to be viewed as popular, despite the fact that they were significantly more physically and relationally aggressive toward peers than their less powerful counterparts. In this regard, this research joins with a growing number of studies suggesting that bullying and other forms of aggressive behavior can be used to enhance and maintain one's status within the peer group (e.g., Espelage & Holt, in press).

Implications for School-Based Intervention Strategies

In considering the implications of these findings for school-based efforts to reduce bullying, it is important to highlight that over half of the students identified by peers as bullies in this study actually enjoyed a substantial level of status and power within the adolescent peer group, and some were even well liked. The relatively high status enjoyed by most bullies, as well as their recognized positive qualities (e.g., leadership, athletic competence) may in part account for why teachers are able to accurately identify fewer than half of the bullies identified by peers (Leff, Kupersmidt, Patterson, & Power, 1999). Perhaps the fact that many high-status bullies display a number of positive characteristics is one reason why teachers, as well as peers, seem to overlook, dismiss, or give them the "benefit of the doubt" with regard to their negative social behavior. Teachers and other adults need to become more aware of the bullying behavior that is perpetrated and possibly legitimized when engaged in by high-status students.

A second, but equally important, implication of these findings concerns the likelihood of changing such behaviors. Indeed, convincing popular students to reduce bullying behavior will be difficult, if not impossible, when such behavior is viewed as a source of privilege, power, and/or status among peers, and when the status afforded them leads them to view their social interactions as effective and successful (see Hughes, Cavell, & Grossman, 1999; regarding aggressive children). This point is particularly true if we consider that being popular and dominant are important pursuits in adolescence (Gavin & Furman, 1989), and that adolescents actually admire aggressive peers (Bukowski, Sippola, & Newcomb, 2000). Zero-tolerance policies and other school-based programs that strive to reduce bullying by establishing negative sanctions against such behavior may be inadequate to counter the status and apparent social "success" associated with such behavior among powerful bullies. High-status and powerful bullies may be particularly resistant to change if they perceive their social interactions to be socially accepted, as well as instrumental. In this regard, it is important to underscore the generally positive self-perceptions expressed by bullies in this study. Olweus (e.g., 1993) has long argued that bullies do not lack self-esteem. These results both replicate and extend these findings by demonstrating that positive self-perceptions are evident across several self-report indices and by offering some suggestions regarding *why* this might be the case. Research on the development of children's self-perceptions of competence across domains (Hymel, LeMare, Ditner, & Woody, 1999) indicates that children's *social* self-perceptions are derived largely from their subjective interpretations of how they are treated within the peer group. Relative to other domains in which more objective information regarding performance is available (e.g., academic test scores, grades), the social "feedback" individuals receive is largely ambiguous and difficult to verify (Bohrnstedt & Felson, 1983), but nevertheless constitutes the primary "data base" on which students base their social self-perceptions. Our results suggest that the feedback provided to bullies by the peer group is largely positive, as peers consider these students to be popular and powerful and acknowledge their positive qualities (e.g., appearance, athletic competence), despite their aggressive behavior. As we have argued elsewhere with regard to the social self-perceptions of aggressive-rejected children (e.g., Hymel, Bowker, & Woody, 1993), such positive peer feedback and treatment make it difficult for bullies to recognize the negative aspects of their behavior and instead contributes to positive perceptions of their own social situation, making it difficult to recognize the need for behavior change. In short, it will be difficult to convince powerful bullies that such behavior is without its own rewards. Similarly, for those students who engage in bullying but do *not* enjoy high levels of status and power among their peers, these powerful bullies may serve as models for the potential "success" of such behavior within the school peer group.

Finally, the fact that bullying is common among high-status and powerful peers also has implications for efforts to enlist the aid of peer bystanders in reducing bullying behavior. Bullying is increasingly recognized as a group phenomenon that can be fully addressed only when one considers the group processes that operate (e.g., Salmivalli, 1999). Indeed, Hazler (1996) argues that peers are a critical, but largely untapped resource in school-based antibullying efforts. Support for such arguments comes from observational studies that indicate that bullying is an underground activity that adults often miss, although peers are present during most bully-victim episodes (e.g., 85-88 percent of the time), and although they seldom intervene on behalf of victims (i.e., 11-19 percent of the time; e.g., Craig & Pepler, 1995, 1997). In fact, Craig and Pepler (1995) found that peers actually reinforce the bully in about 81 percent of the episodes and are more respectful and more amiable toward the bully than the victim following such episodes. Although most students reported that they disapproved of bullies' behavior, Salmivalli and Voeten (2002) found that the majority did nothing to help the victim of such attacks, and that 20-30 percent of children actually encourage the bully, even to the point of joining in (Pepler, 2001). Obviously, such peer responses serve to encourage rather than discourage bullying behavior.

These results provide some insight into how peer group dynamics can serve to *reduce* the likelihood of peer interventions on behalf of victims. First, confronting a high-status and powerful bully may be particularly difficult for more marginal or less powerful members of the peer group. Consistent with these arguments is evidence to suggest that when bystanders *do* intervene on behalf of the victim, such behavior is typically undertaken only by students with high social status (e.g., Salmivalli, Lagerpetz, Bjorkqvist, Osterman, & Kaukiainen, 1996). If only high-status peers are likely to be successful in intervening on the part of the victim, perhaps they should be targeted in school-based intervention efforts. Second, supporting a victim carries considerable risk for loss of social status if the bully is both popular and powerful within the group. For most students, it may be more socially advantageous to support the more powerful and high-status bully. If so, school-based, antibullying programs, especially those that encourage peer bystanders to intervene, will be difficult to implement. Such programs can be effective only if the peer group does not empower the bully by revering and supporting him or her. The fact that over half of the bullies in this sample were viewed as high status (popular) and powerful makes peer support to such aggressors difficult to eliminate.

The results underscore the need for a broader and more ecologically valid approach to the problem of bullying in schools, addressing characteristics of the individual, the family, school and community context in which he or she lives (see Swearer & Doll, 2001). The results also support Sutton, Smith, and Swettenham's (1999) arguments for a reconsideration of our deficit-based model of social difficulties, recognizing that many bullies actually demonstrate rather effective and well-developed social skills. By understanding the positive social functions that bullying and other forms of aggressive behavior serve (e.g., Ollendick, 1996; Prinstein, & Cillessen, 2003), we may begin to develop more effective and valid approaches to intervention.

NOTE

1. Unlimited nominations have been found to yield sociometric scores with superior distributional properties (i.e., less skewed, wider range of scores) than the more traditional limited (three to five) nomination procedures (see Terry, 2000).

REFERENCES

Adler, P. A., & Adler, P. (1998). *Peer power: Preadolescent culture and identity.* NY: Rutgers University Press.

Asher, S. R., Hymel, S., & Renshaw, P. D. (1984). Loneliness in children. *Child Development, 55,* 1456-1464.

Baumeister, R., Smart, L., & Boden, J. (1996). Relation of threatened egotism to violence and aggression: The dark side of high self-esteem. *Psychological Review, 103,* 5-33.

Besag, V. E. (1989). *Bullies and victims in schools.* Philadelphia: Open University Press.

Bjorkqvist, K., Lagerspetz, K. M. J., & Kaukiainen, A. (1992). Do girls manipulate and boys fight? Developmental trends in regard to direct and indirect aggression. *Aggressive Behavior, 18,* 117-127.

Bohrnstedt, G. W., & Felson, R. B. (1983). Explaining the relations among children's actual and perceived performances and self-esteem: A comparison of several causal models. *Journal of Personality and Social Psychology, 45,* 43-56.

Boulton, M. J. (1999). Concurrent and longitudinal relations between children's playground behavior and social preference, victimization, and bullying. *Child Development, 70,* 944-954.

Boulton, M. J., & Smith, P. K. (1994). Bully/victim problems in middle-school children: Stability, self-perceived competence, peer perceptions and peer acceptance. *British Journal of Development Psychology, 12,* 315-329.

Bukowski, W. M., Sippola, L. K., & Newcomb, A. F. (2000). Variations in patterns of attraction to same- and other-sex peers during adolescence. *Developmental Psychology, 36,* 147-154.

Coie, J. D., & Dodge, K. A. (1983). Continuities and change in children's social status: A five-year longitudinal study. *Merrill-Palmer Quarterly, 29,* 261-282.

Craig, W. M., & Pepler, D. J. (1995). Peer processes in bullying and victimization: An observational study. *Exceptionality Education Canada, 5,* 81-95.

Craig, W. M., & Pepler, D. J. (1997). Observations of bullying and victimization in the schoolyard. *Canadian Journal of School Psychology, 13,* 41-60.

Crick, N. R., & Grotpeter, J. K. (1995). Relational aggression, gender and social-psychological adjustment. *Child Development, 66,* 710-722.

Espelage, D. L., & Holt, M. K. (2001). Bullying and victimization during early adolescence: Peer influences and psychosocial correlates. *Journal of Emotional Abuse, 2,* 123-142.

Estell, D. B., Cairns, R. B., Farmer, T. W., & Cairns, B. D. (2002). Aggression in inner-city early elementary classrooms: Individual and peer-group configurations. *Merrill-Palmer Quarterly, 48,* 52-76.

Farmer, T. W., & Rodkin, P. C. (1996). Antisocial and prosocial correlates of social positions: The social network centrality perspective. *Social Development, 5,* 174-188.

Forero, R., & McLellan, L. (1999). Bullying behaviour and psychosocial health among school students in New South Wales, Australia. *British Medical Journal, 319,* 344-348.

Galen, B. R., & Underwood, M. K. (1997). A developmental investigation of social aggression among children. *Developmental Psychology, 33,* 589-600.

Gavin, L. A., & Furman, W. (1989). Age differences in adolescents' perceptions of their peer groups. *Developmental Psychology, 25,* 1-8.

Hayden, L. K. (1989). *Children's loneliness.* Unpublished doctoral dissertation, University of Waterloo, Waterloo, Ontario, Canada.

Hazler, R. J. (1996). Bystanders: An overlooked factor in peer on peer abuse. *Journal for the Professional Counselor, 11,* 11-21.

Hess, L. E., & Atkins, M. S. (1998). Victims and aggressors at school: Teachers, self, and peer perceptions of psychosocial functioning. *Applied Developmental Science, 2,* 75-89.

Hughes, J. H., Cavell, T. A., & Grossman, P. B. (1997). A positive view of self: Risk or protection for aggressive children? *Development and Psychopathology, 9,* 75-94.

Hymel, S., Bowker, A., & Woody, E. (1993). Aggressive versus withdrawn unpopular children: Variations in peer and self-perceptions in multiple domains. *Child Development, 64,* 879-896.

Hymel, S., LeMare, L., Ditner, E., & Woody, E. Z. (1999). Assessing self-concept in children: Variations across self-concept domains. *Merrill Palmer Quarterly, 45,* 602-623.

Kaltiala-Heino, R., Rimpela, M., Marttunen, M., Rimpela, A., & Rantanen, P. (1999). Bullying, depression and suicidal ideation in Finnish adolescents: School survey. *British Medical Journal, 319*, 348-351.

Kovacs, M. (1991/1992). *Children's Depression Inventory Manual.* Toronto: Multi-Health Systems, Inc.

Kumpulainen, K., Rasanen, E., Henttonen, I., Almqvist, F., Kresanov, K., Linna, S., et al. (1998). Bullying and psychiatric symptoms among elementary school-age children. *Child Abuse and Neglect, 22*, 705-717.

LaFreniere, P., & Charlesworth, W. R. (1983). Dominance, attention, and affiliation in a preschool group: A nine-month longitudinal study. *Ethology and Sociobiology, 4*, 55-67.

Leff, S. S., Kupersmidt, J. B., Patterson, C. J., & Power, T. J. (1999). Factors influencing teacher identification of peer bullies and victims. *School Psychology Review, 28*, 505-517.

Marsh, H. (1988). *Self-Description Questionnaire I Manual.* Toronto: Harcourt Brace Jovanovich, Inc.

Merten, D. E. (1997). The meaning of meanness: Popularity, competition, and conflict among junior high school girls. *Sociology of Education, 70*, 175-191.

Nansel, T. R., Overpeck, M., Pilla, R. S., Ruan, W. J., Simons-Morton, B., & Scheidt, P. (2001). Bullying behaviors among US youth: Prevalence and association with psychosocial adjustment. *Journal of the American Medical Association (JAMA), 285*, 2094-2100.

Ollendick, T. H. (1996). Violence in youth: Where do we go from here? Behavior Therapy's response. *Behavior Therapy, 27*, 485-514.

Olweus, D. (1973). *Hackkycklingar och oversittare. Forskning om skolmobbning.* Stockholm: Almqvist & Wicksell.

Olweus, D. (1978). *Aggression in schools: Bullies and whipping boys.* Washington, DC: Hemisphere.

Olweus, D. (1993). *Bullying in school: What we know and what we can do.* Oxford: Blackwell.

Olweus, D. (1994). Annotation: Bullying at school: Basic facts and effects of a school based intervention program. *Journal of Child Psychology & Psychiatry & Allied Disciplines, 35*, 1171-1190.

Olweus, D. (1996). Bullying at school: Knowledge base and an effective intervention program. In C. F. Ferris & T. Grisso (Eds.), *Understanding aggressive behavior in children. Annals of the New York Academy of Sciences, Vol. 794* (pp. 265-276). NY: New York Academy of Sciences.

Parkhurst, J. T., & Hopmeyer, A. (1998). Sociometric popularity and peer-perceived popularity: Two distinct dimensions of peer status. *Journal of Early Adolescence, 18*, 125-144.

Pellegrini, A. D., Bartini, M., & Brooks, F. (1999). School bullies, victims, and aggressive victims: Factors relating to group affiliation and victimization in early adolescence. *Journal of Educational Psychology, 91*, 216-224.

Pepler, D. (2001, May). Peer group dynamics and the culture of violence. In S. Hymel (Chair), *Culture of violence.* Paper symposium for the annual meeting of the Royal Society of Canada (Academy II) and the Canadian Society for Studies in Education, Quebec.

Perry, D. G., Kusel, S. J., & Perry, L. C. (1988). Victims of peer aggression. *Developmental Psychology, 24,* 807-814.

Prinstein, M. J., & Cillessen, A. H. N. (2003). Forms and functions of adolescent peer aggression associated with high levels of peer status. *Merrill-Palmer Quarterly, 49,* 310-342.

Rigby, K. (1999). Peer victimization at school and the health of secondary school students. *British Journal of Educational Psychology, 69,* 95-104.

Roland, E. (2002). Aggression, depression and bullying others. *Aggressive Behavior, 28,* 198-2002.

Rubin, K. H., Bukowski, W., & Parker, J. G. (1998). Peer interactions, relationships and groups. In W. Damon (Series Ed.) and N. Eisenberg (Vol. Ed.), *Handbook of child psychology: Vol. 3, Social emotional and personality development* (5th ed., pp. 619-700). New York: Wiley.

Salmivalli, C. (1999). Participant role approach to school bullying: Implications for interventions. *Journal of Adolescence, 22,* 453-459.

Salmivalli, C., Lagerspetz, K., Bjorkqvist, K., Osterman, K., & Kaukiainen, A. (1996). Bullying as a group process: Participant roles and their relations to social status within the group. *Aggressive Behavior, 22,* 1-15.

Salmivalli, C., & Voeten, M. (2002). *Connections between attitudes, group norms, and behavior in bullying situations.* Manuscript submitted for publication.

Schwartz, D. (2000). Subtypes of victims and aggressors in children's peer groups. *Journal of Abnormal Child Psychology, 28,* 181-192.

Sletta, O. (1998). *Social Self-Efficacy Scale for adolescents.* Unpublished scale.

Sutton, J., Smith, P. K., & Swettenham, J. (1999). Bullying and "theory of mind": A critique of the "social skills deficit" view of anti-social behaviour. *Social Development, 8,* 117-127.

Swearer, S. M., & Doll, B. (2001). Bullying in schools: An ecological framework. *Journal of Emotional Abuse.*

Terrell-Deutsch, B. (1999). The conceptualization and measurement of childhood loneliness. In K. J. Rotenberg and S. Hymel (Eds.), *Loneliness in childhood and adolescence* (pp. 11-33). New York: Cambridge University Press.

Terry, R. (2000). Recent advances in measurement theory and the use of sociometric techniques. In A. H. N. Cillessen & W. M. Bukowski (Eds.), *Recent advances in the study and measurement of acceptance and rejection in the peer system. New Directions for Child Development* (No. 88). San Francisco, CA: Jossey-Bass.

Vaillancourt, T., & Hymel, S. (2002). *Understanding sociometric status: What does it mean to be popular?* Manuscript submitted for publication.

Wheeler, V. A., & Ladd, G. W. (1982). Assessment of children's self-efficacy for social interactions with peers. *Developmental Psychology, 18,* 795-805.

Chapter 19

Correlates of School Victimization: Implications for Prevention and Intervention

Noel A. Card
Jenny Isaacs
Ernest V. E. Hodges

Over twenty-five years of research has amassed a wealth of information regarding the correlates of peer victimization. We begin this chapter with a summary of known concurrent and longitudinal correlates of victimization, especially those related to academic adjustment and the school context. We then review interactive process models, highlighting how the strength of associations between certain correlates and victimization depend on (i.e., are moderated by) other factors. Finally, the implications of this work will be considered, and recommendations for multilevel prevention and intervention will be provided.

CORRELATES OF SCHOOL VICTIMIZATION—CONCURRENT AND LONGITUDINAL LINKS

In this section, we review the research base that has primarily examined concurrent correlates of victimization within five domains: personal, academic, interpersonal, familial, and school contextual. In addition, we highlight extant longitudinal findings demonstrating that correlates likely cause and/or are consequences of victimization. Table 19.1 provides a summary of the concurrent and longitudinal findings that we review.

Bullying, Victimization, and Peer Harassment
© 2007 by The Haworth Press, Inc. All rights reserved.
doi:10.1300/5808_19

TABLE 19.1. Correlates of school victimization.

Correlate	Magnitude of concurrent association	Antecedent of victimization	Consequence of victimization
Personal			
Gender	Small to moderate	—	—
Race	None	—	—
Physical strength	Moderate	Yes	No
External deviancies	None or small	—	—
Internalizing problems	Strong	Yes	Yes
Externalizing problems	None to moderate	Yes	Yes
Socially skilled behavior	Small	Yes	Unknown
Self-concept	Small to strong	Yes	Yes
Academic			
Disliking school	Small to moderate	No	Yes
Perceived safety at school	Moderate	Unknown	Probably
Absenteeism	Small to moderate	No	Yes
Academic ability & achievement	Small	Unknown	Unknown
Special education	Moderate	Unknown	Unknown
Interpersonal			
Peer acceptance	Moderate to strong	Yes	Yes
Peer rejection	Strong	Yes	Yes
Friendship quantity	Moderate	Yes	Probably
Friendship quality	Moderate	Unknown	Unknown
Antipathetic relationships	Small to moderate	Unknown	Unknown
Familial			
Parenting behaviors	Small to moderate	Probably	Unknown
Attachment style	Small	Probably	Unknown
Family structure	None to small	Probably	Unknown
Socioeconomic status	None	Unknown	Unknown
School contextual			
Staff approachability and training	Probably moderate	Unknown	Unknown
School physical structure	Small	—	—
School size	None	—	—
School location	None to small	—	—

Personal Correlates

Personal correlates of victimization include various demographic and physical attributes, behavioral and adjustment variables, and various aspects of self-concept.

Perhaps the most commonly studied correlate of victimization is gender. Research converges to suggest that boys are more commonly victimized than girls, though the size of this gender differential depends on the form of victimization examined. Boys are considerably more likely to be the victims of physical forms of victimization such as hitting, pushing, or kicking and verbal forms such as name calling and teasing (e.g., Crick, Casas, & Ku, 1999; Crick & Grotpeter, 1996; Kochenderfer & Ladd, 1997; Mynard & Joseph, 2000; Paquette & Underwood, 1999; Schwartz, Chang, & Farver, 2001). There have been some claims that girls are more often than boys the victims of social (e.g., intentional exclusion from the group) or relational (e.g., hurtful manipulation of interpersonal relationships) forms of aggression (Crick & Bigbee, 1998; Crick et al., 1999; Mynard & Joseph, 2000; Pateraki & Houndoumadi, 2001), though the extant literature suggests that girls and boys are approximately equal in amount of social or relational victimization received (Crick & Grotpeter, 1996; Kochenderfer & Ladd, 1997; Paquette & Underwood, 1999; Prinstein, Boergers, & Vernberg, 2001; Schwartz et al., 2001).

Race is another demographic variable that may be expected to be related to victimization experiences. However, there has been little to no support for the association between victimization and status as a racial minority either within the larger society or within the local school population (Boulton, 1995; Hanish & Guerra, 2000a; Hanish & Guerra, 2000b; Olweus, 1978; Peterson & Rigby, 1999; Prinstein et al., 2001; Siann, Callaghan, Glissov, Lockhart, & Rawson, 1994; Wolke, Woods, Stanford, & Schulz, 2001). Instead, race may play a larger role in the content of victimization; for example, while racial minorities may not receive more victimization than racial majority children, their victimization may more center around racial issues, such as racial name calling (e.g., Mooney, Creeser, & Blatchford, 1991). Further, race might be expected to predict who will aggress against whom (e.g., Are students more often victimized by same or different race peers?). The evidence is mixed, however, with some support for greater cross-race victimization (Eslea & Mukhtar, 2000), some support for greater within-race victimization (Boulton, 1995), and another study finding no differences in rates of cross-race versus same-race victimization (Isaacs, Piedrahita, Romero, Card, & Hodges, 2001).

Various physical attributes have been considered as correlates of victimization, but only physical weakness (as assessed by high physical weakness or low physical strength) has consistently been shown to be associated with victimization (Egan & Perry, 1998; Hodges, Malone, & Perry, 1997; Hodges & Perry, 1999; Lagerspetz, Björkqvist, Berts, & King, 1982; Olweus, 1978; Pellegrini, 1995). Longitudinal studies have documented that physical weakness predicts increases in victimization over time, but that victimization does not predict changes in physical weakness over time, suggesting that it is an antecedent of victimization (Egan & Perry, 1998; Hodges & Perry, 1999; Pellegrini, 1995). A closely associated variable, height, shows mixed evidence: Borg (1999) found no difference in height among victimized and nonvictimized schoolchildren, but Voss and Mulligan (2000) found that short adolescents, relative to matched controls, were more likely to be victimized. The relations of other physical attributes, such as obesity, wearing eyeglasses, and other external deviations (e.g., atypical manner of dressing, poor hygiene, atypical hair color; see Olweus, 1978) to victimization are uncertain. Although Olweus's (1978) failure to find clear evidence of such associations is often cited, it merits attention that others have found such associations (e.g., Lagerspetz et al., 1982). Although more data may be necessary before firm conclusions can be drawn, it appears that there exist small, if any, associations between victimization and external deviancy.

Numerous behavioral characteristics have been examined in relation to peer victimization. These can be categorized into three broad classes of behaviors: internalizing, externalizing, and socially skilled behaviors.

Internalizing behaviors include anxiety, depression, loneliness, and interpersonal withdrawal. Numerous studies involving youths of diverse ages and countries have demonstrated that these characteristics are strongly associated with victimization (e.g., Andreou, 2001; Boivin, Hymel, & Bukowski, 1995; Bond, Carlin, Thomas, Rubin, & Patton, 2001; Boulton, 1999; Craig, 1998; Craig, Pepler, & Atlas, 2000; Callaghan & Jospeh, 1995; Crick & Grotpeter, 1996; Crick et al., 1999; Hodges et al., 1997; Hodges & Perry, 1999; Juvonen, Nishina, & Graham, 2000; Neary & Joseph, 1994; Kochenderfer & Ladd, 1996a; Perry Kusel, & Perry, 1988; Prinstein et al., 2001; Rigby, 1999; Schwartz, Dodge, & Coie, 1993; Slee, 1994, 1995; ; Wolke, Woods, Bloomfield, & Karstadt, 2000). Moreover, there is considerable evidence that internalizing behaviors serve as both antecedents and as consequences (Boivin et al., 1995; Egan & Perry, 1998; Hodges, Boivin, Vitaro, & Bukowski, 1999; Hodges & Perry, 1999; Vernberg, 1990; Kochenderfer & Ladd, 1996b; Rigby, 1999) of victimization. Internalizing problems may lead to increases in victimization because children with these characteristics may be seen as easy targets by potential aggressors, may reward aggressors with signs of suffering, and may have less support from peers. This victimization appears to, in turn, lead to further internalizing problems, resulting in a vicious cycle of abuse and internalizing behaviors. One extreme consequence of victimization may be suicide, and chronic abuse by peers has been cited as the cause of several youths' suicides (e.g., Head, 1996). Although empirical tests of the association between victimization and suicidal ideation have been limited to concurrent analyses, consistent, moderate effects have been found (Carney, 2000; Kaltiala-Heino,

Rimpela, Marttunen, Rimpela, & Rantanen, 1999; Rigby, 2001; Rigby & Slee, 1999; Slee, 1994).

Externalizing behaviors include aggression, delinquency, argumentative and disruptive behavior, and hyperactive or emotionally dysregulated behavior. When measured as a broad category, externalizing behaviors have a small to moderate correlation with victimization (Egan & Perry, 1998; Hodges et al., 1997, 1999; Hodges & Perry, 1999; Schwartz, McFadyen-Ketchum, Dodge, Pettit, & Bates, 1998; Shields & Cicchetti, 2001). However, the size of this association varies depending on the specific form of externalizing behavior examined. It appears that there is little or no relation between aggression and victimization (Boulton & Smith, 1994; Crick et al., 1999; Crick & Bigbee, 1998; Hanish & Guerra, 2000; Kochenderfer & Ladd, 1996a; Nabuzoka & Smith, 1993; Olweus, 1978; Pellegrini, 1995; Perry et al., 1988; Pope & Bierman, 1999; Rigby, 1993; Rigby, Cox, & Black, 1997; Rigby & Slee, 1992; Salmivalli, Lagerspetz, Bjorkqvist, Osterman, & Kaukiainen, 1996; Schwartz et al., 1998). Delinquency and conduct problems exhibit small to moderate positive correlations with victimization (Berthold & Hoover, 2000; Haynie et al., 2001; Prinstein et al., 2001; Wolke et al., 2000). However, hyperactive and emotionally dysregulated behaviors show moderate to strong correlations with victimization (Crick et al., 1999; Haynie et al., 2001; Pellegrini, Bartini, & Brooks, 1999; Pope & Bierman, 1999; Schwartz et al., 1998; Shields & Cicchetti, 2001; Wolke et al., 2000). Longitudinal studies have provided mixed evidence that externalizing behaviors serve as antecedents and consequences of victimization (see Boulton, 1999; Egan & Perry, 1998; Hanish & Guerra, 2000; Hodges et al., 1999; Hodges & Perry, 1999; Pellegrini, 1995; Schwartz et al., 1998). Externalizing behaviors, especially hyperactivity and emotional dysregulation, are likely to annoy peers and provoke potential aggressors, thus leading to increases in victimization (Pope & Bierman, 1999; Shields & Cicchetti, 2001). At the same time, the experience of victimization may lead to emotional dysregulation and the formation of hostile attributions, thus contributing to increases in externalizing behaviors over time.

Socially skilled behaviors include prosocial behavior and appropriate handling of conflict. Victimization has been linked to low levels of prosocial behaviors (i.e., friendliness and cooperation) in several studies (Abecassis, Hartup, Haselager, Scholte, & Van Lienhout, 2002; Boulton & Smith, 1994; Egan & Perry, 1998; Rigby, Cox, & Black, 1997; Schwartz et al., 2001), although others have failed to find an association (Crick et al., 1999; Kochenderfer & Ladd, 1996a; Olweus, 1978; Schwartz et al., 1993). Thus, it appears that there exists a small concurrent association between victimization and prosocial behavior. However, Egan and Perry (1998) found that prosocial behavior predicted decreases in victimization over time, suggesting its potential importance in reducing victimization. Victims also tend to be less effective at managing conflict. There is evidence of positive associations between victimization and poor conflict management strategies (e.g., anger and aggression, sadness and worry, submission) and negative associations between victimization and effective conflict management (e.g., assertiveness, problem solving), though this evidence is inconsistent (see Andreou, 2001; Bijtteiber & Vertommen, 1998; Kochenderfer & Skinner, 2002; Schwartz et al., 1993, 1998). Through observations of children's playgroups, Schwartz et al. (1993) found that submissiveness and low levels of assertion emerged in children who would become victims, suggesting that these strategies are antecedents of victimization.

Finally, various aspects of self-concept have been examined as correlates of victimization. Self-esteem and global self-worth have been shown to be negatively associated with victimization in numerous studies (Alsaker & Olweus, 1986; Andreou, 2000; Boulton & Smith, 1994; Callaghan & Joseph, 1995; Graham & Juvonen, 1998; Grills & Ollendick, 2002; Juvonen et al., 2000; Karatzias, Power, & Swanson, 2002; Lagerspetz et al., 1982; Neary & Joseph, 1994; Olweus, 1978; O'Moore & Kirkham, 2001; Prinstein et al., 2001; Rigby & Slee, 1992; Salmon, James, & Smith, 1998). Other aspects of self-concept have also been linked with victimization, including perceptions of social competence (Boivin & Hymel, 1997; Boulton & Smith, 1994; Callaghan & Joseph, 1995; Egan & Perry, 1998; Nansel et al., 2001; Neary & Joseph, 1994; Slee & Rigby, 1993); concepts of scholastic, athletic, physical appearance, and behavioral competence (Andreou, 2001; Austin & Joseph, 1996; Boulton & Smith, 1994; Callaghan & Joseph, 1995; Mynard & Jospeh, 1997; Neary & Jospeh. 1994); and self-confidence (Abecassis et al., 2002). The size of these associations vary widely, however. Graham and Juvonen (1998) have suggested that self-reports of victimization, which assess students' subjective appraisals of victimization status, should be most strongly associated with intrapsychological consequences such as self-concept, and indeed, self-reports of victimization appear to exhibit higher correlations with these measures of self-concept than peer-or teacher-reports of victimization. In a longitudinal study, Egan and Perry (1998) found that low self-concept (i.e., global self-worth and perceptions of social competence) predicted increases in victimization, and that victimization predicted decreases in self-concept. In other words, it appears that low self-concept is both an antecedent and consequence of victimization. Whereas high self-concept may prompt youths to behave assertively when confronted with a potential victimization situation, those with low self-concept may behave submissively and anxiously, thus reinforcing aggressors' attacks. One explanation of low self-concept as a consequence of victimization might be that these experiences are interpreted as a signal that one is devalued by peers, and thus leads to self-devaluation.

Academic Correlates

Four domains of academic functioning will be reviewed in reference to victimization: school enjoyment and perceptions of school climate, school avoidance and absenteeism, academic ability and achievement, and enrollment in special education or similar classes.

Several studies have documented significant correlations between victimization and disliking school or unhappiness while at school (Eslea & Mukhtar, 2000; Forero, McClellan, Rissel, & Bauman, 1999; Kochenderfer & Ladd, 1996b; Slee, 1995), though this association was not found in some studies (Karatzias et al., 2002; Lagerspetz et al., 1982; Rigby & Slee, 1992; Smith & Levan, 1995). Overall it appears that victimization is associated with disliking school, but that this relation is small to moderate in size. Stronger support is found for an association between victimization and perceptions of school as unsafe (Berthold & Hoover, 2000; Slee & Rigby, 1993), with this association being moderate in magnitude. Longitudinal evidence suggests that victimization predicts increases in disliking of school over time (Kochenderfer & Ladd, 1996b) but has not shown that disliking of school predicts change in victimization. Thus, it appears that school disliking is primarily a consequence of victimization. The same is likely true for perceived safety at school, though this has not been evaluated longitudinally.

It might be expected that if students who are victimized dislike and feel unsafe at school, they would be likely to avoid school and have high rates of absenteeism. Indeed, victimization is moderately related to a desire to avoid school (Berthold & Hoover, 2000; Buhs & Ladd, 2001; Kochenderfer & Ladd, 1996b) and there is evidence that this translates into actual school absenteeism (Forero et al., 1999; Juvonen et al., 2000). Longitudinal evidence confirms that school avoidance is a consequence of victimization (Kochenderfer & Ladd, 1996b).

There appears to be a small negative association between victimization and various measures of academic ability and achievement. Although several measures of academic ability and standardized achievement tests have been examined in relation to victimization, results have revealed mixed findings of significance and generally weak associations (see Buhs & Ladd, 2001; Ladd, Kochenderfer, & Coleman, 1996; Perry et al., 1988; Sutton, Smith, & Swettenham, 1999). Two important findings may shed light on this, however. Perry et al. found no association between intelligence and victimization for girls, but a moderate negative correlation for boys, suggesting that gender may moderate this association. Ladd et al. (1997) found an association between victimization and scores on a standardized achievement test in the spring but not fall of a school year—suggesting that this association increases later in a school year. Somewhat more consistent associations exist between victimization and school grades, though these associations are also not always found and tend to be small to moderate in size (Berthold & Hoover, 2000; Juvonen et al., 2000; Olweus, 1978). In terms of temporal primacy, either direction of effect is plausible—victimization may lead to poor academic performance, likely mediated by dislike and avoidance of school, or low academic ability or achievement may draw the attention, and abuse, of potential aggressors. However, Kochenderfer and Ladd (1996b) failed to find support for either model in their longitudinal study of kindergarten children.

Finally, there appears to be a moderate tendency for students in special education/special services classes to be more victimized than their peers (Charach, Pepler, & Ziegler, 1995; Martlew & Hodson, 1991; O'Moore & Hilary, 1989; Nabuzoka & Smith, 1993). Whether this relation would remain if factors associated with special services (e.g., behavioral problems, poor peer relations) were controlled, however, has not been evaluated. It is also unknown whether special education placement serves as an antecedent (e.g., being labeled may prompt harassment) and/or consequence (e.g., victimization may cause students to experience academic and/or emotional difficulties, thus prompting removal from traditional classes) of victimization.

Interpersonal Correlates

Students' sociometric status within the peer group tends to be strongly associated with victimization. Peer rejection (being disliked by a large proportion of peers), is strongly positively related to victimization, whereas peer acceptance (being liked by a large proportion of peers) is moderately to strongly negatively correlated with victimization. These conclusions are based on results of numerous studies and are robust across diverse ages, races, and countries (e.g., Boivin et al., 1995; Boulton & Smith, 1994; Buhs & Ladd, 2001; Crick et al., 1999; Forero et al., 1999; Hanish & Guerra, 2000a; Hodges, Malone, & Perry, 1997; Lagerspetz et al., 1982; Olweus, 1977, 1978; Pellegrini et al., 1999; Perry et al., 1988; Salmivalli et al., 1996). Longitudinal studies suggest that these two variables serve as both antecedents and consequences of victimization (Boivin et al., 1995; Boulton, 1999; Hanish & Guerra, 2000a; Hodges & Perry, 1999; Ladd et al., 1997; Pellegrini, 1995; Vernberg, 1990). Poor group-level relations (i.e., high peer rejection and low peer acceptance) may serve as antecedents of victimization because potential aggressors may expect that targeting these low-status students is unlikely to be negatively evaluated by the peer group. Victimization may also contribute to poor group-level relations because peers may dissociate and develop negative attitudes toward those who repeatedly serve as targets for abuse and ridicule.

Dyadic peer relations are also associated with victimization. Students who have a reciprocated best friend (i.e., the peer they nominate as a best friend reciprocates the nomination) are found to be less victimized than those without a reciprocated best friend (Boulton, Trueman, Chau, Whitehand, & Amatya, 1999; Hodges, Boivin, Vitaro, & Bukowski, 1999; Kochenderfer & Ladd, 1997; Ladd & Burgess, 1999; Ladd et al., 1997). Research has also demonstrated that the number of friends students have is negatively associated with victimization (Boivin & Hymel, 1997; Hodges et al., 1997; Hodges & Perry, 1999; Ladd et al., 1997; Pellegrini et al., 1999; Salmivalli, Huttunen, & Lagerspetz, 1997; Slee & Rigby, 1993; Smith, Shu, & Madsen, 2001). The size of these associations tends to be small to moderate for having a reciprocated best friend and moderate for number of friends. Longitudinal studies provide mixed evidence that lack of friendships serves as an antecedent and consequence of victimization (Boulton et al., 1999; Hodges et al., 1999; Hodges & Perry, 1999; Ladd et al., 1997). Friendships may reduce victimization because friends may protect the child from potential aggressors. Victimization may also lead to a lack of friendships because peers may distance themselves from the targeted child.

Not all friends are alike, however, and the characteristics and qualities of friends are important to consider in relation to victimization. Specifically, victimization is associated with having friends who are themselves victimized (Haselager, Hartup, Van Lieshout, & Riksen-Walraven, 1998; Hodges et al., 1997; Pellegrini et al., 1999; Salmivalli et al., 1997), as well as who are physically weak and exhibit internalizing problems (Hodges et al., 1997). Friends with these characteristics may not be able to play a protective role and thus might do little to prevent abuse. Victimization is also related to low supportiveness and companionship within friendships (Hodges et al., 1999; Rigby, 2000; Vernberg, 1990), as well as low protection (Hodges et al., 1999; Hodges & Perry, 1997; Smith et al., 2001). Longitudinal examination of the associations between victimization and friendship qualities is lacking. Thus, friendship qualities might predict changes in victimization over time (e.g., a protective friendship with a physically strong peer should reduce victimization), and it might also be the case that victimization predicts later characteristics of students' friends and the quality of their friendships.

Finally, antipathetic relationships (i.e., relationships based on mutual dislike) are associated with victimization (Abecassis et al., 2002; Card & Hodges, 2002; Parker & Gamm, 2003; Schwartz, Gorman, Toblin, & Abou-ezzedine, 2003). Moreover, research suggests that these relationships are frequent contexts for victimization, and that victimization is associated with having mutual antipathies who are aggressive, physically strong, and nonvictimized (Card & Hodges, 2002). Again, longitudinal studies are needed before conclusions about temporal primacy can be offered.

Familial Correlates

Familial factors that have been examined in relation to victimization include parenting behaviors, attachment styles, family dysfunction, family composition, and socioeconomic status.

Several components of parenting behaviors have been explored in association with peer victimization. Parents' provision of support (Abecassis et al., 2002; Haynie et al., 2001), involvement (Haynie et al., 2001; Nansel et al., 2001), and responsiveness (Ladd & Kochenderfer-Ladd, 1998) are all negatively associated with victimization. Other correlates may vary depending on the gender of the child. For example, there is mixed evidence that overprotectiveness and intense closeness are positively associated with victimization among boys, but not girls (Finnegan, Hodges, & Perry, 1998; Ladd & Kochenderfer-Ladd, 1998; Lagerpetz et al., 1983; Rigby, Slee, & Cunningham, 1999); whereas intrusive demandingness, coercion, and threat of rejection are positively associated to victimization among girls, but not boys (Finnegan et al., 1998; Ladd & Kochenderfer-Ladd, 1998). Child abuse, a more extreme form of coercive parenting behavior, has also been connected to peer victimization (Duncan, 1999; Shields & Cicchetti, 2001). This relation has been accounted for by elevated emotional dysregulation by abused youths (Shields & Cicchetti, 2001), suggesting the process by which many of these familial correlates may antecede victimization—through the fostering of personal factors that may be expressed in the peer group that increase risk of victimization by peers.

Several aspects of parenting behaviors converge to influence attachment styles, suggesting that attachment styles may be associated with victimization as well. The empirical evidence of this association is mixed, however. Troy and Sroufe (1987) found that preschoolers with an insecure anxious-ambivalent attachment were more likely to be victimized in dyadic laboratory play situations. Similarly, Jacobson and Wille (1986) found that this anxious-ambivalent style assessed at eighteen months predicted victimization in dyadic laboratory play among three-year-olds, but not two-year-olds.

Among school-age children, Bowers, Smith, and Binney (1994) failed to find a significant correlation between victimization and attachment security, but these authors did not differentiate between avoidant and preoccupied (anxious-ambivalent) forms of insecurity. Indeed, when such distinctions are made in middle childhood, preoccupied, but not avoidant, attachment is related to greater victimization, at least for boys (Finnegan, Hodges, and Perry, 1996). Together, these results suggest a small to moderate association between victimization and attachment, specifically with anxious-ambivalent (or preoccupied) attachment. No study has yet examined this association longitudinally. Thus, preoccupied attachment may lead to victimization, perhaps through the manifestation of personal risk factors such as internalizing behaviors (Finnegan et al., 1996), but victimization might also affect attachment quality.

Two components of family structure that have been examined with victimization are family size and intactness (e.g., presence versus absence of father). In several studies, these components have not been found to be significantly related to victimization (Berdondini & Smith, 1996; Bowers et al., 1994; Rigby, 1993), though some have found a small association between victimization and father absence (Bond et al., 2001; Flouri & Buchanon, 2002; Mellor, 1990). The mechanisms by which nonintact family structure leads to victimization may include higher risk of maladaptive parenting behavior brought on by parental distress, and lost opportunities for the child to develop social skills through interaction with a second parent. Across several studies, little evidence supports an association between family socioeconomic status and victimization (e.g., Borg, 1999; Karatzias et al., 2002; Olweus, 1978; Wolke et al., 2001). However, exposure to community violence (direct victimization but not witnessing) is linked to greater peer victimization in the school context, with this association partially mediated by the development of emotional dysregulation (Schwartz & Proctor, 2000). Thus, while socioeconomic status appears to be unrelated to victimization by peers, it may have a distal impact through associations with neighborhood violence which, in turn, may promote the development of personal risk factors that place youths at risk for in-school victimization.

School Contextual Correlates

Whereas studies examining personal, academic, interpersonal, and familial correlates are relatively numerous, few have examined school contextual correlates of victimization. The reason for this is likely due to the scale of such projects. Examination of these other correlates is done at the level of the individual (e.g., Are individuals who are high on internalizing problems also high on victimization?), and can be performed by studying students in one or a few schools. In contrast, attempts to determine whether schools that differ in some aspect (e.g., urban versus rural) also differ in frequency of victimization often require that many schools be sampled. Nevertheless, we can draw some tentative conclusions about associations between victimization and staff approachability and training, physical structure of the school, and school size and location from the relatively few studies that have examined such school-level factors.

Several studies have asked victimized youth if, and to whom, they reported their victimization, and results suggest that a minority report their abuse to teachers or staff members. Specifically, about half of elementary school-age children report victimization to teachers (O'Moore, Kirkham, & Smith, 1997), with numbers falling to about one-third in middle school (Mellor; 1990; Smith & Shu, 2000) and to as low as 15 percent among adolescents (O'Moore et al., 1997). Thus, it appears that youths generally do not report their victimization to school officials, often because they believe such action will fail to improve, and may even worsen, their situation (e.g., Smith & Shu, 2000). Indeed, in one survey of teachers, only 5 percent felt they had adequate training to deal with bullying situations (Byrne, 1994), and youths may be aware of this uncertainty on the part of school staff. However, schools with lower rates of victimization have teachers that are more aware of school policies on peer victimization, have received training to deal with bullying, and are seen as more approachable and willing to take action against bullies (Hazler, 1996; Siann, Callaghan, Lockhart, & Rawson, 1993; Smith & Shu, 2000).

Youths' reports of where they are victimized vary greatly across studies, with various samples each reporting classrooms, hallways, lunchrooms, playgrounds, and areas near the school (e.g., parking lots) as the most common sites for victimization (Astor, Meyer, & Behre, 1999; Baldry & Farrington, 1999; Mellor, 1990; O'Moore et al., 1997; Smith & Shu, 2000). Congestion has been cited as a correlate of victimization (e.g., Siann et al., 1993), but the most extensive survey of locations of school violence suggests that an absence of adult presence in certain areas during certain times is most strongly related to victimization (Astor et al., 1999).

Neither school or class size have consistently been found to be related to school differences in victimization (Lagerspetz et al., 1982; O'Moore et al., 1997; Olweus, 1978; Wolke et al., 2001). In terms of school location, there may be a small tendency for urban schools to have more victimization than rural schools (Lagerpetz et al., 1982; O'Moore, 1997), although Nansel et al. (2001) failed to find associations between school location and rates of victimization in a nationally representative sample of over 15,000 American youths.

INTERACTIVE PROCESSES AMONG CORRELATES

Although we have categorized the correlates of victimization into personal, academic, interpersonal, familial, and school contextual factors, by no means do they operate in a compartmentalized manner. In this section, we examine interactions among these various correlates.

Within the category of personal correlates, self-concept has been shown to be important in modifying links between behaviors (e.g., internalizing) and victimization. Egan and Perry (1998) showed that global self-worth reduced increases in victimization as a response to high levels of internalizing behaviors and low levels of prosocial behavior. Perceptions of social competence were found to be an even stronger moderator, buffering against the contribution of high internalizing behaviors, low prosocial behaviors, and physical weakness toward increases in victimization. In other words, positive self-concept (i.e., global self-worth and perceived social competence) may protect children with risk factors such as physical weakness, internalizing problems, and low social skills from escalations in victimization. Concurrent evidence has suggested that high self-worth minimizes associations between victimization and anxiety (for boys, but not girls; Grills & Ollendick, 2002), suggesting that positive self-concept may also buffer against the negative consequences of victimization.

Several studies have shown that personal correlates of victimization are moderated by interpersonal factors. There is concurrent evidence that the negative correlation between physical strength and victimization is stronger for youths with negative peer relations (high peer rejection, few friends, friends who are unable to provide protection) and nonsignificant for those with positive peer relations (Hodges et al., 1997), and longitudinal examination suggests that later peer rejection (but not number of friends) moderates the association between physical strength and change in victimization over time (Hodges & Perry, 1999). Similarly, the positive concurrent associations of victimization with internalizing and externalizing problems are maximized for youths who are rejected, have few friends, or have friends who cannot provide protection (Hodges et al., 1997; see also Hanish & Guerra, 2000a), and longitudinal evidence indicates that peer rejection and nonprotective friendships (but not number of friends) heighten longitudinal associations between internalizing (but not externalizing) behaviors and changes in victimization (Hodges et al., 1999; Hodges & Perry, 1999).

These findings suggest that the degree to which personal factors actualize into victimization depends on quality of peer relationships; specifically, that positive peer relations reduce, and poor peer relations exacerbate, the translation of personal risk factors into victimization experiences.

There is also mixed evidence that interpersonal factors moderate the personal consequences of victimization. Vernberg (1990) found that closeness in best friendships buffered the relations of victimization with depression and perceived social competence, and Prinstein et al. (2001) showed that receiving support from a close friend reduces the association between victimization and externalizing problems. However, this last study failed to provide evidence that social support moderated associations of victimization with depression, loneliness, or global self-worth. Moreover, two studies failed to indicate that social support buffered the associations between victimization and general well-being or suicidal ideation (Rigby, 2000; Rigby & Slee, 1999). Ladd et al. (1997) similarly failed to find evidence that social preference, number of friends, or having a reciprocated best friend moderated associations between victimization and loneliness. However, Hodges et al. (1999) demonstrated that having a reciprocated best friend negates longitudinal associations between victimization and increases in either internalizing or externalizing problems.

In terms of academic correlates, Ladd et al. (1997) explored whether social preference, number of friends, or having a reciprocated best friend moderated associations between victimization and school disliking, school avoidance, and academic achievement. Although it might be expected that positive peer relations would buffer against the impact victimization might have on these academic correlates, no evidence of moderation was found. Further research of this buffering effect is needed. Some evidence is available suggesting that associations of various personal and interpersonal correlates with victimization differ for those with learning disabilities (relative to mainstream youths). Nabuzoka and Smith (1993) found that there was no association between victimization and rejection among children with learning disabilities (whereas a strong positive correlation was found among non-learning disabled children); and Boyesen and Bru (1999) found a stronger positive correlation between victimization and various emotional and physical complaints, and stronger negative correlations of victimization with perceptions of acceptance by peers and support from teachers, among students with learning disabilities, relative to those without. Because these two studies provide discrepant results (i.e., learning disabilities minimizing versus maximizing associations), it is difficult to draw conclusions. However, these two studies, as well as that of Ladd et al. (1997), serve as examples of what we believe is an important direction for research—the consideration of how academic factors moderate the association of personal and interpersonal factors with victimization.

Associations between familial factors and victimization might also be expected to be moderated by personal and interpersonal factors, though the empirical examination of these processes has been limited. Finnegan et al. (1998) explored how children's coping styles moderated the prediction of victimization from maternal overprotectiveness and threats of rejection. However, only one significant interaction was detected: among boys maternal overprotectiveness predicted victimization most strongly when a fearful coping style was utilized. Quantity of friends (but not social preference) has been found to moderate relations of restrictive discipline, abuse, marital conflict, and family stress with later victimization (Schwartz, Dodge, Pettit, & Bates, 2000). In addition, quantity of antipathetic relationships exacerbates the association between exposure to community violence and victimization in the peer group (Schwartz et al., 2003). In terms of familial characteristics moderating associations between victimization and personal factors, Flouri and Buchanon (2002) found that father involvement moderated associations between victimization and life satisfaction, such that this negative association was weakest when there was a high level of father involvement. This last study demonstrates that, like positive relations with peers, positive relations with family members may also buffer the negative consequences of victimization.

To our knowledge, only one study has examined how school context may moderate associations between personal risk factors and victimization. Hanish and Guerra (2000a) surveyed students at several urban elementary schools, and found that concurrent associations between withdrawal and victimization were moderated by school disadvantage. Withdrawal was positively related to victimization only in moderately disadvantaged schools, but unrelated in highly disadvantaged schools. These findings suggest that whereas withdrawal may be a personal risk factor for victimization in many contexts, school characteristics may impact the strength of this risk. Moreover, this study points to the importance of examining the various personal, academic, interpersonal, and familial antecedents and consequences of victimization in differing school contexts.

In this section, we have reviewed evidence suggesting that (1) self-concept moderates associations between personal factors and victimization, such that positive self-concept buffers both the translation of personal risk factors into victimization and the personal maladjustment resulting from victimization; (2) positive peer relations moderate relations between personal factors and victimization by both buffering the translation of personal risk factors into victimization and minimizing the maladjustment caused by victimization; (3) processes involving correlates of victimization may differ for youths with learning disabilities; (4) both personal and interpersonal factors moderate associations between familial antecedents and victimization, and that positive family relations may buffer against the personal maladjustment associated with victimization; and (5) associations of personal, academic, interpersonal, and familial correlates with victimization may vary depending on aspects of the school context. In contrast to the main effect correlates reviewed in the previous section, for which there was generally an abundance of literature from which to draw conclusions, we have found only limited literature exploring these interactive process models. Clearly, other moderating processes besides those reviewed in this section can, and should be, explored.

IMPLICATIONS FOR PREVENTION AND INTERVENTION

In this review, we have attempted to demonstrate that multiple personal, academic, interpersonal, familial, and school contextual factors contribute to peer victimization. Moreover, we have suggested that, although there is a paucity of research exploring interactive process models, there is reason to believe that these correlates do not act in a compartmentalized manner, but instead amplify or buffer the influences of one another. Taken together, this research suggests that there are a multitude of factors that contribute to the emergence and maintenance of victimization. Therefore, prevention and intervention efforts can focus on multiple levels.

Many of the personal correlates of victimization, such as depression, anxiety, and emotional dysregulation, are key areas for intervention. Directing intervention at these individual characteristics not only improves children's overall quality of life (e.g., improvements in mood), but may also serve to make them less likely to be targets of victimization. Interventions may also be targeted at aggressive children. For example, aggressive children tend to show deficits and biases that favor aggressive styles of behavior (e.g., Egan, Monson, & Perry, 1998; Guerra & Slaby, 1989). Interventions that have targeted the social-cognitive processes that support aggression have been found to reduce aggressive behavior (see Huesmann & Reynolds, 2001).

The interpersonal difficulties that are associated with victimization are another area that may be amenable to change. By teaching children interpersonal problem-solving skills, effective conflict-management strategies, and prosocial methods of interacting with other children, victimized children may be more capable of fostering friendships and warding off potential aggressors' advances.

In addition to addressing the problem of victimization on the level of the individual, interventions may also be implemented on the dyadic, group, school, and family level. On the dyadic level, it may be helpful to promote the development of friendships with well-adjusted peers or a buddy system, in which at-risk children are paired with another child, that can model more skilled social interactions. New friends or "buddies" may also serve a protective function for the victimized child. Victimized children may also benefit from interventions aimed at working toward resolving conflict with their mutual antipathies, because victimization frequently occurs within this context. Group-level interventions can be implemented for groups of victimized children, aggressive children, or for the general peer group. Group-level interventions allow for constructive feedback from other children and provide opportunities to interact with peers, ideally under the guidance of a trained professional (e.g., psychologist, teacher).

School-wide interventions can promote a broad awareness and vigilance to the problem of victimization. According to Garrity, Jens, Porter, Sager, and Short-Camilli (1996), school-wide interventions are thought to best serve victimized children if, in addition to working with aggressive and victimized children, they involve the entire school community. Many children observe bullying episodes without taking action (Salmivalli et al., 1996) and it may be useful to train these bystanders to intervene when other children are being victimized (Salmivalli, 2001). It is important that teachers and other school staff are involved in prevention and intervention efforts. Staff should be prepared to monitor students' activities and be trained to intervene with effective conflict-resolution skills, when needed.

Multiple familial factors are associated with victimization. As parents learn to engage with their children in a nonintrusive, nonabusive, and responsive manner, they can support their children's healthy emotional and social development. Parents can also model effective conflict resolution and other socially skilled behaviors, and can help to reinforce the skills taught in individual- or school-based intervention programs. Ross (1996) also has provided suggestions for parents to respond to ongoing victimization, which include expressing sympathy, advocating for the child to school personnel, and avoiding making the child feel blamed.

Due to the multitude of factors associated with victimization, a multifaceted, comprehensive program may be the most effective way to manage the problem of peer victimization. Indeed, Olweus (1997) has successfully implemented a large-scale, comprehensive program aimed at providing children a school atmosphere that is characterized as a warm, safe environment with high adult involvement and support. As Olweus's and similar approaches are described in the other chapters of this volume, we will not review his program here. However, it should be noted that the results of Olweus's (1997) program have been extremely promising; based on approximately 2,500 students, located in forty-two Norwegian schools, the results suggest drastic reductions in victimization (50 percent or more) for boys and girls from Grades 4 to 7. In addition to the reduction in victimization, there were also reductions in antisocial behavior and improvements in the attitudes, behaviors, and social relationships of the students. Given the success of this program, it might be considered the benchmark against which the success of other programs is judged.

Although it seems likely that a multifaceted approach to managing the problem of peer victimization would be the ideal route for prevention and intervention, little is known about the relative effects of a single prong approach (e.g., group social skills training for victims) versus a comprehensive program (e.g., individual, group, classroom, and parent training). Most of the studies regarding the correlates of victimization reviewed earlier examine each correlate in isolation. Therefore, little is known about which factors uniquely predict victimization, above and beyond the other correlates. This lack of information may complicate our understanding of how to efficiently design prevention and intervention programs. Before these comprehensive intervention programs can been deemed cost efficient they must be shown to be superior to programs that address the problem on a single level. In a recent study (Eron et al., 2002) an attempt was made to explore this issue by randomly assigning sixteen schools to four levels of treatment: (1) no-treatment controls, (2) social-cognitive classroom level training, (3) social-cognitive classroom level training plus small-group peer-skills training for aggressive children, and (4) social-cognitive classroom level training plus small-group peer-skills training for aggressive children plus parent training. Although the pattern of results showed tremendous variation depending on unique interactions involving level of intervention, type of community, age of children at the time of intervention, and duration of the intervention; this approach points to our need to better understand which individual treatment components are efficacious, in what combinations, and under which personal and environmental conditions they should be delivered.

FUTURE DIRECTIONS

Although tremendous advances have been made in understanding the correlates of victimization and support for the efficacy of certain treatment approaches has been garnered, it is clear that systematic basic and applied research is greatly needed to better understand and manage the problem of victimization. Specifically, we offer the following recommendations.

Examination of Other Correlates of Victimization

Many of the correlates reviewed in this chapter have been the focus of dozens of studies of youths of various ages, races, and in various countries. Given this voluminous extant literature, further studies showing associations between victimization and certain correlates (e.g., gender, internalizing problems) add little to our knowledge unless there is strong reason to question whether previous findings will generalize to the specific population studied or the methodology employed. On the other hand, the associations of victimization with many other correlates (e.g., many of the familial correlates) have not been well explored, and remain a fruitful topic for future research.

Further Longitudinal Research

The number of longitudinal studies is far fewer than concurrent studies; thus, as noted in our review, the temporal primacy between victimization and many of its correlates are unknown or uncertain. Further longitudinal research exploring the antecedents that predict increases in victimization and consequences that are predicted by victimization is, therefore, needed. An important challenge for future longitudinal research is to better consider the time period under study. Most of the longitudinal work has examined time spans ranging in months to a year. However, recent findings have suggested that victimization can also affect day-to-day adjustment (Nishina, 2002; Nishina & Mize, 2003), and others have supported the finding that the chronicity of victimization over the course of several years is predictive of maladjustment (Kochenderfer-Ladd & Wardrop, 2001). These studies suggest that the temporal relations between victimization and its correlates are complex, and longitudinal examination should consider both the short- and long-term relations.

Further Process-Oriented Research

We have noted that the study of interactive process-oriented models of victimization is limited, and is an important direction for future basic research. This focus should also be adapted within the intervention research. For example, if a particular intervention is shown to reduce victimization, what are the mechanisms through which the intervention operates? Two possibilities are that the intervention reduces victims' personal risk factors (in which case the personal correlate and victimization are reduced), or it reduces the translation of these personal risk factors into victimization (in which case victimization, but not the personal correlate, is reduced, but the association between the correlate and victimization is minimized). Similar process-oriented questions can be asked with regard to the various personal, academic, interpersonal, familial, and school contextual correlates and moderators described earlier (and those that will emerge in future research). In short, the challenge is for future research to not only reduce victimization but to explore how the intervention operates in reducing victimization.

Further Intervention Studies

As noted earlier, further work is greatly needed in designing, implementing, and understanding effective interventions for victimized youths. Many of the challenges for such work have been raised earlier, and are described throughout this volume. While challenging, it is our view that such intervention research is necessary not only to reduce the suffering of victimized youths, but also to inform our understanding of the phenomenon. It is our hope that a better understanding of the empirical evidence reviewed in this chapter will be beneficial to both researchers and practitioners alike.

REFERENCES

Abecassis, M., Hartup, W. W., Haselager, G. J. T., Scholte, R., & van Lieshout, C. F. M. (2002). Mutual antipathies and their significance in middle childhood and adolescence. *Child Development, 73,* 1543-1556.

Alsaker, F., & Olweus, D. (1986). Assessment of global negative self-evaluations and perceived stability of self in Norwegian preadolescents and adolescents. *Journal of Early Adolescence, 6,* 269-278.

Andreou, E. (2000). Bully/victim problems and their association with psychological constructs in 8- to 12-year-old Greek schoolchildren. *Aggressive Behavior, 26,* 49-56.

Andreou, E. (2001). Bully/victim problems and their association with coping behavior in conflictual peer interactions among school-age children. *Educational Psychology, 21,* 59-66.

Astor, R. A., Meyer, H. A., & Behre, W. J. (1999). Unowned places and times: Maps and interviews about violence in high schools. *American Educational Research Journal, 36,* 3-42.

Baldry, A. C., & Farrington, D. P. (1999). Types of bullying among Italian school children. *Journal of Adolescence, 22,* 423-426.

Berdondini, L., & Smith, P. K. (1996). Cohesion and power in the families of children involved in bully/victim problems at school: An Italian replication. *Journal of Family Therapy, 18,* 99-102.

Berthold, K. A., & Hoover, J. H. (2000). Correlates of bullying and victimization among intermediate students in the midwestern USA. *School Psychology International, 21,* 65-78.

Bijttebier, P., & Vertommen, H. (1998). Coping with peer arguments in school-age children with bully/victim problems. *British Journal of Educational Psychology, 68,* 387-394.

Boivin, M., Hymel, S., & Bukowski, W. M. (1995). The roles of social withdrawal, peer rejection, and victimization by peers in predicting loneliness and depressed mood in childhood. *Development and Psychopathology, 7,* 765-786.

Bond, L., Carlin, J. B., Thomas, L., Rubin, K., & Patton, G. (2001). Does bullying cause emotional problems? A prospective study of young teenagers. *British Medical Journal, 323,* 480-484.

Borg, M. G. (1999). The extent and nature of bullying among primary and secondary schoolchildren. *Educational Research, 41,* 137-153.

Boulton, M. J. (1995). Patterns of bully/victim problems in mixed race groups of children. *Social Development, 4,* 277-293.

Boulton, M. J. (1999). Concurrent and longitudinal relations between children's playground behavior and social preference, victimization, and bullying. *Child Development, 70,* 944-954.

Boulton, M. J., & Smith, P. K. (1994). Bully/victim problems in middle-school children: Stability, self-perceived competence, peer perceptions, and peer acceptance. *British Journal of Developmental Psychology, 12,* 315-329.

Boulton, M. J., Trueman, M., Chau, C., Whitehand, C., & Amatya, K. (1999). Concurrent and longitudinal links between friendships and peer victimization: Implications for befriending interventions. *Journal of Adolescence, 22,* 461-466.

Bowers, L., Smith, P. K., & Binney, V. (1994). Perceived family relationships of bullies, victims, and bully/victims in middle childhood. *Journal of Personal and Social Relationships, 11,* 215-232.

Boyesen, M., & Bru, E. (1999). Small school classes, small problems? A study of peer harassment, emotional problems and student perception of social support at school in small and large classes. *School Psychology International, 20,* 38-351.

Buhs, E. S., & Ladd, G. W. (2001). Peer rejection as an antecedent of young children's social adjustment: An examination of mediating processes. *Developmental Psychology, 37,* 550-560.

Byrne, B. (1994). Bullies and victims in a school setting with specific reference to some Dublin schools. *Irish Journal of Psychology, 15,* 73-87.

Callaghan, S., & Joseph, S. (1995). Self-concept and peer victimization among schoolchildren. *Personality and Individual Differences, 18,* 161-163.

Card, N. A., & Hodges, E. V. E. (2002). *Implications of dyadic mutual animosity for victimization by peers.* Manuscript submitted for publication.

Carney, J. L. (2000). Bullied to death: Perceptions of peer abuse and suicidal behaviour during adolescence. *School Psychology International, 21,* 213-223.

Charach, A., Pepler, D., & Ziegler, S. (1995, Spring). Bullying at school: A Canadian perspective. *Education Canada, 12*-18.

Craig, W. M. (1998). The relationship among bullying, victimization, depression, anxiety, and aggression in elementary school children. *Personality and Individual Differences, 24,* 123-130.

Craig, W. M., Pepler, D. J., & Atlas, R. S. (2000). Observations of bullying in the playground and in the classroom. *School Psychology International, 21,* 22-36.

Crick, N. R., & Bigbee, M. A. (1998). Relational and overt forms of peer victimization: A multiinformant approach. *Journal of Consulting and Clinical Psychology, 66,* 337-347.

Crick, N. R., Casas, J. F., & Ku, H.-C. (1999). Relational and physical forms of peer victimization in preschool. *Developmental Psychology, 35,* 376-385.

Crick, N. R., & Grotpeter, J. K. (1996). Children's treatment by peers: Victims of relational and overt aggression. *Development and Psychopathology, 8,* 367-380.

Duncan, R. D. (1999). Maltreatment by parents and peers: The relationship between child abuse, bully victimization, and psychological distress. *Child Maltreatment, 4,* 45-55.

Egan, S. K., Monson, T. C., & Perry, D. G. (1998). Social-cognitive influences on change in aggression over time. *Developmental Psychology, 34,* 996-1006.

Egan, S. K., & Perry, D. G. (1998). Does low self-regard invite victimization? *Developmental Psychology, 34,* 299-309.

Eron, L. D., Huesmann, L. R., Spindler, A., Guerra, N. G., Henry, D., & Tolan, P. (2002). A cognitive-ecological approach to preventing aggression in urban settings: Initial outcomes for high-risk children. *Journal of Consulting and Clinical Psychology, 70,* 179-194.

Eslea, M., & Mukhtar, K. (2000). Bullying and racism among Asian schoolchildren in Britain. *Educational Research, 42,* 207-217.

Finnegan, R. A., Hodges, E. V. E., & Perry, D. G. (1996). Preoccupied and avoidant coping during middle childhood. *Child Development, 67,* 1318-1328.

Finnegan, R. A., Hodges, E. V. E., & Perry, D. G. (1998). Victimization by peers: Associations with children's reports of mother-child interaction. *Journal of Personality and Social Psychology, 75,* 1076-1086.

Flouri, E., & Buchanan, A. (2002). Life satisfaction in teenage boys: The moderating role of father involvement and bullying. *Aggressive Behavior, 28,* 126-133.

Forero, R., McLellan, L., Rissel, C., & Bauman, A. (1999). Bullying behaviour and psychosocial health among school students in New South Wales, Australia: Cross sectional survey. *British Medical Journal, 319,* 344-348.

Garrity, C., Jens, K., Porter, W., Sager, N., & Short-Camilli, C. (1996) Bully-proofing your school: A comprehensive approach. *Journal of Emotional and Behavioral Problems, 5,* 35-39.

Gottfredson, G. D., Jones, E. M., & Gore, T. W. (2002) Implementation and evaluation of a cognitive-behavioral intervention to prevent problem behavior in a disorganized school. *Prevention Science, 3,* 43-56.

Graham, S., & Juvonen, J. (1998). Self-blame and peer victimization in middle school: An attributional analysis. *Developmental Psychology, 34,* 587-599.

Greenberg, M. T., Kusche, C. A., Cook, E. T., & Quamma, J. P. (1995). Promoting emotional competence in school-aged children: The effects of the PATHS curriculum. *Development and Psychopathology, 7,* 117-136.

Grills, A. E., & Ollendick, T. H. (2002). Peer victimization, global self-worth, and anxiety in middle school children. *Journal of Clinical Child and Adolescent Psychology, 31,* 59-68.

Guerra, N. G., Eron, L. D., Huesmann, L. R., Tolan, P., and Van Acker, R. (1997). A cognitive-ecological approach to the prevention of violence and aggression in inner-city youth. In D. P. Fry & K. Bjorkqvist (Eds.), *Cultural variation in conflict resolution* (pp. 199-213). New Jersey: Lawrence Erlbaum Associates.

Guerra, N. G., & Slaby, R. G. (1989). Evaluative factors in social problem solving by aggressive boys. *Journal of Abnormal Child Psychology, 17,* 1277-1289.

Hanish, L. D., & Guerra, N. G. (2000a). Predictors of peer victimization among urban youth. *Social Development, 9,* 521-543.

Hanish, L. D., & Guerra, N. G. (2000b). The roles of ethnicity and school context in predicting children's victimization by peers. *American Journal of Community Psychology, 28,* 201-223.

Haselager, G. J. T., Hartup, W. W, VanLieshout, C. F. M., & Riksen-Walraven, J. M. (1998). Similarities between friends and nonfriends in middle childhood. *Child Development, 69,* 1198-1208.

Haynie, D. L., Nansel, T., Eitel, P., Crump, A. D., Saylor, K., Yu, K., & Simons-Morton, B. (2001). Bullies, victims, and bully/victims: Distinct groups of at-risk youth. *Journal of Early Adolescence, 21,* 29-49.

Hazler, R. J. (1996). *Breaking the cycle of violence: Interventions for bullying and victimization.* Washington, DC: Accelerated Development.

Head, R. (1996). Remembering Brian. *Journal of Emotional and Behavioral Problems, 5,* 6-9.

Hodges, E. V. E., Boivin, M., Vitaro, F., & Bukowski, W. M. (1999). The power of friendship: Protection against an escalating cycle of peer victimization. *Developmental Psychology, 35,* 94-101.

Hodges, E. V. E., Malone, M. J., & Perry, D. G. (1997). Individual risk and social risk as interacting determinants of victimization in the peer group. *Developmental Psychology, 33,* 1032-1039.

Hodges, E. V. E., & Perry, D. G. (1997, April). Victimization by peers: The protective function of peer friendships. In B. J. Kochenderfer & G. W. Ladd (Chairs), *Research on bully/victim problems: Agendas from several cultures.* Poster symposium conducted at the biennial meeting of the Society for Research in Child Development, Washington, DC.

Hodges, E. V. E., & Perry, D. G. (1999). Personal and interpersonal consequences of victimization by peers. *Journal of Personality and Social Psychology, 76,* 677-685.

Huesmann, L. R., & Reynolds, M. A. (2001). Cognitive processes and the development of aggression. In A.C. Bohart & D. J. Stipek (Eds.), *Constructive & destructive behavior: Implications for family, school, & society* (pp. 249-269). Washington, DC: American Psychological Association.

Isaacs, J., Piedrahita, J., Romero, P. A., Card, N. A., & Hodges, E. V. E. (2001, August). *Intra- and inter-race aggression in preadolescence.* Poster presented at the 109th annual meeting of the American Psychological Association, San Francisco, CA.

Jacobson, J., & Wille, D. E. (1986). The influence of attachment patterns on developmental changes in peer interaction from the toddler to the preschool period. *Child Development, 57,* 338-347.

Juvonen, J., Nishina, A., & Graham, S. (2000). Peer harassment, psychological adjustment, and social functioning in early adolescence. *Journal of Educational Psychology, 92,* 349-359.

Kaltiala-Heino, R., Rimpela, M., Marttunen, M., Rimpela, A., & Rantanen, P. (1999). Bullying, depression, and suicidal ideation in Finnish adolescents: School survey. *British Medical Journal, 319*(7206), 348-351.

Karatzias, A., Power, K. G., & Swanson, V. (2002). Bullying and victimization in Scottish secondary schools: Same or separate entities. *Aggressive Behavior, 28,* 46-61.

Kochenderfer, B. J., & Ladd, G. W. (1996a). Peer victimization: Manifestations and relations to school adjustment in kindergarten. *Journal of School Psychology, 34,* 267-283.

Kochenderfer, B. J., & Ladd, G. W. (1996b). Peer victimization: Cause or consequence of school maladjustment? *Child Development, 67,* 1305-1317.

Kochenderfer, B. J., & Ladd, G. W. (1997). Victimized children's responses to peers' aggression: Behaviors associated with reduced versus continued victimization. *Development and Psychopathology, 9,* 59-73.

Kochenderfer-Ladd, B., & Wardrop, J. L. (2001). Chronicity and instability of children's peer victimization experiences as predictors of loneliness and social satisfaction trajectories. *Child Development, 72,* 134-151.

Ladd, G. W., & Burgess, K. B. (1999). Charting the relationship trajectories of aggressive, withdrawn, and aggressive/withdrawn children during early grade school. *Child Development, 70,* 910-929.

Ladd, G. W., Kochenderfer, B. J., & Coleman, C. C. (1996). Friendship quality as a predictor of young children's early school adjustment. *Child Development, 67,* 1103-1118.

Ladd, G. W., & Ladd, B. K. (1998). Parenting behaviors and parent-child relationships: Correlates of peer victimization in kindergarten? *Developmental Psychology, 34,* 1450-1458.

Lagerspetz, K. M. J., Björkqvist, K., Berts, M., & King, E. (1982). Group aggression among school children in three schools. *Scandinavian Journal of Psychology, 23,* 45-52.

Martlew, M., & Hodson, J. (1991). Children with mild learning difficulties in an integrated and in a special school: Comparisons of behaviour, teasing, and teachers' attitudes. *British Journal of Educational Psychology, 61,* 355-372.

Mellor, A. (1990). *Bullying in Scottish secondary schools.* Edinburgh: Scottish Council for Research in Education.

Mooney, A., Creeser, R., & Blatchford, P. (1991). Children's views on teasing and fighting in junior schools. *Educational Research, 33,* 103-112.

Mynard, H., & Joseph, S. (2000). Development of the multidimensional peer-victimization scale. *Aggressive Behavior, 26,* 169-178.

Nabuzoka, D., & Smith, P. K. (1993). Sociometric status and social behaviour of children with and without learning difficulties. *Journal of Child Psychology and Psychiatry, 34,* 1435-1448.

Nansel, T. R., Overpeck, M., Pilla, R. S., Ruan, W. J., Simons-Morton, B., & Scheidt, P. (2001). Bullying behaviors among US youth: Prevalence and association with psychosocial adjustment. *Journal of the American Medical Association, 285,* 2084.

Neary, A., & Joseph, S. (1994). Peer victimization and its relationship to self-concept and depression among schoolgirls. *Personality and Individual Differences, 16,* 183-186.

Nishina, A. (2002). *Peer victimization in school: Implications for mental health, physical symptoms, and school adjustment.* Unpublished doctoral dissertation, University of California, Los Angeles.

Nishina, A., & Mize, J. (2003, April). How was school today? Daily reports of peer victimization and adjustment in middle school. In N. A. Card & A. Nishina (Chairs), *Whipping boys and other victims of peer aggression: 25 years of research, now where do we go?* Innovative poster symposium presented at the biennial meeting of the Society for Research in Child Development, Tampa, FL.

Olweus, D. (1977). Aggression and peer acceptance in adolescent boys: Two short-term longitudinal studies of ratings. *Child Development, 48,* 1301-1313.

Olweus, D. (1978). *Aggression in the schools: Bullies and whipping boys.* Washington, DC: Hemisphere.

Olweus (1997). Tackling peer victimization with a school-based intervention program. In D. P. Fry & K. Bjorkqvist (Eds.), *Cultural variation in conflict resolution* (pp. 215-231). New Jersey: Lawrence Erlbaum Associates.

O'Moore, A. M., & Hillery, B. (1989). Bullying in Dublin schools. *The Irish Journal of Psychology, 10,* 426-441.

O'Moore, A. M., & Kirkham, C. (2001). Self-esteem and its relationship to bullying behavior. *Aggressive Behavior, 27,* 269-283.

O'Moore, A. M., Kirkham, C., & Smith, M. (1997). Bullying behavior in Irish schools: A nationwide survey. *The Irish Journal of Psychology, 18,* 141-169.

Paquette, J. A., & Underwood, M. K. (1999). Gender differences in young adolescents' experiences of peer victimization: Social and physical aggression. *Merrill-Palmer Quarterly, 45,* 242-266.

Parker, J. G., & Gamm, B. K. B. (2003). Describing the dark side of preadolescents' peer experiences: Four questions (and data) on preadolescents' enemies. In E. Hodges & N. Card (Eds.), *Enemies and the darker side of peer relations* (pp. 55-72). San Francisco: Jossey-Bass.

Pateraki, L., & Houndoumadi, A. (2001). Bullying among primary school children in Athens, Greece. *Educational Psychology, 21,* 167-175.

Pellegrini, A. D. (1995). A longitudinal study of boys' rough-and-tumble play and dominance during early adolescence. *Journal of Applied Developmental Psychology, 16,* 77-93.

Pellegrini, A. D., Bartini, M., & Brooks, F. (1999). School bullies, victims, and aggressive victims: Factors relating to group affiliation and victimization in early adolescence. *Journal of Educational Psychology, 91,* 216-224.

Perry, D. G., Kusel, S. J., & Perry, L. C. (1988). Victims of peer aggression. *Developmental Psychology, 24,* 807-814.

Peterson, L., & Rigby, K. (1999). Countering bullying at an Australian secondary school with students as helpers. *Journal of Adolescence, 22,* 481-492.

Pope, A. W., & Bierman, K. L. (1999). Predicting adolescent peer problems and antisocial activities: The relative roles of aggression and dysregulation. *Developmental Psychology, 35,* 335-346.

Prinstein, M. J., Boergers, J., & Vernberg, E. M. (2001). Overt and relational aggression in adolescents: Social-psychological adjustment of aggressors and victims. *Journal of Clinical Child Psychology, 30,* 479-491.

Rigby, K. (1993). School children's perceptions of their families and parents as a function of peer relations. *Journal of Genetic Psychology, 154,* 501-513.

Rigby, K. (1997). Attitudes and beliefs about bullying among Australian school children. *The Irish Journal of Psychology, 18,* 202-220.

Rigby, K. (1999). Peer victimization at school and the health of secondary school students. *British Journal of Educational Psychology, 69,* 95-104.

Rigby, K. (2000). Effects of peer victimization in schools and perceived social support on adolescent well-being. *Journal of Adolescence, 23,* 57-68.

Rigby, K., Cox, I., & Black, G. (1997). Cooperativeness and bully/victim problems among Australian schoolchildren. *Journal of Social Psychology, 137,* 357-368.

Rigby, K., & Slee, P. T. (1992). Dimensions of interpersonal relation among Australian children and implications for psychological well being. *Journal of Social Psychology, 133,* 33-42.

Rigby, K., Slee, P. T., & Cunningham, R. (1999). Effects of parenting on the peer relations of Australian adolescents. *Journal of Social Psychology, 139,* 287-288.

Ross, D. M. (1996). *Childhood bullying and teasing: What school personnel, other professionals, and parents can do.* Alexandria, VA: American Counseling Association.

Salmivalli, C. (2001). Group view on victimization: Empirical findings and their implications. In J. Juvonen & S. Graham (Eds.), *Peer harassment in school: the plight of the vulnerable and the victimized* (pp. 398-419). New York: Guildford Press.

Salmivalli, C., Huttunen, A., & Lagerspetz, K. M. J. (1997). Peer networks and bullying in schools. *Scandinavian Journal of Psychology, 38,* 305-312.

Salmivalli, C., Lagerspetz, K. M. J., Bjorkqvist, K., Osterman, K., & Kaukiainen, A. (1996). Bullying as a group process: Participant roles and their relations to social status within the group. *Aggressive Behavior, 22,* 1-15.

Salmon, G., James, A., & Smith, D. M. (1998). Bullying in schools: Self reported anxiety, depression, and self esteem in secondary school children. *British Medical Journal, 317,* 924-925.

Schwartz, D., Chang, L., & Farver, J. M. (2001). Correlates of victimization in Chinese children's peer groups. *Developmental Psychology, 37,* 520-532.

Schwartz, D., Dodge, K. A., & Coie, J. D. (1993). The emergence of chronic peer victimization in boys' play groups. *Child Development, 64,* 1755-1772.

Schwartz, D., Dodge, K. A., Pettit, G. S., & Bates, J. E. (2000). Friendship as a moderating factor in the pathway between early harsh home environment and later victimization in the peer group. *Developmental Psychology, 36,* 646-662.

Schwartz, D., Gorman, A. H., Toblin, R. L., & Abou-ezzedine, T. (2003). Mutual antipathies in the peer group as a moderating factor in the association between community violence exposure and psychosocial maladjustment. In E. V. E. Hodges & N. A. Card (Eds.), Enemies and the darker side of peer relations, *New Directions for Child and Adolescent Development.*

Schwartz, D., & Proctor, L. J. (2000). Community violence exposure and children's social adjustment in the school peer group: The mediating roles of emotional regulation and social cognition. *Journal of Consulting and Clinical Psychology, 68,* 670-683.

Shields, A., & Cicchetti, D. (2001). Parental maltreatment and emotion dysregulation as risk factors for bullying and victimization in middle childhood. *Journal of Clinical Child Psychology, 30,* 349-363.

Siann, G., Callaghan, M., Glissov, P., Lockhart, R., & Rawson, L. (1994). Who gets bullied? The effects of school, gender, and ethnic group. *Educational Research, 36,* 123-134.

Siann, G., Callaghan, M., Lockhart, R., & Rawson, L. (1993). Bullying: Teachers' views and school effects. *Educational Studies, 19,* 307-321.

Slee, P. T. (1994). Situational and interpersonal correlates of anxiety associated with peer victimization. *Child Psychiatry and Human Development, 25,* 97-107.

Slee, P. T. (1995). Peer victimization and its relationship to depression among Australian primary school students. *Personality and Individual Differences, 18,* 57-62.

Slee, P. T., & Rigby, K. (1993). Australian school children's self appraisal of interpersonal relations: The bullying experience. *Child Psychiatry and Human Development, 23,* 273-282.

Smith, P. K., & Levan, S. (1995). Perceptions and experiences of bullying in younger pupils. *British Journal of Educational Psychology, 65,* 489-500.

Smith, P. K., & Shu, S. (2000). What good schools can do about bullying: Findings from a survey in English schools after a decade of research and action. *Childhood, 7,* 193-212.

Smith, P. K., Shu, S., & Madsen, K. (2001). Characteristics of victims of school bullying. In J. Juvonen & S. Graham (Eds.), *Peer harassment in school: The plight of the vulnerable and victimized* (pp. 332-351). New York: Guilford Press.

Sutton, J., Smith, P. K., & Swettenham, J. (1999). Social cognition and bullying: Social inadequacy or skilled manipulation? *British Journal of Developmental Psychology, 17,* 435-450.

Troy, M., & Sroufe, L. A. (1987). Victimization among preschoolers: Role of attachment relationship history. *Journal of the American Academy of Child and Adolescent Psychiatry, 26,* 166-172.

Vernberg, E. M. (1990). Psychological adjustment and experiences with peers during early adolescence: Reciprocal, incidental, or unidirectional relationships? *Journal of Abnormal Child Psychology, 18,* 187-198.

Voss, L. D., & Mulligan, J. (2000). Bullying in school: Are short pupils at risk? Questionnaire study in a cohort. *British Medical Journal, 320,* 612-613.

Wolke, D., Woods, S., Bloomfield, L., & Karstadt, L. (2000). The association between direct and relational bullying and behavior problems among young primary school children. *Journal of Child Psychology and Psychiatry, 41,* 989-1002.

Wolke, D., Woods, S., Stanford, K., & Schulz, H. (2001). Bullying and victimization of primary school children in England and Germany: Prevalence and school factors. *British Journal of Psychology, 92,* 673-696.

SECTION V:
SCHOOL-WIDE APPROACHES

Chapter 20

Changing the Contexts of Peer Victimization: The Effects of a Primary Prevention Program on School and Classroom Levels of Victimization

Tom Woods
Kim Coyle
Wendy Hoglund
Bonnie Leadbeater

A majority of school-based violence prevention programs have focused on improving individual children's problem-solving skills, social and emotional competence, and capacity to resist bullying. These programs are typically centered in classroom curricula and are delivered by teachers, occasionally supported by mental health professionals (see reviews in Miller, Brehm, & Whitehouse, 1998 and in this volume). While many of these programs show promising results for individual children's competencies, their effects on children's behaviors in unstructured and less supervised settings outside of the classroom—including halls, playgrounds, routes to and from school—are less well studied. In this chapter, we suggest that the reach and effectiveness of these individual-focused programs could be extended by

.   This research was supported by grants from the Canadian Institutes of Health Research (#CAR-4327), the Social Sciences and Humanities Research Council of Canada (410-2000-0748), and the British Columbia Ministry of Education.

Bullying, Victimization, and Peer Harassment
doi:10.1300/5808_20

369

greater emphasis on creating school and classroom contexts that actively support nonviolent solutions to peer conflicts.

Recognition of the need for community-based, school-wide approaches for the reduction of peer violence in schools has been slowly developing and there is growing evidence of the effectiveness of these universal, multi-setting approaches (Aber, Brown, & Jones, 2003; Comer, 1985; Conduct Problems Prevention Research Group, 1992; Hawkins et al., 1992; Kellam, Ling, Merisca, Brown, & Ialongo, 1998; Olweus, 1993). However, obstacles to the widespread implementation of multi-setting programs are hard to overcome given that they tend to be expensive and often require family cooperation, specialized counselors, and extensive staff training (see Miller et al., 1998).

In this chapter, we give a practical example of a relatively inexpensive elementary school program that involves a collaboration among community police officers, university student athletes, elementary school staff (including principals, teachers, playground supervisors, and librarians), and university-based researchers. The "WITS Rock Solid Primary Program" was designed by a community police group (The Rock Solid Foundation, www.rocksolid.bc.ca), local school district, and university-based research center (The Centre for Youth and Society, www.youth.society.uvic.ca). The WITS acronym stands for "*W*alk away," "*I*gnore," "*T*alk it out," and "*S*eek help."

We briefly review past research on the effects of classroom and school contexts on children's aggression and victimization. We then detail how the community–school–university collaboration for the WITS program was established, what some essential ingredients are for preparing schools and communities for this kind of collaboration, and how the program evaluation has focused on changes in peer relational victimization (e.g., social exclusion, manipulation) and physical victimization (e.g., hitting, pushing) at the classroom level.

BACKGROUND RESEARCH

Classroom Characteristics

Growing evidence highlights the centrality of classroom environments for shaping children's experiences of peer aggression and victimization. Classroom compositions determine the peers who children are exposed to and interact with most directly and continuously (Bukowski & Sippola, 2001), and can influence the effectiveness of violence prevention programs

(Aber, Jones, Brown, Chaudry, & Samples, 1998; Kellam et al., 1998). For instance, groupings of aggressive, deviant children may reinforce each others' negative behaviors and undermine intervention efforts (Dishion, Poulin, & Burraston, 2002).

In a long-term follow-up study of a classroom-based prevention program, "The Good Behavior Game," Kellam et al. (1998) found that aggressive boys' (but not girls') placement in Grade 1 classrooms with higher aggregate levels of physically aggressive peers contributed to their behavioral problems in middle school. Similarly, Leadbeater, Hoglund, and Woods (2003) found that higher classroom levels of behavioral problems in Grade 1 increased children's risks for peer victimization beyond individual-level risks by the end of Grade 2. In addition, children who showed high levels of emotional problems reported increases in relational and physical victimization by the end of Grade 2 when they were in Grade 1 classrooms with high levels of socially competent children. These effects suggest that emotionally distressed children either withdraw from or are excluded by their more competent peers.

In a one-year follow-up study, Aber et al. (1998) investigated the effects of classroom and neighborhood contexts on the effectiveness of the "Resolving Conflict Creatively Program" violence prevention program for children in Grades 2 to 6. The findings showed that the positive effects of a high number of program lessons focused on limiting children's aggressive thoughts were diminished for children in classrooms where more children rated the use of aggression as acceptable and for children living in poorer, violent neighborhoods. The second-year follow-up showed that high levels of program lessons were associated with decreases in conduct problems, hostile attribution biases, and aggressive interpersonal negotiation strategies; and a slower rate of growth in depressive symptoms (Aber et al., 2003). However, children in classrooms where teachers received high levels of training, but taught few program lessons, showed a faster rate of growth in aggressive behaviors and a slower rate of growth in competent behaviors.

Classroom-based programs that increase cooperative, prosocial peer group behaviors at the classroom level also appear to reduce risks for peer aggression and victimization while improving competent behaviors. The classroom-based "Good Behavior Game" that rewarded cooperative behaviors buffered the effect of classroom levels of aggression on boys' risks for behavioral problems in middle school (Kellam et al., 1998). In a follow-up evaluation of a kindergarten to Grade 4 program directed at creating classrooms that students experience as communities (where classmates care about and are supportive of one another), Solomon, Watson, Battistich, Schaps, and Delucchi (1996) found levels of social understanding and conflict-resolution skills were higher for children in the intervention group in Grades 4 to 6 compared to children in the control group. Vitaro, Brendgen, Pagani, Tremblay, and McDuff (1999) further highlighted the importance of positive peer affiliations in a follow-up study of aggressive boys who were targeted for an intervention program to improve social and problem-solving skills in Grade 2. Boys who associated with nondeviant peers showed lower risks for conduct disorder in Grade 6 relative to program boys who associated with deviant peers.

Characteristics of Schools

Aspects of the school context, including the presence of violence prevention programs and the proportion of poor children attending the school, have also been linked to levels of competent and problem behaviors and peer victimization within the school setting. Research shows that positive school social climates (the quality of interpersonal interactions and feelings of trust and respect that exist within the school community) are associated with lower levels of emotional and behavioral problems in children (Kuperminc, Leadbeater, Emmons, & Blatt, 1997). School-wide programs that work to create a positive school social climate may reduce risks for problem behaviors and victimization, at the individual, classroom and school levels, while also improving children's competent behaviors (Comer, 1985; Olweus, 1993; Solomon et al., 1996).

Past studies also indicate that schools with high numbers of students from families on income assistance may have a more difficult time limiting levels of aggression and victimization than schools where most children come from higher income families. For example, Hanish and Guerra (2000) showed that the school level of poverty (proportion of children eligible for free lunch) correlated positively with children's reports of peer victimization in elementary school. Hoglund and Leadbeater (2004) reported that children in schools with higher levels of student poverty showed decreases in social competence and increases in emotional and behavioral problems over the course of Grade 1 compared to children in lower poverty schools. Lower classroom levels of peer prosocial acts and higher classroom levels of peer victimization also contributed to increases in emotional problems for children in higher poverty schools.

School levels of poverty also appear to influence the effectiveness of prevention programs targeting peer aggression. Kellam et al. (1998) showed that attending a school with a higher level of poverty (proportion of children eligible for free lunch) in Grade 1 increased children's risk for behavioral problems in middle school, regardless of whether they were in the intervention or control group. The reasons for these effects are not completely clear but may be related to a range of factors, including differences in neighborhood, peer and family values concerning the acceptability of aggression; levels of children with emotional and behavioral problems in the schools; parental participation; or instability in the school population due to family moves that disrupt children's friendships and attachments to the school community.

Hence, while characteristics of classrooms and schools appear to influence children's experiences of aggression and victimization, the question remains whether these contexts can be changed. We have been collaborating in the development of a theory-driven, community-based and school-wide program for the prevention of peer victimization, "The WITS Rock Solid Primary Program," that takes the challenge of changing contexts seriously and shows promise for reducing peer victimization. We next describe the history of this collaboration and the program, and follow this with a report of our two-year, follow-up evaluation of this program.

DESCRIPTION OF THE WITS ROCK SOLID PROGRAM

WITS Conceptual Framework

The WITS program is a coordinated initiative between elementary school educators, community groups, and developmental psychologists that takes a comprehensive, multi-setting approach to reducing peer victimization and enhancing social competence at the school- and classroom level. This program is linked to the school district's mission of creating responsive and safe school environments that enhance students' social and emotional competence, social responsibility, and learning outcomes. "Using your WITS to Walk away, Ignore, Talk it out, and Seek help" can become code words with school-wide visibility and parent and community support. The ideal is to create school, classroom, and family environments that speak with a uniform voice to promote positive conflict-resolution strategies. The WITS program has multiple components (see Table 20.1 and later) and is set out in an easily accessed manual that is available on our website, www.youth.society.uvic.ca. The manual provides suggestions for multisite activities that invite creativity and can be adapted to the needs and interests of a particular school and community.

The WITS program builds on the characteristics of effective violence prevention and social competence development programs that have been identified by prevention scientists, developmental psychologists, and edu-

TABLE 20.1. WITS program components.

1. Teacher curriculum	Directs teachers to a wealth of early childhood literature and activities that can be used to reinforce WITS messages in the classroom. The curriculum addresses the learning outcomes required for elementary school curricula concerning social skills and responsibility, personal planning, language and visual arts, and drama.
2. Police curriculum	Walks police through the swearing-in-ceremony where kindergarten to Grade 3 children are "deputized" as police helpers to keep their school safe and help other children. A stuffed walrus mascot (Witsup) is given to each school. WITS activity books, bookmarks, etc. are given to the children as reminders and to take these messages home.
3. Library curriculum	Details curriculum and activities for a list of popular picture books. It also includes information that is central to a librarian's curricula including effective literacy techniques used in the stories, vocabulary building, etc.
4. University athlete curriculum	Uses student athletes to provide positive role models from the community who advocate "using your WITS" in short visits to elementary school classrooms over the school year. The students are organized and supervised by a community liaison hired by the police group and are supported by the police officer assigned to the school.
5. WITS for siblings and friends	Guides parents in using WITS to resolve conflicts between siblings or children and their friends, using books and TV programs, to identify WITS strategies. Time outs prescribe "walking away" to think about good solutions to deal with problems.

See Web site manual at www.youth.society.uvic.ca

cators. These characteristics include a focus on underlying factors that can enhance and undermine both violence prevention and competence promotion; teaching developmentally appropriate, targeted skills for resisting inappropriate behaviors and utilizing competent ones; starting in the early school years and continuing through the primary grades; using varied teaching methods to link with existing school curricula; providing occasions for children to build positive relationships by actively involving peers, parents, teachers and community members; and including a systematic evaluation of the program implementation and effectiveness (Consortium on the School-Based Promotion of Social Competence, 1994; Nation et al., 2003).

History of WITS

The Rock Solid Foundation was developed in the fall of 1997 by several police officers in conjunction with a local lacrosse team, the Victoria Shamrocks, which is highly visible in this community. An interactive program created by this police group presented positive messages to young people, urging them to understand that they had rights to protection from peer assaults and threats of violence. Unfortunate circumstances in the community as well as growing partnerships led to the expansion of the Foundation activities that included the WITS program.

On November 14, 1997, the Greater Victoria Region was devastated by the tragic murder of a fourteen-year-old girl, Reena Virk. Reena was badly beaten and ultimately drowned by a group of her peers beneath a bridge in the city core. This horrific incident created tremendous media attention and raised questions about what types of youth violence prevention programs existed, with many questions directed to the Foundation. Since Reena's death, members of the Foundation have spoken to over 500,000 young people in Grades 4 to 12 about proactive solutions to peer violence, threats, intimidation, and harassment. A video documenting this initial program ("Rock Solid Children Youth and Families: Creating a Responsive Environments for the Prevention of Youth Violence") was created in collaboration with the Centre for Youth and Society at the University of Victoria and was distributed to schools both within and outside of our local community. The video and accompanying manual were directed at helping communities find their own solutions to peer violence. However, after viewing this program many educators in the local school district stated that these messages would have a greater impact if they also targeted children in the primary grades. Consequently, a partnership was formed between the Foundation, educators from the Greater Victoria School District, and the Centre for Youth and Society for the creation of a primary educational program.

WITS Classroom Component

In the late 1990s, under the leadership of Judi Stevenson (principal of a local elementary school), a committee of teachers was formed to develop curricula materials for using the WITS acronym in the primary grades. This acronym gives younger children simple, developmentally appropriate strategies to make safe and positive choices when faced with peer conflicts. The classroom curriculum has a literacy focus that is integrated into the school district's learning objectives for language arts, interpersonal understanding, and social responsibility for Kindergarten to Grade 3 children. The curriculum directs teachers to a wealth of early childhood literature in which child characters resolve interpersonal conflicts by using one or more components of the WITS message (WITS story books). The manual identifies which WITS message(s) the story book promotes and provides ideas for creative classroom activities teachers can complete with students to reinforce the WITS messages. Activities include role-playing, drawing, and creative writing that get children to use their imagination to identify ways that using your WITS has and can help resolve peer conflicts. The program is not intended to be prescriptive in terms of the number of WITS storybooks read or activities teachers complete per month. Rather, the program encourages teachers to select WITS books for their story times, incorporate activities that focus on WITS messages into daily lesson plans, display students' art and creative writing projects that illustrate WITS messages, recognize children for using their WITS, and capture the "teachable moments" that deal with conflicts as they occur between children (e.g., asking a child how he or she used or could have used his or her WITS when the child informs them of a conflicted interaction with another child).

School staff (including teachers, principals, and playground assistants), were initially trained to deliver the WITS program in a two-hour in-service training session in February of 2000. This training session was led by Judi Stevenson and Tom Woods (co-author and Director of the Rock Solid Foundation). Training centered on rallying schools to adopt the child-friendly WITS program, how to deliver the program successfully to students throughout the school, and how to incorporate it into existing classroom curricula (rather than as an add-on program that created extra work for teachers). Curriculum manuals were given to all the participants and are made available to schools upon request, and are available online, www.youth.society. uvic.ca.

WITS Police Component

The primary goals of the police component are to show children that the police are community adults who are available to help children deal with peer conflicts peacefully, to reinforce that WITS messages can be used outside the school community, and to emphasize the importance of telling an adult early when faced with an interpersonal problem or concern. The police school-liaison officers were initially trained to deliver the WITS messages to young children in a two-hour training session held in November of 1999 that was led by Tom Woods and Bonnie Leadbeater. A police manual is given to all the police school-liaison officers.

At the beginning of the school year, an initial police visit is held in the school auditorium and all kindergarten to Grade 3 students are "sworn-in" as "WITS Special Constables" to keep their school safe and to help other children. During this visit children are read story of Witsup the Walrus (the WITS mascot), taught how to salute and stand at attention like a police recruit, how to give the secret WITS handshake and password ("huddy, huddy"), are given their own personal "WITS Special Constable" badge, and are advised that the police will be back to visit them to see how the new deputies are doing using their WITS. Teachers, principals, and other school personnel are encouraged to attend this swearing-in-ceremony. Each participating school is also presented with the WITS mascot, a stuffed walrus named Witsup.

The time commitment for the police school-liaison officers is approximately one hour per school for the initial swearing-in-ceremony and approximately one hour per class for the follow-up five to ten visits over the course of the school year (about ten minutes for each visit). The follow-up visits are informal, flexible, fun, and absorb little time or resources. These visits maintain the momentum of the program by encouraging the children to use their WITS and reinforce that the WITS messages are also important outside the school community. The police bring clothing items for Witsup (such as a baseball hat, shorts) and leave every child a WITS "gift-reminder" (including book marks, pencils, activity books, tree decorations) as a reminder to use their WITS and to help take the WITS messages home. These small items are corporately sponsored and cost approximately $5 per child per year.

Varsity teams from the University and local athletic groups are now taking part by adopting a class or entire schools for WITS visits. Using the same format, and in conjunction with the police, athletes visit classes regularly to provide other positive, community role models who reinforce the WITS messages.

Overall annual costs to administer the program are relatively low because of the commitment from local police departments to support the salaries of a community police coordinator and the police school-liaison officers. Tasks for a part-time coordinator include scheduling the swearing-in-ceremonies and assigning schools to police and community volunteers. The development of program materials and the evaluation work has been independently funded through research grants.

EVALUATION OF THE PROGRAM'S FEASIBILITY

Participants. In the spring of 2000, the schools that were represented at the February 2000 training session were visited by university researchers to assess the level that the program had been implemented. Of these, thirteen schools received a high rating; indicating satisfactory teacher training and buy-in to the program, the presence of a school champion for the program, implementation of the program in a majority of kindergarten to Grade

3 classrooms, endorsement by the school principal, and use of police visits. These schools were invited to participate in the program evaluation. Two schools declined because other research was already in progress in the schools, leaving eleven program schools. Six schools in the same district that had not yet implemented the program agreed to act as matched control schools for three years. One of the control schools adopted a modified WITS program, replacing "*I* statements" for the "*I*gnore" and did not use the police component (a primary ingredient of this program). Because the status of this group was not clear, measures involving the children ($n = 23$) from this school were not included in the current evaluation. All of the program and control schools had additional programs promoting social skills (but none specifically targeted peer victimization or classroom level behaviors) and all had policies for dealing with excessively aggressive behaviors, primarily through suspensions.

Baseline data were collected at the start of Grade 1 (fall of 2000) from 409 children (290 in program schools and 119 in control schools; 49 percent girls; mean age 6 years, 3 months) in 41 classrooms. Follow-up data were collected at the end of Grade 1 (spring of 2001) from 400 children in 41 classrooms, and end of Grade 2 (spring of 2002) from 374 children in 40 classrooms. Attrition was due primarily to children moving out of the school district. Consent was sought from the parents of all Grade 1 children in the participating schools. Overall parental consent rate was 64 percent across participating schools (range 47 to 91 percent), and did not significantly differ between program and control schools or between high- and low-poverty schools.

Parents' demographic questionnaires indicated that 65 percent of the children lived with both parents, and 47 percent of the children's mothers had completed some training beyond high school and 28 percent had received a bachelor's or graduate degree. Children's ethnicity or race was 73 percent Canadian and European Caucasian, 9 percent South East and East Asian, 7 percent Aboriginal, 4 percent East Indian, 5 percent Other (e.g., Hispanic, Caribbean), and 2 percent reported no ethnicity or race. English was the only language spoken in 73 percent of the homes. Demographic characteristics did not significantly differ between children in program and control schools (one-way ANOVAs, $Fs [1, 398] = .41$ for living with both parents, $= 1.72$ for mothers' education, and $= 1.39$ for ethnicity).

Procedure

Children completed questionnaires in groups of nine to twenty during class time (the number of children in the class who had parent consent), tapping peer victimization and prosocial behaviors, and strategies for resolving peer conflicts. Only the victimization items were used in the current study. A graduate research assistant read the questions aloud and other assistants circulated in the classroom to ensure that the children understood each item and filled them out correctly. Children who needed extra assistance were individually interviewed. For each child who had parental consent, teachers completed questionnaires rating children's social competence and emotional and behavioral problems, while the children's questionnaires were being administered. Children without parental consent were supervised by research assistants in a different room and participated in drawing, writing, and reading activities.

MEASURES

Peer Victimization

The Social Experiences Questionnaire (Crick & Grotpeter, 1996) was used to assess children's experiences of *relational victimization* (e.g., "How often does another classmate tell lies about you to make other kids not like you anymore?") and *physical victimization* (e.g., "How often do you get hit by another kid at school?"). Children rated five items for each subscale on a 3-point scale showing how often the events occurred (0 = never, 1 = sometimes, 2 = almost all the time). Internal reliabilities were good for each subscale (α = .72 for relational victimization and α = .76 for physical victimization). *Classroom levels* of victimization were computed for each child individually by summing the subscale scores for all the other children in the classroom (i.e., excluding scores for that child) and dividing by *n* minus 1. This creates a classroom-level variable for each child that reflects the classroom environment the child is exposed to and prevents the child's own score from influencing the class measure. Because not all of the children in a class were participants in the study, data was used only for classes that had five or more participating children (average = 10.68 children at Times 1 and 2; average = 9.14 at Time 3). This slightly reduced the overall N (N = 395 at Times 1 and 2; N = 352 at Time 3) and could underestimate the effects of classroom contexts on victimization.

Social Competence and Emotional and Behavioral Problems

The teacher version of the Early School Behavior Rating Scale (Caldwell & Pianta, 1991) was used to assess children's *social competence* (e.g., "gets along with other children," "is aware of others' feelings," "is a leader in groups"; fourteen items), *emotional problems* (e.g., "appears unhappy or depressed," "feelings are easily hurt," "is shy or bashful"; seventeen items), and *behavioral problems* (e.g., "fights with other children," "has poor attention span," "has temper tantrums"; nine items). Teachers rated the forty items on a 4-point scale (1 = hardly ever to 4 = almost always). Internal reliabilities of the subscales were good (α = .90 for social competence, α = .84 for emotional problems, and α = .88 for behavioral problems). *Classroom levels* of social competence, emotional problems, and behavioral problems were computed as shown earlier. Data were used only for classes that had five or more participating children. We also computed difference scores (Time 3 scores minus Time 1) to reflect changes in the class variables from the start of Grade 1 to end of Grade 2.

School levels of poverty were measured at Time 1 from School District records of the "proportion of students receiving income assistance" in the school (a composite of schools' neighborhood-level SES indicators, including levels of education, single-parent households, household income, and receipt of social assistance; Hoyle, 1998). The mean proportion of students on income assistance was 1.75 percent higher (one-way ANOVA $F(1, 407)$ = 8.02, $p < .01$) in the control schools (M = 12.77, SD = 5.21, range 5 to 24 percent) than in the program schools (M = 11.02, SD = 5.7, range 3 to 19 percent). This could confound program effectiveness as program schools may look better because they have fewer high-risk children. School levels of poverty are included in all analyses. Based on the district average of 10 percent of students on income assistance, we distinguished between "low-poverty" (student poverty less than 10 percent) and "high-poverty" (student poverty 11 percent or more) schools in the general linear model analyses.

Level of implementation of the WITS program was assessed in the spring of 2001 and 2002 using principals' and teachers' ratings on an implementation questionnaire. Indicators of implementation remained satisfactory in all program schools. All schools had the swearing-in-ceremony and regular police visits, all principals endorsed the program strongly, and all school libraries had a section of the library designated for WITS books. Teachers reported on how many times in the last three months they had (1) read and discussed a WITS storybook (80 percent of Grade 1 and 52 percent of Grade 2 teachers said three or more times); (2) done a WITS classroom activity (58 percent of Grade 1 and 40 percent of Grade 2 teachers said three or more times); (3) recognized a student for using his or her WITS (94 percent of Grade 1 and 82 percent of Grade 2 teachers said three or more times); (4) displayed students' WITS projects (59 percent of Grade 1 and 13 percent of Grade 2 teachers said three or more times); and (5) had a police school-liaison officer visit their classroom (88 percent of Grade 1 and 93 percent of Grade 2 teachers said one or more times).

RESULTS

Predicting Changes in Classroom Levels of Victimization

Hierarchical multiple regression analyses were used to investigate the effects of changes in classroom characteristics (social competence and emotional and behavioral problems) from the start of Grade 1 to the end of Grade 2 on changes in *classroom levels of relational and physical victimization* from Time 1 to Time 3. The moderating effect of the WITS program on victimization was also examined.

Increases in classroom levels of social competence from Time 1 to Time 3 predicted *decreases* in *relational victimization* (see Table 20.2, Model 1). A significant interaction showed that the effect of social competence on victimization was moderated by WITS program status. Specifically, increases in classroom social competence contributed to declines in relational victimization only in the program schools ($\beta = -.38$, $p < .001$ in program schools; $\beta = -.03$, *ns* in control schools), suggesting that having the WITS program buffers the effects of classroom-level differences on changes in relational victimization. In addition, higher levels of school poverty predicted *increases* in *relational victimization* over time.

Similarly, increases in social competence and in emotional problems from Time 1 to Time 3 and the WITS program predicted *decreases* in *physical victimization* (see Table 20.2, Model 2). Significant interactions showed that the effects of social competence and emotional problems on victimization were moderated by WITS program status. Specifically, classroom characteristics contributed to declines in physical victimization only in the control schools ($\beta = -.47$, $p < .001$ for social competence and $\beta = -.56$, $p < .001$ for emotional problems in control schools; $\beta = -.02$, *ns* for social competence and $\beta = .13$, *ns* for emotional problems in program schools). Again, this suggests the WITS program buffers the effects of classroom-level differences on changes in physical victimization. As above, higher levels of school poverty predicted *increases* in *physical victimization* over time.

TABLE 20.2. Hierarchical regression analyses predicting changes in classroom levels of relational and physical victimization from the beginning of Grade 1 to the end of Grade 2.

Step variables	Model 1: Relational victimization			Model 2: Physical victimization		
	β^a	ΔR^2	ΔF	β^a	ΔR^2	ΔF
1a. Classroom relational victimization (T1)	−.06	.00	1.36			
1b. Classroom physical victimization (T1)				−.10*	.00	0.29
2. Classroom social competence (T3-T1)	−.51**			−.40*		
Classroom emotional problems (T3-T1)	−.14			−.56**		
Classroom behavioral problems (T3-T1)	.13	.04	4.74**	.15	.07	8.15***
3. WITS program[b]	.00			−.24***		
School levels of poverty	.45***	.18	37.64***	.32***	.14	30.63***
4. WITS program × social competence	.61***			.42**		
WITS program × emotional problems	.22			.66***		
WITS program × behavioral problems	−.03	.04	6.28***	−.14	.04	5.61***
Models 1 and 2, $df = 9, 327$		.27	13.08***		.25	12.34***

Note. [a]β values are standardized coefficients. [b]WITS program schools = 1, control schools = 0. *$p < .05$, **$p < .01$. ***$p < .001$.

Effects of the WITS Program on Average Classroom Levels of Victimization

The findings from the regression analyses earlier suggest that classroom characteristics, the WITS program, and school levels of poverty can affect classroom levels of victimization. In the next analyses we ask how much having the WITS program effected changes in mean levels of classroom victimization in both high- and low-poverty schools. The effects of the WITS program on classroom levels of relational and physical victimization were assessed separately in repeated measures general linear models comparing changes in average levels of victimization in program and control schools with similar levels of school poverty (see Table 20.3).

TABLE 20.3. Repeated measures GLM analyses of the effects of the WITS program and school levels of poverty on average levels (and standard deviations) of classroom victimization from the beginning of Grade 1 to the end of Grade 2.

	Time 1		Time 2		Time 3	
	Program	Control	Program	Control	Program	Control
1) Relational victimization						
Low-poverty schools	2.62 (.07)	2.34 (.12)	2.15 (.05)	2.39 (.09)	1.91 (.05)	2.06 (.10)
High-poverty schools	3.19 (.09)	2.52 (.12)	3.41 (.10)	2.73 (.13)	2.47 (.08)	2.75 (.10)
Total	2.85 (.06)	2.45 (.09)	2.67 (.06)	2.59 (.10)	2.14 (.05)	2.47 (.08)

Low-poverty schools, Time × intervention group, univariate $F = 5.84$, $p < .01$, $\eta^2 = .03$.
High-poverty schools, Time × intervention group, univariate $F = 18.37$, $p < .001$, $\eta^2 = .10$.

	Time 1		Time 2		Time 3	
	Program	Control	Program	Control	Program	Control
2) Physical victimization						
Low-poverty schools	2.69 (.07)	2.61 (.12)	2.41 (.05)	2.12 (.09)	1.89 (.06)	2.01 (.11)
High-poverty schools	3.17 (.10)	2.58 (.13)	3.30 (.10)	2.97 (.13)	2.24 (.07)	2.96 (.09)
Total	2.89 (.06)	2.59 (.09)	2.78 (.06)	2.63 (.09)	2.04 (.05)	2.58 (.07)

Low-poverty schools, Time × Intervention Group, Univariate $F = 3.35$, $p < .05$, $\eta^2 = .02$.
High-poverty schools, Time × Intervention Group, Univariate $F = 26.33$, $p < .001$, $\eta^2 = .14$.

Classroom levels of *relational victimization* decreased significantly in the *program schools* compared to the *control schools* with similar levels of school poverty (see Figure 20.1). The corresponding effect sizes were low to moderate, with stronger program effects evident in the high-poverty schools ($\eta^2 = .03$ for low-poverty schools and .10 for high-poverty schools). Relational victimization decreased in the low-poverty program schools but remained stable and then decreased in the low-poverty control schools. Relational victimization increased initially and then decreased in the high-poverty program schools but increased and then remained stable in the high-poverty control schools.

Classroom levels of *physical victimization* decreased significantly in the *program schools* compared to the *control schools* with similar levels of school poverty (see Figure 20.2). As mentioned earlier, the effect sizes were low to moderate, with stronger program effects in the high-poverty schools ($\eta^2 = .02$ for low-poverty schools and .14 for high-poverty schools). Physical victimization decreased more in the low-poverty program schools than in the low-poverty control schools. Physical victimization decreased in the high-poverty program schools but increased and then remained stable in the high-poverty control schools.

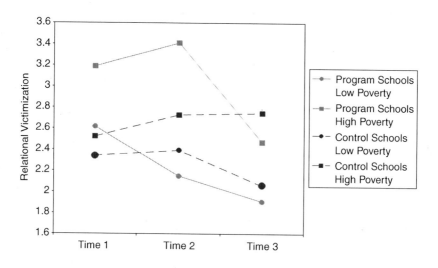

FIGURE 20.1. Average levels of relational victimization by intervention group and school levels of poverty.

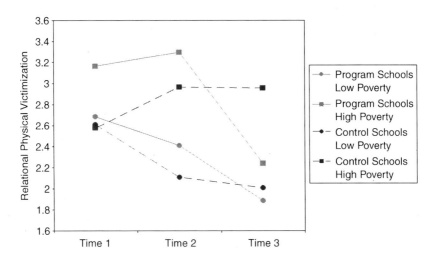

FIGURE 20.2. Average levels of physical victimization by intervention group and school levels of poverty.

CONCLUSIONS AND RECOMMENDATIONS

Consistent with other evaluations of comprehensive school-based programming (Aber et al., 2003; Comer, 1985; Olweus, 1993), our findings suggest that peer victimization can be reduced in high-poverty schools through universal, multi-setting programs that directly target both the prevention of peer victimization and the promotion of social competence; teach children developmentally appropriate, targeted skills; integrate schools' learning objectives; have the support of local community-based groups; and promote positive relationships for children with peers, school staff, and community members. In this study, children in schools with higher proportions of poor students were at greater risk for ongoing victimization, particularly in the absence of this school-wide, multi-setting program. Specifically, classroom levels of relational and physical victimization increased in the high-poverty *control* schools, but declined in the high-poverty *program* schools. Victimization also declined in the low-poverty program and control schools, but significantly greater decreases were observed in the *program* schools. Overall, stronger program effect sizes were evident in the high-poverty schools.

It is of note that classroom characteristics effected victimization in the control schools only. Through its multi-setting approach, the WITS program directly targets the prevention of peer violence and promotion of prosocial behaviors. Previous research with this sample showed declines in classroom levels of social competence in the control schools relative to the program schools (Leadbeater et al., 2003). Direct efforts to support social competence may be needed to reduce classroom levels of victimization. The WITS program's emphasis on prosocial, helping, behaviors may be one ingredient that sustains social competence.

It should be restated that all of the schools in this evaluation also had a variety of other programs (primarily targeting the development of individual levels of social skills) and suspension policies for dealing with excessively aggressive children. These additional programs could have influenced our findings. However, none of these programs directly targeted peer victimization and WITS was the only program consistently found in the program schools and not in the control schools. The low-to-moderate program effect sizes observed indicate that the WITS program holds promise for reducing peer victimization beyond programs focused on individual levels of social skills, particularly in high-poverty schools. Unexamined characteristics of teachers and schools and the number of children in the classrooms who did not participate in the evaluation may have also influenced our findings and require further study. The schools volunteered to participate in the evaluation and individual teachers affected the level of program implemented. Also our nonrandom design limits the generalizability of our findings. However, the feasibility of implementing this kind of intervention is confirmed. A more detailed examination of the intervention dosage could help to determine whether specific patterns and levels of the WITS program components are particularly effective or not (Aber et al., 1998, 2003).

Zero tolerance school disciplinary policies can be common reactions to failures of prevention programs, but suspensions rarely suggest positive alternatives to children who are struggling with the need to respond to the values of the many different "cultures" that surround them. Classroom, playground, school, home, and neighborhood cultures can vary widely in their tolerance for aggression. While further research is clearly needed to unravel the effects of contexts on peer victimization, our findings suggest that creating school, family, and community cultures that speak with a uniform voice about peaceful solutions to peer conflicts hold promise for reducing peer victimization—particularly in schools with higher levels of student poverty.

REFERENCES

Aber, J. L., Brown, J. L., & Jones, S. M. (2003). Developmental trajectories toward violence in middle childhood: Course, demographic differences, and response to school based intervention. *Developmental Psychology, 39,* 324-339.

Aber, J. L., Jones, S. M., Brown, J. L., Chaudry, N., & Samples, F. (1998). Resolving conflict creatively: Evaluating the developmental effect of a school-based violence prevention program in neighbourhood and classroom context. *Development and Psychopathology, 10,* 187-214.

Bukowski, W. M., & Sippola, L. K. (2001). Groups, individuals, and victimization: A view of the peer system. In J. Juvonen & S. Graham (Eds.), *Peer harassment in school: The plight of the vulnerable and victimized* (pp. 355-377). New York: Guilford Press.

Caldwell, C. B., & Pianta, R. C. (1991). A measure of young children's problem and competence behaviors: The Early School Behavior Scale. *Journal of Psychoeducational Assessment, 9,* 32-44.

Comer, J. P. (1985). The Yale-New Haven Primary Prevention Project: A follow-up study. *Journal of the American Academy of Child and Adolescent Psychiatry, 24,* 154-160.

Conduct Problems Prevention Research Group. (1992). A developmental and clinical model of the prevention of conduct disorder: The Fast Track Program. *Development and Psychopathology, 4,* 509-527.

Consortium on the School-based Promotion of Social Competence. (1994). The school-based promotion of social competence: Theory, research, practice, and policy. In R. J. Haggerty, L. R. Sherrod, N. Garmezy, & M. Rutter (Eds.), *Stress, risk, and resilience in children and adolescents: Processes, mechanisms, and interventions* (pp. 268-316). New York: Cambridge University Press.

Crick, N., & Grotpeter, J. K. (1996). Children's treatment by peers: Victims of relational and overt aggression. *Development and Psychopathology, 8,* 367-380.

Dishion, T. J., Poulin, F., & Burraston, B. (2000). Peer group dynamics associated with iatrogenic effects in group interventions with high-risk young adolescents. In D. W. Nangle & C. A. Erdley (Eds.), *The role of friendship in psychological adjustment. New directions for child and adolescent development* (No. 91) (pp. 79-92). San Francisco, CA: Jossey-Bass Inc.

Hanish, L. D., & Guerra, N. G. (2000). Predictors of peer victimization among urban youth. *Social Development, 9,* 521-543.

Hawkins, J. D., Catalano, R. F., Morrison, D. M., O'Donnell, J., Abbott, R. D., & Day, L. E. (1992). The Seattle Social Development Project: Effects of the first four years on protective factors and problem behaviors. In J. McCord & R. E. Tremblay (Eds.), *Preventing anitsocial behavior: Interventions from birth through adolescence* (pp. 193-161). Proceedings from the 10th Biennial Meeting of the International Society for the Study of Behavioral Development, Jyvaeskylae, Finland.

Hoglund, W. L., & Leadbeater, B. J. (2004). The effects of family, school, and classroom ecologies on changes in children's social competence and emotional and behavioral problems in first grade. *Developmental Psychology, 40,* 533-544.

Hoyle, W. (1998). *Estimated proportion of students on income assistance by school.* Ministry of Human Resources Administrative Files. Social Equity Programs.

Kellam, S. G., Ling, X., Merisca, R., Brown, C. H., & Ialongo, N. (1998). The effect of the level of aggression in the first grade classroom on the course and malleability of aggressive behavior into middle school. *Development and Psychopathology, 10,* 165-185.

Kuperminc, G., Leadbeater, B. J., Emmons, C., & Blatt, S. J. (1997). Perceived school climate and difficulties in the social adjustment of middle school students. *Applied Developmental Science, 1,* 76-88.

Leadbeater, B., Hoglund, W., & Woods, T. (2003). Changing contexts? The effects of a primary prevention program on classroom levels of peer relational and physical victimization. *Journal of Community Psychology, 31,* 397-418.

Miller, G. E., Brehm, K., & Whitehouse. S. (1998). Reconceptualizing school-based prevention for antisocial behavior within a resilience framework. *School Psychology Review, 27,* 364-379.

Nation, M., Crusto, C., Wandersman, A., Kumpfer, K. L., Seybolt, D., Morrissey-Kane, E., et al. (2003). What works in prevention: Principals of effective prevention programs. *American Psychologist, 58,* 449-456.

Olweus, D. (1993). *Bullying at school: What we know and what we can do.* Oxford, UK: Basil Blackwell.

Solomon, D., Watson, M., Battistich, V., Schaps, E., & Delucchi, K. (1996). Creating classrooms that students experience as communities. *American Journal of Community Psychology, 24,* 719-748.

Vitaro, F., Brendgen, M., Pagani, L., Trembly, R. E., & McDuff, P. (1999). Disruptive behavior, peer associations, and conduct disorder: Testing the developmental links through early intervention. *Development and Psychopathology, 11,* 287-304.

Chapter 21

Teasing, Taunting, Bullying, Harassment, and Aggression: A School-Wide Approach to Prevention, Strategic Intervention, and Crisis Management

Howard M. Knoff

INTRODUCTION

Relative to the schools, "bullying" is defined as a form of repeated aggression where one or more students physically, psychologically, and more recently, sexually harass or harm other students repeatedly over a period of time. More specifically, bullying can include physical aggression; verbal aggression—including persistent teasing, taunting, and threats; or the more subtle or indirect "aggression" that results in social exclusion. Typically, acts of bullying are unprovoked, and the bully is perceived as stronger or as having more power than the victim (Batsche & Knoff, 1994; Hoover, Oliver, & Hazler, 1992; Nansel et al., 2001; Olweus, 1991).

Relative to addressing this problem, programs or approaches focusing on school bullying can be organized in the form of primary (e.g., whole school or school linked to community), secondary (e.g., early intervention groups for potential or "early-indication" bullies or victims), or tertiary (e.g., direct services for existing bullies) prevention programs. Given the multifaceted and multidimensional nature of bullying, and using a systems

Bullying, Victimization, and Peer Harassment
© 2007 by The Haworth Press, Inc. All rights reserved.
doi:10.1300/5808_21

perspective, this chapter describes a primary prevention blueprint that involves more specific primary, secondary, and tertiary prevention elements to help schools organize comprehensive, ecologically based, and situationally sensitive approaches to school bullying. Briefly, the primary prevention element includes the creation and implementation of a school-wide process that results in (1) empowered students who are tolerant, have sound interpersonal, problem-solving, and conflict resolution skills, can disarm or discourage bullying attempts, and who feel comfortable reporting bullying incidents in a safe and confidential manner; (2) prosocial and supportive classroom settings that teach and reinforce appropriate interpersonal interactions between students and between students and adults; (3) safe and secure common areas of the school (e.g., hallways, cafeteria, buses) where peer groups demonstrate and reinforce prosocial interactions and actively deter bullying; and (4) involved parents and community partners who collaborate such that everyone is aware of and engaged in reinforcing a "notolerance-for-bullying" school culture. All of these effects focus on preventing, decreasing, and/or eliminating bullying.

The secondary prevention (strategic intervention) element focuses on students who have previously exhibited bullying behavior or who demonstrate a high probability of engaging in such behavior; peer groups that facilitate, support, and/or reinforce these students; school settings where bullying occurs most frequently; and parents whose children and adolescents are directly or indirectly involved in bullying. These interventions also may target those students who have been bullied in the past, teaching these "victims" successful ways to avoid bullying situations and approaches to use during bullying incidents. Finally, these interventions may include other adults in the school, helping them to successfully recognize and respond to bullying incidents such that they decrease or are eliminated in the future.

Lastly, the tertiary prevention (intensive needs/crisis management) element focuses on students who demonstrate serious and ongoing bullying behavior; peers and parents who continue to resist preventive or prosocial roles in bullying events; or school environments where groups of students are so out of control, relative to bullying, that crisis intervention is essential. Students who bully at this level typically exhibit a wide range of severe problematic behaviors, and their continued inappropriate behavior demonstrates a clear pattern of nonresponse to multifaceted strategic interventions. Ultimately, these students require services that may include alternative placements, intensive levels of psychological and behavioral interventions, and other community- or agency-based services.

REVIEW OF RELEVANT LITERATURE

While a number of empirical studies related to bullying have been published especially in the past decade, there still are many research gaps that need to be filled. Nonetheless, we do have an emerging picture of the (1) characteristics of bullies; (2) developmental patterns of bullying; (3) characteristics of victims and bully-victim relationships; and (4) interventions needed for bullies and to address bullying.

Summarizing much of the recent research, the following characteristics of bullies and developmental patterns of bullying appear most prominently (Bosworth, Espelage, & Simon, 1999; Craig, Pepler, & Atlas, 2000; Henington, Hughes, Cavell, & Thompson, 1998; Loeber & Stouthamer-Loeber, 1998; Nansel et al, 2001; Pellegrini, Bartini, & Brooks, 1999; Tolan, Gorman-Smith, & Loeber, 2000):

1. Bullying can be placed along a spectrum from teasing and gossiping to taunting and bullying to harassment and verbal threats or intimidation to physical aggression and violence. Some associate bullying with a lack of tolerance for diversity.
2. Boys are generally found to be bullies more frequently than girls, although this may be due to researchers' focus on the more overt forms of bullying, which boys tend to engage in more than girls.
3. Bullying appears to peak during the years when students transition from elementary to middle school (i.e., around age eleven or twelve), occurring most frequently from sixth to eighth grade.
4. Bullying behavior has been correlated with indicators of anger, depression, impulsivity, anxiety, and attitudes that support violence. Bullies are more likely to be poorer students and to get involved with alcohol and smoking.
5. Some bullies have been bullied themselves, some are rejected students, and some bullies are considered popular within the broader peer group.
6. Bullying appears to occur very often in unstructured school settings or common areas of the school (e.g., the playground). Relative to school or class size, however, these do not appear to correlate with acts of bullying.

Relative to victims and bully-victim relationships, recent research (Hodges & Perry, 1999; Nansel et al, 2001; Rigby, 2000, 2001, 2002) indicates that:

1. Boys are more likely to be victims of bullying than girls. Girls tend to be bullied more through personal or relational "attacks," while boys experience more physical or aggressive "attacks." Bullying sometimes occurs due to relationship variables between the bully and victim, and not just as a function of initiation by a bully.
2. Students from preschool through age sixteen respond to bullying through a range of negative emotions or reactions: anger, revenge, self-pity, confusion, loneliness, physical and psychological distress, depression, anxiety, somatic symptoms, and lowered self-esteem. These reactions result in these students sometimes feeling abandoned, afraid of school, and worried at school. Victims also are lonelier and have more difficulty making friends. All of this potentially results in school avoidance or absences, difficulties concentrating while at school, and poor school performance.
3. Victims of bullies are more prone to suicidal ideation, severe depression, or to extreme acts of hostility or aggression.

Finally, when considering interventions for bullies and to address bullying as a whole, recent research (Espelage & Holt, 2001; Huesmann & Reynolds, 2001; Swearer & Doll, 2001) indicates that:

1. Adults have been found to be generally unaware of or to underestimate the extent of bullying that occurs in schools, and they tend to intervene very rarely even when aware of bullying. This suggests that adult involvement is necessarily a critical element to preventing and addressing bullying situations and behavior.
2. The peer group needs to be included in any intervention program as students have become desensitized to bullying behavior and incidents over time and, thus, have become less willing to intervene (and more passively accepting of) bullying when it occurs.
3. Relative to bullies themselves, social-cognitive interventions that include social skills, social-cognitive problem-solving, and aggression reduction and replacement training are important elements to a comprehensive, multifaceted program.

In the end, while a fair amount of research has been published identifying the characteristics and the dynamics of bullying in the schools, very few studies, at least in the United States, have addressed research-proven ways to decrease or prevent bullying. Below, an ecologically- and systems-based intervention blueprint is described.

DESCRIPTION OF THE APPLICATION

Many of the characteristics of a "safe and responsive" school (Dwyer & Osher, 2000) are inherent in and depend on the characteristics of an effective school: an emphasis on academic achievement and social–emotional and behavioral success; the involvement of families in meaningful ways; collaborative links to the community; an emphasis on positive, equitable, and respectful staff and student relationships; open and protected discussions on issues of safety; a functional problem-solving process that results in solution-oriented programs and interventions; and extended day, school-to-work, and mental health support services. Thus, it is important to recognize how effective schools, even at the most global level, are actually safe and responsive schools, and how safe and responsive schools help to create environments that support prosocial student interactions while preventing bullying incidents and opportunities.

At a more specific level, and as noted earlier, schools' responses to bullying must be organized along a prevention, strategic intervention, and intensive needs continuum. At the primary prevention level, an effective school's overall focus is on creating protective factors in schools such that bullying is prevented, decreased, and/or eliminated over time. This is accomplished by (1) implementing a building-wide social skills program that teaches students specific interpersonal, problem-solving, and conflict-resolution skills; (2) developing individual teacher, grade-level, and building-wide accountability systems of meaningful incentives and consequences relative to bullying; and (3) reinforcing staff and administrative consistency such that bullying incidents are addressed in a constant and predictable fashion (Knoff, 2000; Knoff, Finch, & Carlyon, 2004).

In addition, recognizing that bullying often occurs in the common areas of a school (e.g., the cafeteria, hallways, on the buses, or on the playground) and that it often is inappropriately supported or reinforced by peers or peer pressure, schools must conduct "special situations analyses." Briefly, these analyses investigate (1) the bullies, the victims, the active peer bystanders, or the passive or uninvolved peer bystanders; (2) the teachers and other staff who relate or respond to the problem; (3) where the bullying occurs or does not occur in the school; (4) the student and staff incentives and consequences relative to bullying; and (5) the potential or existing resources that are available to help solve the problem.

Finally, parent and community outreach is essential at the primary prevention level such that teasing, taunting, bullying, harassment, and aggression are universally recognized as both unacceptable and preventable. Parents, for example, must partner with the school (Raffaele & Knoff, 1999), encouraging all children and adolescents to demonstrate appropriate interpersonal skills and behavior and assisting students who are bullied and being bullied. In addition, parents must feel comfortable in asserting their rights when it is their child who is being bullied—working with school officials to initiate and implement successful intervention plans. Communities, meanwhile, need to engage in public relations, social marketing, social action, and social and public service programs so that consistent "no tolerance" messages and preventive strategies are implemented across the many diverse populations living in a specific area or locale.

Because primary prevention has the greatest probability of impeding, decreasing, or eliminating bullying effectively and efficiently, the primary prevention domains just introduced will be expanded in greater detail later.

Teaching Students Prosocial Skills

The ultimate goal of a social skills program is to teach students the interpersonal, problem-solving, and conflict-resolution skills that they need to get along with each other and to facilitate positive interactions. In a generic sense, then, students with good social skills are unlikely to engage in teasing, taunting, bullying, harassment, and aggression. More specific to bullying, however, good social skills can help students (1) to deal prosocially with situations that might result in teasing or bullying; (2) to respond to teasing or bullying such that existing situations are halted or resolved, their psychological or behavioral impact is minimized, and they occur less frequently (or not at all) in the future; and (3) to intervene effectively when witnessing a bullying event that they are not directly involved in.

With regard to teaching, an effective social skills program:

1. Is based on a social learning theory model that uses teaching, modeling, role-playing, providing performance feedback, and an active focus on the transfer of training across time, setting, people, places, and circumstances for instruction.
2. Connects skill training to a building- or grade-level positive discipline and behavior management system that holds students accountable for their behavior and provides for implementation integrity.
3. Focuses on both grade-level and whole-building implementation.
4. Uses a core (universal) language that is easy for students to learn, facilitates cognitive scripting and mediation, and conditions behaviors and choices leading to more and more automatic behavior.

5. Is explicit and developmentally appropriate, yet flexible and adaptable for students' individual language levels, cultures, maturational levels, and needs.
6. Provides a defined, progressive, yet flexible, sequence of social skills that recognizes that some prerequisite skills must be mastered before more complex skills are taught, and that skills training occurs year round.
7. Employs an evidence-based pedagogical approach to instruction that integrates behavioral teaching, continued practice, and application under increasingly realistic—yet controlled—conditions, and skill-specific reinforcement and especially during "teachable" moments.
8. Has been factually demonstrated to be effective in controlled and independent studies in real schools and school situations.
9. Was designed to be implemented by regular classroom teachers as the primary instructional leaders of the social skills process.
10. Teaches sensible and pragmatic skills that are needed by today's students and that can be applied on a daily basis by preschool through high school students.
11. Addresses behavior problems or situations, as identified by both adults and students, that occur frequently in classrooms and common areas of the school.
12. Contains an evaluation component that assesses treatment and implementation integrity, student and adult satisfaction, and student behavior both when adults are present and/or supervising and when students are either on their own or in transfer of training situations.

While there are many published social skills programs, only a small percentage of them are evidence based, nationally recognized by virtue of an independent evaluation or critical review, and effective given the aforementioned twelve criteria. One of these programs, the Stop & Think Social Skills Program (Knoff, 2001), was developed through and is used within Project ACHIEVE, a comprehensive, nationally recognized school reform and improvement program that (with the Stop & Think social skills) has been designated an evidence-based Exemplary Model Prevention Program through the U.S. Department of Health and Human Services' Substance Abuse and Mental Health Services Administration and the U.S. Department of Justice's Office of Juvenile Justice and Delinquency Prevention (SAMHSA; OJJDP; Knoff, 2000; Knoff & Batsche, 1995; Quinn, Osher, Hoffman, & Hanley, 1998; see www.projectachieve.info). Project ACHIEVE's ultimate goal is to help design and implement effective school and schooling processes that maximize the academic and social/emotional/behavioral progress and achievement of all students. Using a systematic-design and implementation process that involves seven interdependent components (Strategic planning and organizational analysis and development; Functional assessment and data-based problem-solving; Effective school, instructional, and staff development processes; Instructional consultation, curriculum-based assessment, and academic interventions; Behavioral assessment, consultation, and interventions implemented within a School-wide Positive Behavioral Self-Management System; Parent and community outreach; and Research and accountability), Project ACHIEVE exemplifies the earlier point that "safe and responsive" school environments exist most often within the context of effective schools.

Representing a program that includes all of the effective social skills components described earlier and that can address peer teasing, taunting, bullying, harassment, and aggression, the Stop & Think Social Skills Program uses a universal language that facilitates the conditioning and independent transfer of prosocial behavior and a teaching process that is based both on social learning theory and sound pedagogy. More specifically, the Stop & Think process employs a five-step language when teaching, reinforcing, or using any social skill. The five steps are as follows:

- Stop and Think!
- Are you going to make a Good Choice or Bad Choice?
- What are your Choices or Steps?
- Do It!
- Good Job!

Briefly, the *Stop and Think!* step recognizes that many initial emotional reactions are classically conditioned, and thus, that students need help with impulse control, self-control, and self-management. The *Good Choice or Bad Choice?* step recognizes that even when under emotional control, students need meaningful incentives and consequences to motivate them to make good choices. The *What are your Choices or Steps?* step recognizes that most behavior is mediated by internal language that is taught through cognitive-behavioral scripting so that students can eventually *Do It!*, that is, behaviorally demonstrate their prosocial skills. Finally, the *Good Job!* step teaches and prompts students to reinforce themselves for successfully using their social skills and successfully responding to interpersonal, problem-solving, or conflict-potential situations.

Using this universal script, specific Stop & Think skills are taught by embedding a "skill script" into the third *What are your Choices or Steps?* step. For example, the middle or high school script for the "When You are Teased, Taunted, or Verbally Harassed" skill is as follows:

1. *Take* deep breaths and *count* to five.
2. *Think* about what Good Choices you can make.
   You can:

   a. *Ignore* the person and *turn away* from him or her.
   b. *Tell* the person how you feel and *ask* him or her to stop.
   c. *Move* or *walk* away from the person.
   d. *Find* a teacher or other adult to help.

3. *Pick and plan* your best choice.
4. If your choice doesn't work, *try* another choice.

This skill script is then taught within the five universal steps such that students learn to *Stop and Think*, and then ask themselves if they are going to *Make a Good Choice or a Bad Choice*? After deciding to make a good choice, they then verbalize or cognitively review the aforementioned skill script. Then, they *Do It*, and once successful, tell themselves they did a *Good Job*!

Beyond the universal language and skill scripts, the Stop & Think process works because it uses a teaching process that involves modeling, role-playing, performance feedback, and the transfer of new skills into different student situations. After teaching a specific social skill, teachers *model* or demonstrate the prosocial use of that skill by re-creating an actual classroom or school situation that requires its use for resolution, and then by verbalizing the Stop & Think and skill script while showing students how to perform the "good choice" behavior. Students then are given opportunities to *role-play* or "positively practice" the same social skill in additional recreated situations so that the prosocial choices and behaviors become more automatic over time. Critically, the role-plays typically are done with other students, and different situations are practiced so that the skill transfers into "real life" situations more easily.

While students are engaged in role-plays, they receive performance feedback from teachers and peers. This ensures both the positive practice of the skill in question and additional opportunities to discuss different situations where an adaptation or variation of the skill is needed for success. Finally, the Stop & Think process consciously builds in the *transfer of training*. This occurs as teachers orchestrate *application sessions* where social skills are practiced under more realistic, yet controlled, conditions, and *infusion moments* where actual situations ("teachable moments") that occur in the classroom or school are used to provide positive feedback or needed practice, depending on whether a student successfully uses a necessary social skill or not.

Applying the Stop & Think Process to Bullying

As noted earlier, bullying situations require at least three "parties" to demonstrate good social skills at either prevention or response levels: the bully, the individual being bullied, and the peer group that witnesses the bullying. In order to determine which group requires what skills, bullying situations must be functionally analyzed to determine the reasons *why* each group participates and takes on its specific role. Depending on these analyses, the *Stop & Think Social Skills Program* has many social skills to address most skill-based situations (new or unique social skills can always be created). For example, and based on the research, some bullies may need skills that help them (1) to get along more effectively with peers (e.g., involving the Stop & Think skills of Using Self Control, Staying Out of Fights, Accepting No, How to Share, How to Avoid Trouble); (2) to deal with their anger or other emotions (e.g., involving the Stop & Think skills of Dealing with Anger and Frustration, Accepting a Consequence, Dealing with Losing, Responding to Failure); and/or (3) to access more appropriate peer or adult attention (e.g., involving the Stop & Think skills of Beginning and Ending a Conversation, Giving and Accepting Compliments, Asking for Help, Convincing Others). For the victims, we may need to teach them skills that help them to avoid bullying situations, to respond appropriately and safely to bullies, and to problem solve through situations where bullying has occurred in the past (e.g., involving the Stop & Think skills of When You are Teased, Taunted, or Verbally Harassed, Standing Up for Your Rights, Being Able to Say "No," Dealing with Peer Pressure, Walking Away from a Fight, Dealing with Fear, When You are Excluded or Rejected, Evaluating Yourself). Finally, for the peer group, we may need to teach them skills that help them confidently and positively intervene in bullying situations, both addressing the actions of the bully and supporting the needs and safety of the victim (e.g., involving the Stop & Think skills Being Assertive, Identifying Another Person's Feelings, Dealing with Peer Pressure, Helping Someone with a Problem, Dealing with Fear, Being a Good Leader).

Once a bullying situation has been analyzed and specific social skills identified, the teaching, scripting, and role-playing process can begin. For example, a Stop & Think skills script to help a student to "Deal with Bullying" might include the following in a role-played situation between an actual bully and victim:

> Here comes Jason. He's always picking on me. Oh no—he saw me! [Jason starts to bully. . .] I need to Stop and Think. Am I going to make a Good Choice or Bad Choice? If I make a Bad Choice, then Jason will think that I'm afraid of him, and he'll bully me for the rest of the year. I need to make a Good Choice. What are my Choices or Steps? Well, first I need to take a deep breath, stand up straight, and look right at Jason. Next, I need to tell him in a firm voice that I don't want any trouble with him and that I am going to walk away from him. Last, I need to keep my eyes on him, back away from him, and then walk away as soon as I am a safe distance away. OK—I'm ready to Just Do It. Here I go . . . [Potential Target implements the social skill's steps.] Great!—I did a good job. Hopefully, he'll stay away from me from now on.

Critically, when Stop & Think skills are role-played by an actual bully and victim, both parties learn how to proactively or prosocially handle certain situations and what each other's behaviors might look like if a similar situation occurs in real life.

Accountability

Significantly, just because a student *possesses* certain social skills does not mean that they are *demonstrated* all or most of the time. Indeed, while *skill-deficit* students need more teaching, practice, and skill mastery, *performance-deficit* students do not always (choose to) exhibit available skills in their repertoire. Often, performance-deficit students are either not motivated to display certain skills at important times, or there are competing dynamics (e.g., peer versus adult attention or reinforcement) that increase the probability that certain (not always positive) behaviors and not others will occur. Given all of this, schools need to establish and implement grade-level and building-wide accountability systems that include progressively tiered and developmentally appropriate incentives and consequences that are meaningful to students and that motivate them toward "good choices" and away from "bad choices," respectively. While these accountability systems are needed for all students to address all expected behaviors, they also should inherently address teasing, taunting, bullying, harassment, and aggression—all unfortunate but fairly typical peer-mediated events.

When initially developing an effective accountability system, Project ACHIEVE, through its School-wide Positive Behavioral Self-Management System, uses a systematic process to help schools to create, formalize, and implement a "Behavioral Matrix" that is eventually included in the building's "School-wide Discipline Policies and Procedures" document. Created by staff, student, parent, and community representatives, this matrix explicitly identifies, for all grade levels and then more generically for the entire building, expected student behaviors tied to positive responses, incentives, and rewards, and different "intensities" or levels of inappropriate student behaviors connected with negative responses, consequences, and interventions as needed. This matrix and discipline document eventually helps everyone to know the behavioral expectations and responses at different grade levels and across the school, and they help create a consistent atmosphere that reinforces student responsibility and self-management.

Relative to incentives and consequences, a number of "fundamental evidence-based principles" are practiced in effective schools:

1. All students in the school experience five positive interactions (collectively, from adults, peers, or themselves) for every negative interaction. Thus, school staff are responsible for their own positive interactions with students (and other staff), they need to teach and reinforce peers to positively interact with each other, and they need to identify and respond to students who have "self-esteem" issues such that they give themselves too many negative self-statements.
2. Students are largely motivated through positive, proactive, and incentive-oriented means.
3. When consequences are necessary, the mildest possible consequence needed to motivate students' "good choices" are used.
4. It is recognized that consequences are not the same as punishment. Punishment is motivated to respond to and stop a student's inappropriate behavior (not to teach and reinforce prosocial behavior), and it often models anger or aggression, retribution, and/or poor problem-solving. Punishment, moreover, typically does not result in a prosocial or desired behavior. If it does, the prosocial behavior is demonstrated usually (a) after one to three applications of the punishment, and (b) because the desired behavior already is in the student's repertoire. Finally, for a student who does not possess the prosocial skills that a punishment is attempting to elicit, the result often is a suppression of the inappropriate behavior targeted, and then the *substitution* of another inappropriate behavior that is also in the student's repertoire (or the absence of any prosocial behavior at all).

Consequences, meanwhile, are logically connected to the original "offense," they are used only when a student has mastered or near-mastered the desired skill or behavior, and they focus on (re)teaching and motivating future appropriate behavior.

5. Staff recognize that the building's discipline and behavior management system has not "failed" when students make bad choices. Instead, the staff view "failures" as continued teaching, reinforcement, and problem-solving opportunities. Relatedly, incentives and consequences may not work immediately, especially if a student comes from a very inconsistent environment or developmental/learning history.

6. Accountability works best only *after* students have learned *and mastered* specific social skills. That is, without skills and skill mastery, accountability is meaningless (except, perhaps, to motivate a student to learn the skill). Thus, teachers must make sure their students have learned, practiced, and mastered the social skills they have chosen *before* using incentives or consequences to motivate their use.

Specific to bullying, schools need to integrate meaningful incentives and consequences for bullies, victims, and involved peers into their Behavioral Matrix to motivate everyone to prevent bullying situations and/or to respond appropriately to bullying instances when they occur. That is, beyond social skills training, schools need to identify meaningful incentives and consequences to motivate students to demonstrate prosocial and tolerant behavior, use their "bully prevention and response" skills, and reinforce and support others when they actually demonstrate these skills.

Consistency

Finally, school staff need to recognize that skills and accountability are necessary but not sufficient conditions for effective discipline, behavior management, and self-management. Interdependently, staff need to teach, apply, and reinforce their social skills program and the implementation of meaningful incentives and consequences *in a consistent manner*. Ultimately, this consistency reinforces the importance and need to use prosocial skills, it helps to maintain the integrity of the accountability system in the students' eyes, and it maintains the entire process, especially when students are trying to undermine it through active or passive resistance.

Critically, staff and students must recognize that consistency is more of a process than something that teachers explicitly teach (as in skills) or provide (as in incentives and consequences). And, consistency involves staff communication, coordination, collaboration, trust, commitment, and evaluation. However, relative to bullying, consistency also necessarily involves the students, parents, and community who collectively create a prosocial atmosphere of prevention and a "no-tolerance" reaction when bullying occurs. Thus, schools need to create conscious and explicit values, expectations, norms, procedures, and interactions that prevent or respond to teasing, taunting, bullying, harassment, and aggression. This is best done through the involvement of all stakeholders and parties within a school and its extended community. Sometimes, this involvement includes an active, representative committee that becomes the driving force for analysis, implementation, change, reinforcement, and institutionalization. Always, regardless of structure of implementation and change, involvement includes system, large group, small group, and individual participation.

Special Situation Analyses: Analyzing Building-Wide Behavioral Situations

As noted earlier, it is necessary to recognize that school bullying is multifaceted and multidimensional in nature, and that preventive and reactive solutions require a systems and ecological perspective that involves comprehensive and situationally based approaches. Using the skills/accountability/consistency elements as a foundation, Project ACHIEVE's School-wide Positive Behavioral Self-Management System uses "special situation analyses" to functionally analyze and address both primary and secondary aspects of bullying circumstances.

Two types of "special situations" are used relative to bullying and other types of multifaceted, school-wide events or circumstances: setting-specific situations for the school, cafeteria, hallways, buses, and other common areas of the school, and student-specific situations for peer-mediated "events" that include teasing, taunting, bullying, harassment, and aggression. In order to develop strategic interventions for these situations, they must be functionally analyzed using or considering the following domains: (1) Student Characteristics, Issues, and Factors; (2) Teacher/Staff Characteristics, Issues, and Factors; (3) Environmental Characteristics, Issues, and Factors such as the physical plant and logistics within the specific setting; (4) Incentives and Consequences; and (5) Resources and Resource Utilization. For student-specific special situations, analyses of Peer Group Characteristics, Issues, and Factors are added. These domains are briefly described later relative to student bullying.

Student Characteristics, Issues, and Factors

Consideration here involves specifically analyzing the "who, what, where, when, why, and how" specific students (the bullies, the victims, and the other peers) are involved in bullying prevention, action, and response activities. At a primary prevention level, part of this analysis includes the skill, accountability, and consistency elements described earlier. At a secondary prevention level, part of the analysis includes (1) looking at what the three specific groups of students are doing to contribute to the problem, completing a functional assessment of their relevant interactions; (2) analyzing the strengths and weaknesses of the different groups of students and their skills and abilities, beliefs or expectations, and motivation or resistance relative to the problem situation; and (3) evaluating other situational issues or factors that, again, contribute to the problem or to its possible resolution. In essence, just like the functional analysis of individual student behavior, assessment here involves a functional analysis of individual, group, and contextual or situational behavior.

Teacher/Staff Characteristics, Issues, and Factors

Consideration here involves specifically analyzing the "who, what, where, when, why, and how" administrators, staff, and other adults are involved in bullying prevention, action, and response activities. Paralleling the student domain, this involves functionally analyzing the primary prevention elements, and then such secondary prevention elements as: (1) what administrators, teachers, and/or other adults contribute to bullying situations relative to their interactions and responses; (2) the differential strengths and weaknesses of different groups of teachers and/or staff and how their skills and abilities, beliefs or expectations, and motivation or resistance contribute to or could help solve bullying situations; (3) how teachers or staff who are absent from bullying situations actually contribute to the situation through their absence or indifference; and (4) the interactional or situational patterns, issues, or factors that, again, contribute to the bullying problem or its potential resolution.

Environmental Characteristics, Issues, and Factors— Physical Plant and Logistics

Consideration here involves investigating the settings where bullying predominantly occurs, the dynamics of and conditions (both positive and negative) within those settings or environment(s), and how these conditions are contributing to or causing different facets of the problem. Depending on the environment, this assessment could involve analyses of (1) the physical layout, condition, and organization of furnishings within the setting; (2) how students and others move into, out of, and within the physical plant; (3) the organization and logistics of student and adult presence in the setting (e.g., when and under what conditions students and adults are present in the setting, what grade levels of students are in the setting and where, how quickly students must enter and exit the setting); (4) student-staff ratios and the deployment of staff within the setting; and (5) other related and relevant factors. Once again, information from these assessments must be merged with the information collected in the students and teachers/staff domains such that an integration of the strengths and weaknesses, problems and potential solutions within the "ecology" begins to crystallize.

Incentives and Consequences

Consideration here involves analyzing the incentives, consequences, and reactions of individuals, groups (both peer and adult), and the system as a whole as they relate to bullying situations, their occurrence, their resolution, or their nonresolution. From a primary prevention perspective, the ultimate question is: "What will motivate everyone in the school to create a positive, nurturing, supportive environment where everyone interacts in tolerant, prosocial, and proactive ways relative to interpersonal, problem-solving, and conflict-prevention situations?" From a secondary prevention perspective, the collective incentive and consequence patterns of individuals, (present and absent) groups, and others must be differentially analyzed to understand how bullying occurs in some, but not all, situations. For example, some students might not recognize that their failure to become involved in a bullying situation (e.g., they see themselves as "innocent bystanders") actually reinforces and/or strengthens the bullying behavior such that they might become the next victims. Other students might not get involved for fear that they will be teased or bullied by other students later because of their involvement. Similarly, some teachers might be indifferent to bullying situations because it is an "administrative issue," while others actually fear some physical harm if they were to become involved.

Regardless of how difficult the problem may be to solve (this is often a resource issue—see later), the functional analysis of special situation incentives and consequences still must occur. Too often, staff short-circuit the problem-solving process because they see no hope of solutions or because their "apparent" solutions cannot be implemented. A more effective process, however, fully analyzes why the problem exists, what changes are needed, *and then* how (and with what resources) these changes will be realized. Critically, many staff discontinue their problem solving because they focus on implementation issues (that they don't believe can be overcome) *before* the "high impact" solutions that are generated and linked to a functional analysis.

Resources and Resource Utilization

For any organization, potentially available resources most often include time, money, materials (e.g., books, videos, equipment), activities, people, space, and ideas, creativity, or motivation. Like incentives and consequences, assessment here involves analyzing individual, group, setting, and situational resources and *how they are used*. But, this assessment also identifies potential resources that exist in the setting, but are not being used, and other resources that are *available* to the setting (e.g., from other schools, the district, the community) but have not been considered or used. Thus, a resource analysis here looks at (1) what resources are available in or to the problem situation or setting; and (2) whether the existing resources are being used effectively, ineffectively, or not at all. Critically, the "deployment" of existing resources must be part of this analysis. For example, some student bullying occurs when certain teachers, who are supposed to monitor students as they pass through the hall between periods, do not consistently perform this responsibility. While this does not "cause" the bullying, it certainly contributes to it, and it must become part of the global solution to the problem. Similarly, some schools have teachers who are absolved of "hall duty" because of teacher contracts. And yet, they still are impacted when students come into their classrooms not ready for immediate academic engagement because they are emotionally or behaviorally unprepared due to a bullying incident in the hallways. These teachers are potential resources to the bullying ecology. Ultimately, they need to decide whether it is more important to hold to the "letter of the contract" or to the "intent of the educational process."

Peer Group Characteristics, Issues, and Factors

As noted earlier, it must be recognized that some peers passively or actively support other students' bullying actions (passive support occurs, e.g., when peers either ignore the bullying of others, or they do not support the responses of those who try to stop another's bullying). More important, though, is the fact that bullying is best addressed when student peer groups agree that bullying will not be tolerated, and they take an active and concerted stand to respond immediately to such activities. Thus, the consideration of the peer group in the special situation analysis acknowledges that the peer group often directly or indirectly reinforces or supports teasing, taunting, bullying, harassment, or aggression—or, it actively prevents or responds to it. Assessment here, then, involves determining the presence, contribution, and impact of the peer group in these areas, as well as its willingness to become part of the solution. If willing (or motivated to become willing), a skills assessment follows to determine the peer group's ability to help prevent, diffuse, and/or disengage bullying and other precursor situations. Within the context of an effective school, this typically involves training, infusing, and reinforcing strategic Stop & Think social skills. This also often involves identifying, empowering, and utilizing peer leaders in both bullying prevention and response processes. Finally, given the demographics of most schools today, it critically involves direct attention to issues of gender, race, disability, multiculturalism, socioeconomic status, sexual orientation, and sometimes, even place of residence.

Tertiary Prevention: Intensive Need Students and Crisis Management

The cascade from social skills to building-wide accountability systems to staff and student consistency to special situation analyses forms the foundation of a school's comprehensive, integrated primary prevention "package" addressing teasing, taunting, bullying, harassment, and aggression. When implemented with integrity and intent, this package generally handles 90 percent of a school's actual or potential difficulties in this area either at the moment or within a reasonable period of time. At the secondary prevention level, this cascade provides a problem-solving structure that can be used to functionally analyze the reasons why a school has continuing, persistent, or more serious bully problems (7 percent) so that effective and efficient strategic interventions can be successfully implemented. The remaining 3 percent part of the student body or a number of critical, widespread, or serious incipercent situations involve either small, yet significantly disruptive or resistant, dents. These require intensive, tertiary prevention services or responses and/or crisis management.

While the cascade above is still relevant at the tertiary prevention level, when intensive need and/or crisis management responses to serious bullying incidents are necessary, functional problem-solving must initially give way to a school-wide stabilization process. That is, like the medical team in an emergency room that stabilizes the patient before moving on to more strategic and needed medical procedures, schools in crisis need to quickly identify the pivotal sources of the problem(s) and begin immediate action.

The intent of this action is not "to solve" the problem or prevent future incidents; the intent is to de-escalate and disarm the crisis situation and reassert enough control so that intensive problem-solving and crisis management services can begin. Eventually, tertiary services will likely be needed, as well as possible additions or adaptations at the secondary and primary prevention program levels.

Using the special situations analysis matrix as a guide to respond to a racially motivated bullying incident that escalated into a large-group racial confrontation in the halls, examples of stabilizing and then tertiary prevention strategies might include the following:

Domain	Stabilization strategy	Tertiary prevention strategy
Students		
Bully	Immediate suspension	Evaluation/treatment/behavioral intervention plan/possible alternative placement
Victim	Removal to principal's office/counseling support/call and debriefing conference with parents	Social skills training, mediation sessions with bully and others in the peer group
Peers	Separation into different rooms of the school for debriefing, separate and joint meetings with parents	Sensitivity/tolerance training, behavioral contract
Adults		
Administrators	Implementation of relevant crisis intervention plan(s)	Planning meeting with relevant administrative, security, mental health, and other district, school, and community resources to develop plan of action
Teachers/Staff	Lock-down of building with students not involved in incident	Implementation of developed action plan
Parents	Notified of incident and its resolution via communication sent home with all students	Involvement in community problem-solving and action meetings
Community	Notified as needed through district Public Information Officer	Involvement in community problem-solving and action meetings, social marketing and outreach initiative on tolerance and no tolerance for bullying
Physical Plant/ Supervision Logistics	Immediate lock-down of building, supervised release of students at end of the day	Increased security/adult in hallways, staggered passing of students between periods
Accountability	Immediate delivery of district-set consequences for involved students and peers	Discussion of incentives and consequences with entire peer group relative to tolerance and bullying
Resources	Police/other district resources involved as needed to gain control of the building and situation	Priority use of building, district, and community resources to implement Action Plan as designed

Critically, all schools need to prepare in advance for possible crisis situations in areas related to bullying. Part of this preparation involves anticipating situations, developing intervention systems, gathering needed resources, training everyone involved, and designing an evaluation system that formally debriefs the response process whenever it is used and that extends the process to include responses to unanticipated situations when they actually occur. Critically, any crisis management system should include a "crisis response" system that deals—for students, staff, parents, and community—with any emotional fallout that remains after a serious event occurs. At times, this response system will need to extend days, weeks, or months after a crisis. Sometimes, the system will need to include support for those still impacted on the (one-year) anniversary date of the event in question.

RESULTS

As noted, Project ACHIEVE has been designated an evidence-based Exemplary Model Prevention Program through the Substance Abuse and Mental Health Services Administration (SAMHSA) and the Office of Juvenile Justice and Delinquency Prevention (OJJDP). Among other recognitions, it also has been cited as a "Key Select" model program by the Collaborative for Academic, Social, and Emotional Learning (CASEL) and an Exemplary Program at the White House Conference on School Safety in October, 1998. While not a "bully prevention" program per se, as a comprehensive school-wide prevention, improvement, and strategic intervention program, Project ACHIEVE does address the conditions and characteristics that often prompt bullying and other forms of aggression, and it has demonstrated its success in improving student behavior and school climate.

While components of Project ACHIEVE have been implemented in hundreds of schools nationally, longitudinal data has been collected at three schools in particular: Jesse Keen Elementary School in Lakeland, Florida since 1990, Cleveland Elementary School in Tampa, Florida since 1993, and Hotchkiss Elementary School in Dallas, Texas since 1994 (see the Project ACHIEVE website for more specific data: www.projectachieve.info). In general, Project ACHIEVE activities typically result in decreases in discipline referrals to the office and school suspensions and expulsions, decreases in referrals and placements into special education, increases in positive school climate, and increases in student academic achievement. Relative to the discipline offenses most related to this chapter, at Jesse Keen Elementary School, for example, (1) fights decreased from 215 incidents during the 1990-1991 school year, the first year of Project ACHIEVE implementation to 70 incidents during the 1999-2000 school year; (2) abusive behavior decreased from 50 incidents in 1990-1991 to 25 incidents in 1999-2000; (3) disorderly conduct decreased from 256 incidents in 1993-1994 (the first year this category was used) to 24 incidents in 1999-2000; and (4) there were only 2 sexual offenses during the 1999-2000 school year.

CONCLUSION AND RECOMMENDATIONS

This chapter has outlined an evidence-based primary, secondary, and tertiary prevention blueprint to help schools analyze, develop, and implement a school-wide process that addresses student-related teasing, taunting, bullying, harassment, and aggression. The primary and secondary prevention parts of the blueprint emphasize the importance of (1) implementing a building-wide social skills program that teaches students specific interpersonal, problem-solving, and conflict-resolution skills; (2) developing an individual teacher, grade-level, and building-wide accountability system of meaningful incentives and consequences relative to bullying and other related incidents; and (3) reinforcing staff and administrative consistency so that such incidents are addressed in a constant and predictable fashion. This part of the blueprint also uses special situation analyses to deal with the reality that bullying often occurs in the common areas of a school and that its ecological context includes the victim(s) and other peers or peer pressures. The elements of a special situations analysis then were described. Moving toward the tertiary prevention level, the blueprint addresses the need for crisis intervention and response systems, finally noting the importance of intensive services and/or responses for the students who exhibit the most extreme and resistant behavior and for the small number of critical, widespread, or serious incidents that unfortunately still occur.

At all three prevention levels, it is critical to involve parents and community stakeholders and partners. Relative to the home, outreach activities help to reinforce parents' support of schools' comprehensive school safety and discipline programs, and they may involve training so that parents can use the same social skill and (adapted) accountability approaches as the school. Relative to the community, outreach might involve police, social service and community mental health agencies, government and juvenile justice personnel, the business and faith communities, and formal and informal neighborhood networks and associations. At the primary prevention level, the ultimate goal is to have parents and community agents universally recognize that teasing, taunting, bullying, harassment, and aggression are both unacceptable and preventable. At the secondary level, community resources might provide the pivotal components that decrease the potential for continuing incidents among at-risk groups of students. Finally, at the tertiary level, parents and community agents must collaborate to stop future extreme behavior or critical incidents.

To accomplish all facets of a comprehensive prevention system, six processes are needed: awareness, support, training, application, partnering, and regeneration. When done using systematic and systems-oriented strategic planning, implementation, and evaluation, existing incidents involving teasing, taunting, bullying, harassment, and aggression can be decreased or eliminated; students at risk of being bullies or victims can learn prosocial approaches to prevent these potentials; and all students and staff can create and celebrate positive and supportive school settings and climates that facilitate personal and interpersonal success.

REFERENCES

Batsche, G. M., & Knoff, H. M. (1994). Bullies and their victims: Understanding a pervasive problem in the schools. *School Psychology Review, 23,* 165-174.

Bosworth, K., Espelage, D. L., & Simon, T. R. (1999). Factors associated with bullying behavior in middle school students. *Journal of Early Adolescence, 19,* 341-362.

Craig, W. M., Pepler, D. J., & Atlas, R. (2000). Observations of bullying in the playground and in the classroom. *School Psychology International, 21,* 22-36.

Dwyer, K., & Osher, D. (2000). *Safeguarding our children: An action guide.* Washington, DC: U. S. Departments of Education and Justice, American Institutes for Research.

Espelage, D. L., & Holt, M. K. (2001). Bullying and victimization during early adolescence: Peer influences and psychosocial correlates. *Journal of Emotional Abuse, 2,* 123-142.

Henington, C., Hughes, J. N., Cavell, T. A., & Thompson, B. (1998). The role of relational aggression in identifying aggressive boys and girls. *Journal of School Psychology, 36,* 457-477.

Hodges, E. V. E., & Perry, D. G. (1999). Personal and interpersonal antecedents and consequences of victimization by peers. *Journal of Personality and Social Psychology, 76,* 677-685.

Hoover, J. H., Oliver, R., & Hazler, R. J. (1992). Bullying: Perceptions of adolescent victims in the Midwestern USA. *School Psychology International, 13,* 5-16.

Huesmann, L. R., & Reynolds, M. A. (2001). Cognitive processes and the development of aggression. In A. C. Bohart & D. J. Stipek (Eds.), *Constructive and destructive behavior: Implications for family, school, and society* (pp. 249-269). Washington, DC: American Psychological Association.

Knoff, H. M. (2000). Organizational development and strategic planning for the millennium: A blueprint toward effective school discipline, school safety, and crisis prevention. *Psychology in the Schools, 37,* 17-32.

Knoff, H. M. (2001). *The Stop & Think Social Skills Program (Preschool – Grade 1, Grades 2/3, Grades 4/5, Middle School 6-8).* Longmont, CO: Sopris West.

Knoff, H. M., & Batsche, G. M. (1995). Project ACHIEVE: Analyzing a school reform process for at-risk and underachieving students. *School Psychology Review, 24,* 579-603.

Knoff, H. M., Finch, C., & Carlyon, W. (2004). Inside Project ACHIEVE: A comprehensive, research-proven whole school improvement process focused on student academic and behavioral outcomes. In K. Robinson (Ed.), *Advances in school-based mental health: Best practices and program models* (pp. 19-1 to 19-28). Kingston, NJ: Civic Research Institute, Inc.

Loeber, R., & Stouthamer-Loeber, M. (1998). Development of juvenile aggression and violence: Some common misconceptions and controversies. *American Psychologist, 53,* 242-259.

Nansel, T. R., Overpeck, M., Pilla, R. S., Ruan, W. J., Simons-Morton, B., & Scheidt, P. (2001). Bullying behaviors among U. S. youth: Prevalence and association with psychosocial adjustment. *Journal of the American Medical Association, 285* (16), 2094-2100.

Olweus, D. (1991). Bully/victim problems among schoolchildren: Basic facts and effects of a school based intervention. In K. H. Rubin & D. Pepler (Eds.), *Development and treatment of childhood aggression* (pp. 411-438). Hillsdale, NJ: Erlbaum.

Pellegrini, A. D., Bartini, M., & Brooks, F. (1999). School bullies, victims, and aggressive victims: Factors relating to group affiliation and victimization in early adolescence. *Journal of Educational Psychology, 91,* 216-224.

Quinn, M. M., Osher, D., Hoffman, C. C., & Hanley, T. V. (1998). *Safe, Drug-Free, and Effective Schools for ALL Children: What Works!* Washington, DC: American Institutes for Research.

Raffaele, L., & Knoff, H. M. (1999). Improving home-school collaboration with parents of children at-risk: Organizational principles, perspectives, and approaches. *School Psychology Review, 28,* 448-466.

Rigby, K. (2000). Effects of peer victimization in schools and perceived social support on adolescent well-being. *Journal of Adolescence, 23,* 57-68.

Rigby, K. (2001). Health consequences of bullying and its prevention in schools. In J. Juvonen & S. Graham (Eds.), *Peer harassment in school: The plight of the vulnerable and victimized* (pp. 310-331). New York: Guilford Press.

Rigby, K. (2002). Bullying in childhood. In P. K. Smith & C. H. Hart (Eds.), *Blackwell handbook of childhood social development* (pp. 549-568). Malden, MA: Blackwell Publishers.

Swearer, S. M., & Doll, B. (2001). Bullying in schools: An ecological framework. *Journal of Emotional Abuse, 2,* 7-23.

Tolan, P. H., Gorman-Smith, D., & Loeber, R. (2000). Developmental timing and onsets of disruptive behaviors and later delinquency of inner-city youth. *Journal of Child and Family Studies, 9,* 203-220.

Index

Page numbers followed by an "i" indicate illustrations; those followed by a "t" indicate tables.

Bullying, Victimization, and Peer Harassment
© 2007 by The Haworth Press, Inc. All rights reserved.
doi:10.1300/5808_22

413

Order a copy of this book with this form or online at:
http://www.haworthpress.com/store/product.asp?sku=5808

BULLYING, VICTIMIZATION, AND PEER HARASSMENT
A Handbook of Prevention and Intervention

_____in hardbound at $69.95 (ISBN-13: 978-0-7890-2218-9; ISBN-10: 0-7890-2218-4)

_____in softbound at $39.95 (ISBN-13: 978-0-7890-2219-6; ISBN-10: 0-7890-2219-2)

412 pages plus index   Includes illustrations

Or order online and use special offer code HEC25 in the shopping cart.

COST OF BOOKS_____	☐ **BILL ME LATER:** (Bill-me option is good on US/Canada/Mexico orders only; not good to jobbers, wholesalers, or subscription agencies.)
POSTAGE & HANDLING_____ *(US: $4.00 for first book & $1.50 for each additional book)* *(Outside US: $5.00 for first book & $2.00 for each additional book)*	☐ Check here if billing address is different from shipping address and attach purchase order and billing address information. Signature_____
SUBTOTAL_____	☐ **PAYMENT ENCLOSED: $**_____
IN CANADA: ADD 6% GST_____	☐ **PLEASE CHARGE TO MY CREDIT CARD.**
STATE TAX_____ *(NJ, NY, OH, MN, CA, IL, IN, PA, & SD residents, add appropriate local sales tax)*	☐ Visa ☐ MasterCard ☐ AmEx ☐ Discover ☐ Diner's Club ☐ Eurocard ☐ JCB Account # _____
FINAL TOTAL_____ *(If paying in Canadian funds, convert using the current exchange rate, UNESCO coupons welcome)*	Exp. Date_____ Signature_____

Prices in US dollars and subject to change without notice.

NAME_____

INSTITUTION_____

ADDRESS_____

CITY_____

STATE/ZIP_____

COUNTRY_____ COUNTY (NY residents only)_____

TEL_____ FAX_____

E-MAIL_____

May we use your e-mail address for confirmations and other types of information? ☐ Yes ☐ No
We appreciate receiving your e-mail address and fax number. Haworth would like to e-mail or fax special discount offers to you, as a preferred customer. **We will never share, rent, or exchange your e-mail address or fax number.** We regard such actions as an invasion of your privacy.

Order From Your Local Bookstore or Directly From
The Haworth Press, Inc.
10 Alice Street, Binghamton, New York 13904-1580 • USA
TELEPHONE: 1-800-HAWORTH (1-800-429-6784) / Outside US/Canada: (607) 722-5857
FAX: 1-800-895-0582 / Outside US/Canada: (607) 771-0012
E-mail to: orders@haworthpress.com

For orders outside US and Canada, you may wish to order through your local
sales representative, distributor, or bookseller.
For information, see http://haworthpress.com/distributors

(Discounts are available for individual orders in US and Canada only, not booksellers/distributors.)

PLEASE PHOTOCOPY THIS FORM FOR YOUR PERSONAL USE.
http://www.HaworthPress.com   BOF07

Dear Customer:

Please fill out & return this form to receive special deals & publishing opportunities for you! These include:
- availability of new books in your local bookstore or online
- one-time prepublication discounts
- free or heavily discounted related titles
- free samples of related Haworth Press periodicals
- publishing opportunities in our periodicals or Book Division

❏ OK! Please keep me on your regular mailing list and/or e-mailing list for new announcements!

Name _____

Address _____

_____

STAPLE OR TAPE YOUR BUSINESS CARD HERE!

*E-mail address _____
*Your e-mail address will never be rented, shared, exchanged, sold, or divested. You may "opt-out" at any time. May we use your e-mail address for confirmations and other types of information? ❏ Yes ❏ No

Special needs:
Describe below any special information you would like:
- Forthcoming professional/textbooks
- New popular books
- Publishing opportunities in academic periodicals
- Free samples of periodicals in my area(s)

Special needs/Special areas of interest:

_____

_____

_____

_____

Please contact me as soon as possible. I have a special requirement/project:

_____

_____

_____

PLEASE COMPLETE THE FORM ABOVE AND MAIL TO:
Donna Barnes, Marketing Dept., The Haworth Press, Inc.
10 Alice Street, Binghamton, NY 13904–1580 USA
Tel: 1–800–429–6784 • Outside US/Canada Tel: (607) 722–5857
Fax: 1–800–895–0582 • Outside US/Canada Fax: (607) 771–0012
E-mail: orders@HaworthPress.com

GBIC06

The Haworth Press Inc.

Visit our Web site: www.HaworthPress.com